Black Sabbath

A MARTIN POPOFF BIBLIOGRAPHY

Riff Kills Man: 25 Years of Recorded Hard Rock and Heavy Metal (Power Chord Press, 1993)

The Collector's Guide to Heavy Metal (Collector's Guide Publishing, 1997)

Goldmine Heavy Metal Records Price Guide (Krause Publications, 2000)

20th Century Rock 'n' Roll — Heavy Metal (Collector's Guide Publishing, 2000)

Southern Rock Review (Collector's Guide Publishing, 2002)

The Top 500 Heavy Metal Songs of All Time (ECW Press, 2003)

The Collector's Guide to Heavy Metal Volume 1: The Seventies (Collector's Guide Publishing, 2003)

The Top 500 Heavy Metal Albums of All Time (ECW Press, 2004)

Blue Öyster Cult: Secrets Revealed! (Metal Blade Records, 2004)

Contents Under Pressure: 30 Years of Rush at Home & Away (ECW Press, 2004)

The New Wave of British Heavy Metal Singles (Scrap Metal, 2004)

UFO: Shoot Out the Lights (Metal Blade, 2005)

Rainbow: English Castle Magic (Metal Blade, 2005)

The Collector's Guide to Heavy Metal Volume 2: The Eighties (Collector's Guide Publishing, 2005)

Dio: Light Beyond the Black (Metal Blade, 2006)

Black Sabbath

DOOM LET LOOSE

AN ILLUSTRATED HISTORY

BY **MARTIN POPOFF**

ECW PRESS

Published by ECW PRESS
2120 Queen Street East, Suite 200, Toronto, Ontario, Canada M4E 1E2

LIBRARY AND ARCHIVES CANADA CATALOGUING IN PUBLICATION

Popoff, Martin, 1963–
Black Sabbath : doom let loose : an illustrated history / Martin Popoff.

ISBN 1-55022-731-9

1. Black Sabbath (Musical group)—Interviews. 2. Heavy metal
(Music)—England—History and criticism. I. Title.

ML421.B627P82 2006   782.42166'092'2   C2006-901701-8

Developing editor: Jennifer Hale
Cover and Text design: Tania Craan
Back cover photo: Paul Johnstone
Cover poster from the collection of Doug Roemer
Cover background: Jamie Farquarson / Getty Images
Typesetting: Gail Nina
Production: Mary Bowness
Printing: Transcontinental

DISTRIBUTION

CANADA: Jaguar Book Group, 100 Armstrong Avenue, Georgetown, ON, L7G 5S4
UNITED STATES: Independent Publishers Group, 814 North Franklin Street,
Chicago, Illinois 60610

PRINTED AND BOUND IN CANADA

ECW PRESS
ecwpress.com

TABLE OF CONTENTS

ACKNOWLEDGMENTS

I'd like to thank the following for their crucial contributions to this project.

The Sabs. Unfailingly polite in conversation, to a man, anybody involved in the band I talked to, and anybody on the fringes of the story . . . it was a pleasure.

Joe D'Agostino — Although I never ended up visiting Joe in Las Vegas (damn!), my phone calls with him were always a blast, especially when we turned 'round to politics.

Leif Edling — Candlemass' spiritual leader is, I suppose unsurprisingly, a huge Sabbath fan and provided a swack of memorabilia shots cheerfully, quickly and with a high level of expertise unexpected from a doom icon. Tied for second spot in a death match for Trouble as the greatest doom band of all time, Candlemass returned with a crowning, resounding self-titled reunion album in mid-2005. A good forty percent of the memorabilia you see pictured in this book came from the collection of Mr. Edling.

Mike Pritchard — Keeper of the metal lair that is better than yours by a Marshall mile, Mike supplied shots of some of the 45 and LP variants you see in this book. Plus he's bloody smart on the subject of Black Sabbath. Damn . . . you should see his record collection.

Tim Wilson — Canada's keeper of the Sabbath, Tim supplied most of the 45 sleeve shots you see in this book. As well, he came up with some nice fan club material and offered them happily in service of the Sabs. A true fan and meticulous collector.

King Fowley — King, like Mike, is a huge record collector and Sabbath fan. And not just that, he is the leader of the legendary Deceased. King supplied a bunch of records for photographing as well. This guy lives metal.

Heather Harris — Quite simply, we couldn't have done this book without Heather. With Doug and I bumbling around drooling over his collection and regaling each other with Sabbath stories, Heather quietly went about scanning everything we tossed her way. She's the brains of the operation, and was the crucial link in getting everything of Doug's, King's and Mike's into useable form. Organized and gracious, Heather rules.

Doug Roemer — Ah, what can one say about Doug? He is the Sabbath expert with the most-est, and that's just the start of his collecting and academic interests. Doug was extremely generous with his time and knowledge on all things Sabbath, as well as the willing source of all manner of Sabbath audio rarity I may otherwise never have heard. Plus the guy loves Ronnie, so he's a friend for life. An immense help, and . . . ha ha . . . a little closer in politics to me than to Mr. D'Agostino.

Finally, for those who dug deep into their archives and supplied photos for the book, we salute you!

Had a dream last night that demonstrated for me that I'd better knock this book on its head.

I was looking in a rack, outside at my cousin's house, mounted on a work-bench among rusting machine parts, and found an 8-track of *Paranoid*. First thought was "Cool, something else we can take a picture of and shove in the book." Then I looked more closely and each song had one of those extra song bits/subtitles I've been wracking my head to verify/get straight for the last few days — and they were all pretty long and silly. I thought with a sly chuckle, "No one knows this — this is new terrain, baby!"

Then, man, right below the art for *Paranoid*, I see that this is a two-fer! Yes, two albums on one 8-track, the second being . . . *Sabbath Plays Purple*. It's the cover of *In Rock* adapted with the Sabbath guys in there, with slashing Sabbath typography everywhere, the band running through classics from *In Rock*, *Fireball* and *Machine Head*. My cousin tells me, yes, we've got an old 8-track home deck around here somewhere, and it works. And then I wake up.

Anyway, like anything, you gotta know when enough is enough, so I'm cuttin' 'er off here, today — heck, along with dreaming about Sabbath, man, I don't know if there is much Sabbath left I can ever listen to again without being thoroughly sick of it.

But it wasn't always that way. I remember first hearing Sabbath and loving it, though finding it a mess. It would have been about '71 when I was eight, and that mess was the first album, a record that sounded old and not in a good way. Quickly it was onto *Paranoid* and me an' the buds were certifiable metalheads, with the most immediate headbang for pups that age being scary monster song "Iron Man," which also had a riff dumb enough for us to absorb.

The first Sabbath album I ever bought was *Vol 4*, and decades later, I realize how smart we were ignoring the guff about the two mellow tracks, realizing this was heavier than the debut, and about as heavy as *Paranoid*. This was also the heaviest band we knew, our older brothers' and older cousins' Zeppelin, Iron Butterfly, Steppenwolf and CCR (!) records paling in comparison. Significantly, Sabbath was our band, not the domain of our elders.

We loved that Oz looked our age, and that the other guys had these big han-dlebar moustaches.

Anyway, *Vol 4* was the first to call my own, then *Master of Reality* blew our minds, although I don't think I had a copy to call my own for a while. *Sabbath Bloody Sabbath* I recall as almost too scary — we're talking mainly the album cover here — with the music sounding uneasy in a different way, not exactly always heavy, kind of druggy, a concept we didn't get at all. *Sabotage* was more of the same, and for some reason, I talked a buddy into buying it first. I must have had something else to spend our dollars on that day. Anyway, Geoff came home with it and we thought Sabbath had made another weird record. It took us a while to get into it. "Supertzar" was classical, "Am I Going Insane" was singsongy, there were mellow bits they were trying to hide on us (but oh, we found them out). Bear in mind, me an' the buds were only 12. Kiss — *Alive!* was more our speed (and yes, we were Kiss veterans by this point — *Hotter Than Hell* was the first bought as an anticipated new release).

Oddly, my favorite *Sabotage* memory is racing back home on my bike for lunch, hoping intensely as a 12-year-old metalhead in the '70s did, that the new *Circus* had arrived. It had, and it was red, and there was a cool shot of Oz in a brown jacket. This was the best *Circus* cover ever, better than a Kiss cover. Inside was a *Sabotage* feature, but groovier was the ad for the album, featuring a bunch of sorta 1940s heavies in suits perusing a train wreck. Turns out this had nothing to do with the album art, and I was over the moon — my favorite ad ever.

Technical Ecstasy was a grave disappointment, but I soon grew to love it. The cover art mesmerized me and the music depressed me. *Never Say Die* . . . I fondly remember staring out our picture window waiting for my buddy Mark across the street to return from an orthodontist trip to our record-buying mecca, Spokane, two hours directly south of us in scary America. His instructions were to locate and buy me *Never Say Die* and The Saints — *Eternally Yours*. He was successful on both counts. *Eternally Yours* was the slightly better album, a pleasant surprise because it improved on *(I'm) Stranded*. *Never Say Die*? I don't remember being too pleased with it. In fact, I recall struggling to hear what was going on through the noise of it. We were pretty sure it was heavier than the last one, but this would take a mathematical comparison to verify.

I do remember thoroughly digging the cover art, as well as the higher gloss put on U.S. copies of albums versus our Canadian issues, along with the less angled way the plant folded and glued the covers together. Years later I still have my original copy, and now it's signed by all four guys. I have a bunch of stuff signed by all of them, but this is my prized collectible, cause the way the autographs are arranged is nothing short of beautiful.

Come *Heaven and Hell*, I remember the hype. At 17, I was a friggin' metal expert and had followed the reports leading up to it. And there it was, a stack of them at Vancouver's A&B Sound. For a long time A&B was all of British Columbia's favorite place to buy music — literally, without exaggeration, for years, A&B had the cheapest record prices in the world. I plucked one off the stack and flipped it over and there was that oddly aristocratic shot of the band. I liked it, and once home in Trail, loved the album — me and a growing Sabbath legion at our high school. We were rooting for Sabbath at this point, even though it was almost dizzyingly disorienting that they had hired Dio. I don't remember anybody thinking this was sacrilege though. We all loved Ronnie and were rewarded in that love by Black Rainbow turning in a glossy, professional, heavy record.

Years later, I actually prefer its denigrated predecessor *Never Say Die*. *Heaven and Hell* soon sounded manufactured, machine tooled to precision. *Never Say Die* sounded like a tiny figure skater giving birth to an anvil. Whether it was the end of the Ozzy years or my loss of innocence as an already world-weary encyclopedia of metal, or indeed, metal's loss of innocence given the commercial prospects afforded the New Wave of British Heavy Metal, I'd never feel that rush again when buying a Black Sabbath album.

But, as you can see, Sabbath had been getting absorbed into my circuitry for a long time, and now I finally get to put together a book on them. What I've done is focus primarily on the music, as I've done with previous books, going record by record, song by song, touching on touring as well. I suppose the main reason I do these books at all is to get a bunch of the known facts down in one place, along with my opinions (because I really, really want to convince you to buy Black Sabbath albums), so I can purge them from my trivia-cluttered head.

And in terms of my trademark, if you will, the format you see here is one I've used in all my "biographies" thus far, and I see no reason to change it. I've always felt that what we can all experience together, and have experienced together, are the actual albums — less so the shows, even less so the makers of the music and their private lives. Additionally, I've always felt that a judicious analysis of the albums at hand, if done right, makes you want to revisit those records, hopefully with renewed appreciation given the things you've learned about them. You've spent this money, those records are sitting there. Why not get more use out of them, enjoy them more, mathematically and quantifiably, make yourself happier?

In any event, enjoy the book, I hope you learn something, and thanks for letting me wistfully reminisce for a bit. Email me at martinp@inforamp.net if you wanna say hi. Next stop, Birmingham.

Martin Popoff, June 2006

"MUSIC WAS OUR WAY OUT"

— the punks from Birmingham

Chris Walter/WireImage.com

Just like the iconic punks who would come along a mere seven years later, the four lads known as Black Sabbath had no clue as to the history they would make. Yes, the Sabs invented heavy metal, plain, simple, unassailable.

Like those of the punks, their aims were rudimentary, blessed with an innocence. For the boys of Black Sabbath, the blues provided only a cursory blueprint, while The Beatles and their backwater Liverpool experience offered an enticing taste of escape. Almost as an afterthought, walls of power chords pushed forth in a wave of doom.

So yes, there was a period of futzing about, of loitering, followed by a random, fateful sonic earth-shattering . . . both of these hapless happenstances would underscore the sorry fact that these four Birmingham bashers were punks railing against their soot-obscured lot, looking for a way out through volume and the crude delivery thereof.

In more dire straits than the punks — who at least had an art school, socio-political sense of their own importance — incredibly, Sabbath would make record upon record before they could even look back with any sort of filmy recognition and say that yes, they had invented a new, doomy kind of music emphatically relegated to the lefthand path as heavy metal.

But as it began, this was just a case of four guys knocking about under the iron-dusky, smoke-cloaked skies of Birmingham's drab, satanic mills. In fact, Anthony Frank Iommi, William Thomas Ward, John Michael Osbourne and Terence Michael Butler were the same age, born within a year and a half of each other from 1948 through '49, and all had hailed from the dreadfully conformist Birmingham suburb of Aston, the industrial seed of this very industrial town. Birmingham also had the distinction of having the daylights bombed out of it by the Germans in World War II.

In 1965, rock 'n' roll was goosing Britain in a big way. America had waned in its ascendance, and jolly ol' England was birthing bands like mushrooms. Birmingham participated competently through The Move and The Moody Blues, but in the early days, it was London that shone. The Midlands would, of course, bounce back with contributions from Traffic, Denny Laine, the well-traveled Clem Clempson, two locals by the names of John Bonham and Robert Plant, and then later on, Judas Priest, who, in more of a primary-colors fashion, would assume Sabbath's heavy metal mantle in a more commercial time and space.

Each of the lads worked jobs after leaving school at the age of 15, so music was an immediate draw. Prophetically, their ears tweaked at the louder music around them. "Oh definitely," muses Bill Ward, the man who would become Black Sabbath's drummer. "There are some major people that have to be credited [for influencing us]. Those first chords from Dave Davies in 'You Really Got Me,' to me, that was just so incredibly heavy. Cream I think were incredibly influential, an outstanding band. The Who with 'Substitute.' Lyrically I thought The Who were amazing — they were going into places that were almost taboo — they didn't play safe. And just listening to the power of some of the blues singers from the United States — Muddy Waters, the growl out of Howlin' Wolf."

Ozzy Osbourne would find work at the car factory his mum worked in, as well as biding time in plumbing, tool and die, the mortuary, and famously, an abattoir, where he slaughtered upwards of 250 animals a day. He lasted a mere two months. Ozzy's family nestled somewhere between working class and dirt poor. Six children, two jobs, small row house . . . stories of going shoeless proliferated.

In 1966, a six-week stay at the local prison (for stealing "a load of women's clothing," which Oz sold in pubs) would punctuate his ongoing failure at yet another career, that of breaking and entering — and it was in jail that Ozzy would get his signature O-Z-Z-Y tattoo across his fingers. "Grand larceny," mused Oz in 1976. "I was in Winston Green for two months. Once I stole a telly and I was balanced on top of this wall, one of them walls with glass along the top, and I fell off; this 24-inch telly was sitting on top of my chest and I was screaming 'Get me out, get me out!' I had nothing to do inside. You did about two hours work a day and the rest of the time you're locked in your cell. That's why I did my tattoos, with a sewing needle and a tin of gray polish." Asked in 1975, to describe his body paintings, Ozzy said he went with "just a few signs and symbols. One's a dagger, one's the number three. It's just something I did when I got bored or pissed off. You get a tin of gray polish, not ink, and melt the polish and inject yourself with a fuckin' needle." Ozzy mentions another cool tattoo he saw in the slammer. "I've seen this one of a hunt with a fox's tail disappearing up a guy's ass and 500 horses chasing him. My grandfather had a tattoo that went from the top of his head and ended at the bottom of his foot. It was a snake going all around his head and around his body to his foot. Its head went around and down between his eyes." Of his famous smiley face knee tattoos, Ozzy said they were "to cheer me up when I looked down."

On a whole different career tack, Terence "Geezer" Butler would establish himself as a numbers guy (helpful in later years), working admin at an Aston factory. Guitarist Tony Iommi, from a comfortably middle-class background (his family ran a general store), would become a sheet metal worker, soon to receive the crush and cut to two of his fingertips that would become the heavy metal handicap he managed to turn right 'round. With Bill

BIRMINGHAM WAS VERY ROUGH WHEN WE WERE GROWING UP ... WE WERE ALL IN GANGS BUT WE DIDN'T WANT TO BE — WE WANTED TO BE IN BANDS."

Daragh McDonagh/ Retna Ltd.

Tony Iommi's right hand of doom

MUSIC WAS OUR WAY OUT

ensconced in the field of coal delivery, a soiled, smudged and sweated picture is painted of an impossibly, comically heavy metal apprenticeship — nay, enslavement. Is it any wonder that doom was born?

"Birmingham was very rough when we were growing up," recalls Tony. "There were gangs, and it was very hard to move away from that. Music was our way out, but it was something that we really wanted to do as well. We were all in gangs but we didn't want to be — we wanted to be in bands."

"When I had my accident, all my hopes had gone down the drain," adds Tony, describing his machine shop mishap. "I really wanted to play and I couldn't. I got really depressed for a period. Finally, somebody brought me a Django Reinhardt record. That really inspired me to start playing again. I went to several hospitals and they told me that they couldn't do anything, that I should basically give up. I just couldn't accept that. I thought there has to be a way. I went home and I made myself a set of thimbles out of a Fairy Liquid bottle. I melted it down into a ball and sat there with a hot solvent on and made a hole in it so it would fit over my finger. I filed it down so it looked like the shape of the finger. I needed something to grip the strings, so I came up with leather to stick on there. It was very crude but it enabled me to be able to play. You couldn't trill the strings or anything, but it was a start. I still use the same type of thing now."

"He was working in a place that had a guillotine," is Geezer's recollection of the tale. "He used to cut things, and his hand got stuck in the machine and the guillotine came down and chopped the ends of his two fingers off; the bones stick out. That's why he has to wear those thimbles. And that's why he got into Django Reinhardt. Of course, Django had only three fingers. It sort of inspired him and encouraged him to carry on."

As the '60s blossomed chaotically, mods and rockers gave way to the British blues boom and psychedelia. The blues, in the hands of big British egos, eventually developed a certain bloat, followed by a reaction against it. The predictability at the heart of the blues, something that had once been an endearing and comforting asset, now began to bore clubgoers. Psychedelia went the way of enlightened idealism and became progressive or art rock. Or it didn't. A ragtag, grumbling, cynical, disconnected mob of mean mindset, not one predisposed to Jon Anderson's sunny flower power sentiments, went dark — picking up the newspaper was enough to galvanize their fatalism. Psychedelia formed an uneasy alliance with bad-assed American garage rock and a predilection for misfit menace to become not so much heavy metal, but simply the redheaded stepchild of psychedelia — the nasty end of a gray-and-getting-grayer scale.

But, being the punks they were, Black Sabbath were oblivious to this sea change, their collective bile churned to a different set of home-grown and world-worn circumstances. Like other punks, they formed bands indicative of random fandoms. Tony, now ex of The Rocking Chevrolets, The In Crowd, The Birds and the Bees, and The Rest (which also featured Bill), joined a preexisting Cumberland act called Mythology.

Ozzy's personal assistant in later years, David Tangye, puts some clarity to Tony's pre-Sabbath years. "We wanted to put the record straight on Mythology. It had been totally dis-

Mythology→

HRIS MITH

BILL WARD

NEIL MARSHALL

SWINDON LOCARNO
This Thursday
THE TASTE
plus THE EARTH

By " KIE "

The Birmingham group "Earth," well-known to their Cumberland fans as the former Mythology group, are now being acknowledged in London as one of the new "in-groups."

A short while ago they visited the Border area playing at Carlisle, Dumfries and a number of schools. But, it is down in London where things are really beginning to happen for the group.

In the near future they will be going into the recording studios to 'cut' their very first L.P. So far they have written two tracks, both without names at the moment. During the last month they have had a number of performances at the Marquee, the place where Fairport Convention, Ten Years After, and a number of

Tony Ionni, guitarist with Earth, who was a member of Jethro Tull for a short time.

"Black Sabbath" dance cancelled

A venture by a Maryport disc jockey to stage a dance with

BLACK SABBATH

Black Sabbath, the Birmingham group with very strong connections in Cumberland, have just signed an

Workington fans will be the next in this area to hear Black Sabbath, who will appear at Banklands Youth Club on Tuesday, February 10. The following Friday, they are booked for the Workington division of the West Cumberland College of Science and Technology, a venue they had to cancel in December because of German television commitments.

torted in other publications and it wasn't fair on guys like Neil Marshall, who started Mythology. He really worked hard to get that band going. And Tony actually came to that band. It was an accredited band before he got there. Tony basically came up to Cumberland to work and that's how it was. But they didn't have managers in those days or itineraries. I even remember touring around, and you would go into the town you're supposed to be playing, looking for the posters showing you where you're supposed to play. Because you had no idea."

Was there a hint of the roots of heavy metal evident at that time in Mythology? "Certainly not in The Rest, but in Mythology there was, yes," notes Tony. "It was more guitar-oriented blues. I'd been doing lots of solo guitar work in those days. But blues played a major part; that was my main influence, blues and jazz. I love to hear good blues players."

Backing up, Bill had this to say about The Rest: "We were just playing basic cover songs, but the cover songs we would play were a bit out of the norm, unusual, if you like."

In February '68, Mythology would also absorb Bill into the band. However, a sobering pot bust effectively ended the bluesy band's trajectory, and a dejected Tony and Bill shuffled back to Birmingham, where a psych band

I WAS SORT OF A RELIGIOUS MANIAC WHEN I WAS A KID. I USED TO COLLECT CRUCIFIXES AND PICTURES AND MEDALS AND EVERYTHING, AND I WANTED TO BECOME A PRIEST.

called Rare Breed featured Geezer o'er on the fat strings. After the band's singer left, Rare Breed answered an ad in a music store announcing cryptically "Ozzy Zig needs a gig. Own PA system." This is usually the clincher in such negotiations.

But the hookup never happened, and Rare Breed became fully extinct. The ad was still posted in the store, and Tony was next to answer, who, along with Bill, pulled up in his blue van to Ozzy's door in Aston (Ozzy's dad thought it was the cops), privately hoping it wasn't the same Ozzy that Tony used to terrorize back in high school. Turns out, it was.

"There's a long history because they were at school together when they were kids," laughs Geezer, on Ozzy and Tony's odd relationship. "Tony always intimidated Ozzy at school together when they were kids [laughs], and there's always been a history of that throughout the band. And when things happen in childhood, you always think about it. You never quite blow it out of your system. So Ozzy's always had this thing about Tony intimidating him. In recent years, they've had a good talk and resolved everything. For now anyway.

But yes, it was the old school thing. They hated each other when they were in school. Tony used to beat up Ozzy at school, and it was just a continuation of that. It wasn't really on the surface, but underneath. And when push came to shove, all the old tensions would come out."

Ozzy seems to have blocked it out of his mind, denying that it had ever happened, but he admits that Tony was a fighter, a kid who could take care of himself. He stayed out of his way, but also was quite stricken by Tony showing up at school and playing Shadows songs on his red guitar. In the band, Ozzy felt a bit of an odd wheel, due to being the only non-musician of the four, and Tony in particular putting him down. As well, Tony was known to crave the limelight (Geezer had been described as a bit of a peacock as well), and any front man, especially one with Ozzy's almost panicked desire to get crowds on his side, is always a threat to the prominence of a band's guitarist.

Geezer had been a guitarist up to this point, but by switching the strings on his Fender Telecaster to bass strings (and then graduating to a three-stringed bass!), a bobbing, weaving legend was born. Ozzy came with his PA system (Triumph amp, mic and two column speakers). Hitting the road, already under the protective wing of roadie Geoff "Luke" Lucas, the band gigged as a brassy, proggy, jazzy, meandering beast known as the Polka Tulk Blues Band, the name derived from that of a Pakistani clothing store. The band's August 1968 show was one of two (the guys have also suggested six, and even nine) featuring the band as a six-piece, the two strap-ons being a

sax player and a second guitarist for slide and rhythm work.

"The number one inspiration for me as a bass player is Jack Bruce," notes Geezer, on his conversion from six strings to four. "I didn't even consider playing the bass until I went to see Cream. I used to see Cream whenever they came to Birmingham. Up until then, I was playing rhythm guitar. I saw Jack Bruce, what he could do with a bass, and it just gave new meaning to the whole instrument. And I just swapped me rhythm guitar for a bass guitar."

Years later, Geezer looked back on that same defining moment. "Up until then, bass players used to just stand there and use the pick, be in the background; you would never notice them, and then when I went to see Cream, it was so different to anybody else I had ever seen. I'd never seen anybody use the fingers before, and just his whole presence on stage . . . it was amazing to me."

Seeing Cream live wasn't the first religious experience Geezer had had. "I was brought up strictly Irish Catholic," he adds. "I was sort of a religious maniac when I was a kid. I used to collect crucifixes and pictures and medals and everything, and I wanted to become a priest. I used to sing in the school choir. I just literally loved God. I was just fascinated by the whole thing. I used to read about it and go to every class I could concerning religion. And that developed into sort of wanting to know more about other religions, and other spirituality, more about the occult and everything else."

Geezer later added, "In the end, I just got sick of going to Mass every Sunday, surrounded by a lot of drunks and idiots taking the piss out of me hair [laughs]. And so, I just didn't want to go there anymore. It was terrible; I was one of the few people with long hair back then, and all these Irish guys used to take the piss out of me something rotten. And in the end, I just couldn't stand it.

"When I first saw The Beatles, I was probably 12 or 13," adds Geezer, citing a root music influence for so many budding rockers his age.

"And that sort of took over from where religion left off. It was like reality — you could touch it. It was four people from exactly the same background as where I was from, being able to rule the world. It gave everybody that was from the working classes in England some hope. So that almost took over from religion, and became religion in itself. I saw them in Birmingham, but as soon as I heard 'Love Me Do,' the first single on the radio, I was just completely taken over by it."

He added later, "Eventually, when The Beatles started getting into all the transcendentalism, there were a lot of magazines and assorted publications about the different religions, including Satanism, white magic and black magic, and I just got interested in the whole spiritual thing. And I suppose it rubbed off in me lyric writing with Sabbath."

Canning the idea of a six-piece, the Polka Tulk Blues Band became Polka Tulk, then the Earth Blues Band and then Earth, playing their first gigs by September of '68. A remarkable wrinkle in Black Sabbath history occurs next, with Tony leaving the band for Jethro Tull. The happenstance was even caught on camera for the *Rock 'n' Roll Circus* TV performance, an event headlined by the Stones, for members of that band's fan club, and other acts included John Lennon, The Who and Cream. While Tony can be seen somberly trying to fit in (strumming, prophetically, a doomy sort of blues), he had, in fact, already quit the band, then asked to rejoin, only to be told by Ian Anderson that he had already been replaced, and that the TV gig would be his last.

"When they [Jethro Tull] asked me if I was interested in joining, I talked to the other guys," explains Tony on his brief side trip. "They told me that I should go for it. We were just starting out and we hadn't gotten anything going. I actually joined, but I changed my mind. I wanted to come back and get the band going again. I learned quite a lot from Ian, that

Tony Iommi (far right) with Jethro Tull at the *Rock 'n' Roll Circus*

you have got to work at it and rehearse. When I came back, I made sure that everybody was up early in the morning and rehearsing. I used to go and pick them up. I was the only one at the time that could drive. I used to have to drive the bloody van and get them up at quarter of nine every morning; which was, believe me, early for us then. I said to them, 'This is how we've got to do it because this is how Jethro Tull did it.' They had a schedule and they knew that they were going to work from this time 'til that time. I tried that with our band and we got into doing it instead of just strolling in at any hour."

What also rankled Tony about the Jethro Tull situation was his impression that the band didn't feel very much like a gang — Ian ate his lunch at one table, the other three ate at another — as well as the sentiment drummed into him by the band's manager that he was so lucky to be part of this hallowed act. By late December '68, Earth were again gigging around Birmingham and Cumbria. January 3, 1969 saw the band's first gig in London, with Ozzy establishing what would become the band's trademark penchant for wearing cruci-fixes — except that this first time, what Ozzy had around his scrawny neck was an X-shaped tap from a kitchen sink. After a period of men-torship by Alvin Lee and Ten Years After, the band found management with Jim Simpson,

THERE WERE THREE PEOPLE IN THE WHOLE CLUB FOR OUR ENTIRE FIRST SET.

who would be instrumental in launching them. "When we were Earth," notes Geezer, "we were doing lots of old blues, from Howlin' Wolf, Muddy Waters, John Lee Hooker, and even some soul — Sam & Dave and Wilson Pickett. And a lot of the English blues like the Cream, John Mayall; some jazz as well."

While managing Bakerloo Blues Line, Tea & Symphony and Locomotive, Jim Simpson also played trumpet for the latter, who scored a minor hit with "Rudi's in Love." Locomotive's Norman Haines would be proffered as a potential writer for Sabbath, penning "When I Came Down," which Sabbath can be heard jamming competently through on a recent acetate that has turned up.

"I remembered the song once I heard it, but I had completely forgot about it," muses Geezer, on this yet un-marketed early Sabbath session. "Jim kept playing us that sort of thing, because he was a jazz player, and his favorite band was Chicago; they had just come out with their first album. He had been a trumpet player, so he loved brass sections. So he kept playing us all these jazz records saying, 'This is what you should be doing.' No thanks."

"Yeah, we just did that the one time," says Bill of the track. "We were trying to get songs to get us a recording contract, so Norman — good songwriter — had written up this pretty cool song. But it was plain, right from the get-go, that we really didn't like doing other people's music. We did Crow's version of 'Evil Woman' and I didn't particularly like that."

So who taught the band to be so heavy? It seems the sound just happened by accident. "We didn't have anybody who taught us that," Bill says. "The songs, when they came about, just sounded right. We just used to show up and play aggressively. It was just more the aggression that came out than anything else. We just pretty much turned up the volume. I didn't have a PA back then, for my drums or anything, so there were no microphones. I had to play as loud as possible, and I think that sometimes the guys thought I was playing too loud [laughs], so they turned up. So we all just got louder; it wasn't planned."

There was volume, plus jazziness from Simpson, and also, as Tony recalls, an overt jam ethic. "I used to do these ridiculously long solos because every song was like a 12 bar [laughs]. And it'd be like a five-minute guitar solo in there, which was great for me, because it gave me the opportunity to learn new stuff, new parts."

Gigging regularly up and down England, Earth would soon embark on their first overseas jaunt, to Germany and Hamburg's Star-Club, influential of course due to its association with The Beatles, but also important with respect to Sabbath, for this was the locale at which a selection of the early Black Sabbath classics were written — live. After a second European trip, landing with hijinx in Denmark then over to Hamburg again (as well as Sweden and Belgium), the band returned home enthusiastic and not without a sizeable buzz. Hamburg beckoned a third time in August '69 for a three week stay, amidst publicity that the band were recording their debut album — with Gus Dudgeon, of Bonzo Dog and Locomotive fame. Gus later improved on that resumé through work with David Bowie and Elton John.

The Star-Club stints hardened the band incredibly, and served as a creative launch pad. Playing upwards of five, maybe even seven, 45-minute sets a night to a mostly indifferent crowd ("six people, and three of them were nutcases, plus a prostitute," quipped Geezer), Sabbath would bring on stage barely written originals and then finish them off o'er the hours. As well, extended solos would be taken by all (except Oz), sometimes with one of the guys blowing it alone for an entire set.

And, as Ozzy regales, touring in the early days could turn nasty. Especially in Northern Scotland. "It was one of those horrible little towns — you know the type, three shops and about ten boozers. To get there, we had to drive for hours over these bumpy dirt roads. There were three people in the whole club for our entire first set. It got to be ten o'clock and that's the hour when the pubs close, so pretty soon all these farmers started coming in. They're all drunk out of their minds and started shouting things like, 'Play something we can dance to, you cunt!' Some of them had these pennies they would heat over a flame and throw at the stage. There we were trying to play music and they were pelting us with these horrible bloody hot coins that stick your skin when they hit you. Then they started complaining about our volume. They sent up a note: 'Turn down or . . .' and below that was a large bloodstain."

What did you do?

"We turned up!"

"We had to," added Geezer. "After all, we're only in it for the volume."

On the way o'er the channel, August 9, 1969, Earth decided to change their name, due (perhaps?) to the existence of another "rock and blues at high volume" band called Earth. Other reports have the band contemplating the name change due to potential confusion with the bands Rare Earth or Mother Earth. Still others say the band believed the name was a bad omen because a few of the guys' relatives had recently died in quick succession, this story usually revolving around Geezer and some aunts and uncles, his dabblings with black magic cited as the cause.

Thirty-five years later, Geezer clears the air. "The proper story is, when we were called Earth, we turned up at this gig one day, and there were all these older men and women, all dressed up nicely, suits and dresses. Then we started playing and the promoter came up and told us to shut up and play our proper stuff. And we go, 'What proper stuff?' And he said, 'The single that you've got out.' And we go, 'What single?' And there was another band called Earth, and they were like the ultimate pop band, really teeny bopper kind of crap, middle-of-the-road stuff, like The Archies. We were wondering why we were getting so many gigs at the time, and it was because of this other Earth."

In any event, the change wouldn't happen right away, but the guys were fond of a song they already had in their repertoire, a song based on the Boris Karloff movie called *Black Sabbath*. Back in England, the boys discussed the new name with manager Simpson, who countered with Fred Karno's Army as a more worthy moniker — Joe Leg was also kicked around. However, Black Sabbath stuck, although the band's first professional record-

ings would still be under the guise of Earth. Gus Dudgeon was indeed along for the session, and the band was to record "The Rebel," accompanied by Norman Haines of Locomotive, the song also written by Norman, and forcefully suggested for the band by Jim Simpson. Dudgeon was soon replaced by Roger Bain, and "The Rebel," along with "A Song for Jim," were recorded and then never issued, "A Song for Jim" (the first song Sabbath ever recorded) because it was too jazzy, and "The Rebel" (the second song Sabbath ever recorded) because it was too commercial. In interviews, Sabbath has been known to call "Evil Woman" the first song they ever recorded.

"When I Came Down" became the third song Sabbath ever recorded and it too was never issued. The only 7-inch acetate of that track (handed to a mate and helper of Tony's in 1969, after he had given Tony a ride home from the pub) is backed with an early version of "The Wizard," making that likely the fourth track Black Sabbath ever recorded. A radically different, and lighter, version of "When I Came Down" would emerge on a rare album credited to the Norman Haines Band, consisting of material from Haines' post-Locomotive band Sacrifice recorded in 1970 — the track is renamed "When I Come Down." Very brief snippets of both "A Song for Jim" and "The

Rebel" can be heard on the *Black Sabbath Story Volume One* video. Tony is famously disinclined to issue Black Sabbath rarities, although he's also said, with respect to these two tracks, he doesn't know where the original recordings are anyway.

"They ended up on the video," said Tony, offhandedly. "No, we wouldn't release anything we weren't proud of. I've got stuff at home, 24 multi-tracks donkey's years old. There are tracks we did with Gillan that have never been released. There's really no point. You release the stuff you think at the time is the best for that album. It would probably have collectors' value. I've never really given it a thought. I'm not going to start releasing stuff just to make money out of it."

An early capture of the band punk-rocking their way through "Blue Suede Shoes" live, now widely available, rounds out the very-early-days oddities. "'Blue Suede Shoes' is something we'd done when we played Germany, The Beat Club," says Tony. "We just wanted to check the sound and camera shots, so we just played 'Blue Suede Shoes' for a laugh, and it's there forever now! So you've really got to be careful. It was just one of those things we did, just joking around, as we always did. Christ, if they'd taped some of the Shadows numbers and stuff we did . . . my God!"

After informing a crowd a few nights previous of the band's impending name change, Black Sabbath would play their first gig under the new, dark moniker on August 30, 1969, in Worcestershire — to seal the deal, Luke had spelled it out in black electrical tape on Bill's bass drum head.

"THE BELL AND THE RAIN"

– Black Sabbath

Before Black Sabbath got down to the brief business of shocking the rock world with their self-titled debut, they had to write (often live) the songs that would stud that sledge. The guys set about gradually replacing their long list of protracted blues covers with originals, one by one. Eventually, "The Wizard," "N.I.B.," "Black Sabbath," "Warning," and even second-record classics such as "Fairies Wear Boots," "Rat Salad" and "War Pigs" would form from clumps of clay, all before the debut record would come to pass.

WE USED TO HAVE BATTLES WITH
PRODUCERS AND ENGINEERS ABOUT
DISTORTION AND WHAT BASS IS
SUPPOSED TO SOUND LIKE. IT WAS
AN ARGUMENT ON EVERY ALBUM.

"We'd played the majority of them at gigs," remembers Tony, of the songs that would make the debut Black Sabbath record, which was tracked October 16th of 1969 and issued on a spooky Friday 13th the following February, (though not until June 1st in the U.S.) "So we were familiar with them by the time we went into the studio. We were playing Europe quite a lot. In Hamburg, the Star-Club, we actually broke The Beatles' record, which we were thrilled about. I think the first record was done in about eight hours, because at the time, for us, it was just like doing a gig. We'd walk in, get the gear set up and play [laughs]. And Ozzy would sing in a little box and that was it. You would do one guitar overdub and that was it, you're out, finished."

As compared to later albums, where Tony would perform his magic right in the control room, the sessions for the self-titled album indeed had the band set up in the same room as their amps, playing as if it was just another live show. Tony had also quipped that "you couldn't do your guitars in the control room back then even if you wanted to, because the control rooms were so tiny."

"A lot of people think the bass player is supposed to be more melodic, like Paul McCartney, playing all these nice things to give everything more depth," said Geezer, on the early establishment of his heavy, guitar-ish sound. "I couldn't do it that way so I just followed along with Tony's riffs. In addition, when we used to go into the studio, they'd say I couldn't have this much distortion on my bass, because bass players don't do that. But that's my sound. We used to have battles with producers and engineers about distortion and what bass is supposed to sound like. It was an argument on every album."

"In the studio they would always try to separate the guitar and bass sound," agrees Tony. "They get into the control room and listen to our tracks separately and complain that Geezer's bass sounded so distorted. They didn't understand that what we had together was the sound we wanted. You just can't start listening to the parts individually, because together they created our sound."

"Nobody gives an unknown group a lot of money to make an album with," said Ozzy, on the record's whirlwind session, which took place at a four-track facility off London's Tottenham Court Road. The band was said to have been turned down by 14 record labels before respected progressive rock label Vertigo relented. Vertigo had been conceived by Phonogram, who had seen EMI's Harvest label skillfully tap into the zeitgeist of pioneering British rock and folk. It was a mini boom for boutique labels, and a lot of good signing got done. But if commercial success for Vertigo acts was patchy at best, the last laugh comes in the fact that the label's many obscure records are now highly collectible among discerning hard progressive rock aficionados.

Backing up a bit, Geezer and Tony helped lay the administrative groundwork for the first album. First, Geezer: "We'd been put down by everybody, from our parents, onward. They said we'd never do anything with our lives. I was going to college, and they thought I was going to be the one to end up training in a good job, accountancy. It was a good professional job to be in. There were seven kids in my family, and I was the only one that sort of did well at school and went on to college. And when I left to form this band, they went nuts. Everybody

to play there once a week, once every couple of weeks. He got a few people down to listen to us, and a lot of them weren't interested. But Tony Hall was. All he was really interested in was making an album. We said, 'Oh that's great!' We didn't know anything more than that. And Tony Hall was willing to sign us for an album."

"I don't think they really have those kinds of people now," adds Geezer, when asked about Tony Hall. "He was like an A&R man, but A&R people had a lot more power back then, and he was a broker between different record companies and publishing companies. He would say, 'I think you should go with this,' more like a manager really.

"We auditioned for lots and lots of record companies but nobody would have us. I mean, in the end, we'd go with anybody, to get the record done. And Vertigo . . . they just gave us 1000 pounds to go and record the album. We kept about 100 quid each, and the rest of it went on the studio. Vertigo was like the new progressive label, because there were a lot of bands coming out that they couldn't classify as pop, so there were quite a few new labels. Harvest was created by EMI, Vertigo was Phillips, and it was quite prestigious to get on that label at the time."

At the production helm (at the behest of Hall and his Tony Hall Enterprises) was Roger Bain, who wasn't so much there to produce as to capture the band correctly enough. Roger had seen the guys play at Simpson's club, Henry's Blueshouse, famously saying that they had "the biggest balls in Britain." The stated aim for the work they were to do together was to out-heavy Led Zeppelin's recently issued and much vaunted *II* record.

Says Tony, "It was a new thing for Roger as well, because we were sort of his first project. And because we were very green, we didn't

thought, 'Well, it's just a pipe dream. He can't possibly do anything with it. There's no way you can ever have it as a career.' And when we finally wrote a whole album's worth of stuff, the record companies wouldn't let us into the building. They'd tell us to piss off and go away and write proper music. Everybody hated us! In the end, we went through this independent person that was like a broker for record deals. He saw something in us, and signed us up. He was like a professional A&R person. He liked what we were doing and sold us to a record company. And when we finally got into a studio, that was like the greatest thing that we could possibly do. Because we were showing everybody that we could do it. That was one of the best memories."

Tony Iommi: "This chap Jim Simpson was our contact and he ran his blues club. We used

RECORD COMPANIES WOULDN'T LET US INTO THE BUILDING. THEY'D TELL US TO PISS OFF AND GO AWAY AND WRITE PROPER MUSIC.

know any different from who was going to come from the record company or what. So they just sent Roger Bain along to work with us, to produce. So it was his test as well, really, for the record company. But he was very good, because we knew absolutely nothing. By today's standards, he probably wouldn't know a lot, but he did at that point, certainly a lot more about production than we knew. He worked a lot with the engineer we had at that time. I think it was Tom Allom, who was very helpful as well. It worked as a little team, to come up with ideas, like on 'Black Sabbath' with the bell and the rain. But he didn't have much input musically, because all that was basically done. But the little effects and sounds were down to them."

Ah yes, the bell and the rain. Opening Black Sabbath's debut self-titled record was the earthquaking namesake track, an excruciatingly slow, yet inexorably advancing mud wall of doom. Relentless rain and metronomic tubular bells accompany the band as they play the Devil's music, scaring the bejesus out of an unsuspecting rock public ill-attuned to such overt tales of Satan. All the while, Tony crouches behind a simple, lightly strummed riff that is the soundtrack to Chinese water torture, a riff that explodes in metal glory periodically, and then gives way to a thrilling, staccato, even more metallic squall of post-flower-power profanity.

Still, the band knew they had something, as Bill explains. "When we did the song 'Black Sabbath,' I think we knew we were definitely on to something different. Just by the audience reaction at the pubs we were playing. We loved the heavier stuff. We were all into Hendrix and Cream and Zeppelin. The one thing that appealed to us was taking that sound and making it heavier than everybody else, although not consciously."

"Well, certainly Cream, I liked, but more so John Mayall's Blues Breakers," says Tony, again underscoring the band's almost imperceptible graduation from heavy blues to heavy metal. "And when Clapton joined Cream of course, I wasn't too keen on that. But that was our early blues influence."

"The Shadows," laughs Tony, trying to articulate the influences that improbably had taken rock 'n' roll from the American black experience to Black Sabbath. "I don't know what makes you come up with that sort of music. The music just formed the way it did. And we never termed ourselves as heavy metal anyway. It's always been just 'rock' or 'heavy rock.'"

How about more specifically, the minor keys, the . . . doom? "Nothing I can think of. We just liked it. It just sounded heavy and ominous. It just materialized from the stuff we were doing at that time, which was all blues. We were just dabbling around and said, 'Oh I like that sound,' and it formed the basis for all those songs — 'Wicked World' was the first song we wrote, then 'Black Sabbath.'"

"On the first album, we never had any input," Iommi once said. "That was how we played, and that's how they taped us. Our sound was based on the guitar. The initial riff I'd come up with would set the scene for the song. And I sort of had more influence than anybody else, probably because I'd been with Jethro Tull. They looked at me like, 'Oh well, he left them and come back with us, so we gotta listen to him.'"

"The 'Black Sabbath' lyrics, Ozzy came up with them," notes Geezer, who would proceed to write almost all the Sabbath lyrics through all the records during the ensuing Ozzy era. "He just wrote them on the spot. We didn't even write them down. That was the first thing

out of his mouth. He knew I was into the occult and things, so we used to talk about it. I told him about some weird things that were happening to me, and I think that stuck in his mind. And when we did 'Black Sabbath,' it had a doomy riff anyway, so he just came out with those lyrics, as a warning to me about Satanism. It was about how you had to be aware of what happens to yourself when you get mixed up in black magic. My lyric writing came about because no one else in the band could do it. I think Ozzy did two sets of lyrics

on the first album, but then when it came down to coming up with something else, he was stuck [laughs]. Tony and Bill couldn't do lyrics, so it was left to me. So I got the knack for them. But 'Black Sabbath' was another bass riff. We knew it was different. Bass players wrote stuff before like that. At the time, Paul McCartney was the most famous, but The Beatles didn't write riffs on bass. I think we sort of set a precedent. Everything was bass riffs. Even when Tony wrote them on guitar, it was like how the bass would be."

"Black Sabbath" includes a third verse that was rarely used (one can experience it on the Ozzy rarities/hits package *The Ozzman Cometh*). Fleshing out the short tale of an ill-meaning witch, Satan by her side, the additional text adds a nasty image of a child watching its mother in flames, with the narrator ultimately added to the bonfire. Comments Ozzy, "Those lyrics, I didn't know what the fuck I was on about. We'd do a lot of

writing on the way to the gig, or the morning of. We'd have the melody line and that's it."

The fact that any rock band was writing about Satan was a hair-raising rarity. In fact, during the decade following the issuance of *Black Sabbath*, only a handful of bands would dare follow. Monument, Coven, Bram Stoker, Pentagram, Black Widow, perhaps Alice Cooper . . . but there was next to nothing. Before Sabbath, you had Arthur Brown, Screaming Jay Hawkins, and certainly avowed magick man Graham Bond, who was to die mysteriously, hit by a subway train in 1974. But the sum total is paltry, and none of it com-bined malevolent words with the stomach-churning volume and electricity of heavy metal quite the way Sabbath did.

Leicester's Black Widow bears special mention. Incredibly, the similarity of the name to Black Sabbath almost caused the Sabs to change their name for a second time. Also, Black Widow were the real satanic deal, or at least more enthusiastically showy about it than Sabbath. Their 1970 United Artists debut *Sacrifice* included titles such as "Come to the Sabbat," "In Ancient Days," "Conjuration" and "Attack of the Demon," and live, the band did feature satanic ritual as part of their act, resulting in all sorts of press. The two bands would be constantly confused for a couple of years; a famous mainstream Black Sabbath record review denigrated the singer on the album, Kip Trevor, who was, of course, none other than Black Widow's lead singer. Musically there was no getting the two confused. Black Widow was a jazzy, light, progressive act with flutes, who over three records became vaguely louder but still very much prog. Sabbath, on the other hand, started hard and just got impossibly harder.

As Geezer has said, there certainly was a level of interest in the dark arts, culminating in Butler painting his apartment black. "That was when I was into the ol' black magic stuff," affirms Geezer. "I'd left home, and I'd always wanted, like most teenagers, to have a garish-colored room, so I decided to paint my room totally black and have inverted crosses over the place — totally into the black magic thing. I think the ceilings were orange [laughs]. It was like a Halloween museum. Plus I had some posters, psychedelic stuff. I used to read on the subject a lot as well, plus a lot of fiction. I was into things like *The Hobbit*, *Lord of the Rings*, which was really popular in the late '60s."

Geezer explains, 35 years after the event, that a line soon had to be drawn in the sand. "Ozzy had brought me this really old black magic book, and it was all in Latin and Greek or whatever. Somebody had sent it to him, and he knew that I was interested in all that stuff. I was looking through it, and then I hid it in the cupboard, where I was living. Because I just got a weird feeling from it. And the next day, I went to get it out of the cupboard, to reread it, and it had disappeared. Completely gone into thin air. And then, I was lying in bed one night and I just felt this presence. I woke up and I saw this black shape, standing at the bottom of me bed

IF THERE IS A SATAN, HE ISN'T GOING TO HAVE FIRE COMING OUT OF HIS ASS AND HORNS ON HIS HEAD AND A FUCKING FORKED TONGUE. HE'S GOING TO BE JUST LIKE YOU AND ME.

staring at me, and it just totally freaked me out. I told Ozzy about it, and that was when I went off black magic [laughs]. This was like 1969. I took it as a warning to get out while I can."

And you never saw that book again? "Never. Totally disappeared. And it was only me in the house at the time."

Geezer's account differs slightly from the apocryphal black cat story told by Sabbath fans, in which Geezer is actually looking at the book (described as 400 years old and hand-written), turns and is startled by a black cat, turns back to the book, and the book is gone.

"Geezer's done all sorts of bloody things," laughs Tony. "We did actually live this sort of life at first. We were very interested in the other side of life, particularly Geezer and myself. We used to go and watch the horror movies and really talk a lot about the other side of life. It got to a stage in the band where we were frightened to say anything, because things were happening when we were saying them. So it became sort of a bad penny. But his apartment . . . he would do stuff like that, have all his candles burning. Black walls. He would live the

part. We used to go around the black magic shops as well, when you can find one, of course. So there was a lot of interest. Not a lot of practice, but interest."

"In those days, we didn't hang with Jimmy Page," clarifies Tony, when asked if he or Geezer ever went so far as to commiserate with the noted occultist over such matters. "It was more Robert and John we hung out with. Because Jimmy . . . you never saw Jimmy that often at all."

Speaking to *Hit Parader*, Tony elaborated on the band's penchant for the dark side. "Things we've written about in the past have just been things that have happened, but people don't mention — things that are happening in the world. Satanism and a good bit about drugs and the bomb and things like that. Geezer's had dreams. This particular instance, he had a dream that I was stuck in a lift and couldn't get out, and right next day, I got stuck in a lift and couldn't get out. Which was really weird, because the night before he had this dream and he told me about it and the darn thing happened the next day. Just like that. It's happened a few times. He can dream of things and they'll happen. Even in the early days with the things we got into on the first album, there was something pushing us into doing those sorts of things."

Geezer says he's had these dreams "from when I was a little child. I don't know if there's anything in the fact that I was born on the 17th day of the seventh month, 1949, 49 being seven sevens. I was the seventh child of a seventh child. And I always had these dreams, premonitions, that would come true. Sometimes I'd see ghosts."

"A lot of people, when we first went over to the States, realized how different the band was," continues Tony, on the band's sense of mystery. "It was like a new thing for them, because we were writing about things that were actually happening that people didn't really write about. Satanism and the like. People really got into it. We were trying to throw things up to people so that they'd realize what was going on."

The band's baring of black witchery extended to the debut album's front cover, which featured a grainy photo of a green-tinted "witch" in front of an old English house. Open the original gatefold vinyl, and you have the album's credits and a short spooky tale housed within an upside-down cross.

"Certainly, the upside-down cross was not our idea," notes Tony. "When we saw the album cover, that was in there, but I suppose what it was, was that they were asked to do an album cover, and it went with the name of the band, and they put this image together, whoever designed it. From then on, of course, we had all sorts of things happen over the years. Because, playing under the name of Black Sabbath, you can imagine the sort of people we attracted." In original — and now quite rare — UK issues of *Black Sabbath*, the gatefold art was black with gray type. Later issues were white with black type. North American issues were housed in standard, non-gate sleeves and didn't include this artwork in any form.

The mysterious lady on the cover soon revealed herself. "It was at a gig in, I believe, Lincolnshire in England," says Geezer, "and this girl came up to us, dressed just like the cover. And she was allegedly that person. Whether it's true or not, there's no way of proving it."

"We didn't know her at the time," affirms Tony. "She said 'I was the lady on the front of the album.' And we went, 'Oh!' [laughs]. But no, we didn't see her at the time."

"I just found out, again, from the Internet," adds Geezer in 2005, on the locale of the infamous cover shoot. "Someone had gone there and got a photograph taken there, and I was actually going to use that as the album cover for my new album [*Ohmwork*]. I was going to have the band stand in front of that mill. It's a place in Oxfordshire, not far from where I live in England." In fact, the structure is the Mapledurham Watermill, located on the River Thames.

Ozzy's kitchen tap necklace, and then the inner gatefold's surprise crucifix, were early examples of what would become Sabbath's penchant for crosses. Ozzy's handy father, Jack, would end up making about a hundred of them for the band, and from there on in, you always saw shots of the band, crucifixes around their necks — prime stated purpose, to stave off evil, which the band frankly attracted through their actions, mainly their early lyrics and their ominous new invention, heavy metal.

"Ozzy's pop, who was a toolmaker, forged the first ones," said Bill on the subject in a mid-'70s interview, muddying the subject of the metals. "They were made of iron and very heavy. They were made to protect us against the evil spirits, the Satanists. It was so strange. Satanists were calling us to complain about our using Black Sabbath as a name. At Christmas, Pat Meehan, our manager, is getting us crosses in platinum! The rest have been either in gold or in aluminum. Can you believe it, platinum!" "I think they were in payment for the album we had out at the time," laughs Geezer.

From the collection of Doug Roemer

"Sometimes we've felt that God could be Satan," continued Rev. Ward. "What I mean is we are living in an evil world. Therefore Satan could be God. But let's leave it at that, please. I have a concept of God that isn't just Christ, but is a God for everybody. That's why we all wear crucifixes. God is neither good nor evil. There's some of the Devil, or Abraxas, in God. That's why Black Sabbath can be into God, why we can worship him and wear these crucifixes. If he was supposed to be only good, we couldn't believe him."

"We thought to ourselves, we need to get a new angle," recalls Ozzy. "There was all this flower power and wishful thinking, that the world was so great. If you were in the sunshine with flowers in your hair, smoking pot, that was great, but the world isn't all sunny. And we thought, 'Isn't it amazing that people pay to get

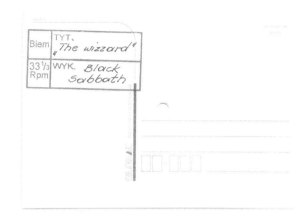

the shit scared out of them?' So we just decided to do an opposite angle to all the flower power stuff. Because that's really more satanic; if there is a Satan, he isn't going to have fire coming out of his ass and horns on his head and a fucking forked tongue. He's going to be just like you and me. He's going to be cunning and baffling — if you actually believe in that kind of thing. I think heaven and hell are on this earth. You can make anything you want out of it. But more people have died in the name of God than anything, and as far as I'm concerned, any kind of violence achieves nothing."

Back at the first album, *Black Sabbath*'s second track is jumpy, progressive proto-metal classic "The Wizard." Opening with harmonica, the song then goes into rule-breaking jam mode before settling into a pounding, metallic Bill Ward showcase of a verse, evocative of Keith Moon and his pioneering, rarely copied "lead" drumming technique.

"I really liked 'The Wizard,'" reminisces Bill. "That was a real sod to figure out. There are a lot of movements, just like 'Symptom of the Universe.' Doing those live, you had to be pretty physical to be able to play both of those. Especially 'The Wizard' because it actually doesn't stop for me as a drummer from beginning to end. There's no actual time, so I'm actually just pushing it through with all the different rolls and things like that from top to bottom."

Emphatically, "The Wizard" houses one of those Sabbath lyrics that is good, rather than evil, although all that ominous power chording around it might smokescreen the casual listener

Polish issue postcard that plays "The Wizard" on flower side

to its benevolence. Bottom line, this is a good wizard, spreading his magic, making the sun shine, making the people sigh happily. Only the demons worry. "I was reading *Lord of the Rings*, funnily enough, at the time," laughs Geezer. "The lyric came from Gandalf and all that."

Blue Öyster Cult would famously rip off "The Wizard" for their semi-hit/crowd favorite "Cities on Flame with Rock and Roll," Buck barely disguising the riff. Columbia had been jealous that they had lost out when Sabbath went with Warner Brothers U.S., and bellowed that they had wanted their own, all-American version of Black Sabbath. Blue Öyster Cult had been a psych band that had gone through as many crazy name changes as the Sabs, eventually arriving at one last weird moniker, but they possessed a sound that, indeed, approximated a version of the thunder owned by Black Sabbath. BOC would begin a period of commercial success following 1976's *Agents of Fortune*, a stadium-level run that would last through the early '80s. The two bands collided for the bickering, bad-blood *Black and Blue* tour that darkened much of the second half of 1980, with Sabbath out presenting *Heaven and Hell*, the Cultsters wielding *Cultosaurus Erectus*.

Blue Öyster Cult drummer Al Bouchard cops to the nicking. "Patti Smith was loft-sitting for Johnny Winter and that was the first time I had met her. We rehearsed there in Johnny Winter's loft and, that first day, we wrote 'Cities on Flame with Rock And Roll.' That was our first attempt at imitating Black Sabbath. And of course we stole the lick from 'The Wizard'; it's well documented. We stole the first part from 'The Wizard' and the second part from '21st Century Schizoid Man.' So, two of our favorite licks."

Returning to the originators, next on *Black Sabbath* came a tangle of music that is partitioned differently depending on what version of the record one owns. Essentially, the two full tracks are "Behind the Wall of Sleep" and "N.I.B." The original European issue of the album lists just those two tracks. The original North American issue calls the vaguely psychedelic 32-second wash of music preceding "Behind the Wall of Sleep," "Wasp," and calls the funky, iconoclastic, highly memorable 41-second bass solo from Geezer that precedes "N.I.B.," "Bassically." This issue grabs all four titles and assigns them a time of 9:44 and also bands them as one track. The European version bands them as two tracks, assigning 3:40 and 5:58 respectively. Apparently, all of this tomfoolery has to do with higher royalties being paid in England if you could get ten "songs" on an album.

"Behind the Wall of Sleep" is an unheralded, underrated Sabbath track, Ozzy crooning (in that strange low register he quickly left behind post-debut) a cryptic, poetic, almost proto-environmental tale of death and dying.

Often erroneously said to stand for Nativity in Black, "N.I.B." gets its title in a less sinister manner. "That's the one we threw together in Switzerland in 1968," begins Bill, "and actually 'N.I.B.' is named after me. The guys nicknamed me Nibby. Tony still calls me Nib to this day. It

came from a time when we were doing a lot of opium [laughs]. We were all high and for some reason through the hallucinogenics of it all, Geezer and Ozzy thought I looked like the top of a pen. A pen nib. They totally got lost behind the idea of that, cracking up, and it just stuck. And that's been it for the last 30-odd years. But it's just a real good, hard rock song. I like Ozzy's lines; the 'Oh yeah's' showed up. That was the stamp of approval on that one."

Still the Nativity in Black thing makes sense: this is probably Geezer's most patently evil lyric. "'N.I.B.' was supposed to be a humorous song about Satan falling in love with a woman. Because at the time, there were all these corny old films about the guys saying we'll give you the stars and the moon, like to your girlfriend. Whereas Satan could actually do that [laughs]."

"It was totally spontaneous in the studio," adds Geezer, on "Bassically," the aforementioned intro to "N.I.B.," "because I had just gotten a wah-wah pedal, and I was playing about with it, and the producer at the time really liked it, and 'N.I.B.' was one of my riffs, so he just said, 'Do your bass solo and then go into 'N.I.B.'"

Side 2 of the original vinyl begins two different ways, depending on which version of the record one purchased. European issues featured a cover of Crow's "Evil Woman."

Why a cover? "Because that's what we thought we had to do," relates Bill. "We we're really naive, I mean, even to this day. But as soon as we did it, everybody was just so uncomfortable. All of us were just going 'Ugh, this feels horrible.' It was like going to the dentist or something. So we knew we had done the wrong thing."

Nonetheless, the track works. In this considerably heavied up form, it makes sense for the leaden band at hand, both through its pur-

poseful rumble and its evil woman theme. The chorus is a little melodic, a little obvious, but the overall melody is, all things considered, pretty dark. "Evil Woman" was released as a single on January 9th of 1970. The album, as mentioned, came out a few weeks later, selling five thousand copies in its first week and hanging around the UK charts for 13 weeks at onset (peaking at Number 8), and 42 weeks

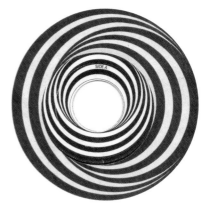

over various time periods. The album would eventually go platinum in the U.S., for sales of over one million copies.

North American issues of the album included another Sabbath original called "Wicked World," which was also the B-side to the "Evil Woman" single. Once past a spirited but jazzy and dated intro, a characteristically doomy verse infects and spreads, with Ozzy's vocal back in low register mode, nearly to the point of sounding like the work of someone else, someone wiser.

"Certainly, 'Wicked World' was a 'make it up as you go along,' definitely the solo part," explains Tony. "It was very much a jam, so that would vary from night to night. When we actually did record the album, it was actually longer than it is on the record, because I went on a bit [laughs]. And I wanted to do it again, but it was like, 'Oh, no, no, there's no time,' and that's the way it was in those days. It was such a long number for them and for that time, if you do it again, that's another 10 or 15 minutes. 'No, no, that's enough' [laughs]."

Lyrically, Geezer is on his way to establishing himself as cynical documenter of the world's many plights. In a very short space, he speaks of war, disease, and finally a single mother trying to earn a living.

"There are quite a few," reflects Geezer, on

his many themes. "That song was influenced by Vietnam. Elsewhere, I think science fiction played a big part, things like 'Iron Man.' Science fiction, fantasy, the supernatural, and a lot of politics as well. The one thing we didn't want to do was normal love songs, because everybody in the world was doing them. And our whole band was against all that anyway, everybody talking about splitting up with their girlfriend. But the reason we got together and made our music in the first place was because nobody else was doing it. So I just wrote about things that were interesting to me. If I'd read a particularly good book, I'd condense that down to a song."

Closing the album is another tangle of tracks with jams. European versions cite "Sleeping Village" and "The Warning," an

Aynsley Dunbar Retaliation cover, as separate tracks, the former at 3:50, the latter at 10:30. North American copies list "A Bit of Finger," "Sleeping Village" and "Warning" (not "The Warning") as one track at 14:32.

In any event, what you get is an extended blur of jamming, albeit somewhat structured and well recorded. "The Warning" has a depressing love-gone-wrong lyric, but an appropriate enough doomy blues for the fit of the album. Still, the blues is something Sabbath had outgrown, and their ensuing catalogue had little to do with the genre. "We started out as a blues band," affirms Geezer, "and many of the songs on the first album were quite blues-based. But there were never any songs where we were thinking about another band or their style. Our biggest influence was Led Zeppelin."

Polish issue postcard that plays "The Warning" on flower side

From the collection of Doug Roemer

"The Warning" quickly collapses into additional bouts of psychedelia and even boogie rock (think pre-Schenker UFO), before mercifully drawing to a close with a reprise, culminating in the song's powerful chorus clang. All told, though, not the most inspired or purposeful pile of music from the Sabs, and, given its nearly full-side girth, a large part of why the first Black Sabbath album is arguably the dodgiest — unarguably the most meandering — of all the Ozzy-era albums.

The legendary Lester Bangs, writing for Rolling Stone at the time, was not that impressed either, indicating that "across the tracks in the industrial side of Cream country lie unskilled laborers like Black Sabbath, which was hyped as a rockin' ritual celebration of the satanic mass or some such claptrap, something like England's answer to Coven. The whole album is a shuck — despite the wooden Claptonisms from the master's tiredest Cream days. They even have discordant jams with bass and guitar reeling like velocitized speedfreaks all over each other's musical perimeters yet never quite finding synch — just like Cream! But worse."

Which proves — through the obvious inability of the language to quite identify what was going on — that there was this emphatic invention of heavy metal taking place, a breath of hot black air that hadn't been there before. "Black Sabbath," "The Wizard," "N.I.B.," and "Wicked World" . . . this was about as much as Led Zeppelin had accomplished for the heavy metal cause, through double the work — not that they were trying, noses upturned. Whether, purposely attempting something or not, Led Zeppelin had turned in the seminal "Communication Breakdown," along with "Whole Lotta Love," "Heartbreaker" and "Livin' Lovin' Maid," through *Led Zeppelin* and *II*, issued March 1969 and October 1969 respectively. Less convincing metal behemoths "Dazed and Confused," "Good Times Bad Times" and "How Many More Times" were also laid down (and all three from the debut), but nobody had quite put the package together the way Sabbath had.

In the end it, however, is of no concern, because Sabbath's next 1970 album would summarily annihilate the above comparative, and bring on two more — Deep Purple and Uriah Heep.

"I THINK I'M A NATURAL WORRIER"

– Paranoid

There wasn't really so much of a pronounced tour for Black Sabbath's debut album, nor, for that matter, for its resounding, head-pounding followup *Paranoid*. Recording the self-titled record was no more than a sidetrack amongst pub gigs. After the second day of that, the band soldiered on with business, the record was released, and on they went. Indeed, the songs of the set were as much selections that would show up on record number two anyway. The band had played sporadically through 1969, then intensified the pace in early 1970, playing every corner of the UK imaginable through March, April and May of that year. Early June saw more of the same, with mid-month marking the making of *Paranoid* ("in a couple days, three days," says Tony), followed by a handful of German dates, all in June.

The album was recorded at Regent Sound, also studio of choice for the debut, Roger Bain again at the production helm, black magic lyrics dropped from the itinerary due to all the press hassles from the first record 'round.

Paranoid was to be the album that set Sabbath up for life. Fans would show up in droves and the critics would begin what became an endless debate over the evils of heavy metal, touching down hither and thither on the sorry, scroungy, depressive state of the band's fans; whether Tony could play guitar or not; the band's bulldozing lack of dynamics or subtlety; whether all those spooky lyrics were merely designed to shock and sell, or whether they had any sort of poetic or perhaps even social value; and most quaintly, whether Sabbath had created some sort of new thing called "downer rock."

The first inklings of the quaking record to come arrived in the form of an advance single, featuring the album's mercilessly simple and point-blank title track, issued July 17th of 1970. But once the record proper dropped (on September 18th for UK fans; not until January 1, 1971 in the U.S.), a much more bombastic and overarching song greeted the ears.

"War Pigs," provisionally named "Walpurgis," had already been a live favorite for the band, and indeed, the lyrics changed completely over time from something much more brutal and witchcrafty, to the ugly, aggressive antiwar classic now considered one of Sabbath's top two or three most enduring compositions. Asked about the alternate lyrics, Ozzy says that "what we'd do is get the melody line, and the lyrics were always the very last thing to be written. I'd get comfortable with the melody line, and Geezer or I would write them in the studio. But other than that, I don't know where they're from."

"That was totally against the Vietnam War," offers Geezer, "about how these rich politicians and rich people start all the wars for their benefit and get all the poor people to die for them. Which is still happening now." In fact, the album was going to be called *War Pigs*, but the label got cold feet due to the hostility it perceived for the band in the U.S., given the fractious debate over the merits of the Vietnam War. Adds Tony, "the album cover was designed with the guy with the shield and sword, and it was supposed to have at least some resemblance to "War Pigs," and then they banned the title. So we had to come up with a title quick, and they said, 'Oh, *Paranoid*.' So suddenly we were stuck with a cover that didn't have anything remotely to do with somebody who was paranoid."

"We used to sort of jam around with 'War Pigs,'" offers Tony on the song's very early origins. "Again, we used to play at these clubs in Europe playing seven 45-minute spots a day, and we would get bored, because there would only be a handful of people in them, and we would start making songs up. And "War Pigs" was one of them. And we might have had 'Fairies,' as well."

Adds Bill, "The first memory I have of working on 'War Pigs' is at The Beat Club, Hirschen, which I think was in Zurich, Switzerland. But it was a real horrible place, basically full of prostitutes and some of the johns that used to come in for the prostitutes. This would be roughly 1968. We would've fin-

I THINK POLITICIANS ARE JUST PUPPETS TO THE HANDFUL OF PEOPLE WHO RULE THE WORLD ANYWAY.

ished 'Iron Man' and 'War Pigs' at Monmouth, where we did all of our early stuff."

"It's just a reflection of society, real life," says Geezer, repeating a theme Sabbath would often bring up with the press in defense of their more virulent pronouncements. "Everyone has their point of view. I used to write like that. 'War Pigs,' 'Lord of This World,' even 'Paranoid.' It's just an observation of society. I'm not preaching or trying to come up with any answers. But 'War Pigs' is such a strong song. That's why we start concerts with it. It has absolutely everything in it. It's a great song and it gets you up to play the whole concert. From there it's full steam ahead."

"I think you have to be a fan of politics if you live in the world," muses Geezer. "You are subjected to politics and it's always a good subject to write about [laughs] — good for musicians and comedians. Back then, it was more about the Vietnam era. Because we used to get a lot more things on the television in England than anybody ever did in America. They would show like all the propaganda that was going on. And people didn't know what I was talking about, when I came over here, because they weren't allowed to see that on TV. And we just thought England was going to be next to be dragged into the Vietnam War. I grew up post-World War II, and the area we lived in in Birmingham was bombed out during the war, and it was still being rebuilt when I was growing up. I knew a lot of families whose fathers were killed in World War II. My uncle was shot in World War II, so war really affected me. And me brothers had to join the army; one of them had to go fight in Egypt, so it was all very real to me, and it was scary, in a way. And with Vietnam, people were saying it was really bad and England was going to join in. So that's why we wrote 'War Pigs.'"

Geezer's political tendencies also came from his father. "He had been brought up in Dublin, when the British were shooting everyone over there, being Catholic. So he was very much working class, 'of the workers' and that kind of thing. He didn't like government whatsoever. But on the other hand, there was no work in Ireland, so he actually joined the British army — he was in that for about 20 years. So, on one hand, he was for the military, but for the working class as well."

"War Pigs" is of course intensely catchy due to its verse construction, Tony's slamming, simple chording spanned by nothing more than Ozzy's admonishing, sanctimonious bleat and Bill's timekeeping high hat. But as the song grinds on, Sabbath prove themselves capable of sophisticated, almost progressive rock maneuvers. Some copies of *Paranoid* list the amorphous blob of instrumental intro to "War Pigs" as "Luke's Wall." Or not. The U.S. original

resorts only to the record centerpiece for the designation (no mention on the back sleeve or within the gate), messily going with "War Pigs — 7:55 Luke's Wall."

"There is always war going on somewhere in the world," says Geezer, ruing the song's accursed universality. "You can relate that to any war going on at any time. Unfortunately, wars are always with us. We're just wasting our time; it's out of our hands. Just look what is happening with the Iraq thing, with all the ordinary people dying over that crap. You vote for a person who promises one thing and then turns around and does another. I think politicians are just puppets to the handful of people who rule the world anyway. There is nothing we can do about it, unfortunately. It's always going to be the little people who get sent to war and die for all these rich idiots. Why would anyone care for Iraq when the American health systems need money? Why spend all the money that could help fix that problem in Iraq? We have enough poverty in our own countries we need to worry about before going anywhere else."

Black Sabbath's biggest (yet arguably tiniest) song of all time, "Paranoid," followed up the grand gestures of "War Pigs." Beyond being Sabbath's signature track, "Paranoid" won top heavy metal song of all time, in a worldwide poll conducted for this writer's *The Top 500 Heavy Metal Songs of All Time* book. (Sabbath had fully 28 different songs crack the Top 500; the source album notched Number 6 in the companion albums-based book).

But, as Geezer explains, "Paranoid" is famously known for being an off-the-cuff afterthought. "We'd finished the album and had packed up all our gear and the management said they needed an extra three or four minutes to put on the album. We said we didn't have

anything, and they said, 'Can you write something?' And Ozzy would literally be singing the lyrics as I wrote them. I was looking through the basement the other day and I found all the original lyrics from the *Paranoid* album, and verses from the song 'Paranoid' that weren't used. It might be interesting for people to see the original versions some day. Lyrically, 'War Pigs,' 'Iron Man,' 'Paranoid'. . . I used to try and give a message of hope or something at the end of each song, and now I don't bother. Now I realize I can't change anything!"

"It was about 12:30 in the afternoon," adds Bill. "We were down at Regent Sound, in the heart of London, Soho. We stopped working, went out to the pub, had a couple pints and a sandwich and really had no idea what to do for the song. Anyway, as always, we get back into the studio and Tony immediately came up with the main riff you hear in 'Paranoid.' And as we got around our instruments, we started

to jam. We hadn't been jamming for more than five minutes and we started to get an arrangement. And then we ran down from top to bottom, like 'OK, here we go; this is fun.' Oz put a bunch of lyrics straight on it and Geezer put a bunch of lyrics there, and he had a melody and Ozzy had a melody and that was it. Top to bottom, the whole song took about 25 minutes." Indeed Geoff Lucas (the Luke of "Luke's Wall") has said that he and Spock Wall had gone to Birmingham to pick up some equipment, gone for not much more than a couple hours, and by the time they got back to London, the song was done.

"Paranoid" is of a certain, then quite modern metal construct that improves upon a formula cast virtually for the first time through Led Zeppelin's "Communication Breakdown." One might call it proto-punk, a staccato chugger, its riff a machinegun riff. Whatever the descriptive, Tony's quick hitting of the power chords became a signature metal maneuver, good for a couple of songs on most metal albums through the rest of the decade

and into the '80s. Lyrically, the song is deeper than the credit usually given it. "I used to suffer a lot with depression," explains Geezer. "I used to go in and out, happy one day, down the next. And I was just going through a bad time at the time, so I wrote those lyrics. I just couldn't seem to get through to anyone."

"It's not so much of a problem now, because they've come up with some really good things like Prozac and stuff," adds Geezer, on his current state. "But when I was growing up as a kid, I used to get these weird, strange moods, and people thought I was being miserable and standoffish, and I didn't know what the hell was happening to me. It wasn't until the mid-'90s, when I was going through a really bad depression. I was living in St. Louis at the time and I went to the doctor there, and he says you've got depression. And that's when he put me on to Prozac, and after all these years I realize how bad I'd been, once I'd gotten back to sort of normal again. I realized that I'd been suffering from it for 20, 30 years."

Setting the focus on Sabbath's Ozzy years,

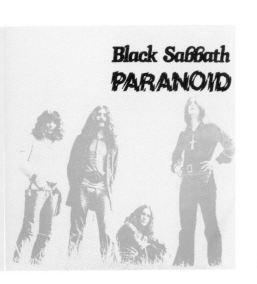 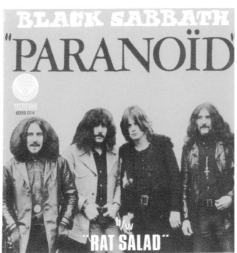 

I HOPE THEY SACRIFICE SOMETHING TONIGHT. A HUMAN SACRIFICE WOULD BE GOOD. I'D DO IT MYSELF IF I WOULDN'T GO TO JAIL FOR IT.

Geezer recalls that "It was all right in the '70s. It was all the drugs I was taking [laughs]. That sort of made it go away. So it was mainly in the '60s, I had it worse. There was a time when Sabbath first started and it just hit me in Germany for some reason; I was in a really bad state and didn't know what was going on. Nobody talked about it or explained it to you, and I managed to get through that. And in the '70s I wasn't too bad; I think I just had one bout of it. The '80s were OK. It was mainly the '90s where it came back. All of the lyrics in 'Paranoid' sort of summed up the way I felt at that time. 'Finished with my woman because she couldn't help me with my mind.'"

In that light, one can find a richness of imagery within the song, imagery that offers insight into the nature of depression, alienation, being locked within one's own mental prison. It was all the more grist for a certain, often-repeated critical accusation that Sabbath's dire, drunken, often riotous fan base was having their dead-end depressive moods reinforced and solidified. Part and parcel of this denigration was the perception that the band was empathetic but irresponsible, dishing the downer rock because they were down themselves, no apologies, this is the real world, welcome to it. Critics were quick to point out that this yoke of sullenness was shared with an almost exclusively teenage male fan base — what could they know about good music?

Supporting such an oscillating view between nihilism and unvarnished reality, journalist Robin Green gathered some fan reactions back in 1971. Said one follower, "I'm scared of them; they're evil and strange. I like to be scared. I hope they sacrifice something tonight. A human sacrifice would be good. I'd do it myself if I wouldn't go to jail for it." Another said, "It's freaky. It makes you think you're in a graveyard; it makes you feel more alive while you're there." A third added, "We dig Black Sabbath. You can get high on their music without even being stoned."

Green also obtained comment from some of the Warner brass. "Their music is loud; it's painful. I've been driven out of places by the noise. They play to a young crowd, say 14 to 17 years old. Who knows how they hear about them? The word just gets around that this is a group to go see." Another label honcho said "It's incredible. They're not like our other performers, and we don't understand their popularity; no one can figure it out. They haven't had that much publicity, but their concerts are sellouts and their albums sell millions. The baby teenyboppers all just boogie up in the balconies and then run out to buy the records, and we love 'em."

"They're just a greaser band," added another rock journo. "No one knows how they got started. They're loud and electronic and get an ugly audience — not your Grateful

Dead audience, not even your Poco audience — kids on reds, the Johnny Winter audience."

"They're metallic, like a magnet. I like their words, they're weird, about death and Satanism, but I kind of like it," said one teen fan. Another added, "They have drive. They have a better three-piece sound than any group since Cream. They're not musically inclined, but they're basic and powerful. And they're kind of sadistic."

"People feel evil things," replied Geezer, "but nobody ever sings about what's frightening and evil. I mean the world is a right fucking shambles. Anyway, everybody has sung about all the good things." To which Bill added, "Most people live on a permanent down, but just aren't aware of it. We're trying to express it for people."

"We like to see people enjoying themselves, and if we come across doomy and evil, it's just the way we feel," was Tony's assessment.

Back on planet *Paranoid*, "Planet Caravan," Black Sabbath's first ballad (although more of a funeral dirge), came next, its soundscape drifting along gauzily in stark contrast to the cold steel of the two previous tracks. "We did that in a rehearsal room in Birmingham," recalls Tony. "It was a time when I had just gotten this flute. I started playing this thing on the guitar first, and it was very light sounding,

and I didn't think anybody would like it, really. 'No, we like that,' and Ozzy started singing and that was it. I played a flute on it, just to make it a bit different."

"Ozzy's using the famous tremolo from the Hammond organ system," explains Bill. "We put his voice through it, a Hammond reverberation effect. Tony had that weird sound, and Geez just got in somewhere. It was something that was made up in the studio and totally worked."

"That was about visiting planets, in your own sort of spacecraft, getting away from Earth," says Geezer. "It would be a good idea to do that now with all the hatred in the world. It was about how there was so much hate in the world, and these people wanted to get away from it, to find a better world."

"We do that to add a bit of light and shape to the album," says Tony, on the band's balladeering tendency, "Planet Caravan" marking their first attempt at it. "When I first started doing quiet stuff, the others were like, 'Well, where's that gonna go?' And I try to explain, 'Well, it's good to do that, because that makes the heavier tracks sound even heavier.' It gives a bit of strength to the album. I would always try and do something on an album like that. As

I say, it was a bit of a jump in the deep end, as far as being questioned, 'Ooh, is that gonna go on the album? Do you think it's a bit too opposite?' But I think it worked to have a few acoustic things in."

If "Paranoid" is Sabbath's "Communication Breakdown," then "Iron Man" is undoubtedly the band's "Smoke on the Water," both tracks living on the big, dumb riff no self-respecting guitarist would dare be so audacious, so devoid of sense, as to write. Of course, sometimes the simplest ideas are the most timeless (ask AC/DC).

"I thought it was a really stupid concept," laughs Geezer in his inimitable sardonic style. "The title was from a comic book, *Iron Man*; it was an ecological theme. We were all very environmental at the time, and it was about this entity that turns into metal and is incapacitated at the end, just lying there. He can't talk at the end of it, but he has all this knowledge that can save the earth from catastrophe. I think I'm a natural worrier [laughs]. Some people are political, others are totally apolitical. I think me dad was very political, so I was sort of brought up very politically minded."

"I was into English comics but not really American comics," he adds, clarifying who did what. "I think Ozzy just came up with the title 'Iron Man.' When we were writing that song, Ozzy just threw in a line about 'Iron Man.' It was just like a throwaway line for him, and I said, 'Let's write about that' and I just made it up. I didn't really know about the comic at the time, though."

In a separate interview, Geezer adds another slant to the tale. "There was a lot of space exploration being done by NASA and a lot of things in the news about pollution and nuclear war at the time as well. It was about a guy who had gone into space exploration and had seen

Black Sabbath's "Iron Man"
Black Sabbath's "Iron Man"
Black Sabbath's "Iron Man"
Black Sabbath's "Iron Man"
Black Sabbath's "Iron Man"
Black Sabbath's "Iron Man"
Black Sabbath's "Iron Man"
Black Sabbath's "Iron Man"
Black Sabbath's "Iron Man"
Black Sabbath's "Iron Man"
Black Sabbath's "Iron Man"
Black Sabbath's "Iron Man"
Black Sabbath's "Iron Man"
Black Sabbath's "Iron Man"
Black Sabbath's "Iron Man"

Photo of a group who needs a hit single like you need termites. But who's getting one. Just in case.

"Iron Man" issues from "Paranoid", the second of Black Sabbath's three gold albums from Warners, and on Ampex—distributed Warner Bros. tapes. It is single #WB1530, brought to you by the gang that can shoot straight.

If you want to improve this country, register to vote. Or else.

SINGLE-WISE
"IRON MAN" BY
BLACK SABBATH
IS THE PEOPLE'S
CHOICE

TOUR-WISE
BLACK SABBATH IS AT IT AGAIN

		3/16	Tucson, Arizona
		3/17	San Bernardino, California
		3/18	San Diego, California
		3/19	Las Vegas, Nevada
3/1	Fayetteville, So. Carolina	3/21	St. Paul, Minnesota
3/3	Miami, Florida	3/22	Detroit, Michigan
3/3	Jacksonville, Florida	3/23	Quebec City, Quebec, Canada
3/4	West Palm Beach, Florida	3/24	Montreal, Quebec, Canada
3/6	St. Petersburg, Florida	3/25	Rochester, New York
3/6	Raleigh, North Carolina	3/26	Salem, Virginia
3/7	Charlotte, North Carolina	3/27	Pittsburgh, Pennsylvania
3/9	Columbus, Ohio	3/28	Huntington, West Virginia
3/10-11	San Francisco, California	3/30	New Haven, Connecticut
3/12	Vancouver, British Columbia	3/31	Charleston, West Virginia
3/14	Spokane, Washington	4/1	Greensboro, North Carolina
3/15	Los Angeles, California	4/2	Columbia, South Carolina

the future of the world. He came back to warn everyone about what was going to happen to the world, and he got caught up in an electronic type thing when he was entering the earth's atmosphere and he got turned into iron, but his brain was still working. It was really just a science fiction story."

Evocations of both *Frankenstein* and The Who's *Tommy* reside within Geezer's unknowing portrayal of this comic book "Armored Avenger," who, as the actual comic-based source character, was unwieldy and slow, a bit of a joke as a superhero.

Says Bill, "I wanted 'Iron Man' to be really heavy, from a drum point of view. So I came up with that slow bass drum thing, which feels different every time we do it live. That's because I can never get the bass drum the right way. But that's just my internal struggle for the rest of my life to live with."

Side two of the original vinyl opens with "Electric Funeral," a doom-drenched downer rock classic if there ever was one. Geezer is in fine ghoulish form, describing the particularly nasty effects of an atomic blast, the world's utter annihilation to be followed by some sort of supernatural conference on the fact between the forces of good and evil. Comments Geezer, "The big Cold War thing was going on at the time and it just seemed like any second it could happen." In fact, this is another one of those underrated and underappreciated Geezer lyrics, poetry flowing from nearly every line.

"Hand of Doom" follows, with Sabbath, or more specifically Geezer and Ozzy, laconically handing out more downers, before Bill and Tony explode with "War Pigs"-style metal mania. And like "War Pigs," the song houses unexpected additional movements. "We wrote that in Wales and I was feeling quite ecstatic about the track after it was complete," remem-

bers Bill. "We must have played it five or six times a day; we all liked it that much that we would go back and play it. It's still one of the band's favorite tracks from the early days."

Geezer remarks on the band's graphic antidrug lyric. "In me former band, before Sabbath, and in the early days of Sabbath, we used to play a lot of American military bases around Europe, and in England. We used to talk to the soldiers who had just come back from Vietnam, and they used to always talk about the drug use over there. A lot of them were on heroin, and they used to have this stop-off point in England where they had to come off heroin before they could go back to America, because the government didn't want the American media to see the troops were on heroin. And I used to talk to a lot of the soldiers about the drugs, and that's where 'Hand of Doom' came from."

"The lyrics are true to life," said Geezer back in '81. "The words we write are about things that are happening. A lot of bands write about things like love. We write about things that are true but that people don't necessarily like to talk about. I suppose we prick a few consciences in a way." Added Tony: "Raw words to

go with raw music. People think about evil all the time, and feel evil things, but rarely do they sing about what's evil. Most people live on a permanent down but aren't even aware of it."

"'War Pigs' and the drug songs are just our opinions," remarked Tony back in the day. "We're not trying to influence people. We don't know if people will take it all in. One of the biggest problems in the music scene today is the kids that try to read things into songs. They often create things that aren't there. The music of Black Sabbath is simple, basic stuff; the lyrics are plain, laid on with a plate. But with those kids, it's like a big battle with the mind trying to sort things out. We haven't got the power to try and direct people in politics or anything else."

"Because it's happening all around us," says Ozzy, when asked about "Hand of Doom" and the other drug lyrics. "People take drugs just like they breathe air, in one form or another. It's better than boy meets girl, boy loses girl. We like to write about other things happening around us. Like describing someone lying there with a needle in his arm, wondering if he's going to get out of this mess. You can't avoid these things. Geezer wrote those

WE WRITE ABOUT THINGS THAT ARE TRUE BUT THAT PEOPLE DON'T NECESSARILY LIKE TO TALK ABOUT.

grotesque lyrics to 'Hand of Doom.' They were meant to be shocking like that, about people who take drugs all the time. I take drugs sometimes to get high, to escape reality, but I don't make a habit out of it because I've got responsibilities, to my family, to my band. Something's wrong with people who have to depend on them, and maybe through lyrics like 'Hand of Doom,' we can make some of them realize, 'Hey, that's me they're talking about.' You can't just treat them like pieces of shit; they need to be helped."

Next up was a bit of a respite called "Rat Salad." In effect, this one is a Bill Ward showcase (pair and compare with Led Zeppelin's "Moby Dick"), though it's not as if he doesn't get to stretch out in numerous other places on the album. "Everybody was a star back then; everybody got their chance, for 30 seconds, or a couple of minutes, to play solo. I just love the way the concerts were back then because the bass player had his bass solo et cetera. That was the art at the time; that was the fashion. So I got to take my little drum solo and put it on a record. We really didn't know what to do with it lyrically. There were some nice little cuts that

Tony and Geezer were doing so we just said fuck it, let's do this. And the title fits things very well because inwardly, Sabbath have a lot of inside comedy, a lot of inside jokes; name-calling is definitely a big thing for us."

Rat was one of Bill's pet names, Ward being the main beneficiary of most of the name-calling (and practical jokes), some of the other jibes being Nib, Nibby, Stinky and Smelly. "I'd been called Smelly for years and that's like a drop-off from Rat, like a little cul-de-sac. They called me Smelly because I played so fucking hard on stage and the sweat is just unbelievable [laughs]. There's lots of unmentionable names. Everybody got their own abusive name."

Closing the record is another swingin' Sabbath classic in "Fairies Wear Boots," with the dreamy, jazzy, psychedelic intro called, on some issues of the album, "Jack the Stripper."

"That one, like 'N.I.B.', and some of the really early Sabbath stuff, was done at the Aston Community Center," remembers Bill. "I think the idea came from the Mods and the Rockers, which was big back then. It originally might have been aimed toward the skinheads. But again it was Geezer and Ozzy who put the lyric together, and it's very much a '67, early '68 Sabbath feel in the sense of the jazz and really no solid sense of time. We kind of just clumped my drums around Geezer and Tony [laughs]. Every time we do that song I can never play the same thing twice. It's probably pretty close but every night I never know what I'm going to do, because it's based on wherever I am physically and mentally at the moment. I seem to be lacking in whatever it is you have to have to get it perfect every night."

Adds Geezer, "'Fairies Wear Boots,' Ozzy wrote that. We got set upon by a gang of skinheads. And skinheads in England used to wear these great big Doc Marten boots. The higher

up the leg meant how hard they were. So skinheads used to have these almost knee-length Doc Marten boots on. So we got attacked by about 24 of them one night and we beat the hell out of them. There were about five of us against 25 or 24 of them. We murdered them, so we call them a bunch of fairies." This event is possibly the time Sabbath had a bunch of equipment stolen in Newcastle, after which they were set upon by skinheads, with Tony sustaining injury to his right arm, which caused the cancellation of a gig the next night. Other versions report that Tony had received a black eye, at which point the crew came to the rescue swinging mic stands.

By the end of 1970, Black Sabbath had the music industry up in arms over their daring, blaring music. But competition was in the wings. Three months before *Paranoid* hit the

streets, a newly reconstituted Deep Purple (Ian Gillan and Roger Glover had replaced Rod Evans and Nick Simper respectively) had formulated their shockingly heavy *In Rock* album. In many ways, *In Rock*, with its speed, precision and pyrotechnics made *Paranoid* sound dated. It was the new perfect heavy metal album, and the critics gave it the nod, further positioning Sabbath as the heavy band for shiftless ne'er-do-wells, while Deep Purple and/or Led Zeppelin were both loud and wild, but haughtily sophisticated. But most often, the cage match was set between Sabbath and Zeppelin. As the generation before had split itself into warring factions of Beatles and Stones fans, high schools across North America defined sociable, smart, literary, possible musician types as the Zeppelin fans, while the jean-jacketed longhairs smoking dope behind the backstop were more likely to have in their possession stolen 8-tracks and cassettes featuring the hopeless anthems of Ozzy, Tony, Geezer and Bill.

"I suppose it automatically became a rivalry," reflects Tony, "because we were both heading for the charts, and we were the only few bands that were like that. I didn't know Ritchie [Blackmore] at the time, but I know him now. We knew Zeppelin well, because they were friends of ours in the early days and we were from the same town. So we used to see them a lot, certainly Robert Plant and John Bonham. When they started Zeppelin I

remember Bonham saying, 'We've got this band; we're joining with Jimmy Page.' And I remember the days from before he joined Zeppelin. He used to play in different bands around Birmingham, and he was always getting fired because he was too loud. So one week he would be with a band. We used to play these alternate weeks; this was before I was with Sabbath and before he was with Zeppelin. Bill and myself had another band. So we used to see him every other week playing at this place called The Midland Red Club in Birmingham, and he'd be there one week, and then the week after that, he wouldn't be there. 'What happened?' 'Oh, he was too loud; we fired him.'"

"Some of our fans would like Zeppelin and Purple," continues Tony, "then there was the other side who just liked what we did. So I think we all had our individual things, then we had a joint thing where some bled onto the other. We were classed as more of the heavier, doomier, downer rock sort of band — and working class; Purple were more rock, jolly rock if you like [laughs]."

"I saw Deep Purple as a pop band," muses Bill. "Again, no disregard to the fellas, but I could hear that sort of pop mainline through it. We were singing about shooting heroin and 'Hand of Doom,' 'Children of the Grave.' We were inside a lot of hardcore issues. And I mean, I love Purple; I saw them as a real solid rock unit, but I didn't get the rest of it. And it was the same with Zeppelin, and I love Zeppelin and I totally admire John Bonham as a percussionist. But Robert's lyrics were kind of like love lyrics. And that's not a put-down. But Ozzy was screeching his balls off singing 'What is this that stands before me?' And we were serious about it. It was a very serious band as well as a happy band. But those lyrics meant all the world to us. That line still means a lot to me every day [laughs]. So I could hear some really good rock units forming, but I always felt we were the odd band out. We'd come in under the gun all the time [laughs] and I just loved it."

"I knew we were doing something different because everybody hated us," continues Bill. "We were thrown out of most places. I felt very alone, along with Tony, Ozzy and Geezer, which created tremendous unison, by the way. That was one of our strengths. It was us against the world, and as a teenager, of course, one can feel that way a lot. I knew deep down inside that we were into something that was not a part of anything else I'd been hearing. I felt like an oddball. One could look back and go, 'We did that and that got created and fashion came from this, and so much came from hard rock which then turned into metal.' But we were raw. When Led Zeppelin's first album came out, one of the things I was particularly fascinated about was the smoothness of it. And ours, when I compared, was so raw and almost punkish, gritty — there's mistakes all over it."

Adds Geezer dismissively, "I liked Deep Purple *In Rock*, but I don't really like anything else that they've done. We didn't really like Deep Purple, to be honest [laughs]. That wasn't one I'd really listened to, although I think I had the album eventually."

Released that same month was Uriah Heep's *Very 'Eavy Very 'Umble*, known in the U.S. as simply *Uriah Heep*. Savaged in the press as a mere Deep Purple clone, their record nonetheless was roughly as heavy and riffy as *Paranoid*, perhaps even more accomplished and efficient, although, granted, neither was a match for *In Rock*. "We didn't even recognize them," notes Geezer on Heep. "We didn't even think of them as a legitimate band."

One could argue that *Paranoid* was inferior to both of the above records, most clearly in

comparison to *In Rock*. Indeed *Paranoid* contains many echoes of that debut record's morose bluesiness, its jammy qualities, its competent yet raw and somewhat chilly recording values. There's a bleakness to *Paranoid*, even a sort of mean-spiritedness, that puts it second to last in this writer's opinion with respect to rankings of the Ozzy-era albums. Part of that summation surely must come from the fact that in terms of airplay, it is the band's Led Zeppelin *IV*. If one is to be sick and tired of any Black Sabbath songs, the list will very likely include "Paranoid," "War Pigs,"

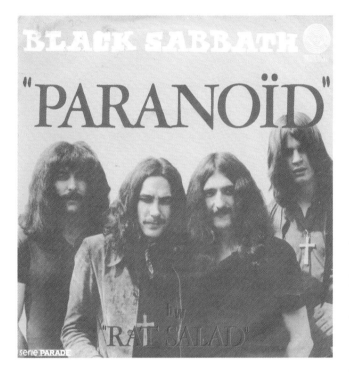

"Iron Man" and "Fairies Wear Boots," a happenstance not helped when any given Sabbath show through any era is likely to include most or all of these in its predictable set list.

Sabbath's friendship with Led Zeppelin eventually spawned the rumor of the Black Zeppelin Tapes. It begins with a conversation between a book publisher and an unnamed ex-manager for the band, in which the curious publisher points to a box in the corner of the office marked Black Zeppelin Tapes. An explanation ensues that, at one point, Black Sabbath and Led Zeppelin were rehearsing just down the street from each other, and that, for a lark, they decided to switch singers for a bit of fun. The results, apparently, were caught on tape.

"No, we never, ever did that," counters Ozzy. "No, what happened on one occasion, when they had Swan Song and we were floating between management and record companies, they came and tried to get us to sign to Swan Song, and we had a jam session in the studio, but we never recorded it, as far as I know." Did Robert Plant ever sing with Black Sabbath? "I believe so, but I don't think it was ever recorded. It might have though. Jimmy Page wasn't there. It was John Paul Jones, John Bonham, Robert Plant and us guys."

Adds Geezer, "We'd grown up with Planty and Bonham. Bonham was Tony's best man at his wedding. I'd been around to Planty's house and jammed with him, but the only time the two whole bands got together was when we were doing *Sabbath Bloody Sabbath*. They came down to the studio to see us and we just had a jam, for some reason. That was the only time the two bands actually got together. I think we just did some blues stuff; we both started out being blues bands."

Sadly, no one recorded the events, according to Geezer. "I can't even remember what we played. We were probably all stoned out of our minds [laughs]. Our manager recorded everything we ever did live, but not that."

"There was some crossover stuff that went down between Sabbath and Zeppelin," affirms Bill, adding a bit of intrigue in a different direction. "Only in the sense that collaborations started to sprout up between members of their band and members of our band. I think the strongest collaboration was between Geezer and Robert Plant. I mean, they were working on songs together and working things out! I do know that [laughs]. I'm just thinking of John right now, God bless his heart. I do know that John came down to visit with me one day and we actually talked about it. John was a little bit

concerned about the collaborations that were going on in the sense that 'Hang on a minute; is this right? Where do you stand on this Bill?' And I said, 'I don't know John, I haven't really taken a lot of notice. I know that Robert wants to do some stuff with Geezer.' But it all fell by the wayside; it wasn't heavy or anything. We were just sitting over a pint discussing it. But we never actually exchanged recordings, not that I'm aware of anyway. If there are tapes, then I'd love to hear them."

A good part of the condescension suffered by the Sabs, as compared to Zeppelin or Purple, was fueled by the band's fairly constant flow of bad press. It is very likely that there was some baggage on the part of the media when it came to their dealings with Sabbath. It is well documented, that the band could blow off interviews, treat them frivolously, or simply lack the organization to make sure they happened on time, or at all. Then there's the band's insular nature, their particularly odd form of quietness, their brevity with words and their variously sardonic, ironic and grim senses of humor, especially on the part of Geezer and Ozzy. As well, you'd probably find some bald-faced skepticism on the part of the press, given Sabbath's quick, almost manic rise to the upper ranks.

To top it off, somebody at "the office" had surely caused bad vibes by making the band unavailable. "Certainly in the early days, we had hardly done any press," remembers Tony. "We were kept away from doing press, really, purposely. They just didn't want to us to do press. Later on, of course, people would have input, saying 'Do this, do that,' but we decided for ourselves what we did. That's why at one period we managed ourselves, took over the reins."

Geezer refutes Tony's assessment. "No, we did all the press we could. But then again, maybe Tony remembers it better than I do. I know the English press was against us at first, because a lot of it was based in London, and the press had never heard of us because we made our name outside of London, and we were the first band ever to do that in England. They just dismissed us. It's like, unless you've made it in London, you can't make it in England. And we totally proved them wrong."

Resoundingly so. *Paranoid* was to hit Number 1 on the UK charts and Number 12 in the States. Over time, *Paranoid* spent 27 weeks on the UK charts. Even its "reissue" in 1980 took it to Number 54, where it stayed for two weeks. The "Paranoid" single would hit Number 4 in the UK and Number 61 in the U.S. By far the band's most successful album of all time, *Paranoid* stands at quadruple platinum in the U.S., testimony to the power of hit singles.

Touring for *Paranoid* found the band visiting the U.S. for the first time, Sabbath touching down in New York on October 29, 1970, playing their first gig the next night — Traffic was on the plane with the boys and a right drunk was had. Preceding these dates, the band was in Europe, with Chapter III and label mates Manfred Mann as support, before a handful of dates back home in the UK. The U.S.

stint saw the band play upwards of a couple dozen dates, the highlight being extended stays at both the Whisky A Go Go in Hollywood and Bill Graham's Fillmore West in San Francisco.

A Warner Brothers executive said that when Sabbath "first came to Los Angeles, the Whisky was packed two shows a night. I don't know where people heard of them. The word just seemed to be out." Indeed it was. Upon the release of *Paranoid*, the debut had apparently already shifted 40,000 units in America. Tony also had said in the press that playing European festivals, especially in Germany, had been a boon for the band, although logistical hassles made touring America preferable.

With regard to the Fillmore shows, Bill Graham initially booked the band at the Fillmore East, for November 10, 1970, and reportedly saw them and hated them. But when he saw the size of the crowds they were bringing, he relented happily. He sold out the ensuing Fillmore West run three weeks in advance.

Notes Geezer, "I remember the Fillmore West and Fillmore East. We supported Rod Stewart at Fillmore East; Fillmore West, it was the James Gang and Love. I think we were in the middle; Love was headlining, we were second and James Gang was third. We hadn't really heard much about where you would play in America. There was the Fillmore West, the Fillmore East and

The Whisky in L.A. and I think that was about it; those were the most famous places, for a band coming from England."

"The first U.S. gig ever was a place called Ungano's in New York," recalls Tony. "We came over, brought all our gear, sound system, the lot. It was all big stuff then. We weren't aware of what sort of sound systems you'd have over here. Which is, obviously far better than what we'd brought over. So the first thing we do is plug all the amps in, and they blow up! Because of the power difference. We were so thick, we didn't know what we were supposed to do. So promptly, bang! The stuff blew up. And here we are stuck in this little spot called Ungano's, a tiny little place. These were the sorts of places we'd be playing at. We were really disillusioned. We thought when we got to the States, we'd see these big venues. And we get to this place, which is about twice as big as this room. Bloody hell! We were there for two nights."

"We had heard all this stuff about America," interjects Geezer. "Like, you've got to make it in America, Carnegie Hall, Madison Square Garden. And at that point, we'd had a Number 1 album in England with *Paranoid* and a Number 2 single. So we were playing the real decent gigs in England and Europe, nice places. And we got to New York; we're thinking it was going to be Madison Square Garden, and it's like the worst club we've ever played in! I think capacity was 300 or 400 or something. It was this horrible, dingy dump. I'll always remember . . . I don't know whether it was at the club, or at this place where we went to eat, there's this guy frying hamburgers. And a fly landed on the wall, and he smacked it with the thing that he was using to pick the hamburgers up with. I've never seen anything like that before! Killing flies with the hamburgers spatula."

"We just thought, 'What the hell is this?' But

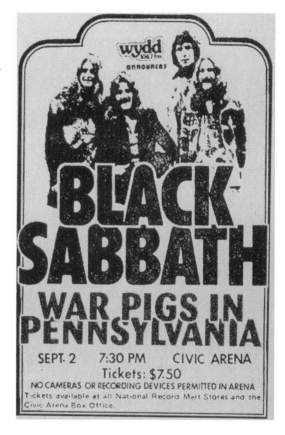

what we didn't know is, the whole club was filled with agents who were there to see what we were like, and to see if they were gonna book a tour on us. And that's all we really played to, all these agents and record company people that we'd never even seen before, or heard of. That was our welcome to New York."

"The third night we did the Fillmore East," continues Tony. "And of course, that was great. We were like, 'Oh God yeah, this is more like it!' And we'd never used a monitor system before. So it was great for us, because we could hear what everybody was doing through his monitors. It was real good fun to see all that, to build up to these stages, learn about things like that."

Additional support on the *Paranoid* tour came from an impressive batch of acts including Savoy Brown, Curved Air, J. Geils Band and Humble Pie, as well as lesser known "baby bands" such as Freedom, Patto, Quatermass, Sir Lord Baltimore, Jonathan Swift, Cactus. A band called Steel Mill included among its ranks a young Bruce Springsteen. Eight months of touring this venomous, garrulous record ended in late April of 1971, the band exhausted and exasperated at the distances they needed to travel in the U.S. to get their point across. "I had to go to the hospital, my nerves were getting in such a state," complained Ozzy. "It was all that travel that shook me up. Flying 3000 miles from New York to Los Angeles and then back again."

Headliners over Sabbath included Canned Heat, Fleetwood Mac, Jethro Tull, Emerson, Lake & Palmer, Rod Stewart & The Faces, Alice Cooper, James Gang, Mountain and, at the L.A. Forum in late February '71, Grand Funk Railroad, who Geezer recalls as the band who treated them most shabbily throughout Sabbath's long touring history.

Gearing up for the release of the next record, Ozzy spoke a bit about his early influences, as well as his impression of Grand Funk Railroad. "I used to like what everyone else did: The Beatles and Rolling Stones. Geezer was into heavier things like The Mothers. We just started playing 12-bar blues and 12-bar jazz about four years ago. I used to like anything that was heavy. The Kinks' 'You Really Got Me' did something to me, and I used to dig the early Who and Led Zeppelin. I dig anything that makes the hairs in the middle of my spine stand up. We just started writing our own stuff and our sound just evolved into what it is today; it wasn't planned. I suppose we are similar to Grand Funk Railroad, but I hadn't heard of them until our third tour here. Nobody knew who Grand Funk were in England. We didn't realize how big they were until we played The Forum with them and they just packed the place — two nights! They turned the crowd on, but musically they didn't do anything for me. I'm not saying they're a bum group, because they've got to be a good group for people to dig them. Personally, I like to hear music which is considerably different than what we play."

"When we played with Cactus," recalls Geezer, "that's when they got some of their Sicilian friends down to shoot us, because Tony had beat one of them up. They came off stage, and their dope was rolled up in a towel, and they accused us of stealing it. Meanwhile, we hadn't even been there. And this guy came in, I think he was the singer or something, and started shouting at Tony, which is the wrong thing to do, and the next thing, the guy went straight through the wall. Tony smashed him around the head. And we just beat hell out of them, because they thought they were tough and we found out that they weren't. So when we went on, we had all these motorbikes turn up outside, and somebody passed us this message that we were going to be shot in the middle of the set. So we went on and just kept our eyes open, and we saw all these guys making their way to the middle of the hall, and just at that moment, somebody tipped a can of Coke into Tony's amp [laughs], and blew it up, so we had to finish the show. So we'll never know if we were going to get shot or not."

"There was a wee skirmish, aye, aye," recounts Cactus bass legend Tim Bogert, going on to actually invert the key detail of the tale. "What happened was, we were on stage. And our roadie went back, who was a little, tiny guy — smaller than Vinny is — a really thin man.

He went back to the dressing room to get us towels or water or whatever it was. And he goes off stage, doesn't come back in the appropriate amount of time. Rusty goes back, and he's all beat up. They had accused him of taking their stash, which we did not, which, he wasn't a user; we couldn't care less. And Rusty and Jimmy went flying off the stage and by the time Carmine and I got there, most of the melee was over. But yeah, it got heated. People got pushed around."

A piece in *Circus* ultimately explained that Sabbath had had two towels, Cactus one, in a joint dressing room, and Sabbath accidentally grabbed the Cactus towel, which was identical to theirs, save for the fact that Cactus' drugs were wrapped up in it. The roadies summoned both bands, and Tony punched the Cactus roadie, having taken offense at being called a thief. After the towel was returned and apologies were made, tensions still simmered, with Cactus sticking up for their 110-pound roadie. Legend has since turned the aftermath into an all-out war: Cactus allegedly looked into getting a gun; a hundred guys were being gathered to attack Sabbath, possibly onstage; turpentine was added to the band's onstage water glasses. Regardless of the veracity of any of these statements, guards were posted, songs were played, and the power went out . . . twice. Five songs were proffered before the show was knocked on its head. It's no surprise Black Sabbath haven't forgotten Cactus.

Another New York band, Mountain, would make an impression on the Sabs. "The first real band who I really loved, before we got to America was Mountain," says Geezer. "'Mississippi Queen' and all that stuff. And they were really good guys, showed us the ropes. When we came to America, we didn't know who we were going to be on tour with,

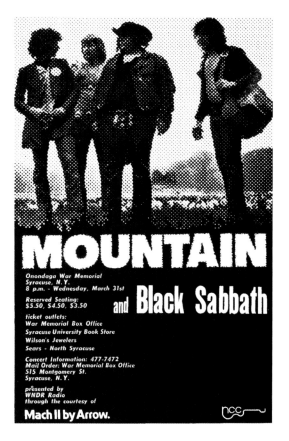

and when that was put together, we loved it."

Indeed, one could add Mountain to our previously discussed trinity of heavy acts. Leslie West and crew made their deafening mark through two albums as of spring 1970, the Leslie West — *Mountain* album from September '69, and the classic *Climbing!* record from March '70, the latter including the seminal "Mississippi Queen."

"Nobody would touch Black Sabbath," recalls Mountain drummer Corky Laing. "They were too heavy in those days. We had a theory that when you're a headline band, get the strongest opener you can, because it keeps you on your toes. And Black Sabbath . . . they weren't a great band but they were very cutting edge, the gothic thing. Nobody went near them. Because don't forget, in those days you had Nixon in the White House, it was a very Republican, conservative era. As a result, the underground was very underground. And Black Sabbath were having a very hard time cutting it in America. In those days it was pretty heavy stuff. You go down to Texas in those days with Black Sabbath and you can get your car blown up. We were one of the few bands to take them on the road because we were hooked up with an English agency that had Jethro Tull, Humble Pie, Ten Years After. If you play with those kinds of musicians you tend to be competitive."

"They were trying to break them over in America, summer of '70. And especially in Texas, nobody wanted to know about Black Sabbath — just too freaking weird. And Ozzy was just so thankful after every show. He would run back and give us all kisses on the lips and stuff. He was just so boisterous, even though the crowd booed him. The fans really didn't understand Sabbath. The cops were looking at Ozzy like he was some kind of fucking alien. They were just a very different kind of band; the first gothic band to come out. This was a whole month, in the south and in Texas. We were still touring Mountain *Climbing!*, which was recorded in the fall of '69, and came out in the first quarter of '70."

"It was just very awkward," continues Corky. "The police were there. Don't forget, they looked pretty strange. They weren't your pretty boys. The only thing was, we had to keep an eye on Tony Iommi because he lost his fake fingers. One gig, we had to look for them. I remember that because we found them like a minute before the show. They didn't really know what they were going to do, because he only had one set at that time."

"Bill Ward is a very solid drummer," offers Laing, speaking with obvious authority. "He never considered himself a well-rounded drummer. He was just really great with the Sabbath. He had a plodding nature about the way he played. Everybody would bounce their heads really slow, you know, like sort of dolls or dogs at the back of the car, the way that doll goes up and down. He wasn't a speed freak at all. He's a plodder."

Mountain also hooked up with the Sabs on their own turf. "When they were in England, they invited us over," notes Corky. "I'm serious, they played so loud — I was a block away driving to the studio, in London — I just followed the sound. It was like three or four blocks away, and it was so loud, you could open your window and all of London could hear it. This was when they recorded the second album. We were over there touring or something. I remember going to the studio over there, with their manager and their agent. We hung around quite a bit. For some reason there was an affinity there. Oddly enough, my father was born in Birmingham, and this is where they're from. It's a real blue-collar worker upbringing, a tough place, like Manchester. These guys had to be hard-assed. Quite frankly, I always thought Ozzy could do better singing-wise. He didn't consider himself a singer as much as an entertainer, you see? So that's why he sort of did all that stuff at the front of the stage, but I thought he had a great voice."

"I CHOKED ME BLOODY SELF"

– Master of Reality

With a shuddering hack, Black Sabbath found themselves back in business, the bulldozing *Master of Reality* slamming into record store shelves, July 21, 1971. The band's first two albums had been certified gold in the U.S. for a couple of months, and sold-out shows had become commonplace. Advance orders for *Master of Reality* already had the band shipping gold, with official certification sorted out by late September. As testimony to the band's unorganized business dealings, long-overdue platinum certifications wouldn't be obtained until 1986.

Featuring a now iconoclastic (but at the time, sort of stupid) pitch-black cover, band name eerily painted in purple, title of the record neatly but obscurely embossed, *Master of Reality* looked as ominous as it sounded. Printing the lyrics on the back of the album was a nice touch, however, and original issues of the album had the sleeve constructed as a thin box, opening with a flap at the top. Housed inside was a large, psychedelic poster featuring a sinister shot of the band standing under a tree. Some later non-box issues also included the poster. Black and purple were chosen as the theme to represent the colors of mourning.

"During *Master of Reality*, we were moving so fast," says Bill, when asked about the cover. "When we completed that album, we were truly veterans, multiple world tours under our belt, absolutely nonstop. There were signs of exhaustion showing. We'd not come off the road, and in some respects, I see *Master of Reality* as the end of one era before we entered another, but I didn't know it at the time. I know that when we saw the album cover, we just loved it. Everybody loves fucking black in our band. I think we took a glimpse of it between an airport and a limousine. It really was like *Spinal Tap* [laughs]."

Master of Reality found Sabbath recording in better facilities than the locales of its two predecessors, and the band was rewarded with a fat, powerful, round guitar sound, yet they retained the gorgeous separation of Iommi's brilliant tone with that of Butler's bass frequencies. Which is fortunate for us, because Geezer turns in a truly inspired performance, groovy, bobbing, slinky, yet still precise — picture the man's most excellent stage presence and that's what these songs sound like.

"We had a lot more time to do that album," laughs Geezer. "The first album was two days. *Paranoid* was five days, and I think *Master of Reality* was a whole week. Plus we'd been on nonstop touring, so we knew the direction we want to go in. We got used to the studio. It was the first real studio we'd been in, because the other ones were sort of like four-track demo studios, and this was a proper 24-track professional studio."

As the band prepared for the recordings, Ozzy warned the press that the new record was going to be "the heaviest we've done. It's going to be heavier than before because that's what people want. I don't know whether Led Zeppelin made a big mistake or not with their third album, but personally I think a lot of people were disillusioned. If we ever decide to go acoustic with the band, we would do it gradually. But at the moment, people want heavy music, the heavier the better."

Roger Bain was again at the production helm, third record running. Says Tony, "Up till then, we had such a restricted amount of time in the studio, he could really just sit there and record us live in the studio. We finally had a chance to put in extra instruments. But Roger was great, just like a member of the band, same kind of humor as us; really nice."

And that title? "I came up with that," says Geezer. "Because when you do an album, you've got the master tapes. So it was the master of the album, and all the lyrics were about reality."

Explains Tony, "From *Master of Reality* on, it got more and more bloody complicated. Every album was getting longer and more involved. *Master of Reality* . . . we used to experiment a lot in the studio, so consequently it took longer. In those days, you had to make all your own effects. You couldn't go buy a machine where you could press a button and get an anvil sound or water or whatever. And some of those would take bloody hours just to get a little sound. That album in particular, we used an anvil. We tried to create a 'deeeoooo' sound, so we had to get a big tub of water, fill the tub with water, and then lift this anvil over it, hit it, and then drop it into the water slowly to get this effect."

> THE CHURCHES, FOR A LONG TIME IN DIFFERENT PLACES, TRIED TO BAN US, BECAUSE THEY THOUGHT WE WERE EXTREMELY EVIL.

"We always used to do mad things," affirms Geezer. "We used to lower this great big gong into water as well, and have the bottom of the water tank mic'ed up. Because back then, there were no synthesizers or samplers, so any obscure sounds, you had to make them all yourself."

Bill puts into perspective the band's recording career thus far. "I think *Paranoid* represents the late '60s, and where we were in the late '60s. Because a good portion of the material on *Paranoid* was actually starting to be written, or was written, in '68 or '69, maybe even '67. But *Master of Reality*, you're hearing a band that are already pretty much veterans. I think we probably already had at least one tour of the world under our belt, tours of America, multiple tours of Europe. So the band on *Master of Reality* was a band that had lived together and had been playing together nearly every single day. We hadn't left each other's sides. So it's a definite upgrade in musicianship. And Ozzy's voice is just incredible. So we were probably at our peak of working the hardest we had ever worked."

Addressing the huge, enveloping sound of the record, Bill says that "recording procedures change quite a bit very quickly. *Master of Reality* was done on a 24-track board, so that brought us up to a kind of Beatle-esque level, whereas *Paranoid* was done on an 8-track board."

The album opens with a hacking cough from none other that Mr. Iommi. "You really want to know?" laughs Tony. "I was doing some guitar part in the studio, and Ozzy brought me a joint out, and I took a couple of tokes on it, and I choked me bloody self. I started coughing, and of course, they let the tape run, and that tape became 'Sweet Leaf.'"

After that legendary but jarring intro, Tony rips into another massive, highly tuneful riff. "I will probably cut my own throat by saying this, but I have never had any problem coming up with riffs," he said looking back. "It seems to be easier than ever now. I don't know what it is. I must have written some horrible ones. I have thousands and thousands of riffs here at home that will never see the light of day. I just play something and throw the tape into a box and it never sees the light of day for years."

The riff for "Sweet Leaf" was indeed a keeper, turning the lumbering paean to pot into son of "Iron Man," but without that track's cold and rusty clank. Oddly, another Vertigo act recording in 1971, Clear Blue Sky, had as the opening track of their self-titled debut, a song (actually a song part), called "Sweet Leaf."

"We were in Wales when we wrote that," says Bill. "And it was either Geezer or Ozzy that first came up with that lyric: 'When I first met you, I didn't realize.' And I realized it was about having a relationship with marijuana. And I thought, this is fucking incredible. At the time it was like, man, this is real hardcore, to be talking about a relationship with oneself getting high. It was basically us saying, 'Hey, we stand up for marijuana.' And then we did

'Snowblind,' which again was putting a seal of approval on yet another drug. I'm certainly not ashamed of that because we went through that, but as you know, I'm an addict as well, so in my life now, that is something that is absolutely discouraged."

"'Sweet Leaf' was obviously about smoking dope," affirms Geezer. "I'd just come back from Dublin, Ireland, and they used to sell these cigarettes over there called Sweet Afton [laughs], which I used to smoke, and we were trying to think of a title for that song, and on the packet of cigarettes, it had, 'It's because of the sweet leaf that they taste so good.' And I went, 'Oh yeah, "Sweet Leaf," that's good' [laughs]."

One of this writer's top five Sabbath tracks of all time, "After Forever" winds up one of the heaviest songs Sabbath ever wrote, insanely groovy, pounding, and with an excellent hippie-fried solo break. The nicely layered, eminently hummable intro is pure genius as well, as is Geezer's bulbous bass work throughout.

"We probably tuned down on that album," answers Tony, when asked why the guitars are so hard-charging on *Master of Reality*. "I think as time went on, I spent more time working on the guitar. The first couple of albums were very, very quick; we didn't have time to work on the guitar sound [laughs]. We were in, done it and out."

This was the album where the practice of down-tuning began. "When I chopped the end of my fingers off, I found it difficult to bend strings. On the first couple of albums, of course, in those days you couldn't get gauge strings. They were all sort of heavy strings. So I had to make my own setup. I had to come up with ideas that would work for me. So I made my own set of light-gauge strings. I got two first banjo strings, and then I got a regular set, and I dropped it down, until I found the right gauge for me. Instead of using the sixth string that was in the set, I would throw that away and then use the fifth as the sixth, and do it like that, until I found one that was comfortable for

me. And of course, it was a problem tuning it. My old Gibson in those days, you could bend the neck, you could move it easily, as soon as you touched it. So tuning was very awkward. But I had to do it. I realized that I had to change my whole style of playing, play in a way that suits me and not anybody else. Later on, I tried using every string tuned down, to get the same effect. Again, it's an experiment, just to get a different mood for songs. And of course, when you do it live, you have to do the same live. The last tours we've done with Ozzy, when we play 'Into the Void,' I had to have a guitar ready that is tuned down a step."

Also on the subject of down-tuning, Tony has stated the following, having been asked specifically about the number of guitars he was using live on the reunion trail of the late '90s "Probably about six or eight. We use different tunings because some of the albums were played in different tunings in the early days. We never went by the rules and just tuned the way that sounded right for that track. We've always tuned a semi-tone down, but on the *Paranoid* and *Black Sabbath* albums, we tuned to pitch. On *Master of Reality*, we tuned down three steps. We didn't have any rules, because everybody else made the rules up. We just broke them. Onstage we tune down a semitone. We always tried things that weren't the norm. We were the first to tune down, and nobody could understand that. I also went to many guitar companies years ago when I wanted light-gauge strings and was told they couldn't make them because they wouldn't work the same. I had to explain that I'd already been using them and that I'd made up the sets myself."

Offers Bill, with respect to "After Forever," "I really liked that one, especially Geezer's 'Would you like to see the pope on the end of a rope?' line. At first I thought that song was a little too poppy. But I really like the backwards gong at the beginning and the phase-shifting. I still have that gong. We just washed it up a little bit with the sound effects and we put it on backwards."

With respect to other sound effects the band got up to, Bill recalls the following. "I think one of the nuttier things, there was a studio right behind The Marquee Club in London, and we were recording there. Somebody came up with the brilliant idea of let's all walk upstairs at the back of the club. There was a lot of echo and reverberation on the stairs, and so we were walking up and down the stairs, trying to record what it might be like, give the feeling of an army marching or something. There were so many stupid things we came up with [laughs]. But I don't think they ever got used."

What about innovative ways of recording your drums in the studio?

"I've tried all kinds of different things. I've used what we called a cannon effect on the bass drums. When the sound comes out of the bass drum, it starts to reach its strongest point about six to ten feet away from the bass drum; that's where you get the real gut reaction. So that's where we put all our mics. I have a couple of mics inside the bass drum, but that's not my favorite pickup point. When you hit the bass drum, you move the air, and the sound is peaking about six to ten feet away from the drum. So we used to build columns that were six to ten feet long, so the sound would travel

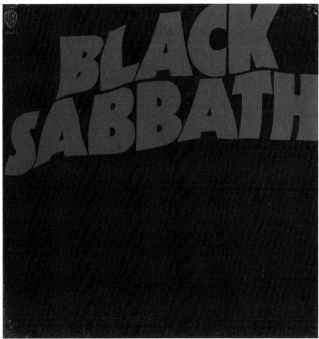

Master of Reality on reel to reel

down these columns and we'd have microphones placed six feet away from the bass drum heads. But I've never really enjoyed the sound of my drums, on any of the Sabbath albums. They've either been compressed or . . . at the time they sounded OK. But I'm like that; I'll never be happy with the drum sound, probably until the day I die."

"We were getting accused of all sorts of things, the whole Satan thing," remarked Geezer on another occasion. "And 'After Forever' is just about all these people that were following us around that were into the occult, and all the so-called Jesus freaks. I used to talk to these people that supposedly had dedicated themselves to Jesus. And I knew more about Jesus and the Bible and God than they did. Most of them had, like, done too much acid. So as a response to them, I wrote 'After Forever.' It raises the question: 'When you're on your deathbed, who ya gonna call, God or the Devil?

Are you going to be prepared for what you find? Have you lived a good life?"

Geezer's lyric is point-blank pro-Christianity, further demonstrating the enigma that was Black Sabbath. Still, there's incongruence, even a bit of misguided motivation. That other great doom band, Trouble, would tread this slightly aggressive, confrontational path a decade later, to almost thuggish effect.

Like Geezer, Tony rolls his eyes when recalling the strange situations Sabbath got into with both the far right and those doomed to the left-hand path. "We had all sorts of people. We had witches, Bible pushers, the church, of course . . . lots of different types of people. The churches, for a long time in different places, tried to ban us, because they thought we were extremely evil. And then we had witches coming to the shows and camping out in the hallway of the hotel."

Did the anti-Sabbath demonstrations actually ever work? Did you have gigs canceled? "If anything, it created more interest. It made people more interested to see what was going on, especially the young kids. The parents of course, would stay away [laughs]."

One mustn't forget that the late '60s and early '70s was a boom period for Satanic hysteria, with very real good reason. The hippie

era had resulted in all sorts of spiritual experimentation, and both white and black magic were at the top of the list. The horror movies were particularly chilling, with Roman Polanski's *Rosemary's Baby* leading the way, and *The Exorcist* to come shortly — in the press, Ozzy would claim to have seen that devilish classic 25 times, also professing that he would have appreciated if Sabbath had been asked to score Kenneth Anger's *Lucifer Rising*, a job that went to Jimmy Page. *Race with the Devil*, starring Peter Fonda, was also a trip, documenting a fairly plausible chain of events that might occur had one purely by happenstance witnessed a satanic ritual. British writer Dennis Wheatley, with his book *The Devil Rides Out* was an influence on Geezer's very earliest lyrics, and Wheatley enjoyed renewed fame (as well as movie adaptations of his titles) due to all things devilish being in vogue.

Back in the nonfiction world, Charlie Manson and his bald, cross-headed posse were all the rage as well, with Sabbath having to answer tiring questions about whether there was some sort of affinity or like-mindedness there (in defense, Bill had said that the band had tried to put a peace message in the *Master of Reality* album). In any event, this was the post-hippie landscape in America, and Sabbath's music thrived in it, more so even than back home in England, where depravities were less intense and imaginative.

The righteous harassed Sabbath, but so did the damned. Once at a theater show in the U.S., the band had to contend with the threat that they would be shot when they got to their third song, three being a significant number in occult studies. Indeed all the lights suddenly went out as the evening's third selection arrived, but the band survived the occasion, though they were spooked for a time thereafter.

"Yeah, in the early days, that was the Druids," recalls Geezer, of another episode regarding witch folk. "The black magic people were doing a Walpurgis, which is a satanic black mass, at Stonehenge. They'd heard about us and wanted us to go down and play some songs while they were doing it [laughs]. And we just didn't want to. You know, we weren't involved in all that crap anyway. And then the head of the white magic church in England phoned us up and says he's heard that they're gonna curse us, and that the only way for us to ward off the curse is for all of us to wear crosses. And that's where all the crosses came from. We still wear them now."

Back at *Master of Reality*, another crunching Sabbath classic, "Children of the Grave," was preceded by 26 seconds of medieval instrumental music called "Embryo." Along with "Sweet Leaf," this is *Master of Reality*'s big hit. Like "Paranoid," it establishes a heavy metal plateau, Sabbath perfecting the archetypical heavy metal gallop, also arguably creditable to Deep Purple's "Hard Loving Man."

The song is known for its extra layer of percussion, which lends the track an inexorable, apocalyptic critical mass. "I used two tracks of drums," affirms Bill, "but now I just play all that live. We use timbales on stage. I just play them with my left hand and keep the groove going with my right hand. I liked some of the things I was doing on *Master of Reality*. I was doing stuff with my bass drums and toms which were things I hadn't heard anybody else doing. And there's a lot of counterpoint drumming on *Vol 4*. The sixteenth note bass drums are being played against a four cowbell, which was again an interesting combination and not that common at that time. I'm not saying I invented it or whatever, but it wasn't that prominent. There were some great drummers

that I knew at that time, John Bonham, Carmine Appice, Ginger Baker. Those influences would rub off. But I found myself always staying with the jazz and blues roots. I'd use big band swing drumming. It was orchestrational, reactive drumming, just reacting to Tony and Geezer. You have to work when you're playing with such great players. Keeping focus and energy was incredibly important."

"They're all the same theme aren't they?" laughs Geezer, examining the "After Forever" lyric. "That was about how if we don't watch how we're polluting the earth we're all going to end up dead. I think there was hope in most of the lyrics, so it always had a positive ending. In 'Children of the Grave' you have to do something, or otherwise you wouldn't have it, sort of thing. So it was like, there is still hope for the human race. There is some bleak stuff, like 'Hand of Doom,' but you try to vary it."

"Birmingham was the industrial center, the first place to have a factory," says Geezer on the origins of his environmental themes. "In fact, where we lived, in Handsworth, was the actual original place to build a factory; Matthew Boulton built his first factory there. That's where the Industrial Revolution started. So,

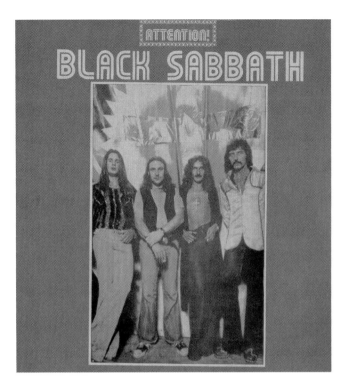

where we grew up, it was all factories and a lot of smoke and grime. Basically, everybody I knew used to have asthma and suffered with colds, emphysema. So it directly affected us. Politicians weren't too bothered about it, because they were safely ensconced in the Houses of Parliament away from all that stuff, but we had to go through it. Me uncle died; where he used to work, he inhaled a lot of vapors from rubber, Dunlop Tires, so he died of this thing on his lungs when he was only 50. And there was a lot of stuff like that going about, so it did directly affect us. Plus it was on the news as well. I was training to be a custom works accountant. This was just after I left school when I was 15, and then I went to college and had this job in the offices of the factory at the same time."

Side 2 of *Master of Reality* opened with a two-minute acoustic instrumental called

"Orchid." Says Tony, "That was something I had done at home and played to the others, saying, 'I've got this little acoustic bit.' Because with Sabbath, you never want to get too far the one way. They liked it and said, 'Why don't you put it on the album?' Those are little trinkets I do for my own self."

"Lord of This World" is introduced with a watery bit of guitar, but very quickly the majestic full band explosion occurs, Bill highly groovy, until the band settles down for yet another oppressive doom verse pattern. Ozzy is recorded thin, frantic and urgent, perfect for the storyline, which finds the Devil himself gloating over yet another damned soul. "'Lord of This World' was about Satan," explains Geezer. "Because, the way the world was going at the time, it wasn't God's world, it was Satan's world, which is the way it is now."

Indeed, Geezer had returned to fatalistic, apocalyptic themes — the Final War was ruefully inevitable. No surprise need register; it would smack too much of hope destined to be smacked down. Ozzy could flash peace signs all he wanted, and the witnessing throngs could flash him right back, but all of that wilted amidst the sonic carnage billowing from Sabbath's warlike stage.

And then things get eerily quiet. "Solitude" is essentially a sequel to "Planet Caravan," containing the same gloomy, wandering vibe, a nomadic, depressive lyric, similar in musical structure, even employing flute. Surprisingly, the odd vocal is indeed Ozzy, heavily treated.

Closing out *Master of Reality* is a song all about finality . . . and new beginnings. Tony Iommi's favorite song on the record ("a real cracking track"), and an undisputed heavyweight champion among the five mountains of muscle that make the album so classic, "Into the Void" has also been collared by Bill as his favorite Sabbath track of all time. "That was Black Sabbath at its height, when it was absolutely coming alive," enthuses Bill. "At that point Geezer was writing really strongly. The band was unbelievably tight. We were really becoming confident, due to all the touring we'd done."

Says Geezer, with typical succinctness, "That was a science fiction one about how we were all fed up at the time and wished we could just get into a rocket ship and blast off."

The guitars heave to a stressful breaking point, Bill and Geezer struggle to hold the inevitable implosion in check, and Ozzy turns in a terse, monotone vocal. Geezer's message of our doomed planet reverberates long after the bad vibrations have waned. As the album was taking shape, Tony had told the press that "Into the Void" and "After Forever" were the first songs the band had come up with, and that they were a bit funkier, but still heavier than the songs on *Paranoid*.

In press at the time, Geezer came off like a bit of a hippie, but with a disposition blacker than black — "Into the Void" seemed like the final solution to his sincerely held views. "It's a satanic world," reflected Butler. "The Devil's more in control now, and happier than ever before. People can't come together; there's no equality. The higher you climb, the more people you have to cut down. You feel you're better than other people, that they're inferior to you, and it's a sin to put yourself above other people, and yet that's what people do. Even in freak communities, people are trying to be

THE WHOLE CAR INDUSTRY IN ENGLAND IS BASED IN BIRMINGHAM, AND SHE WORKED ON THE CAR SEAT SECTION, SO THE STUFF FROM THE CAR SEATS, SHE WOULD TURN INTO LEATHER TROUSERS FOR US.

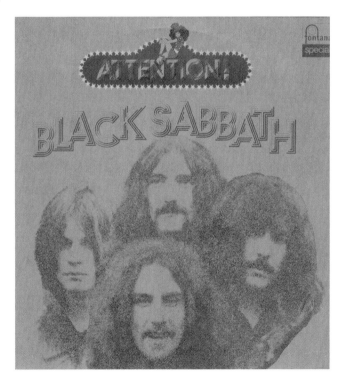

freakier than the other person, to be one up on them, to be better. That's the Devil's work; that's why there's war. We all live with a shadow over us — the shadow of the next world war. You're not going to get out of life alive, so it's not worthwhile. And people don't live a spiritual life. They only live for now; the Devil rules them. That's what my poems are about, things that are happening now. War and paranoia, death and hate. It gets people thinking about what's going on."

Sabbath wasn't yet dreading the prospects of their next American tour. The tour for *Master*

of Reality kicked off in the States, in the summer of '71, Tony summing up the experience shortly after the fact. "America was amazing. Although we'd been there before, the impact is more impressive this time. Our first trip was to tell them what Black Sabbath was all about. A high-pressure promotional tour, if you like. This time though, we were really able to take stock of the States and get to know how the scene works. Venues were a lot bigger for instance, and because of the album's success we were more widely known. American fans will travel miles to see a group. They think nothing of traveling 50 or 100 miles, even by air to catch a concert. Then they're patient and orderly and make the gig really great for us."

"Even really bad reviews haven't stopped the albums from selling," said Tony, in another contemporary interview. "I don't know why they sell so well. Maybe people like the songs words-wise, or maybe they buy them because they're simply heavy. I'm also pleased with our tours. Apart from one time in New York where we were really tired and just couldn't get into it, the reaction we got was great. We have one or two gigs where they were screaming, but the rest, they are just quiet and appreciative. Maybe the critics go to the six o'clock shows. If you're doing two shows a night, it's a known fact that the second one is better. Another thing you've got to consider about the critics is that if someone is looking for an audience reaction, they may not think we're going down so well, when the kids don't rave all the time. In certain places in America, the kids are afraid to get up and rave because the police might hit them over the head with a truncheon! The police can be very cruel like that."

"We've still got a hard core of British fans and our records do well," says Tony defending against accusations — also those leveled at Deep Purple and Led Zeppelin — that Sabbath had somehow abandoned the host country fans to concentrate on America. "I don't think

ONE TIME THE HOTEL WAS ON A LAKE, AND OZ WAS FISHING OUT THE WINDOW. I'M SITTING THERE, HAVING ME TEA, AND A HUGE FISH FLIES THROUGH THE WINDOW.

we are being unfaithful to them by going to America. You can only play certain venues in Britain; the Albert Hall in London is great, for instance. But we reckon it's worthwhile going to America and it's not just because of the money. The first tour we ever did, we made very little money. Now we do make some, and our records sell well. The albums get advance orders of around 200,000, which isn't bad at all. But then America is such a vast place. With each succeeding tour, we like to cover parts that we haven't already visited and, even this way, we still haven't been everywhere. We've done well in America, the gold discs and all that, and the American kids seem to know more about the band. When we play England, we get slugged by the journalists, but not by the people. *Paranoid*, that LP got bad reviews and sold well. But we can't complain about English audiences. They've always been good to us."

Actually, both the UK and the U.S. were good to Sabbath, with *Master of Reality* rising to Number 5 on the UK charts (a residence of 13 weeks in total) and Number 8 in the U.S. No singles were issued from the album, which

didn't stop it from being the second most successful record of the band's career in America, where it currently sits at double platinum.

Tony says touring for Sabbath didn't include the extracurriculars, like say, Deep Purple with their soccer. "For us, we took music very, very seriously. And it overtook our lives, really. Geezer had an interest in football. I don't know if he actually went out and played, but he certainly watched football a lot, Aston Villa. Bill and Ozzy and myself weren't so much into soccer. I was into more gruesome sports, I suppose; boxing, wrestling, anything where there's beating somebody up [laughs]. But as I say, most of our efforts were channeled into music. Everything we were interested in before got pushed aside when we went into music."

With the relentless work and experience adding up, were there still confidence issues within the band? "I think we all had problems to a degree, in the early days. Because we worked as a band. We weren't the sort of musicians to get up and jam with people. We tended to be like a unit and work as a unit. I think inside, everybody was 'Oh, I'm not very good at this or that,' but you work as a band and you work as a team."

Addressing the subject of stage wardrobe in the early days Geezer laughs, "I saw one the other day, and I can't believe I wore it. It was black-and-silver trousers that were about 40 inches wide at the bottom, and I'd totally forgotten about them. And at an autograph signing, this kid came up and showed me this picture. God, it's unbelievable I went onstage with them things on. It was like curtain material or something. You used to have to have things made back then; you couldn't really buy them. Nobody would want to buy them anyway, nobody else. So you would have somebody make them for you."

Was it usually somebody's wife or girlfriend?

"It started off that way when we couldn't afford it, like the first album. Bill's wife, she made us all the leather stuff, but it was out of old car seats, so like, the leather was about three inches thick, and you could hardly move in it. And then the more money we got, the better tailors we found. But this leather, it was mainly like the trousers. You can't really see them in the photographs because it's usually the top half of us. Yeah, old car seat leather. Because there again, she worked in a factory in Birmingham that made car parts. The whole car industry in England is based in Birmingham, and she worked on the car seat section, so the stuff from the car seats, she would turn into leather trousers for us."

Dragging themselves across America, both Bill and Ozzy tried valiantly to keep their long-distance marriages alive. Letters from home would be delivered, issues would have to be dealt with slowly, and at geographical odds. "It's all so horrible," said Ozzy, speaking in the midst of the U.S. tour, "flying around and around, landing again. The hotel room's the same, everything's the same, the walls . . . it drives me mad. I really freaked out on the last tour. I got pissed off; those hassling bastard groupies screwed me up for one. We have a lot of nervous trouble in our family; I'm very high-strung. On the last tour I had blackouts."

"I'm quite sane now, but I won't be sane for long, after I take this pill," continued Oz. "Metrospan, they're called. They really give you a hit on the head. A doctor gave them to me for depression a few days ago. They must have some ups in them; they make me crazy. I'll be OK as long as there is me and my wife, and my kids and my group. But sometimes I start to wonder if my family's going to wait for me. I wonder if she'll get pissed off while I'm run-ning around, recording and all. I don't know what I'd do without her."

"Our music is aggressive; people can get off on it," added Ozzy. "It gives them a release. I can see it happen at concerts. We get people's aggressions out. Then they won't go out and beat some old lady over the head. It works for me too. Like when I'm at home for a while, not working, with no outlet for me energy, my wife and I are hammer and tongs at each other 'cause I'm all pent up. But our music gets it out, for me as well as the audience."

"They're crazy mad in love," volunteered Bill, on the drama in Ozzy's marriage. "He really can't stand being away from her. The problem they're having is something too com-plicated and personal to talk about now. It has to do with something that happened some time ago."

Temptations on the road were most defi-nitely causing resentment — the band, each of the boys raised conservatively but flung into this wicked world, seemed to be in a fight for their very souls. "Fucking groupies," spat Ozzy. "I'm telling you, the next one who pushes her-self at me, I'm going to piss all over her. Me and Bill decided to do that. Ain't that right, Bill? Just piss all over them. They're disgusting. Remember Bill, that time in Atlanta, Georgia? This bitch calls me on the telephone and said, 'I'm the best plater in the world' — you know, blow job — 'Can I come up to your room?' So

I gave her Geezer's room number, and told her to come up, just for a laugh. Well, she went up to Geezer's room, and without a word, took all her clothes off, and lay down on the bed with her legs apart, Billy, me and Geezer looking on. 'Well, isn't somebody going to fuck me?' she says to us. We all just stood there looking at her, kind of horrified. She looked pitiful and disgusting. Finally, she got pissed off when no one went near her, got up and dressed. 'You English boys are disappointing.' A bunch of fags, she called us, and left the room. But the next time I'm not going to stand there. I'll fucking piss all over them. Wait till me mother reads that; she'll never speak to me again."

"We used to have fun in the old days," sighed Bill, Ozzy adding, "before we got all exploited and things. It used to be anything goes and we'd have fun. But now it's more of a business. We've got to watch what we say and do — more people watching. You've got to be clean English boys. Well, not exactly, but we've got to be more cautious now that people are aware of us. Before, we really didn't give a damn. We played small clubs in England and Germany. Like the Star-Club in Hamburg. Remember that night that chick gave Geezer some pills, told him they were ups? But it turned out they were laxatives, and Geezer had to run off the stage to shit every five minutes. His ass was fucking raw! We finished playing, we did five sets a night then, and we'd go out on the town and tear the place apart. We could have parties then, but we can't do that anymore. We have to get up early and fly somewhere to do a concert the next day. It's more a money thing now. I'm going to make as much money as I can, then shoot myself. I'll die before I'm 40."

"Oz gets up too fucking early," groused Bill, "eight o'clock, and turns the TV on. One time the hotel was on a lake, and Oz was fishing out

the window. I'm sitting there, having me tea, and a huge fish flies through the window. He caught a mud shark. We put in the tub, but it died by the time we got back that night. We cut it up and threw it out the window, back into the lake."

On the *Master of Reality* tour, Black Sabbath shared stages with a myriad of acts in a myriad of styles, as was the tradition in the '70s. Along for the ride were the likes of Alice Cooper, Humble Pie, Yes, Three Dog Night, Black Oak Arkansas, Bloodrock, Gentle Giant, Ten Years After, and Nazareth, along with acts now forgotten to various degree, such as Brewer & Shipley, Grease Band, Sweathog, Eleven, Ultra Violet, Stoneground and White Witch. Wild Turkey greatly exceeded any other band in the number of Sabbath dates it logged on the tour. The bluesy, fairly hard-hitting and Free-like act was the band of choice for the UK leg in January and February of 1972, and then a second U.S. leg in March, Yes also along for that tour-closing stint. Press reports at the time sniffed that Wild Turkey and Yes got the good reviews and Sabbath got most of the "bread," the reporter also adding note of the divide between the band's young fans and the older folk of the critic class. But Sabbath got the final just desserts, crying all the way to the top of the charts.

"THE EERINESS OF THE COCAINE"

– Vol 4

Already gravely burnt-out from the long, continent crisscrossing tours, the boys in Black Sabbath decided to court a fully crisped form of burn-out by writing and recording their fourth record in three years lounging in the den of iniquity known as Los Angeles.

"We were totally mental," recalls Geezer, shaking his head at the thought. "It was when we were really into cocaine. We used to have like queues of women every night outside the house [laughs], and the studio was the downer part. That was probably Sabbath at our most debauched. I remember when Ozzy sat on the alarm bell, and the police came up to the house. We had a great big bowl of grass on the table and loads of vials of pharmaceutical cocaine all over the place. We didn't know that Ozzy had set the alarm off, because it was a silent alarm. All these coppers turned up outside, so we flushed everything; it was like a mad dash. We must have flushed about 10,000 dollars worth of cocaine and two grams worth of grass, and it was just like a false alarm [laughs]. The police were outside, knocked on the door; we thought they were busting us, but they said, 'Your alarm's going off. What's wrong?' And we said, 'Nothing.' And they just left. Didn't even come in the house."

About *Vol 4*, Geezer said, "I can't even remember the lyrics on that record. We were all cooked out of our brains every day. It was just mad. That was the peak of our lunacy. The first

three albums had been incredible successes and we were all like young kids with loads of money and loads of drugs, living in a great big house in Beverly Hills and just going wild. And I think the album kind of wrote itself. We were very productive, because we were all living together at the time. Parties every night, more drugs than the average drugstore, and we were experimenting a lot with different sounds. We had a grand piano in the house; that's where 'Changes' came about. We had a Mellotron, all different kinds of instruments at our disposal."

"It was like Disney World really," adds Tony. "It was a lovely house, had a ballroom and everything, fantastic. There was like a bar downstairs and we set up the equipment in there and just wrote the album. We'd be up all bloody night tooting coke . . . oh, we just went berserk. It was a joyride, really. We had a fantastic time. And when it came down to seriously recording the album, we got down to it and did it — in Los Angeles as well, at the Record Plant."

Bill is quite fond of the resulting album, but adds, "I think what overpowers me when I listen to it is the circumstances that surround it. My second wife and I were going through some rough times. We weren't fighting or anything. There were just problems going on with her being American and thus living in England. And the use of cocaine had escalated, especially with me. I had become completely and totally involved in cocaine at that time. When I listen to the album, I can feel all the eeriness of the cocaine."

Tony denies that this was one of those rock star situations where dealers are so plentiful that no one can get any work done. "To be honest, we used to have stuff flown in privately. So that wasn't such a problem for us. But actually, yes, all around the studios in those days

Black Sabbath
Vol. 4

you'd have somebody trying to sell you one thing or another."

Bill figures that *Vol 4* marked yet another notch up in sophistication for the band. "We had this change of attitude where we had decided to slow down a bit and feel less hurried about getting an album out and going on tour. As we've said, we recorded a majority of the album at the Record Plant on La Cienega Boulevard in Hollywood. But yes, my cocaine addiction was pretty darn heavy. I know I'm not successful at this, but I do try to be careful about talking about the other guys, the way they might have been partying. But I don't mind speaking for myself. I was pretty much loaded. And I think a lot of the songs are influ-

enced by the narcotics we were using. 'Snowblind' for instance, I mean, give me a break. That was a direct song that came from the use of the narcotic cocaine. But there was some thought going into the album. It was the first time we ever used strings — at the end of 'Snowblind,' there's a little string quartet. From a drummer's point of view, I thought I had progressed into some new bass drum work."

"That was the first album where I nearly got kicked out of the band," continues Bill. "We took the remainder of the album and we went to London and I was pretty solid gone. I was good at getting so far out of it that I was forgetting what we were doing. I was pretty critical of the songs, and I said 'Look, let's get into some old-fashioned blues. Let's do some blues jams.' And that didn't go down too well. And there was kind of a cold eeriness in the studios and I definitely realized that I was under the gun. It was like, 'Uh-oh, I think I'm causing some trouble here.' And I had nowhere to live. I was with my girlfriend, and we were leading

like a Sid and Nancy lifestyle, living in hotels and wherever we could, just running around London and doing stupid things, loaded all the time. Cocaine was just ruining me, a day at a time. I thought it was making me productive, but it would take ages to get anything done."

Vol 4, issued September 25, 1972, opened with a lumbering yet markedly less malevolent epic track for the band called "Wheels of Confusion" — originally titled "Illusion." Ozzy's vocal is starkly melodic, and there is a slight increase in nuance and subtlety to the band, especially come the jammy closing section — which is separately named "The Straightener," but only on some copies of the album. Revolving Leslie speaker cabinets are used for this textured portion, which prompted observations that this was quite a psychedelic record for the band.

Vol 4's gatefold existed in variants. The full version features a stitched-in booklet, a Geezer page and a Tony page as the actual inner gate, an Ozzy page and a Bill page as part of the booklet, and then a live shot from behind as the center spread of the four-page booklet. Later issues deleted the individual player pages, leaving a standard gatefold using the live shot, but some issues went out with the booklet simply removed, leaving the Geezer and Tony pages as the sum total of the inner gate.

Geezer's "Wheels of Confusion" lyric seems to sum up the loss of innocence and the fatigue the band had experienced over the whirlwind few years since their debut album was recorded in not much more than a day. It is of note that Roger Bain, producer of all three Sabbath records thus far, had been ousted. *Vol 4* was produced by "Patrick Meehan and Black Sabbath," which essentially means it was self-produced, as Patrick was the band's manager. At the time, Ozzy dismissed Roger as "someone the record company gave us when we signed with the company. It was really a clash of egos. He got it into his head that he was more responsible for our hit status than we were. He wanted, to a moderate extent, to control our music."

"Tomorrow's Dream," which can best be described as a deep album classic, is the album's second track, the band once more

residence of ten weeks), Number 13 in the U.S., with the record eventually reaching platinum in America.

Next up was a track so saccharine that it became bitter, especially in the context of who this band was. Piano, strings . . . are they being used ironically or with sincerity? Certainly the melody and the lyric possess a mournful quality, but, unlike "Planet Caravan" or "Solitude," this was emphatically not a dirge, although one can still envision "Changes" being played at a funeral or somber church service.

When asked if that's him playing piano on the track Tony laughingly admits it. "Actually, that was the first thing I'd ever played [laughs]. Because I'd never really played piano. In Bel Air, they had a piano there in the ballroom, so I used to play that at one and two o'clock in the morning, and I had come up with this idea for 'Changes.' I played it for the guys, and they liked it, and we ended up recording it that week. First thing I'd ever done."

"I tried other things, other instruments," says Tony on the subject of branching out beyond the guitar. "I think everybody in the course of playing tends to get to that stage. And I am included in that. I played the piano and flute. I bought a sax and I made a right row with that! Then I bought a sitar that I couldn't play at all. Geezer and myself, when we had done either *Vol 4* or *Sabbath Bloody Sabbath*, we were going to use strings on a track. So we never thought of hiring anybody — we were going to play them ourselves. Geezer was going to play the cello and I was going to play the violin, and we started trying to play these

underscoring their penchant for rumbling, massive, elephantine structures that seem to shake the earth when they move — Bill calls the song "a great one to play, a drummer's dream." Geezer's lyric can be seen as a break up story, but one with hope, one that includes the promise of fulfilling dreams to go along with the sense of grief. "Tomorrow's Dream" was launched as a single, backed with "Laguna Sunrise." It failed to chart, although the album proper rose to Number 8 in the UK (with a total things and the sound was fucking horrible, sounded like dead cats, like someone had trodden on a cat! We just assumed we would be able to play them. I thought, 'Oh fuck it, let's get a string section in.' But it was funny. You get to that stage — you want to be like Roy Wood and play everything."

Upon the impending release of *Vol 4*, Ozzy addressed the subject of changes in the band, as well as the incendiary new track "Changes." "I think everybody peaks. Not only does the crowd get fed up of hearing the band, but the band gets tired of gigging. It's not like we're jukeboxes or records that can play forever. When you're a new band, it's like you get a tinge of stardust on you. It's born, then accepted, and after leveling it off, it dies. Anything's like that. Our new album still has the Black Sabbath sound, but it's more

melodic. Instead of me singing the guitar riff like on 'Iron Man,' I'm singing different melodic things and it's all building up. Tony just composed a guitar piece with strings. It's a nice piece of music, and we wanted to write a happy song. People call us 'downer rock' — you take the reds, man, and drink the wine, and blow out, get high on the decibels . . . all that's a lot of rubbish. Whatever people do at our concerts is none of our business as long as they enjoy it. I'm just up to entertain people, a good old show business trip."

"So there'll be a lot of gentle things on the new album," continued Oz. "'Changes' is about a guy — whether he's with the band or not, I'm not gonna say — who quits with this woman; it's the ultimate in the way I feel about things. It's more of a song rather than a frustration-reliever screamer. It's just a pretty, slow ballad."

Polish issue flexi-disc that plays "Changes"

Ozzy goes on to address the novel, contrary nature of the band's lyrics. "When we started writing things, we didn't want to present rubbish like 'I'm gonna see my chick and we're gonna get it on.' It's all hypocritical. Let's face it, you only remember the good times because you don't wanna remember the bad. You can have a whole month of downer and only one good night, and you remember the good night. If you feel positive, that's fine; though we wanted to write things the way they really were. Geezer furnishes most of the lyrics. This love trip is so grossly distorted. One week you fall in love, the next week you fall out and start doing dope and blow your mind out. I don't believe

there's anyone in this world who is one hundred percent in love. I don't think anyone is totally happy; you can't really wake up in the morning free of hassles and do what you want as long as you don't harm anybody else. If you wanna stick needles into your arm, it's your own life. Like, I'm not into taking heavy dope, although I have taken dope. People who take it just have hang-ups that they can't deal with.

"If you haven't got your own mind and you can't do what you want, you're not an individual, just part of a mass. The society trip in England is that you go to school, then get a job, and at the age of 21, you get married. You work the rest of your life in a factory and when you retire at the age of 65 you get a gold watch; 45 years in a factory with stinking oil, polluting the land. I used to work in a factory, and I used to see these blokes dying on their machines. That just blew my mind. They're saying you should cut your hair and get a good job — for what? So people can suck off you? They're picking your bones, getting all that energy out of you, when it could be put to much better use. But I'll tell you one thing, I've got children, and if such a day ever came, I'd dig holes to feed them. I believe in giving your children a good start and a lot of love."

German 1970

Spain 1970

Holland 1970

France 1970

Belgium 1970

Brazil 1970

Germany 1977

Israel 1970

Germany 1980

Germany 1983

Germany 1970

Thailand 1970

Australia 1972

Belgium 1978

Belgium 1979

German 1972

France 1972

Holland 1972

Sweden 1972

Ozzy next tackled the incongruence of delivering the band's "downer rock" with such giddy abandon, when it comes to the concert stage. "When someone identifies with the downer song that I'm singing, they're able to put their energies into the music and relieve their frustrations. It's good therapy. If I make people feel good, I feel good. The band and the crowd get off on each other and it's a tremendous trip: peace power. I don't wanna see people get busted on the head. I've been through that whole trip, been knifed a couple times and it's not much fun. Music is my life; I am music. It gets into your body. The stage becomes like a cancerous growth in your mind; if I'm not working for a time, I get so aggressive because the frustration builds up to a tremendous level."

Back to "Changes," Ozzy remarks, "I sing on it, and I'm so pleased with it because I'm able to sing in a different way than, like, screaming. It's a gentle, sad song, very un-Black Sabbath."

"It drove me nuts in the end," says Ozzy, on constructing *Vol 4*. "I used to freak out. I was dreaming there was like a tape machine coming into my room and eating me. The album's not a change from heavy to soft. It's still very heavy, but it's just going in a different direction. It's more . . . worked out, if you like."

"English bands tend to play dirty, earthy, vicious type music," he continued. "Like our type of music, it's like trying to get back or get at or blow it out at someone. When I'm on the stage, my feelings come out when I'm singing. Like for instance, if we're playing the song 'Black Sabbath,' and somebody annoys us or something goes wrong, I just sound against the guitarist. Bill, once, we were playing a jam, and Bill, he thought we were going to kill everybody. You see, we're just four ordinary guys and we come from a really rough area of Birmingham, all the Irish people fighting, everybody always fighting everywhere. Our environment shows in our music. And when you're playing, you can build a little wall around yourself. You just play and your emotions come out. You really go mad."

"Changes" was eventually brought into the live set during the Tony Martin years, for the *Forbidden* tour. As well, in 2003, Ozzy's duet on the song with his daughter Kelly hit Number 1 on the UK singles charts, the track showing up on Kelly's album *Changes*, a reissue of *Shut Up* from the previous year, renamed, with that track added.

Back on *Vol 4*, a short spell of sound effects called "FX" arose next, as preamble to "Supernaut." "That's Tony standing and playing his guitar in the nude," laughs Geezer. "He took all his clothes off in the studio and he was hitting on his guitar strings with the crosses that he wore around his neck."

"Supernaut" is another classic great-escape lyric from Geezer. Filled with (drug-fueled?) motion, the song sounds like a rocket taking off, Supernaut laughing maniacally as the g-forces paste him to his seat. "John Bonham really liked that song," laughs Ward, presumably referring to the Black Zeppelin Tapes story discussed earlier. "It was one of his favorite songs. He came to Morgan Studios in London one time when we were recording, and they wanted to jam. There was Planty and

Bonham. They came down and they were jamming, and we got together and Bonham wanted to play 'Supernaut,' and he had it down. We know there's never been a recording of it, but it just sounded really cool. I love the beginning of that song. Tony's riff totally rips, and I love the lyrics. Again, Ozzy and Geezer were totally on. 'The dish ran away with the spoon' — I love that."

Side 2 of *Vol 4* opens with the aforementioned "Snowblind," this album's most famous song, a track that lumbers and then lilts, the band turning in melodic, acoustic-structured passages rendered full electric, their oft-purported but elusive bluesiness making a rare if obtuse appearance. The track's cocaine lyric lacks the celebratory vibe we saw back at "Sweet

Leaf." "We were going to call the album that but the record company wouldn't let us," laughs Geezer. "We'd been through grass and hash and acid, and cocaine was the big new drug at the time. We were recording in L.A. and coke was very big there, so we wrote about it."

"At the time I thought it was a good album, although a bit tighter than our other albums," muses Bill. "We spent more time on sounds. You know, we would take a few takes rather than like, three takes and that's it. So there was more time to use overdubs, to get a steadier, tighter sound. And I think it's quite noticeable, particularly on 'Snowblind.'"

"We just had the fucking packages up to here," regales Oz, on the snowblinded state of the Sabs. "It would come in like big gallon bottles with a spoon on it, covered with a seal of wax. This coke was the best coke that I've ever had. I'm lying by the pool one day and I met this guy and I asked him, 'You wanna do some coke?' He goes, 'No, no, no.' I'm whacking this stuff up my nose, it's a brilliant sunny day, and this guy sitting there with one of those reflectors under his chin getting a suntan. I say, 'What do you do?' He says, 'I work for the government.' 'Uh . . . what do you do with the government?' 'I work for the drug squad.' I sez, 'You're fucking joking.' He shows me his badge. I fuckin' flipped. I was fuckin' . . . flames were coming out of my fingers, man. He says, 'Oh, you're all right. I'm the guy that got you the coke.' We got all fucked up [on drugs], but me and Bill went a little bit further. Bill ended up in a psychiatric place. Bill's antidrug, anti-drink, anti-everything now. He don't mince his fucking words either, you know. With the coke and all these chemicals, I got a chemical imbalance in my brain. I'd become really shaky. I have to take Prozac and various medications just to stabilize me. One thing about cocaine though, it used to isolate you and you used to stay in your room paranoid. You buy a bag of white powder and the paranoia soon follows. And when you hear those birds going in the morning, tweet tweet, you want to get a fucking machine gun and shoot every bird in sight. When the day breaks, it's horrible. And what do you do when you wake up? Snnnniiiiffff! Like a fiend, you know."

After "Snowblind" was "Cornucopia," and the doom got blacker. Beginning as a denigration of consumer society, the track ended with an antiwar message, apparently incited by Geezer hearing about the latest casualties in Vietnam, a report that "only" 25 Americans had been killed that week. Another one of the band's solemn, mellow moments comes next, with acoustic instrumental "Laguna Sunrise" sounding so sepulchral, one feared that a death in the band was near. "I don't play acoustic guitar that much, so I'm not a very good

THE DOCTOR WAS IN, AND HE SAID WE'D HAVE TO GO HOME, SO WE HAD TO CANCEL THE DATES. I DIDN'T KNOW ANYTHING

acoustic player, quite honestly," says Tony. But the song achieves its goal, calming the band's crazies, before the practical joke of volume kicks in with a cackle, in the form of "St. Vitus Dance," named for a childhood affliction related to involuntary muscle spasms. The "St. Vitus Dance" lyric, however, is surprisingly this-worldly, revolving around love gone wrong; the music almost funky; the song all but forgotten in the catalogue.

"Things come out in the music," mused Tony, doing press at the time, on whether the band's increasingly complicated lives had affected the music at all. "Your scope widens. Like from the early days of Sabbath up until now, we've seen a lot of the world; we've seen a lot of everything that goes on. Like in this last album, there's a thing called 'Laguna Sunrise,' which is over there, Laguna Beach. It's about the beach and the sea. You just write about things that are in your environment at the time. Obviously we all live a lot better. In the early days it was a lot rawer because of the environment we were in. We were all down in the dumps and that had a lot to do with it. It certainly changed the music. At the time of the first album we were pretty much upset, as I said, and it was all very aggressive. The new album is different, really. It's basically heavy but it doesn't have the rawness like the first one."

BLACK SABBATH
SHATTERING SOUNDS FROM 4 ALBUMS
"PARANOID," "MASTER OF REALITY," "BLACK SABBATH," "BLACK SABBATH VOL 4"

Closing *Vol 4* is an epic called "Under the Sun," with a frantic closing section called (on some of the printed copies and in some of the printed locations on those copies) "Every Day Comes and Goes." Lyrically, this one is akin to "After Forever," Geezer proposing this philosophy of *tabula rasa* through nihilism; or on the positive side, freedom from all creed through knowledge and enlightenment — maybe just through drugs, maybe from cold-blooded cynicism.

"Bill had a terrible time trying to get that song," laughs Tony. "It was a time when we were pretty stressed out. Certainly Bill was. And he had gotten this thing in his head about playing that particular song. He brought it on himself. He just couldn't get it right. Every time

we would start to record it, he would mess it up. And of course, after a bit, he would just lose his temper — 'Ah fuck it!' So we thought we would try another studio, because somehow the studio got blamed. But Bill definitely had his hang-up with that one. Eventually, of course, he got it, but it did really drive us nuts. I think we tried three different studios recording that one."

"Bill's fantastic. He's such a nice guy, Bill," muses Tony, during the same conversation. "You couldn't wish for a nicer guy. Especially these days. Years ago, when he used to drink, God, he was a different story. Drummer, I think he's great; he's fantastic, such an unusual drummer, so unorthodox. He plays all these little bits that you don't hear drummers do nowadays. Most drummers say, 'Oh, I'm a good drummer and I'll just play the beat,' you know? But Bill will really get involved in it, really look into the percussion side of it."

"I hated the bloody thing," affirms Bill. "Tony had this lick [sings it], and at that time I thought it was just horrible. I couldn't stand the song. Oddly enough, today, I think it sounds great. But at the time I just couldn't find a drum part for it, and I thought, 'Oh God, anything but that song!' It was such a struggle with that particular riff. What I wanted to hear was a blues jam more than anything [laughs]. But I think we made some new ground. Geezer was writing really strong on that album, good lyrics, it was very much a band effort."

Musically the song is another very vaguely blues-doomed freight train, and yes, almost entirely metal, but somewhat tinctured by the blues, perhaps mostly in the vocal melody. Mournful passages emerge later, and then there's the strangely singsongy "Every Day Comes and Goes" section, which is not entirely successful, but is indicative of the band's wild

creativity for this involved record.

All told, *Vol 4* was not well received by the critics. The album has a strange uniformity to it, despite all that supposed studio work. The brunt of the album is slow, almost fatigue-inducing, and it has a coldness and dampness to it, unlike *Master of Reality*, which had charm. Vocally and lyrically the band sounds a little haggard and desperate — the doom doesn't leap out of the lyrics as much — although it is certainly there. More so, it seeps from the sounds. Several tracks would slouch off the record into the band's set list for years, even decades, but certainly few fans would characterize these as live favorites. "Snowblind," "Tomorrow's Dream" and "Supernaut" would act more as the glue that held the show together, as one prepared for the blast off of Sabbath's more beloved anthems.

Hitting the tour trail in America in the summer of '72, the band included "Tomorrow's Dream," also adding "Under the Sun," "Cornucopia," "Supernaut," "Wheels of Confusion," and of course, "Snowblind." The album wouldn't actually be issued until

September of '72, at which time the U.S. leg was over (Gentle Giant being the constant main support). The last two dates of the American tour had to be canceled due to Tony collapsing at the Hollywood Bowl gig on September 15th of '72.

Somewhat recovered, the band was off to a memorable one-off festival date in New Zealand (with a ton of unknown locals, and only England's Fairport Convention joining the Sabs from away), followed by five Australian dates. German dates kicked off the European tour in mid-February of '73, followed by UK dates in March, Sabbath backed by Badger and Necromandus, with which the band shared friendship and business ties.

But Sabbath was burnt to a crisp, their exhaustion after touring the U.S. causing a major rethink of the whole process. It was reported in the press that the band had decided to quit touring the states, Ozzy winning no friends saying that "America was the most satanic country in the world. They'll do anything for a dollar. People are living nightmares over there. Everybody in America is crazy." Ozzy was also known to remark that he was surprised fans in America didn't bring their own coffins to the gig.

"We thought we'd go over anyway," said Tony, of the band's reluctance to tour the U.S. "So we did a couple of gigs, and Ozzy's voice went. We had the doctors in, everything, injections, throat sprays, the lot. The doctor said he should have time off, and he did take time off for two days. So we thought, it's getting better, we'll try again. So we did another gig and then he had to have a week off. It just makes me fed up hanging about. It had been just all rush from the beginning, and we just weren't ready for it and then when his voice did come back, we were going out onstage wondering if it was going to go again, all worried like in case it goes. Eventually it all came to a head, and the last night, I collapsed at the Hollywood Bowl. We'd just finished the last number and I come off and I'm just gone. The doctor was in, and he said we'd have to go home, so we had to cancel the dates. I didn't know anything about it. Completely out, I was."

An interesting bit of trivia comes with press reports in January of '73 that Sabbath had plans to issue a live album called *Fire on the Mountain*, in time for U.S. dates in June. The label however, was said to have not liked the tapes, sending the band off to L.A. to write the next studio album instead.

Still, with respect to grueling tours, nothing much had changed. The griping and the drama of the *Master of Reality* tour reached a fever pitch on the *Vol 4* tour. Sure, the number of U.S. dates were reduced, but Sabbath also covered two other continents. The band's gaskets were blown — they clearly couldn't handle it. Ozzy was literally haunted by America, scared of its audiences, horrified at its string of identical hotel rooms and meals, at its groupies, at its stoned throngs wanting nothing more than to drive him crazy and away from his wife and kids (Ozzy's first wife Thelma and family are essentially estranged from him now). Later, in a more sober state, Ozzy would find himself backtracking and saying that he maybe did not loathe America to the extent that was portrayed (most notably in a Barbara Graustark piece in *Circus* called, aptly, "Why Black Sabbath Hates America").

In any event, a wholesale refurbishing was in order — a vigorous and almost damaging shaking of heads — the evidence of this to be offered in great supply come the Sabs' next album, a mind-blowing masterpiece called *Sabbath Bloody Sabbath*.

6

"ONE TYPE OF BEING ON FIRE"

– Sabbath Bloody Sabbath

There's a whiff of finality to the name *Vol 4*, or at least the sense that this is part of a finished set. In retrospect, that sentiment would ring out loud and clear. There's an immense gulf between those songs that came before and ended with *Vol 4*, and what Black Sabbath had up their collective sleeve. *Sabbath Bloody Sabbath* marked a second wind for the band, an explosive record that is very often cited decades later as the finest Sabbath has ever crafted.

BLACK SABBATH

911 157 (EA)
114 62

Face A
paranoid
Iommi - Ward - Butler - Osborne

Face B
sabbath bloody sabbath
Iommi - Ward - Butler - Osborne

Production: Roger Bain, et Black Sabbath pour Excellency Music
Licence: NEMS RECORDS Ltd.
Extrait du LP Eur 913.192

PRODUCTIONS
EDITIONS
MUSICALES
Asbela
P (1978)

Gravé et pressé en France

DISTRIBUTION
wea
bapocch music

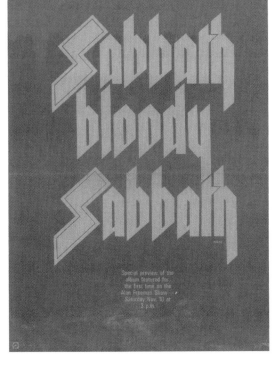

"I really like *Sabbath Bloody Sabbath*; I thought that was a great album," muses Tony. "Because it lifted us up a bit different from what we'd done on the first four albums. We experimented a bit more. We went back to Los Angeles, the same house, tried to create the same vibe we had with *Vol 4*, but of course we didn't. We couldn't create the same vibe. And even the studio changed, that we were going to go into. So we were basically right in the shit. We went back there to write it, and I got a writer's block. I couldn't think of anything [laughs]. Like, 'Oh my God, no!' I mean, we had a couple of songs, but not an album. And with the studio being smaller, we weren't happy at all. So we just packed up and came back to England. I got home and felt really depressed, and thought, 'Oh God, now, that's it.' We left it for a while, and then we had

booked Clearwell Castle, in Wales, and that was an experience and a half again. We all moved down to this castle and set up in the dungeons. Because we want to be miles from anywhere, to concentrate on what we were doing. So we set all the equipment up in the dungeons there, and bloody 'ell, things started happening just like that. I wrote 'Sabbath Bloody Sabbath' first, and that was the benchmark for that album. From then on, it was not a problem. Just the vibe of being somewhere like that created an album. Each one of those [albums] means something special, but I like *Sabbath Bloody Sabbath* because it was different. It was a phase in our lives where we tried something different, and I enjoyed it."

So, to break the Sabs' creative stalemate, a castle came to the rescue, in this case Clearwell Castle near Tintern Abbey in Wales, the band's new and temporary home, complete with practical jokes, hauntings and fires.

"As far as fires were concerned, Ozzy and I were always lighting fires," recalls Bill. "*Sabbath Bloody Sabbath* was made in a castle, and when we first did that track, man, it was phenomenal. I loved it. But the fires, that could have well come about through myself or Oz. It wasn't unusual for me to get drunk and just light a fire whenever I wanted to light a fire. I don't know if you've seen the movie *Sid and Nancy* and sometimes him and Nancy would go on the nod, and that one part of the movie, they didn't even know there was a fire. When I saw that, I thought, oh my God, I totally identify with this. Sometimes the room could have been on fire, and I would have just looked and watched the flames, oblivious to the fact that I could be in danger."

And then there were the hauntings. "Seeing a ghost was not unusual," notes Bill. "Geezer was always in tune to the phenomenon of ghosts. And I've seen ghosts many times. Even today, it's not unusual. My father had seen many ghosts. It's something that is normal, clairvoyance and stuff. My mother had the ability to teach me and pass on things to me. Even as a child, I had clairvoyant instincts and was able to answer questions before the person asked them. I did not understand why I was able to deduct. And I still have that with me, right up until this interview today."

Pyromania wasn't reserved for the stage alone. "Oz and I were firebugs. I might have got sick of my clothes and just took them off anywhere and set them on fire; it was almost like ritualistic. We also had the burning of my coat. Half of Led Zeppelin were there and all the Sabs. So that was one type of being on fire. And there was an inside trick we used to perform at parties. Being set on fire by Oz or the guys was

BEING SET ON FIRE BY OZ OR THE GUYS WAS NOT UNUSUAL; SOMETIMES I MIGHT HAVE BEEN TOO LOADED OR OZ WAS LIKE WAY LOADED AND WE'D HAVE THESE RITUAL BURNINGS OF CLOTHING.

not unusual; sometimes I might have been too loaded or Oz was like way loaded and we'd have these ritual burnings of clothing. Plus we'd build gypsy fires for campfires. And also now in reflection, things fell out of the fireplace and set Ozzy on fire and nobody knew about it. Unbelievably irresponsible. When I look back on it, we're lucky to be alive."

Bill had other problems as well, which saw him move onto Geezer's . . . lawn. "Yes, that was when we were doing *Sabbath Bloody Sabbath*," affirms Butler. "I just moved; that was the same house where I wrote 'Spiral Architect.' And the first day I'd moved in, I looked outside, and Bill had turned up outside. He was just leaving his first wife and was with his soon-to-be second wife, and he'd been thrown out of his house by his wife, so he didn't have anywhere to live [laughs]. So he came up, followed me home, just as I'd moved into my house. I've got no furniture or anything in the house, and Bill says, 'Do you mind if I sleep on your lawn? I've got nowhere to live' [laughs]. I think it was just the night. Until he sorted out his hotel or whatever. I said, 'Do you want to come sleep inside?' He says, 'Oh no, I couldn't do that. I'll just sleep on your lawn,' which he did."

Bill recalls the event this way, although pertinently, thinks it was during the making of *Vol 4*. "I didn't know where to go. One night the guys were just wanting me out of the studio. Period. I can't say I blame them at all; I'm not sure what kind of a state I was in. And I ended up going to Geezer's house and sleeping on his lawn, outside of his house. I went there and slept on the back lawn and I don't think he was too happy to see me and my missus sleeping on the lawn when he got up in the morning. We just didn't know where to go. I was definitely in crisis. I think I was about 23, and I was big-time in trouble — a young guy, already a veteran of the road."

Bill has more "ghost" stories than anyone else. "Oh yeah, thanks to Mr. Iommi and Butler and Osbourne. They used to tie little bits of fishing wire, which you can't see. I mean, they spent more time . . . so elaborate, you know. If there was a picture in the room or a glass on the table — this is my room, of course — they would wrap fishing wire around it. They would go to really elaborate lengths to pull off these tricks, even to the point of actually going up two or three stories on the outside of the building, so they could put the fishing wire from the outside in. And the fishing wire was under the door. So at nighttime, things started to move. And you couldn't see it, because it's like invisible stuff. I managed to get fucking scared to death at Clearwell Castle, as everywhere else, to be honest with you."

Finally, Geezer chimes in on Clearwell's charms. "We had been in America trying to write *Sabbath Bloody Sabbath* but nothing was working at the time. We felt like we were on the verge of breaking up, so we came back to England. After a couple of months we went back to our regular rehearsal place but I think Free were recording there. We had to find an alternative place. They recommended this castle. We had to rehearse in the dungeon of all places. We were in the dungeon playing away and all of a sudden we saw this person walk past the door that had a big black cloak on. We thought, 'What the hell is going on around here?' Tony and one of the roadies ran after the person. They saw him go into this other door at the end of the corridor. They ran after him and they were shouting at him because they thought he was some lunatic that got into the castle. They went into the room where he had gone into and there was nobody in there; he totally disappeared. We asked the owner of the castle about it and he told us, 'Oh that's just the ghost.' Apparently, he was the regular castle ghost. We all saw it. Tony went after him. You couldn't miss him wearing that big black cloak. I went home every night after that."

Sabbath Bloody Sabbath's stunning, incendiary cover art found Black Sabbath firmly back in Satan's downy, matted lap. "The front

THAT'S ONE OF MY FAVORITE ALL-TIME ALBUM COVERS.

of the cover represents a man dying on his deathbed," said Ozzy in 1974. "There are all these distorted figures bending over him and gloating as he lies there. These figures are actually him at different stages of his life. He's a man of greed, a man who's wanted everything all his life and done all this evil stuff. But flip the album over, and the back represents the good side of life. The person dying on the bed has been really good to people. He's got all these beautiful people crying over him as he's

ONE TYPE OF BEING ON FIRE

dying. At the bottom of the bed, he has two tame lions guarding him. All in all, this represents the good and bad of everything." Geezer has supported the basic premise of this interpretation, calling the artwork yet another in a long line of misunderstood anti-black magic messages from the band.

"Oh no, I thought *Sabbath Bloody Sabbath* was incredible," remarks Bill. "That's one of my favorite all-time album covers. On just a personal note, I love the back of that album cover, really nice. I guess if I ever wanted to die, in a certain way, that's how it would be, with all the animals and everybody just around me or whatever."

The cover painting, called *The Rape of Christ*, was done for Pacific Eye and Ear by Drew Struzan who was also responsible for the iconic movie poster art for the first *Star Wars* film. A reading like Ozzy's would make sense: evil on the front, good on the back. As well, one might look at it as a battle for a man's soul at the point of death, with the demons falling away for a peaceful passing. As well, one might look at it as a case of possession, with good winning out on the back, no death involved whatsoever, but instead, recovery. An interesting and somewhat sinister interpretation has been floated, this idea of the man on the bed being tormented. Either by his surrounding loved ones or by a demonic presence, and that what is going on in his head on the seemingly serene back cover, is actually the evil scene from the front. As well, meanings can be ascribed to the sex and age of the "watchers," to the rats and snake on the front as opposed to the translucent God image and the "tame" lions on the back.

The typography for the album was executed by Geoff Halpin, who essentially had touched off a heavy metal firestorm with his slashing Nazi-esque lettering, this and the gothic type-face used on the back cover (and for the tiny band name on the front), which became prevalent for heavy metal covers for much of the '80s.

On a perhaps amusing but real personal note, I remember as a young metalhead in the mid-'70s, spotting an optical illusion to the back cover that I've never been able to shake, that of a "headless" man turned away from the viewer, arms extended Christlike. It works like this: the bottom dark blue rectangle is the "upper butt" of his jeans (the lion's paws could even be pockets), the light blue band above that is a belt, and then all of the orange is the back of a shirt, arms extended to the left and right, hanging down, the collar of the shirt being the area adjacent to the chest of the man lying on the bed. Get it? In order to see it, you have to essentially ignore all the blue, except for the mystery man's belt and jeans.

I asked Bill if the *Sabbath Bloody Sabbath* cover art fanned the flames of the occult controversy surrounding the band. Indeed, one wonders how Warner Brothers even let it hit the racks.

"Yeah, that was something we lived with all the time and I think it scared a lot of people. It was interesting to see what it did do to people. To be honest with you, the people that I feared the most, personally — and I don't think this is a very admiring name — were the Jesus freaks, which is not a particularly nice way of calling people. They're still human beings, you know? But unfortunately they were just caught up in this obsession and I feared them a lot because they could be very violent at the same time. And if anybody was going to try to pull a gun and shoot one of us, I'm sure it would have come from there. But there were attempts on our lives over the years, through different sources. We were well protected at the time, well policed, and the FBI were involved. But it was the people who believed in Jesus Christ who really bothered me. Only because I feared that they were mental enough to go over the top."

"We had good and bad, funnily enough, for that album cover," adds Tony. "We won some awards for it. And then yes, there was obviously criticism from both sides." Again, it's sur-prising there wasn't more outrage at *Sabbath Bloody Sabbath*'s cover art, but then again, the early '70s was a decadent time in the history of popular culture, and the Satanism craze was all the rage. In fact, Sabbath's new record hit the streets one month prior to the launch of *The Exorcist*, that film fully scaring the hell out of everybody throughout 1974. "I was a big fan of it," muses Geezer. "We all were, but it didn't really filter into the music. It was pretty scary, at the time. I mean, people running out of the cinema in fear and puking [laughs]."

Early copies of *Sabbath Bloody Sabbath* (and even later copies in certain territories) were gatefold, with an inner photo depicting the band semi-transparent and naked, arms crossed in front of their faces (Ozzy doesn't quite get it right), in an old, nondescript, typi-cally English house. A partial link is made to

the cover art in that there is a bed behind the band, and, I suppose, because the guys are naked. This photo can also be seen in the Castle mini-sleeve CD reissues of the album. A lyric insert was included with the album.

Sabbath Bloody Sabbath opened with the album's superlative title track. All sorts of tense textures revealed themselves with this song. Bill Ward torments the riff in what is actually one of the best illustrations of his "lead drum" playing, his Keith Moon-ness, reminding us of Tony's summation of the man as more of a percussionist. An urgency verging on desperation is felt, underscored by Ozzy's frenetic vocal, the high range of which was destined to cause Osbourne grief for years; the oft-requested song would be attempted and dropped in the set, as it became increasingly onerous for him to sing.

"That one was about all the management hassles we were having at the time," explains Geezer. "And the Sunday Bloody Sunday thing had just happened in Ireland, when the British troops opened fire on the Irish demonstrators. That was known as Sunday Bloody Sunday, but

I didn't really want to write about that. So I came up with the title 'Sabbath Bloody Sabbath,' and sort of put it in how the band was feeling at the time, getting away from management, mixed with the state Ireland was in."

At this time, the Sabs were starting to move away from Patrick Meehan. Looking back on the band's experience with Meehan, Geezer doesn't mince words. "He's horrible."

Tony contrasts life with Jim Simpson pulling the strings, versus life with Patrick Meehan. "Jim Simpson, for us, in the early days did help us. We had nobody. He used to have a club and he got us rolling, playing at his blues club, Henry's Blueshouse. He started looking after us and helping us, and became our manager. Which was like having the guy next door to you, 'Oh, he'll be a roadie,' you know? And that's what it was based on. 'Well, Jim, you might as well manage us.' But Meehan came along with a lot more ideas and a lot more determination to take over the world, as opposed to take over England. And that was the difference. That Meehan had come in with that power to get us out there. But I don't think we realized how big we were becoming. In America, the album was in the charts and whatnot, and when we first came to America, we knew nothing. So it was probably us as well that got us booked around the world, as opposed to us thinking that Patrick Meehan did it, because of the popularity we were building up."

Geezer has also explained that some of the venom of the song "Sabbath Bloody Sabbath" was directed at the press, and it expressed acrimony over the emptiness of fame. It has also been said that the title came from a headline for a story on the band in the UK's influential *Melody Maker* magazine.

Musically, the track saw Sabbath adding some brave new textures. A daringly dovetailed mellow portion, replete with acoustic guitars, signaled that the rule book had been ritually burned. Tony's guitar tone is newly driving and dangerous, Iommi adding to the effect with a mercilessly doom-filled section late in the song, after a freight train of a guitar solo that is exquisitely musical and composed. During this nightmare, Bill gets truly percussive, a tambourine shakes like a rattlesnake, and Ozzy sings more harrowingly than he ever had to date.

"As soon as Tony came up with that lick, Terry and I just went full tilt," says Bill. "Geezer is such a great bass player; he just puts it where it's supposed to go. I immediately went to the toms, and I just love the power of the song. I think we did a good recording of it; but live, man, it was so powerful. The lyric 'Bog blast all of you' . . . it's just such a neat way of saying

BUT YEAH, MY HOPE, BACK IN '75, WOULD HAVE BEEN FOR BLACK SABBATH TO REMAIN WITH SOME HARDCORE ROCK, AND ALLOW ALL THE THINGS THAT WE COULDN'T DO IN A BLACK SABBATH RECORD TO COME OUT ON SOLO ALBUMS.

screw you, because it's used in such a polite terminology. It absolutely got the point across. Privately — and it's not very private anymore — but I've always referred to Geezer as The Irish Poet. I kind of romanticize like that when I think of him, because his descendency is Irish. Sometimes I see him as this kind of impish, Irish, vagabond writer lyricist, which is a nice way of looking at him."

Next up was "A National Acrobat," a malevolent arch-Sabbath track with a vague psychedelic feel to its lope, especially come its murky wah-wah break. The song breaks into a caterwaul of a jam, with all manner of layering demonstrating again that this was a newly sophisticated Sabbath at work.

"'A National Acrobat,' Geezer came up with a riff in that," recalls Tony, "which I thought was really good. We hadn't swapped ideas much before; it was always me who came up with the ideas. Geezer, you see, always felt a bit embarrassed to play me any of his material.

Merry bloody Christmas

Really, it was silly, but he had this thing in his head, 'Oh, I can't play it to you.' And one day, I made him — 'Come on, you've got to play; come up with something. It shouldn't be me all the time.' And he'd gotten some good stuff, Geezer. You know, he's had music that he's had way back till then, that he's still never, ever done anything with; myself as well."

Geezer confirms Tony's assessment of the situation. "I used to come up with stuff, but it's hard to do when you're in the studio and you've just got your bass. And every time I played a guitar, everybody would bust themselves laughing. I used to feel intimidated, so I wouldn't play it. That's why I love it now. I can just do whatever the hell I like. But yes, I wrote 'A National Acrobat'; I did that whole thing at home. And Tony came over to the house one day and I just played it to him, rather than in a group situation."

"I know we would joke around a lot, and sometimes the jokes would hurt," says Bill. "I know I would bring things forward and kind of wait for the rebuttal. It's not like it was boo-hooed or anything, but yeah, bringing something that is vulnerable to three other guys who are just . . . you never know what kind of mood they're in that day. So I can totally appreciate Geezer saying that."

Geezer admits he wasn't the only one in the band with confidence problems. "I think Ozzy was never sure about his lyrics, which is why he always delegated them to me. The thing is, we

were like, whatever instrument you started out on, that's what you are expected to play, and never move from that. I mean, it took Ozzy a long time to play 'Who Are You,' for instance, on his Moog, for us. And Bill, when he used to play 'It's Alright' on the piano, he came to us and would say, 'I'm thinking about . . . .' You have to say, 'I'm doing this as a solo album' [laughs], and hope that somebody would go, 'Oh yeah, that would be a good Sabbath track.'"

Bill confesses to getting the solo album itch. "Yeah, in fact, what my dream was, because there were a lot of different songs that were showing up, which might not necessarily be what one would call Black Sabbath, so right in the middle of it all, one of the ideas that I was pretty firm on was for us all to do solo albums, but never touch the mother ship. In other words, guide the mother ship with our lives, still carry on with Black Sabbath, and put Black

ul Johnstone

Sabbath songs in Black Sabbath, but at the same time, allow ourselves to do solo albums. I thought that would be a great way of using any pressure of trying to pack a lot of stuff into a Sabbath album.

"Geezer had a lot of stuff. I would just sit there for hours listening to what he had, and I was just blown away. I just thought, oh my God, this is great. There's always that internal argument: 'This is where he is in his private life; this is where Geezer is now.' And if this is where we are, then surely we ought to show this truth in a Sabbath album. But the truth is that when we do get together, we pretty much like to rock. I love showing up and kicking the

WE'RE NOT FED UP OR ANGRY YOUNG MEN ANYMORE. WE'RE GETTING INTO MUCH HAPPIER THINGS NOW.

ONE TYPE OF BEING ON FIRE

8-track stereo

crap out of me drum kit. It's the only chance I get to play drums, because I don't play drums with any other band. But yeah, Tony too — jazz, piano playing, all kinds of stuff!

"But yeah, my hope, back in '75, would have been for Black Sabbath to remain with some hardcore rock, and allow all the things that we couldn't do in a Black Sabbath record to come out on solo albums. But it was an idea that was a pipe dream; it never came to fruition. I think it was a scary proposition to us. 'If we have a solo album, that might tear the band apart.'"

"'A National Acrobat' was about sperm," continues Geezer, addressing the album's reptilian second track. "It's just about what happens to all those spermatozoa that don't make it to the egg. It's their big moment inside this ejaculation or whatever, and nothing happens to them. It's like, what could've been? All those sperms will never meet the egg and turn into people [laughs]. But I loved *Sabbath Bloody*

Sabbath. I mean, I loved the first three, but they were almost done unconsciously [laughs] in every sense of the word. Lyrically I really like 'A National Acrobat' and 'Spiral Architect,' my two favorite lyrics. 'After Forever,' as well."

"Fluff" followed, with Tony turning in an uneasy acoustic track, again — beautiful in a morbid manner, the song so incredibly mellow that few could see it as anything but ironic. This was not the band being pretty, this was Sabbath playing a practical joke. Tony is credited with acoustic and steel guitars, as well as piano and harpsichord. The title is a reference to BBC Radio 1 DJ Alan "Fluff" Freeman.

Closing out side 1 was "Sabbra Cadabra," a curious track that rocked hard but sounded oddly earthly, a bit conventional, with touchstones in blues and boogie. "That was our one love song we ever wrote," laughs Geezer. "We were probably all stoned out of our heads at the time." Geezer has also said that it was about a girlfriend he had at the time, and that the original lyric came from Ozzy cracking up over — and repeating the English voice-overs from — some German porn that had been worked on in the studio in which Sabbath now found themselves.

"Sabbra Cadabra" closes with another interesting, high-relief jam, Ozzy's voice captured hauntingly, Tony reprising his "Changes" and "Fluff" roles by tinkling the ivories. Rick Wakeman from Yes joined in as well. "I just did mini-Moog on two tracks; 'Sabbra Cadabra' was one of them," says Wakeman. "I did the mini-Moog on that at one in the morning one day. That was done at Morgan Studios, which is now in London . . . it was exactly the same week we were doing *Topographic Oceans*."

"He was great," recalls Butler. "The whole thing was just totally accidental anyway. It just happened that Yes were in one studio and we

were in the other, in the same complex. I think he wasn't very happy as far as the rest of the members of Yes, and he would come over and spend time with us, hanging out in the bar and stuff. We were a lot more sociable than them. It just came about."

"We liked Morgan Studios a lot, and went there a number of times," adds Bill. "We used to meet people all the time there. Yes were in and out of there all the time, Ronnie Wood, Charlie Watts would come down, and I used to play darts with Charlie [laughs]. There's a nice little bar there. That's where we bumped into Rick Wakeman and we ended up with 'Sabbra Cadabra.' We became good friends with Rick. It was almost like Rick was part of our band but he was still with Yes."

Officially, Rick is credited only on "Sabbra Cadabra." Tony and Ozzy are credited with the synthesizer work on "Killing Yourself to Live," Geezer and Ozzy on "Who Are You." Also on credits, Spock Wall is thanked prominently on the back cover. "A big help he was," confirms Tony. "All around, he was great. Spock was with us from the very early days. We brought him on as a tech, really, to do guitars. And eventually he was doing the mixing, and had become really good at it. But he was like an extra member; he was a great help in the studio."

Back at "Sabbra Cadabra," Rick can be heard in the quite progressive break section marked by Ozzy screeching "lovely lady," which, given this vintage quote from Bill, might have ended up as the title to the song (the band ultimately

FT.991

KILLING YOURSELF TO LIVE
LOOKING FOR TODAY
WHO ARE YOU

decided it was a little light for a Sabbath title). "We're not fed up or angry young men anymore. We're getting into much happier things now. On our new album, we're into songs like 'Lovely Lady.' We're actually talking about women, which is something we haven't gotten into before. With a lot of other groups, everything they do is related to women. The title track's about big brother. It's a revolution song. We're having a knock at society; there are a lot of things that could be straightened out in it."

In the same interview, Ozzy mused that Sabbath "don't ever try to say we're a bloody downer rock band or anything. We just play music. For the past three years, all I've read about is the same old thing. We come from Birmingham, hard town, and we're a hard band, and all that bull. It makes you sick. It's all too exaggerated. The *Master of Reality* album I didn't like it at all. It was too rushed and the sleeve was a load of nonsense. It was done so quickly, in three weeks, and even the bloody sleeve had been printed. We didn't have the chance to do what we wanted. The first album

was even worse. We did that in just two days! You know Led Zeppelin's second album, the one with all those incredible tracks? Well that was what we wanted for our album, but all we got was flat sounds. After the *Master* album, we said screw all of them, we'll do it ourselves. We didn't want to feel like we were putting out a load of bull. And we were pissed off with people telling us what to do. We didn't start out saying we were going to conquer the world; that's a load of bull. We're trying to achieve quality. It's nice to do something different every now and then, and this LP we've just done has some nice melodic things on it." Tony was in agreement. "It's probably less aggressive and raw than in the old days. The theme is wider too, and I think that with the passage of time, we've improved as musicians. Yeah, it's widening out."

Opening side 2 is another Sabbath classic, "Killing Yourself to Live" possessing some of the inky blackness of "A National Acrobat," its synth pattern under the verse being almost as prominent as Tony's secret agent man riff. The chorus is all Sabbatherian power and might, the band collapsing in a pool of doom, Ozzy again forced to hit notes that would later cause him trouble. Says Bill, "I remember when Ozzy was first doing the vocals, it seemed like a really angry song." Adds Geezer, "'Killing Yourself to Live' was just about the rigors of the road and all the management problems we were having. It just seemed like everything we were doing was going to line the manager's pocket, doing all this and seeing nothing for it." Geezer has also said that the song is about the boredom of hotel rooms, and in those waiting areas, doing too many drugs, or coming down hard off those same drugs.

When the album was but a month old, Ozzy saw it quite differently from his bandmates.

"Everybody is so governed by what they hear on television. Look at Watergate and all. It's hard not to be sensitive to what you hear and read about all around you. One night I was at home watching TV, when I heard some really bad news about people getting their heads blown off, and it was getting very frightening and sickening. So I started writing the lyrics to a song called 'Killing Yourself to Live,' which just about sums up the bloody state of affairs around us. The song is about people who are born to do just one thing in life, and then they die. They don't even care about trying something else. I personally believe that people are here for a reason, not to do what someone's telling them all of their life. I think that's why so many mindless acts are committed. It's like that painting of the man on the bad side of the album. You can give to people all of your life, but they'll never give to you. I guess it's just selfishness."

Subtitles for "Killing Yourself to Live" have been noted on some issues of *Sabbath Bloody Sabbath*, namely "You Think That I'm Crazy" and "I Don't Know If I'm Up or I'm Down."

Sabbath really step outside the box for the record's next track, "Who Are You" living, loving and dying on the strength of a synth riff, although rhythm accompaniment is added to this rare Ozzy Osbourne contribution. The lyric charts typical Sabbath-steeped exasperation at religious issues, the narrator stung, like any misunderstood and outcast metalhead, by the workings of the world, asking an omnipotent being — God or the Devil — what in the hell do you want from me?

"That's a total Ozzy song," says Geezer. "He'd just bought a Moog synthesizer, one of the first ones, and it was just like monophonic, so you could play with one finger, so he put that together and wrote the lyrics. It was fine, so we just left it like that."

Paul Johnstone

Notes Bill, "When Oz originally came down to Field Farm, he drove down overnight from his house, and fuckin' six in the morning, me and the wife are fast asleep, and he's a pretty loud guy, and the door bursts open and it's like, ' Hey!' And I'm like, 'Oh God, it's him, this time in the morning.' And he set it all up. The next thing you know, he's singing 'Who Are You' and he did the vocals and he double-tracked himself in our hallway, because it was a big farmhouse, so the hallway had good reverberation. And I was just in bed listening to him put it together and I thought 'My God. What an incredible fucking song.'"

Ozzy, speaking in 1974, called "Who Are You" the story of a person who is "confused

Paul Johnstone

Paul Johnstone

about everything and didn't know who to trust. You can say that person was sort of like me. I wrote that number at home between bouts of insomnia. I couldn't sleep. I bought this synthesizer and all day and night I would fiddle around with it to keep me busy."

"Looking for Today" serves as a metaphor for this album as a whole, Sabbath finding a way to synthesize (no pun intended) their harder rock with overt melody through this track's verse riff, as well as integrating their challenging new palette of instruments into their central guitar/bass/drums format. All of a sudden, the band is acoustically popping along at the same speed as the harder verse section, even with flutes added to the mix. Then there's

the chorus, which stood out as Ozzy's most sing-songy vocal melody to date. Bill turns in an interesting military march pattern for the verse and then grooves deliciously at the melodic, descending riff chorus. A second track of drums is added for fill purposes within the lush close out of this brave and underrated Sabbath classic.

Geezer offers that the lyrics were "about all these up-and-coming bands who thought they were brilliant and lasted for like about a week," Although Ozzy, on the press trail at the time, again contradicted Geezer's modern-day account. "The album was written in a very rural area, like a piece of nothingness, a void. I remember one night, I just picked up the newspaper, and that inspired me to write. One paper told how somebody had gotten blown up in Ireland and another paper I picked up told how somebody was blowing up a jumbo jet. There was trouble at the London airport, and all kinds of crap. I thought to myself, 'Well, what's it all about?' These people don't even know why they're doing these things. I guess

that's the way I feel. Tomorrow comes and comes, but we're all still looking for today, searching for something that's passed us by."

Settling heavy metal accounts, "Looking for Today" was slightly pop, "Fluff" a full-on baroque acoustic, and indeed, mellow bits emerge like spring flowers in various other incongruous spots all over *Sabbath Bloody Sabbath*. But the band was to end this boldly presumptuous album with what would be their most serious soft rock track ever, "Spiral Architect" sounding like the Moody Blues, albeit of a forceful, darkly pensive mood, orchestrated to the brim by Will Malone and "The Phantom Fiddlers."

"I had just moved into a new house in England," offers Geezer on the writing of it, a process that happened quickly after fully three months of gestation. "When we were recording the album, we used to commute back home on the weekend, and I just couldn't come up with the lyrics for 'Spiral Architect.' I was trying and trying but nothing was happening. I got back to me new house about six o'clock in the

Paul Johnstone

morning, and it used to have these two great big pine trees in the front garden. And I went there and sat between these two pine trees and I was just watching the sun come up, and I just started writing those lyrics. And it sort of wrote itself. It was like looking at the earth and knowing it was good and all that kind of thing."

Bill takes credit for the chorus of the song, having piped up as having written some of the lyrics and the melodies at that juncture. "I came up with the title," notes Bill. "What was neat about that is that Geezer got that straight away. He liked the title and was able to work with it. I wrote the verses in that: 'Of all the things . . .' I wrote those parts and Geezer wrote the other parts."

Paul Johnstone

Also of note, contrary to the credits, neither Tony nor anybody else plays bagpipes on the track, as Tony couldn't squeeze anything out of the instrument. Says Iommi, "During recording, you sometimes get these brain waves. 'Oh yes, let's do that.' We wanted this drone on a track, and I bought some bagpipes. I had this Scottish guy send them out. I started puffing on them, and couldn't get a thing out of them. Nothing. So I sent them back, and said they were broke. He sent them back and said that they were OK. I tried again. Nothing. I even got to the stage where I was going to hook them up

to a vacuum cleaner, to see if it had got the wind. It was disastrous. They sit in the cupboard now."

So there you have it, Black Sabbath had turned in a record that fans might, and did, compare to Led Zeppelin *III*, despite Ozzy's earlier aversions to having his band associated with that sort of record. In essence, Sabbath were admirably above caring about things as base as weighing their records for heaviness. Or at least at this juncture they were. They were looking to prove themselves as artists, but one suspects they were just as much looking to father some music that wasn't so hard on the bloody ears. And this shouldn't have been surprising. Despite playing heavy metal almost by accident, the guys didn't listen to it.

So Sabbath did what they did best, randomly fire off on tangents, experiment, jam, pick up weird instruments, use everything, and almost as pertinently, write a few passages based on the drama of their own lives. And that's what we got with *Sabbath Bloody Sabbath*, an exotic amalgam of the experiences of four lives lived fast and furious with the inevitable surrealism popping out at the seams.

But *Sabbath Bloody Sabbath* included so many fake-outs, there really weren't any seams. Somehow the album came off as heavy, or at least heavy enough that there wasn't a massive revolt from the fans. The biggest fake-out being its torrid emotional force. As further fake-out, the big songs from the record were the impossibly leaden rockers, the title track being launched as a single (and sinking like a stone), before it would become a perennial live favorite, along with "Killing Yourself to Live." In terms of the Charts, *Sabbath Bloody Sabbath* outpaced its predecessor in both the UK and America, hitting Number 4 in the UK, where it stayed for 11 weeks (as mentioned, *Vol 4* peaked at Number 8) and Number 11 in the states (with *Vol 4* reaching Number 13). *Sabbath Bloody Sabbath*, like *Vol 4*, currently sits at platinum status in the U.S.

Sabbath Bloody Sabbath was launched in the UK in November of '73, and North America two months later, but at the time, there were reports that a vinyl shortage, due to the OPEC oil crisis, had delayed its issue, the more immediate source of this shortage having to do with Alice Cooper's hotly anticipated *Billion Dollar Babies* taking priority.

Alice Cooper bassist Dennis Dunaway laughs when told that story. "You know what? If you ever talk to Warner Brothers, anytime we were ready to go back into the studio, they would say, 'Oh, your career is over; you guys are washed up.' And we would have to fight tooth and nail to keep things going with the record company. I liked Warner Brothers; that was just the way they did business. They always made you feel like you were on your way out. I don't think they could believe that we sustained. Maybe that was a realistic point of view on their part. But yes, the price of oil went up, and yes, we were on the road, and there was the trucker's strike, because of the high cost of fuel. We had two semis on that tour, and whenever they would pull into the gas station, there would be all of these truckers picketing, and then they'd have to tell them, 'Oh man, this is for a band — rock 'n' roll,' and then supposedly

BLACK SABBATH

LONDON MUSIC FESTIVAL '73
ALEXANDRA PALACE
THURSDAY, AUGUST 2nd

Paul Johnstone

they would be allowed to fuel up. But we had a few gigs where we had makeshift staging. And vinyl was threatening to be outdated, even though it did come back briefly before CDs took over."

Dennis adds a memory of Alice Cooper playing with Sabbath, rarer than one would expect, given shared label and stylistic similarities. "I do remember a gig where the bill was Black Sabbath and Alice Cooper headlined, and there was this opening band that nobody had ever heard of. And I remember walking into the arena seeing the audience, basically people socializing and finding their seats, and this band was on stage that I thought, 'Oh man, we've got to follow these guys?' And it was Yes. And I was thinking, geez, these guys are playing so good and nobody is paying any attention to them [laughs]. But yeah, I know that we played a lot of festivals where we were on the same bill, but that was the only gig that I can remember that was an actual concert-type lineup. We were pretty much running independently in those days."

Black Sabbath indeed had played many dates with Yes in 1971 and in 1972. It's been said that Tony had been inspired by that band to expand Sabbath's sound, hence the instrumental layering and progressive flourishes on *Sabbath Bloody Sabbath*, even if Ozzy said the two

bands didn't like each other and were worlds apart. The fact that Rick Wakeman lent his services was just a bit of serendipity.

Sabbath's tour for the album began in December of '73 in England with a brief trip to the continent in January before mounting a major American assault in February. Playing through April, Sabbath had on board a diverse selection of bands, including James Gang, Blue Öyster Cult, Lynyrd Skynyrd and Bedlam, whose drummer was future Rainbow and Sabbath member Cozy Powell. With respect to the set list, Sabbath tapped their latest album for "Killing Yourself to Live," "A National Acrobat" and "Sabbra Cadabra," with the title track to the record noticeably absent. "Fluff" was used as chill-out outro tape. In contrast, four songs from *Vol 4* were still part of the band's set list at that time. It is said that "Who Are You" was attempted then knocked on its head because temperature fluctuations caused problems with the Mellotron crucial to the track.

The U.S. leg of the tour was capped off with a quick stop at the first California Jam, April 6, 1974, which attracted a crowd of 200,000 to the Ontario Motor Speedway. In addition to the

SABBATH·
FIRST HERE IN '73!

GO·SET ENTERS ITS 8TH. YEAR ·
POP BOOM PREDICTED · ANY'OW
HAVE A HAPPY NEW YEAR!

I STRIPPED OFF AT ONE POINT
AND GOT IN THE FOUNTAIN RIGHT
IN THE MIDDLE OF SYDNEY.

just an ocean of people. I can't completely explain the feeling I got from it all."

Grossing two million dollars (advance tickets were ten bucks), nonetheless not much profit was to be had by the promoters, although TV rights and a simulcast were part of the deal. It is said that the biggest glitch on the day was when 100,000 cardboard sun visors were dropped from a helicopter, with most being carried by the wind away from where the crowd stood steaming in the hot California sun. Traffic was hell, with cars being abandoned on the freeway (over 700 were later towed), and yet, once weary walkers got to the event, they saw the parking lot was half empty. As well, approximately 30,000 fans knocked down fencing and crashed the event. Still, the paid-attendance figure of 168,000 beat out Woodstock, Altamont and Watkins Glen, even though those two festivals had much bigger crowd counts. The second and last Cal Jam was to occur in 1978, and it is better remembered, due to a double gatefold live album that was issued commemorating the event.

Curiously, the press in late '74 spoke of *Sabbath Bloody Sabbath*'s followup to be delayed to make room for . . . the first Ozzy Osbourne solo album, provisionally titled *Am I Going Insane?* But all was well with the band. After all, Ozzy's three mates were helpfully scheduled to appear on the record.

Sabs, baked fans got to see Earth, Wind & Fire, Rare Earth, The Eagles, Seals & Croft and Black Oak Arkansas, who would tag along as Sabbath played UK dates in May. Headliners for the event were Deep Purple and Emerson, Lake & Palmer, ELP's name held back until late in the game for suspense. The headliners played for 90 minutes apiece, while Sabbath put in a 70-minute set.

"It was the most incredibly well-organized gig that I've seen," said Ozzy in July of '75. "There were no pigs, no busts; everything had a backup system to it so there were no delays. The PA was the biggest that I'd ever seen; you could probably hear it in the next state. It was the first gig that we played in a few months, and I got so high from it all. Going on stage and seeing people as far as the eye could see,

Paul Johnstone

After a break in the schedule, November saw the band hit Australia, where a wee act by the name of AC/DC would back the mighty Sabs. Recalls Tony, "I thought it was some young kid on the guitar. I thought it was a schoolboy. I just looked up to the stage, because it was an outdoor show, and I saw this kid with a satchel on his back. Bloody 'ell, he only looks about nine, I thought. But of course when you get closer you realize he wasn't. But they were a good rock band. They were all a bit wild, I think. They did actually come on tour with us in Europe, and ooh, they were big drinkers, all of them. We both got a bit outrageous, I suppose.

"The band at that point were definitely in their heyday in the sense that nobody had burnt out quite yet. I think on one of my trips to Australia I'd already burnt out for the first time. I know I'd been in bed for about nine months; I think we had to cancel some tours. I'd got hepatitis B and the doctors had told me that if I carried on drinking and using I'd be dead in another year anyway. I can remember coming into Australia and I was carrying a walking cane actually. I'd lost a lot of weight. I was still very, very weak from the illness that I'd been going through."

Adds Bill, when prodded for stories, "I stripped off at one point and got in the fountain right in the middle of Sydney. We came out of a restaurant and I stripped down, completely naked standing in the fountain. There's been many a time when I've walked back into the hotel with my underpants barely hanging on me [laughs] and covered in crap and shit and God knows what else. I know everybody would get a kick out of that, and I would ask for my key in the most polite way and people would look at me and go, 'Oh my God, who is this insane person?'

"We were out playing one day, and the cars ran out of gas, so we drove them into the ocean and just let them float there, and then we hailed a cab and went back to the hotel. I can remember passing out. I was just drunk on my ass, and I think I passed out in Ozzy's room, nude as usual — I spent a lot of time with no clothes on in those days — but Ozzy apparently dragged me back to my room because he couldn't pick me up and I woke up out of this passed-out sleep covered in rug marks, all over my back and all over my chest and my arms. Man, that stung! He'd dragged me all the way down the corridors — I don't even remember him doing it. So I was a bit pissed with Oz because I was just in so much pain; I mean I have literally scars all over me from him dragging me down the hallway! I realized that he was out of his mind as well, so he probably thought he was doing me a favor."

7

"SMASHED OUT OF ME BRAINS"

– Sabotage

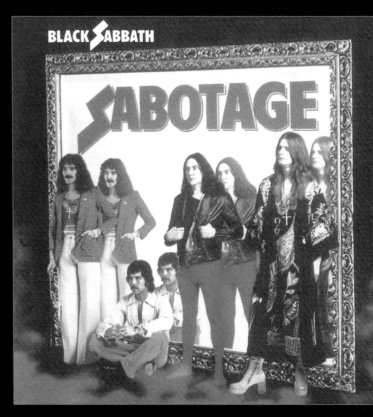

From agony and strife would come a record that many of Sabbath's maddest fans, this one included, consider the apex of the band's career. *Sabotage* (Sabbath felt their career had been sabotaged by bad management) would combine the frantic, ecstatic creativity of *Sabbath Bloody Sabbath* with a returning heft, the band proving beyond a doubt through two cerebral records in a row that they fully deserved to swim with sharks like Deep Purple and Led Zeppelin in any waters, on any given day.

> **WE USED TO TURN UP AT THE STUDIO TO GO AND WRITE A SONG, AND THERE WOULD BE LIKE THREE LAWYERS WAITING FOR US TO PUT SUBPOENAS ON US, STUFF LIKE THAT.**

Beginning with the cover art, what you see (and what has become an iconic image, if not an impressive one), was not the way it was supposed to turn out. Graham Wright was assistant to Bill Ward (with David Tangye, Graham has co-authored the excellent *How Black Was Our Sabbath: An Unauthorized View from the Crew*), and he was in on the initial stage of the design.

Explains Graham, "It was going to be a passageway or corridor in a castle or an old house, and they were going to be standing with black suits on, in front of full-length mirrors, four mirrors that were hanging from the wall, with stained-glass windows, very dark, with the image reversed like a Magritte. So it was their image being sabotaged. Sort of like a really old dingy corridor, like Dracula's castle. And the record company said, 'Oh yeah, we love the idea; we'll organize a photo shoot.' And we ended up in a studio in the middle of London. And we're going, 'What the hell is going on here?!' 'Oh, don't worry about it; we just want photographs of the band.' And they weren't wearing suits. It was taken out of my hands. Because I was the drum tech. And then you've got management

and the record company. They just pushed me to one side, and it was just a disaster. After that, I just said 'Hey, I'm not getting involved.' But it was typical of that period."

"Working on that was fun except for one thing," adds Bill. "Graham and I forgot to let the guys know what to wear, so when we showed up for the shoot, it was a total fucking disaster. That's why we ended up with this very odd looking Black Sabbath. But I love the idea of the mirror. But we just came in and we hadn't focused on wardrobe or anything, which was important. So in that particular shot, you'll notice that Ozzy's wearing a long cloak. Well, he has no underpants on. I'm wearing his underpants, his checkered underpants. Because when we showed up for the session, I didn't have any underpants. I borrowed the red tights from my wife, Mysti, who was at the shoot. So I had a pair of my wife's red tights on, Ozzy's underpants and my black leather jacket which was with me for years. I think Tony looks like he's just come from the office. I think the shot's hilarious to be honest with you."

"They were all going to have the same clothes on," says David Tangye, Ozzy's personal assistant and close friend at the time. "But Ozzy had the kimono on, and they always used to call him the homo in the kimono [laughs]. It wasn't meant to be like that. Graham's idea — he's quite a prolific artist, Graham, and he's had stuff shown in America and all over — but his idea was more like a gothic image. But it certainly worked, because it's one of the most talked about album covers they ever did [laughs]."

As it would turn out, the worst thing about putting together this poison-penned opus of a record was not the cover art, but having to deal with the band's collapsing business empire. Meehan and the Sabs were in a mammoth legal battle, and the paperwork was spilling into the

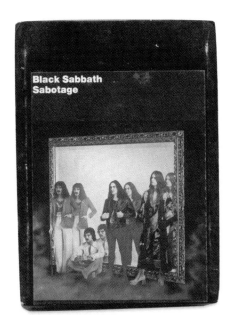

studio, which was maddening for four working-class lads cursed with a voracious, all-encompassing creative streak.

"That was probably the hardest record, the bleakest," begins Geezer, "because we were in the studio and we were having lawyers come in. We were leaving the management at the time and he was suing us, we were suing him. He was trying to stop us from recording and freezing all our money — bad times. We used to turn up at the studio to go and write a song, and there would be like three lawyers waiting for us to put subpoenas on us, stuff like that. It took us about ten months to do the album because of all the interruptions."

Even though *Sabotage* is seen by Sabbath fans the world over as a creative masterpiece (with a sizeable portion calling it their best album), the band is still, 30 years later, so clouded by the tortuous assembly of it, that most gravitate to the similar *Sabbath Bloody Sabbath* as the creative pinnacle, Ozzy going so far as to call that album the band's last.

"I think we changed, purely because of the system, the people surrounding us, the things we were involved with," adds Tony. "We started going through things we knew nothing about, the legal sides of things, all these hassles with management, stuff we really didn't want to be involved with. But we *were* involved in it. And I think that really put a blunt end to what we were doing. Because suddenly here we are, musicians, or supposedly musicians, and then we needed to become businesspeople, which we weren't. And try to work out, bloody 'ell, what do we do now? Here we are having lawyer's meetings, and turning up in court, swearing affidavits, getting sued left, right and center. It was a part of our lives we had never seen before, and I think it really interfered with our music. We were bloody getting writs in the studio, and then we were having to attend court because we were obviously going against Meehan. We were seeing the other side of life we had never seen, so it was not a nice time. We were thinking more about how we were going to get out of this problem, than what we were supposed to be doing."

At this point Bill took it upon himself to try to deal with the monies. "Everybody had a part in the band," laughs Tony, "and Bill's part was to sort out the money, go down to the bank, get the money, pay all the crew and pay each other, the general running of everything. But it went to his head [laughs]. He started dressing up in suits and going down to the bank with his

> WE GOT PISSED OFF BECAUSE OF ALL THESE MANAGERS TREATING US LIKE PRODUCTS INSTEAD OF HUMAN BEINGS. I WAS BEGINNING TO FEEL LIKE A PROSTITUTE, A MUSICAL PROSTITUTE.

briefcase. It was another Bill! He really took it to another level, Bill. We had some bloody laughs over it. But everybody tried to do their part, and Bill worked hard and tried to do what he could. But of course Bill got, in them days, as time went on, more into the alcohol, and became an alcoholic. It's very hard to talk to an alcoholic, even though he's your best friend. When he's drunk, it's very difficult."

"I think he was doing it simply because he was the only one who could be bothered at the time," adds Geezer. "He'd try and go get some money out of the bank for us, and phone up Warner Brothers, that kind of thing."

"I know that I spoke to a lot of lawyers," confirms Bill on his new role. "I worked real close with Spock. Spock took care of the stage, all of our equipment and our sound, even in the studio; he was a major player. But there were still problems and lots of things going on and I just tried to fill in the holes."

Bill insists he didn't take on this role because of any affinity for numbers; he says Geezer was

the numbers guy. "I just had an instinct about it. I was the mother hen; I still am. I'm like a mother hen when it comes to Sabbath."

"We spent a lot of time at it," adds Graham. "I was driving Bill and Geezer down to London to what they call The Inns of Court, to see the lawyers and barristers because they were in litigation. There were quite a few weeks of that. And that's a stressful time for any band. Because they had worked so hard. They got ripped off. It's been well documented. Sure, they carried on, but there was a bitterness towards management. It's like anything: 'Oh, why did we sign this and why did we go with this person?' 'It was your idea.' 'No, it was your idea.' Meehan was a businessman; he was in it to get as much out of it as he could for himself. That breed of person, they're ruthless. There's no loyalty in business. Bands are made up of artists. It's the same old story. Jim Simpson was sort of like a local promoter, from Birmingham, a nice guy. Once the band took off, especially in America, I think he was just out of his league. And then Patrick Meehan jumped in and said 'Hey, come with me; I'm the big shot.'"

"There's nothing you can do," says Geezer, on the subject of watching Bill's drinking getting worse. "If you try to do something with them then you just get abused by them anyway. I am not a qualified person to get somebody out of a drug or alcoholic situation. It is a specialist subject because if you try to do it, you just get abused. Plus, we were not exactly teetotalers either. But Tony and I didn't do it to the same excess that they did. I used to drink and do quite a lot of drugs. Drugs didn't really agree with me. Eventually, I didn't like the way they made me feel. I couldn't do them even if I wanted to because they made me feel horrible. Boozing gave me terrible hangovers, so it wasn't fun anymore. I can drink socially. I go

SABOTAGE!

An insidious plot to undermine all that is safe and secure in modern music. Sixth in a series of dangerous acts perpetrated by Black Sabbath. Contains "Symptom of the Universe," "The Writ" and "Am I Going Insane."

SABOTAGE. New Black Sabbath on Warner Bros. records and tapes.

out and drink once or twice a month but I don't have to do it every day. I never got into the situation like Ozzy or Bill did where they woke up in morning and had a bottle of vodka for breakfast. I could just never get into that — not that I ever wanted to. I didn't see how you could get through an entire day drunk. I got to the peak of the drug thing and booze thing and said so what? I went back to the way I was before. It's like the old saying, 'Drugs don't work anymore.'"

Ozzy's assistant David Tangye explains the movement from Patrick Meehan and the imploding World Wide Artists, to Mark Forster, who has since died. "I only ever met Patrick maybe once or twice, when I was working with Necromandus. He just seemed to be a manager, a London guy. It seemed that he had plenty of money and was just sort of guiding them through. Mark Forster was there when I was; sort of managing the band, tour manager/tour accountant. Mark was a lovely fellow, a great guy for them, very, very well-respected in the music industry, and I think he did a lot for them in America, because he had a lot of contacts. He'd been around the block a few times. After they'd finished with Patrick Meehan, like '74, it was like they were in free fall. When Mark Forster was actually brought in, they said they wanted to manage themselves, and do their own sort of deal, with Mark just helping them along. And of course they had big accountants in America looking after the business side. They were quite happy to juggle management themselves and talk to the record companies themselves. With *Sabotage*, it seemed the band were at their best, I think, because they were under pressure. I just think they worked best under those conditions. Because it all sounded demonic at the end of it, didn't it?"

Ozzy, speaking in 1975, just before the release of *Sabotage*, summed up the band's management hassles, also offering a character-ization of the new record. "After we did a tour of the east coast last July, the band just took a three-month vacation from everything; we just stopped to reassess our whole situation. We don't have a manager as such now; it's changed into a sort of family-type of operation. We were tangled up with the political things, getting rid of our management. The band wasn't stopped from recording, but it was the wisest thing to lay back until the political things straightened themselves out. It's all a lot of rubbish to me, but we couldn't avoid it."

"We just wanted to reduce the whole operation to more manageable proportions," continued Oz. "It got to the stage where people were coming up to us saying, 'Hi, I work for you' and I didn't have the foggiest idea where. I mean, we got pissed off because of all these managers treating us like products instead of human beings. I was beginning to feel like a prostitute, a musical prostitute. Forcing us to go on tour all the time was affecting us physically. We were ill; if we let people down, I'm sorry. It got to the stage where we had to rely on drugs, uppers, just to keep going, just to be able to get on stage. We played music that's false. The energy should come from the music, not from some artificial substance. You can only go so long; you just start going through the motions after a while.

"That's why we had to cut some of them short. The management seems to think that we're Superman; they don't give a shit about our lives. When I'm dead, they'll go and manage someone else. The only times these agents and managers would speak to us was when they wanted us to do something, and then they'd make it sound like they were the ones doing us a favor; that 'We're going to make you rich' line. I don't care about being rich; I just want enough to support my family, to live comfortably with. I mean, it's like when people go, 'Yay, Black Sabbath,' the managers care about us. But when they go, 'Boo, Black Sabbath,' they don't want to know. If they could earn bread by gassing people, they'd be right there on the controls."

"*Sabotage* still emphasizes hard rock," added Oz, getting 'round to the album. "Sabbath couldn't be anything but hard rock. I like to feel my spine curl from our music, from its power. On *Sabbath Bloody Sabbath*, we experimented a hell of a lot with different sounds, orchestra backings. The new ones vary, but we've also tried to keep it as basic as possible. There's various keyboards on most of the tracks; we've hired a keyboard player, Gerald Woodruffe, to reproduce them on tour."

Anything but a "basic" album, *Sabotage* opened explosively with "Hole in the Sky," a dense, purposeful doom classic that pounded the daylights out of anything from the competition circa '75. Though previously not thought possible, Tony's tone had gotten even larger, placed over a looming, surging swing from Geezer and Bill, while Ozzy is forced into another high and dramatic vocal. Indeed, as one walks through this harrowing, chemically induced record, it begins to come clear through the paisley murk that *Sabotage* would mark the finest vocal performance of Ozzy's career, a certain savage anger in his voice cutting through the heroism of the ornate musical backdrop.

"'Hole in the Sky' is great to play," offers Bill. "It's a tough one for a drummer because you want to push ahead but you have to lay back. That one is really behind the beat, kind of tricky. You've got to drive it hard but you've got to keep relaxed on the track, otherwise you'll blow the track." Adds Geezer, "'Hole in the Sky' was just about the environment, pollution, just the way the whole Western world was going at

IF THEY COULD EARN BREAD BY GASSING PEOPLE, THEY'D BE RIGHT THERE ON THE CONTROLS.

the time. I don't think they had discovered the hole in the ozone yet. Or it was a brand-new concept anyway. I must have known something, otherwise I wouldn't have called it that [laughs], unless it was a coincidence."

Says Graham on the writing arrangement, "The lyrics were all Geezer's, apart from the one Ozzy wanted. Geezer would never talk about them, to me or to anybody, really. He just brought them down and Ozzy would sing them. He thought, 'Well, I've written them down; you decide what you think they're about.'"

SOMETIMES I THINK, WITHOUT SOUNDING AGED AND DECREPIT, THE PHYSICAL ENERGY THAT CAME FROM SOME OF THOSE SONGS WAS ABSOLUTELY INCREDIBLE.

"Oz was always sitting down with Geezer, going back and forth with different things," adds Bill, intimating that Ozzy was more involved than we think. "I mean, popular conception is right, that Tony wrote all the parts and that Geezer wrote all the lyrics. There were lyrics and titles that were added, either by myself or Ozzy, and musically there were things that happened as well, where Geezer would introduce ideas — or myself, or Oz. If Ozzy had not been the singer, then lyrically I'm sure these things wouldn't have happened. Ozzy's incredibly almost clay-like. You're able to present some really neat things that you probably couldn't present to another singer. I like to call Black Sabbath a phenomenon and not a band, because the phenomenon does allow for that kind of interaction. What happens is, when us four get together, things like 'Paranoid' happen. Sometimes Oz would just come out with a word, and it would spark a whole thing; he does it to this day. He just comes out with one single word, and if you're listening, it will inspire a complete song."

"Hole in the Sky" comes to a brilliantly abrupt end. Once the shock wears off, Tony can be heard playing a barely audible, torridly exotic bit of acoustic guitar called "Don't Start (Too Late)" (Geezer: "The heavy parts were always sort of the bad vibe and the mellow parts were the good vibe that gave you hope"), before the heavy metal riff of all riffs announces the arrival of "Symptom of the Universe." Sure there's "Smoke on the Water" and even "Iron Man," but "Symptom of the Universe" purely and simply gets at the crux of why doom darkens the heart so inexorably. Again, once the song percolates to a rumbled chug, Ozzy is sent up his register to writhe.

"Well again, we actually show up with jazz parts," comments Bill on this song's shocking dispersal late in the track. "That goes back to our roots. The songs are a little bit unpredictable; we try to make it a bit unusual for the listener. 'Symptom of the Universe' was one of those songs. We had so many people participate in so many different areas of the work. When one would leave off, another one would pick up and move it forward."

With respect to the involved drum fills he gets to perform in this song, Bill explains, "It was just the appropriate thing to do. Tony and Geezer just hammered it out, and as soon as Ozzy's voice got on there and we got closer, it was just the natural thing to do — no preconceived notions. God, I love that song, but physically it's a tough one. Sometimes I think, without sounding aged and decrepit, the physical energy that came from some of those songs was absolutely incredible. When you're 20 years old, it's just like that's being pushed out of you; 22, 23, you can handle that because

physically you're in pretty good shape. When you're playing it past 50 years old, even though we're all fit and my health is really good, I'm still going to feel it. I'm still going to feel 'Symptom of the Universe' physically, at age 53. Because the benchmark that I set when I was 24, that's a lot of energy. And to perform at that level, I'm going to perform as a 53-year-old not as a 23-year-old."

Says Geezer with typical bluntness when he's looking for the short answer, "'Symptom of the Universe' is about love; that's the symptom . . . whatever that means. I don't know; I was probably smashed out of me brains at the time." Despite that dismissal, Geezer proves himself

to be at the height of his lyrical prowess, really, for two records straight now, writing not only longer lyrics but ones that work both poetically and philosophically. Both the "Symptom" and "Hole in the Sky" lyrics prove that songs like "A National Acrobat" and "Spiral Architect," with compactness, intensity, exotic imagery and messages with substance, were no flukes.

Bill is accurate when he speaks of showing up with "jazz parts." The starkly surprising jam at the end of "Symptom" rides a strange hippie terrain, with an added bit of beat generation that borrows from the blues, cocktail jazz and even Tex Mex. It's further testimony to the otherworldliness of an album that, as it unfolds, is going to get weird very quickly; menacingly weird, relentlessly weird, and even cruelly weird through the middle of the second side.

Side 1 of *Sabotage* ends with a ten-minute monster called "Megalomania," the song is this record's "In My Time of Dying," no light comparison, given that four months before the launch of *Sabotage*, Sabbath's up-market rivals, Led Zeppelin, had issued an album this writer considers the greatest record of all time, *Physical Graffiti*. Which is not to slight Sabbath. At various times when prompted for such lists, I've rated *Sabotage* the greatest record of all time — to be sure, at this level, we can just call it a tie (and if you want to tip to the Sabs, they manage the feat with one record instead of a double).

But yes, "Megalomania" is an evil epic of torrid, emotional movements. It opens like a schooner adrift, all but dead or dying, slowly lifting off on a heavy Iommi riff somewhat similar in speed and structure to the one in "Symptom." As the song progresses, different melodies unfold, and the record's goodly production values reveal clever little details of tone and tenacity.

"We were going through a very tricky time, getting ripped off by tricky people," says Bill, affirming that "Megalomania" and "The Writ" revolved lyrically around the band's legal woes. Of course Geezer hides the detail well, and what emerge are songs where you can taste the torment, a torment powerful enough to offer a sense of universality.

"Those two songs are intertwined," adds Bill. "'Megalomania' was about greed or coveting, and then 'The Writ' is kind of like the coveter or the greedy person — the end result was the writ, if you like. I don't know if there's a big difference there. Fantastic guitars; I think the band sounded pretty hot on both of those songs. I liked Tony's solo in 'Megalomania,' and I enjoyed very much putting a very straight beat to it. It was one of the only times I got the opportunity to do a very straight beat for a number of bars [laughs]."

"Like 'Killing Yourself to Live,' which was also written about management and record company people in general," offers Geezer. "It was so long because we couldn't figure out how to end it. We kept coming up with parts that were going to be new songs, but then we figured they would fit, so we used them."

Curiously, despite the tour de force of light and shade all over "Megalomania," and indeed almost all of *Sabotage*'s tracks, back in '75, Tony didn't quite see it that way. "It's more of a basic, raw album really, in the same way that all the albums up to *Master of Reality* were, but we've taken a lot more care in the way that this one is produced. We spent a lot of time on *Vol 4* and *Sabbath Bloody Sabbath*, but they were moving away from a oneness of approach. *Vol 4* was such a complete change; we felt we had jumped an album, really. It didn't follow suit because we had tried to go too far and again *Sabbath Bloody Sabbath* was a continuation from it. We could've gone on into more technical things and fulfill a lot the band is capable of achieving, and which we don't necessarily do on stage either. But we decided we had reached the limit as far as we wanted to go. We felt we wanted to get back to a more basic thing. We'll pick up again and develop from *Sabbath Bloody Sabbath*, but that will come later when we are more ready for it."

"I've always regarded it as important that people should pick up on the words," continued Iommi. "They're not just functional. The lyrics are about things that have happened to us, or dreams, or stages that we've been through. They're true for a lot of people who are actually experiencing them or have yet to go through them. They've felt whatever emotion, depression or whatever, and can relate. Younger kids especially can latch on to what there is and realize that there is somebody else who's been through it. With *Sabbath Bloody Sabbath*, everything was said — on the whole it summed up everything we had done over the years. This album is like starting again — like the music, the lyrics aren't so technical."

"I don't read science fiction," continues Tony, "but I believe Lobsang Rampa's writings about astral traveling in the next life. I believe there is a next life. It's easy to be skeptical, but I get a lot out of reading his books. Geezer was into this kind of thing long before me, and I think the influence is in some of those songs. I don't write the words, but I know the wavelength Geezer is on. In fact, the whole group communicates on a very close level. Like, we have what you could almost call a third eye. We can sense with each other what is going to happen. We've had actual experiences. One, I remember, Geezer was asleep and he must have astral traveled. I was stuck in the lift . . . when [I managed to get out of the lift and] I woke him up, he said, 'I'm glad it's you, because I just dreamt you were stuck in the lift.' These are quite regular occurrences. They used to frighten me at first until I got used to it."

Kicking off side 2 of the album was "Thrill of It All," which begins with a noticeable

downer rock vibe. Before long, though, the band pick up with a second, brighter, more hopeful structure, before the doom invades hard and hard-hearted — Tony's riff on this one is pure dark metal, its pregnant pauses more stillborn than anything.

"I was just reading a book about the 1920s and there was a title, *The Thrill of It All*," says Geezer, Bill adding, "It's one of the songs where, musically everybody got it, but sometimes you have to sit back two months later and realize what the lyrics were."

Late in the track, the band break into a sort of happy hard rock buttressed by synthesizers,

> OZZY WOULD SORT OF COME IN AND OUT THE ROOM, SING FOR A BIT, THEN HE'D GO TO MAKE A CUP OF TEA AND BRING TEA AND BISCUITS BACK FOR EVERYBODY, WHILE WE'RE WRITING THE SONGS.

the sum total of this one sounding like something that would have fit handily on *Sabbath Bloody Sabbath*. "I was a handclap," laughs David Tangye. "Bill had us into the studio clapping — myself, Graham and his brother, Bill's brother Jim. So that's my energy in there."

"Supertzar" is next, and for this one, Sabbath create a Luciferian bridge between classical music and metal that presages those naturalist and folk preoccupations of black metal bands of a pagan ilk. "Supertzar" sounds almost fascist, at least Wagnerian. One pictures a choir in uniform, marching to Bill's military snare and bombastic percussion appointments.

"That was a big production," explains Bill, proceeding to sing it. "Tony had the lick; that's all we had. And again, we were at Monmouth, at the farm. That lick kept coming up, and we all knew something had to be done with it, but we couldn't move on from there. And Tony somehow found out what would be the next indicated chord and push it into a different area. And as soon as he did that, all of us were able to just come into it. I had a field day. I put vibes on there, tympanis, snare drum . . . we

had chimes, we had the English Chamber Choir. Plus we had very professional harp players. We just kept adding more things to it and it just grew. And that was our opening theme for our shows after that.

"It was a bit unusual at that time, putting a big choir sound with the rock 'n' roll feel. Some of the bands were doing it. I'm not saying by any means that Sabbath was unique, but it was a little bit unusual. And the choir loved it. The lady who played the harp, I think she was from the London Philharmonic Orchestra, and she was fucking great, man. And we had an arranger come in, Will Malone, who put it all together really nice. But we knew where we wanted it to go. We were singing for them like a choir, all the low parts."

"When they brought in the choir, it was quite funny," recalls Graham. "The choir was shocked; it was just a session choir. They all piled in, took over the studio, did their bit, and off they went." Adds David Tangye, "It took a couple of hours maybe. There would be more time spent tuning up and blowing the spittle out of the instruments, and they would just sort of do it. The guys had an idea what they wanted, but I don't think there was any score."

While working on the track in Brussels, Bill had had what was later diagnosed as a mild heart attack, no doubt exacerbated by his self-professed alcoholism. Ozzy took the bull by the horns and got a doctor on the case quickly, Bill having crawled to his room in the middle of the night. A month's rest was prescribed, with Bill worrying that if he didn't get his act together quickly, he would be replaced.

Next up on *Sabotage* was another oddity, "Am I Going Insane (Radio)" hearkening back to the preceding album with its overt melody and synthesizer flourishes. Unwittingly, Ozzy had added hugely to the theme of mental insta-

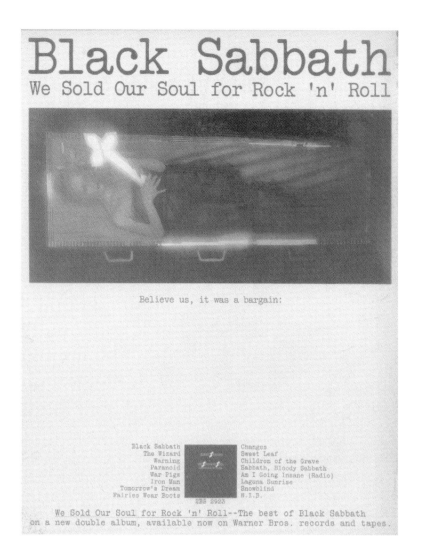

Black Sabbath
We Sold Our Soul for Rock 'n' Roll

Believe us, it was a bargain:

Black Sabbath	Changes
The Wizard	Sweet Leaf
Warning	Children of the Grave
Paranoid	Sabbath, Bloody Sabbath
War Pigs	Am I Going Insane (Radio)
Iron Man	Laguna Sunrise
Tomorrow's Dream	Snowblind
Fairies Wear Boots	N.I.B.

2BS 2923

We Sold Our Soul for Rock 'n' Roll--The best of Black Sabbath on a new double album, available now on Warner Bros. records and tapes.

bility of "Paranoid," finishing the job five years later with "Crazy Train," establishing a caricature that's his for life — this idea of a regular, not-too-bright geezer driven mad by his emotional unfitness for stardom, or at least touring. Musically, the song features more military single-stroke rolls from Bill, while Ozzy sings a weirdly foppish and Shakespearean vocal melody over a soundtrack that devolves into tormented laughing and then crying.

David Tangye: "'Am I Going Insane' was Ozzy's song; he did all that, with his Moog. I don't know if you've been watching *The Osbournes*, but he had the old Moog; he'd bought this synthesizer and he used to muck about with that in the studio in his house. And he actually came with that, 'Am I Going Insane (Radio),' which was radio rental, Cockney rhyming slang for mental." Graham explains further: "That thing in brackets, radio — in Birmingham at that time, there used to be a shop called Radio Rental. And because of the rhyming slang, if you thought somebody was mental, you would say, 'Oh, they're radio rental.' Even if you knew somebody in the pub who was a nutcase, you'd say, 'Oh, he's radio, he is.' Radio rental, which rhymes with mental. It's English rhyming slang."

"I think 'Am I Going Insane' is kind of the blueprint for a lot of Oz stuff to come," says Bill, "the kind of stuff Oz did with *Blizzard of Ozz*. He came down again to Field Farm and we got the roughs down there, and of course, he followed the song all the way through, did a fantastic job. The laughing on that, that's a friend of ours, from Australia, Adrian. The crying is Ozzy's daughter Jessica. We slowed it right down and it was horrible. Everybody knew Jessica, and she was just this beautiful, beautiful kid, and then when we slowed it down, it was like 'Oh God!' We'd be getting high and flipping out behind it, like, 'Oh, don't do that.'"

"We would always jam around as a band and Ozzy would sort of join in," remarks Tony, "He'd sort of come in and out the room, sing for a bit, then he'd go to make a cup of tea and bring tea and biscuits back for everybody, while we're writing the songs. Then we'd do a take of the song, then Ozzy would take it into his room and you'd hear him wailing away there for a few hours, coming up with ideas."

Sabotage ends with a clang, "The Writ" being one of the band's under-appreciated classics.

The song revisits the sparseness and sluggishness of "Black Sabbath," the guys bravely writing and executing a plod, with nightmarish, boiling-cauldron sounds adding to the madness. As with "Megalomania," it's almost detrimental to the enjoyment of the track when one finds out the lyric is rooted in the band's management troubles. But Ozzy delivers the song's spitting venom with manic savagery.

"Recording with a room full of lawyers," says Geezer, remembering "The Writ." "Ozzy came up with those lyrics, and I thought they were really good. But it was this whole situation with everybody suing everybody else. We just wanted out of it."

As with "Black Sabbath," or for that matter "War Pigs," Sabbath pick it up later in the track, adding segues and secret passageways, as they'd learned to do on the preceding album, and they dovetailed in acoustic guitars with a sleight of hand that kept the listener from watching the clock, waiting for the next headbang. It's a trip, a journey, and we're all along for the developing, doomy story and lurching demise thereof.

"No, I loved that!" says Bill, on the challenge

of playing so slowly and simply. "The less the better. For me, that's what metal is about. Doing a slow song really loud, you just put the one down; you just put the bass drum where it has to go. You don't need a lot. You can use the air and you can use dynamics and that is where the song is. Sometimes just not even playing can bring out an incredible sound."

Early copies of *Sabotage* included a 23-second joke song at the end of "The Writ," recorded at low level, called "Blow on a Jug." Bill calls this one of his and Ozzy's "family songs," just something tossed off for light relief when in the mood. That's Bill playing piano and Ozzy and Bill both singing, if you can call it that. "That was just an outro," says Tangye. "They used to muck about. Daft stuff. There was a lot of comedy with Black Sabbath. It wasn't doom and gloom. It was more fun and games, down home. They didn't live that part."

With respect to chart placement, *Sabotage* saw further slippage for this band soon to be deemed out of steam. The record rose to Number 7 at home in the UK, where it stayed for seven weeks, but stumbled to a mere Number 28 in the U.S., eventually going gold for sales above 500,000 copies — it was the first Black Sabbath album to fail to reach platinum status. No singles were issued until five months after release of the full-length, when, in February of '76, "Am I Going Insane (Radio)" came out, backed by "Hole in the Sky" — unsurprisingly, this weird, strangely irritating song failed to chart in either key territory.

The high drama with Patrick Meehan had resulted in a two-LP compilation issued in early 1976. *We Sold Our Souls for Rock 'n' Roll* would creep to the lower rungs of both the U.S. (Number 48) and UK charts (Number 35, for a five-week visit), but its main claim to fame is the ghoulish gatefold image, that of a decadent

I'VE GOT BATS LIVING IN MY HOUSE. I LIVE IN A 300-YEAR-OLD HOUSE AND WHEN I FIRST MOVED IN, THERE WAS TWO OR THREE, AND NOW THERE'S EIGHT OR NINE.

society lady lying in a coffin and clutching a big shining cross. All of the material was previously released with all but two tracks hailing from the band's first four albums. As was the case with *Paranoid*, *We Sold Our Soul* proved the immense power of hit singles to make wallets flop open. Unfortunately, this record appealed to a lot of what one might call the casual Sabbath fan, with its eventual double platinum status trumping the certification of the previous three Sabbath albums, *Vol 4*, *Sabbath Bloody Sabbath* and *Sabotage*, each, of course, studio albums full of new material.

Out on the tour trail, the Sabs played all of *Sabotage*'s Taurean side 1 and none of its Aquarian side 2. "Hole in the Sky" opened the shows, with "Sabbra Cadabra" closing them out, while altered lyrics provided for amusement. "Rock 'n' Roll Doctor" from the forthcoming *Technical Ecstasy* was also boogied about, in roughed-in form.

The tour opened in July of '75 in America, a couple of weeks before the release of the album. Backups included southern raunchers

Ruby Starr & Grey Ghost, along with the Leslie West Band, Lynyrd Skynyrd, Mahogany Rush and Kiss. Back in the UK in October of '75, Sabbath played with Bandylegs, the precursor to Quartz, a band that Tony would produce. Quartz also coughed up one Geoff Nicholls to the Sabbath camp. O'er the strait and Sabbath toured Europe with ZZ Top, Streetwalkers and Chapman/Whitney's.

Recalls Tangye, "The *Sabotage* tour had a massive, big cross, and it had like reflective crosses stuck on it, mirror crosses. Les Martin, Geezer's roadie, his dad made a big coffin to put this in. When the roadies cleared the show for the night, it used to come to bits. It was massive, in two parts, and then it fit into the coffin. It was all part of the effect. They tried everything, including mirror balls. And they had the World War II footage in the background, Adolph Hitler and all that. That might have been *Sabbath Bloody Sabbath*, because for *Sabotage*, they had the big fiberglass shell behind Bill, which was designed to throw the sound out from Bill's drums and stop the feedback from Tony's amps on the stage."

"It was a bloody nightmare," he adds, with respect to the notorious shell. "The roadies hated it because it was more to carry about. They got some company from Huddersfield to build it. And for *Technical Ecstasy*, Bill had the big drum riser and he had lights and strobe machines, which cost a fortune to make, from a studio in L.A. Bill liked a lot of drums and he always had loads and loads of flowers around his kit, red and white carnations. He liked the risers. I think the first riser he had was a funny reflective material, a rainbow effect — mother of pearl, that's it. Prior to that, it was just a little riser on the stage, nailed down eight-by-four-foot sheets. But then when they got to America, everything had to be bigger and better. Because if you're playing at Madison Square Garden, you needed a big riser anyway. The band's got to look big, haven't they?"

"I liked the shell," laughs Bill, calling it his favorite Sabbath prop of all time. "It acoustically held in my drum sound. I just built it purely to enhance the sound onstage. We were looking for different ways to grab the sound of the drums. But it was a pain in the ass to the roadies [laughs]. They hated me, and it became like a joke, Bill's shell. I mean, the comments from those guys . . . because they were just so dry with their humor. So I got a lot of laughs. But in practicality, it really worked well for me. But it was a crap idea when it came to the auditoriums with the audiences that wrapped around, because they couldn't see me. I like the effects we used to have in the song 'Black Sabbath.' I always found that Black Sabbath is better just standing up and playing. I don't think it needs a lot of effects. Just get up there and play our balls off. Kiss are the best at effects, quickly followed by Pink Floyd, but they're in a class of their own. But I've often said, why even bother putting anything up there?"

"When Bill came up with the shells, we all laughed and thought it was bloody ridiculous," adds Tony, "and quite honestly, I thought it was good. It was good for sound, for acoustics, because it bounced back the sound of the drums, which otherwise would just disappear behind the stage. I don't even know if it was intended as that, but it worked really well."

Bill's assistant Graham, explains the flowers strapped to Bill's kit that created an eerie, funereal effect. "Throughout the time I worked for Bill, after I finished setting up his kit, I always used to tie flowers to the drum kit and then throw them into the audience after the show. And on the rider, there were always so many bunches of flowers. There'd be like six large bunches of flowers. And to be honest, it was any old flowers we could get [laughs]. But carnations tend to last the longest. Usually we would end up with carnations. And as soon as the band went offstage and the lights came up, I would throw the broken sticks into the front rows and I'd rip the old flowers off and throw them, usually at the girls."

"We were playing this baseball stadium in the States," said Ozzy, in press at the time, relating a road story from the tour. "We were in the middle of a huge field, and there's a high wire fence all 'round, with the kids outside. So I say to them, you know, come on, come inside, and suddenly they're all climbing over the fence and running towards us like a human stampede, and we're playing away, waiting for them to get up to us. But when they do, they don't stop! They just trample right over the stage, bust up all our equipment, and rush away across the rest of the field and out of the stadium doors! 'Cause the police are after them, see."

Ozzy also recalls that on this tour, audiences began throwing crosses to him on stage. "I've got a drawer full of them. I couldn't hazard to guess how many I've got. I got them all over the house. People throw them on the stage at me and I pick 'em up and save 'em. I've got some really beautiful ones thrown at me, and they're very personal to me because I've communicated with somebody in the audience. Sometimes they throw a cross and I didn't see it and it didn't work. When I pick one up, I've picked up the vibe of the person who'd thrown it. I've got seven or eight to take back with me from this tour."

Things then got a little silly in this same *Sabotage* tour press interview, Ozzy remarking, "I've got bats living in my house. I live in a 300-year-old house and when I first moved in, there was two or three, and now there's eight or nine. Also in the Greenwich house, there are eight or nine stray black cats. I live in the middle of the country and they appeared from nowhere. It freaks me out, so I've got crucifixes all over the house." When asked what he would like etched on his gravestone, Ozzy answers: "I was just thinking about that the other day. I'd like to have a great stone made for me of me as a young man instead of an old man. I'm gonna have a gravestone made with a statue of me and the position that I'm in on the cover of *Vol 4*. I've got to find out what stone is my stone."

Bill talked to the press about his home life as well. "I live on this farm in the countryside. I love to hunt and ride across the fields. But Ozzy here, he's dangerous with guns. Ozzy goes hunting with John Bonham, you know, the drummer from Led Zep. Sometimes we bring our families to one of our homes and have a huge outdoor feast or cookout. One time Ozzy got carried away with his guns. Almost shot off everyone's head, he did — of course Ozzy was drunk at the time."

As Oz had mentioned earlier, Black Sabbath had hired Gerald "Jezz" Woodruffe as a keyboardist for the *Sabotage* tour. Here Jezz charts his joining up with the boys. "The drummer that was in my jazz trio, Mike Evans, who unfortunately got killed, was a very close friend of Bill Ward's. And when Sabbath were looking for a keyboard player in 1975, Mike Evans said to Bill, 'You should check Jezz out, because he can play anything.' I got a phone call from Bill, and met him at a drum shop in Birmingham, went to Ozzy's house, and played with the band, who were just there. Ozzy had this room on the side of his house that was a special place for rehearsing, like a studio, but there was no recording equipment. And I walk in there, and they were all there, luckily, just a kid off the street, really, and it was quite mind-blowing. But I thought, 'Right, I've got to do this,' so I just ripped into the keyboards, and they said 'OK, you're coming with us to America.'"

The band toured constantly for three years, and Jezz remembers well the gear that went with them. "I just had masses of keyboards, because in those days you had to have a keyboard for each sound. And they were just all over the place. My Moogs were the key to doing the *Sabotage* songs. I had four Moog synthesizers and I spent hours programming those to get as near and as close a sound as I could. But I think the most successful thing was a Fender Rhodes going through a fuzzbox. That sounded very much like the backing chords, the heavy riffs, if I got it right."

Surprisingly, Jezz confirms that the band had played "Am I Going Insane (Radio)" live. "Yeah, we did. And I used Ozzy's ARP 2600 to do that, the one that he actually has at home, that he's standing next to on *The Osbournes*. There's the one where he's trying to get the noises out of his synth. It's the same synth because I remember sticking the tour sticker on it where it is on that one. And it's worth a fortune now, because those old synths are collectible. Otherwise, I used to try to copy Tony's original guitar parts on keyboards, so he could do the solos and the riffs would keep going."

Jezz admits that he didn't sing. "I can't sing. I sound like Ringo Starr."

A further UK leg of the *Sabotage* tour had to be postponed when Ozzy smacked himself up in a motorcycle accident, although December dates back in the States would go ahead, Sabbath playing with the likes of Aerosmith, Manfred Mann, Savoy Brown, and, once more, both Kiss and Ruby Starr. The *Sabotage* tour, though not a particularly long one, ended back in England with the rescheduled dates from November performed in January of 1976, the year that would mark a miserable downward slide for the band that would render it virtually unrecognizable.

8

"LOTS OF DOPE ON THE FIRE"

– Technical Ecstacy

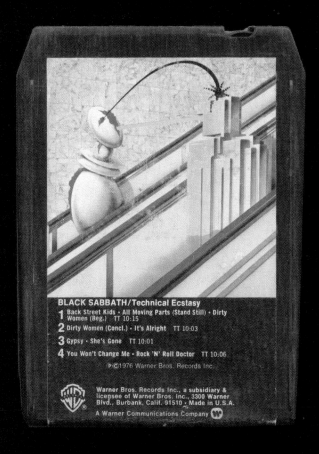

Everybody's got their Sab favorites, but, as with other monumental greats like Zeppelin or Purple, once sick of the usual old rotters, the discerning fan digs deep into the dark-horse albums, finding treasures along untrampled pathways. *Technical Ecstasy* is one of those treasures, an album that is oddly, uneasily mainstream in its construction and lyrics, but somehow cloaked in a thick, damp blanket of doom, and a hacking flu is the inevitable result. It is a record of corruption absorbed and then Oz-mosed through the pores, a corruption more sophisticated in its seduction than the shouting and pointing version represented by the overt horrors of records like *Sabbath Bloody Sabbath* or *Paranoid*. *Technical Ecstasy* will rot the brain if loved too obsessively.

In fact, the album was recorded in sunny Florida, temporarily lifting the spirits of a band desperate for a hit, a band reeling from drug and drink, increasingly at each other's throats (or smoldering, or at least vaguely aware of discomfort) over the workload. "The album was written in England at Ridge Farm," says Tony. "We lived there for six weeks while we wrote the album, which was pretty quick for us. When we were done, we had all really liked it and were playing it all live, and it sounded really good live. So basically when we went in the studio we had done the same thing — we played it live and recorded it. So it was pretty painless from that side of it." The pain, like the record it would produce, was more insidious — it came from having to operate at manic warp-speed as Black Sabbath, other identities strewn about. Bill was not too bad, Tony overworked . . . really it came down to Ozzy who had become increasingly surly. The presence of keyboardist Jezz Woodruffe deep into the writing also upset the familial, years-old balance.

Technical Ecstasy, now somewhat written, was carried away to be recorded at famed southern rock locale Criteria Studios. But none of the usual technical Criteria folk were on board. The album came out self-produced and quite satisfying sonically in light of *Never Say Die* and about half the starchy records from

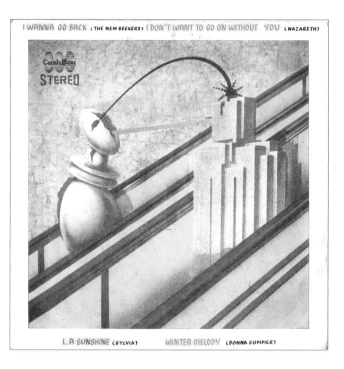

earlier in the catalog. Much of the task, including mixing and mastering, fell to Tony who has often and vociferously made clear over the years that he resented doing as much work on that album as he was forced to. "Criteria Studios was really great," recalls Tony. "It was a great atmosphere and I think we really had a good thing going. But I remember being stuck in the studio a majority of the time while everybody's out sunning themselves. But I do like that album."

Adds Tony, "It's the old thing. You get to a lovely place and you sort of tend to take a bit longer. You tend to be on the beach during the day and working at night. But I liked it. I remember trying a few different amps on that one. I used a transistor amp a lot, which was very unusual for me. I think the engineer we were using almost went around the twist; we were driving him up the wall. But definitely, I was left to do that album more or less on my

own, so I did feel a bit left out on a limb. I followed it all the way through."

Bill Ward also recalls the experience as being basically enjoyable. "We were in Miami and I might have been having too much of a good time [laughs]. It was the first time we ever went to Criteria Studios. We were attaching ourselves to a lot of experimenting, moving into new areas, seeing if there were things that could work, also going back to things we knew worked and we enjoyed, but at the same time saying let's stretch it here. For instance, 'It's Alright' is just this really soft song, but I liked the idea that it was a risk."

Explains David Tangye, charting the process from writing through to completion, "I think first off we went to a place called Glaspant in Wales, an absolute dump, this place. And everybody started scratching and itching saying, 'Well, we've got to get out of here.' So the band pulled roots and went to Ridge Farm Studios, on Rusper Road in Sussex. It wasn't a

full-blown studio as it is now. Ozzy did his first three albums there. They rehearsed there and then took it over to Miami. We were there for two or three months. And then Tony went to L.A. to do the final mix with Robin Black. Robin Black sort of coproduced on that. Robin had worked with Jethro Tull; he used to do quite a lot of stuff with the Rolling Stone Mobile. I think they did some of the mix at Sounds Interchange in Toronto as well.

"It was a funny time for Black Sabbath. They were going through a lot of changes in their personal lives. Tony really worked hard on that album. He was bringing new stuff in, and of course Gerald Woodruffe had come out. He had come to do the keyboards, which was excellent. Gerald is a brilliant musician. He injected a lot of creative stuff into that album because he could play. And that's why it was so different. A lot of the fans didn't like it because there was more melody and strings. They did that track 'She's Gone,' with strings, and of course they had Bill singing 'It's Alright.' I love that album, but a lot of people have knocked it. Tony and Geezer were working on it hard, and then of course Ozzy went in in the end and overdubbed everything, got his vocals down. We had quite a bit of fun, because there were a lot of people in the studio at the time, like The Eagles who were doing *Hotel California*."

"The Eagles were in Studio 3 and Fleetwood Mac were in Studio 1," confirms Jezz. "Micky Fleetwood used to call me into their studio to listen to what they were doing, which was nice — great bloke. But what really impressed me was the rows and rows of guitars in the other studio that belonged to Joe Walsh. There were about 30 vintage guitars, and this one roadie, who had only two fingers on one hand, was in charge of them all."

David Tangye comments further on the presence of Robin Black, who had also co-engineered *Sabotage*. "Robin was in there, more engineering than producing, because Tony and Geezer would probably do the majority of the production. And of course Spock Wall would be assisting him as well. But Robin was a lovely fellow, a quiet fellow. And then Robin and Tony went to California to do the final mix, the mastering and that. The majority of the time, I looked after Ozzy and that was it. There were loads of different camps in Black Sabbath [laughs]. Tony, Geezer, everyone had something to do. And of course Ozzy, although he was busy working on the album, he still had his bits of time off. We had our things to do. We weren't necessarily screwed to the floorboards in the studio."

"I think they were just experimenting," Tangye continues, reflecting on the tenor of the record at hand. "*Sabotage* was a really big turning point for Black Sabbath — absolutely brilliant. That was Sabbath at its best, really. I think they got a lot of aggression out with *Sabotage*. And *Technical Ecstasy* was a different thing altogether, because they had gone to Miami. All the other albums, they'd either been in Record Plant or London, basically, Morgan Studios. So for *Technical Ecstasy*, they went to a warm climate. And climate changes you; it gives you a different perspective. Sure, they had the ideas in England originally, but I think they just expanded them, and *Technical Ecstasy* was the end result."

Geezer's celebrated creativity extended to the album graphics this time out. "I just gave [noted UK album cover artists Hipgnosis] a rough thing of what I wanted and let them go at it. I wanted the sort of robots, but with an art deco feel."

Adds Tony, "Geezer came up with that title, as he did with most, and I thought it was good. If you remember the cover, it has the two robots going past having sex, technical ecstasy [laughs]." Ecstasy technically speaking perhaps, but the communication within the cover art comes off as blind, machine-like, functional and mindlessly procreative at best, a perfect visual wrap for the hypnotic, fascinating sleepwalk enclosed.

"I think we saw a couple of things, as far as the artwork goes," adds Bill. "It was one of those situations where somebody magically was coming up with the artwork and it kind of drifted past our eyes, so to speak. Everybody settled on the album cover. It was like, well, that makes some kind of sense. We were all attracted to it. I liked it for about ten minutes [laughs] but I'm used to it now. I pretty much went along because Geezer thought it was great. We influenced each other. If Geezer thought it was OK, then it was OK."

Technical Ecstasy opens with a bold gallop of a rocker, a song that amounts to the album's pure metal moment, "Back Street Kids" discharging an immediate blast of up-tempo precision metal that was almost too energetic for a band laboring up the road low on motor oil. "I love 'Back Street Kids'; that's so fun to play, man," offers Bill. "We were actually messing around with that one during rehearsals a couple of weeks back (this interview was conducted April 11, 2001), but it's very high vocally for Oz." Geezer had also noted that bringing this song to life in '01 wasn't exactly working out for the band, this blustery, hard-charging rocker joining "Symptom of the Universe," "Hole in the Sky" and "Sabbath Bloody Sabbath" as tracks that were off-limits late in Ozzy's career.

David Tangye, given his role as Ozzy's P.A. at the time, offers a glimpse into the working methodology of the Oz-man. "'Back Street Kids' and 'Rock 'n' Roll Doctor' were good ones for him, in terms of a personal stamp. Because a lot of the stuff they didn't put together when we were in England. Usually it was a big jam sort of thing, and then record everything, and then basically the words would come on top. Tony would come up with riffs and Ozzy would just sing anything that came into his head. And they would have it all recorded and played back maybe at the end of the day's rehearsal. And then Geezer would be thinking about it. And we'd just let them get on with that, because that was band stuff; that was their creative period. Lyrically, they were quite close and they worked together. Ozzy would have some good ideas. If you read a lot of these newsletters that kids post, they say 'Ozzy had nothing to do with this, and he didn't do that,' but he did, you know? He was there. And he wouldn't have survived, if he hadn't. And he did survive.

"But after *Technical Ecstasy*, that's when things were really going downhill. It's like familiarity . . . they'd been together a long time. And when you start making money, I think you

OZZY JUST DISAPPEARED AND NOBODY KNEW WHERE HE WAS; HE WASN'T INTO IT AT ALL. WE HAD TO DRAG HIM INTO THE STUDIO.

get ideas that you want to do something else. I remember when I came back from Miami, we went back to Ozzy's house, and that's when he told me he wanted to get the guys from Necromandus down, the band that I had looked after and managed before I started to work with Sabbath. I think it was more of a band that he wanted to try some of his creative stuff out with, an experiment, to see how he would work with other musicians. I mean, he's worked incredibly well with other musicians as times got on [laughs]. The band had worked hard those few years. I think they weathered the storm really well."

Noting Ozzy's dissatisfaction with Sabbath at this point Tangye says, "I think Ozzy's idea was more down-to-earth solid rock like the first album; get in, get it done. As the albums went on, it got more complicated. Recording techniques changed and there was more stuff in the studio to play with. Ozzy wasn't really over-keen on having the keyboards. I got the impression at the time he wanted the four guys doing it, the guitar, bass, drums and vocals and that was it. Although they brought Gerald in to sort of fatten the sound out, I think Ozzy is more inclined to the earlier stuff."

Tangye doesn't believe Ozzy was insecure about the writing. "I think he had problems with dyslexia, but that was never an issue. Ozzy would come up with some good words and great ideas. He liked to put his two pennies in. But I think collectively, they got everything down that they wanted to. They were quite happy with each other. They were all quite involved. In rehearsals, Spock would be there with the Revox tape and everything. They were quite intense when they were working. There would be jam sessions, all banging away, putting in their own ideas. It was like building a house. You would put the foundation down, put bits in, take bits out."

"I think they were really into it," adds Jezz Woodruffe, regarding Bill's and Geezer's involvement with the record. "At that time *Presence* came out by Led Zeppelin, and they couldn't understand that. They were going, 'Why is this number one?' And I was saying, 'This is unbelievable!' So they weren't on the same level musically as bands like Led Zeppelin. It was much more simple than that. None of them had any musical education. But I had, you see. I'd been sent away to public school, and I was in the school orchestra and I'd done theory and grades on woodwind instruments and piano and all the rest of it. So I had this big advantage, which they used. You know, they used me to help them get to that next edge further. So no, everybody at that point was putting in what they should be doing, apart from Ozzy. He was never there."

And where was Ozzy?

"He was probably out with a shotgun shooting chickens [laughs]. He just disappeared and nobody knew where he was; he wasn't into it at all. We had to drag him into the studio. We had to push him onto the stage when we were touring. He just wanted to go home. At that stage in his life, I don't think he was interested in anything. He and Tony were really at loggerheads. But it was Tony's band; he'd taken over the role as head of the band. He was definitely in control of Black Sabbath, because Ozzy was not interested. Bill was taking care of business, always on the phone to L.A. sorting out deals."

"Ozzy is just music; that's all he's ever done and that's all he knows," sums up Tangye, "getting up on the stage and performing. He's very, very intense. Quite a complicated chap. They had the time of their life, really. They were doing what they wanted to do and they had a lot of success. There wasn't anything else. Ozzy just lived the role; he lived Black Sabbath and that was it. I suppose he was two people. He was John Osbourne and Ozzy Osbourne, like an alter ego. I don't see much of him now, but when we do meet up, we have a laugh. Ozzy is as you see him; that's him. There are no airs and graces about him. There are no back doors; that's him. He's in your face and that's him. He's a rock star and he's a singer in a heavy metal band."

Back at *Technical Ecstasy*, things slow down with a deathly lurch for "You Won't Change Me." There's something a little obvious about this song. To their credit, Sabbath create a dirge that is as depressing as they've ever done, no small feat given the misery-ridden back catalog — it's what they do best. But then again, the

AND WHEN WE'D JUST FINISHED IT AND
BILL HAD DONE THE VOCAL, WE WERE
GETTING READY TO DO ANOTHER TAKE,
AND OZZY CAME INTO THE STUDIO AND
SAID, 'WHAT'S THAT FOOKING RUBBISH?!'

song is written somewhat conventionally, it is accessible and it's almost a ballad (of a bludgeoning sort), Bill dropping bombs, the band bashing in resignation of an end to come. But you never quite feel the song could support a sour, head-scratching wigout like those all over the late stages of songs from the last two records. Instead, the break is Beatle-esque. Tony, however, turns in not one but two ripping yet still sorrowful and bluesy solos, choosing a tone that scrapes the heartstrings until they recoil.

"I think it's about just sticking to your principles," remarked Geezer on the uncharacteristically straightforward lyric. "And no matter what people try to do to change you, nobody's going to be able to do it."

Jezz sings the melody to "You Won't Change Me," and says, "That's all keyboard patterns. You can spot them a mile off. They don't come from the guitar like that," intimating he had a big writing presence in the song. Beyond debate is the *Exorcist*-esque keyboard line Woodruffe

puts into the track, adding to its creepy mystique — it's almost shocking to hear this song placed at the second position on the record.

"He was helpful, yes," recalls Tony on the contentious issue of Jezz in the band. "I wanted somebody else to play with. Ozzy was going, 'Oh, we don't need a keyboard player.' But I just thought it would be helpful for me, for writing songs, to bounce off somebody. Because it was always me that had to come up with the riffs, I thought it would be a nice touch to widen our scope by using a wider variety of sounds, with the keyboards. I think in the day, it was a lot of pressure, because there was a lot of responsibility, and somebody had to come up with the ideas and somebody had to get it down, so I started getting more and more things put on me on the production side, and booking the studios and whatnot. Because at certain stages, we didn't have management. I was supposed to know more than anybody else in the band about the studio, and it was left to me to book the studio and book the people involved in that.

"I think it's good to have someone for the other members to turn to. If there was any problem, they used to come to me. Sometimes, it wasn't a good thing for me because I couldn't go out and get drunk when they did. Somebody had to stay straight to see that things happened correctly."

Tony also felt, however, that this was a really fertile period for him with respect to his playing abilities. "I felt, sometimes on stage, as time went on, yeah, you feel like you can play anything. I was playing things and I didn't even know what it was I was playing [laughs]. It was becoming second nature. Things were coming up and I couldn't remember what it was, so of course, I couldn't play them again. I felt things stepping up, which is, yes, probably around *Technical Ecstasy*."

"It's Alright" is unarguably the most left-field track on the album, a fully Beatle-esque ballad written by Bill and, astonishingly, sung by Bill. "Actually I started that one some time before," notes Bill. "I wrote it at Field Farm, our first house in England, the house I shared with my second wife. That's where we used to rehearse as well. Oz would come down and write stuff of his own. It was a kind of commune-type place for a while."

It took some coaxing to get Bill to come out of his shell for that song. "I was scared to death!" he laughs. "I had it in the house and the guys knew about the song and Ozzy kind of

liked it, but it was like, 'Oh my God, am I going to play in Sabbath one of my own songs?' Because it's one thing being a cowriter, supporter and a semi-arranger, but then moving into your own material and being supported by your bandmates, it's pretty scary. Tony was doing it with 'Laguna Sunrise,' but he didn't have to sing them."

"I liked it," adds Tony. "I thought it was really good. We tried to encourage Bill, yeah, you should record that. It was quite different for us. Bill wrote all the lyrics on that and the music, and I just wrote the solo part in the middle."

"When we were in Miami, Bill never surfaced," says David, remembering the working dynamic of the drummer. "He was the only Englishman to go to Miami and come back lighter than when he left [laughs]. It was just how he was. He's a creature of the night, Bill. Fairly nocturnal. Because we were booked in the studio in the nighttime, from six until six, we'd get back in the early morning, have a couple hours sleep, and then of course we're up around the pool. But whenever Bill came onto his veranda after his deep sleep, he used to get a big rapture of applause. And the other guests used to think, well, maybe it's his birthday. Because we used to sing 'Happy Birthday' and all sorts of things, just a bit of a joke."

Bill pleads, of all things, sobriety. "What happened, in the weirdest way, when we were down in Florida, there was a lot of cocaine use then, and I wasn't using [laughs]. So I got to watch them. Some of them were pretty out of it, and I couldn't hang with the all-nighters, stoned with the blow. I used to isolate anyway, but I just didn't join in the big cocaine parties and things like that. Because by the time I was 25, I was burned-out. I had already had hepatitis. I guess at that time I was the band member most likely to fucking die before he was 30. Which is nothing to be proud of, but I just couldn't hang where the only talk's about what drugs we were going to do and things like that. I became quieter; I just watched."

"Ozzy hated it right from the start, never wanted it on the album," notes Woodruffe, contradicting the above, on Bill's big number "It's Alright." "And when we'd just finished it and Bill had done the vocal, we were getting ready to do another take, and Ozzy came into the studio and said, 'What's that fooking rubbish?!' And Bill went absolutely ballistic and trashed his drum kit. He'd just spent hours getting a drum sound and he just smashed the whole lot, the microphones, the whole lot. The whole studio was a wreck. And a few weeks later, they decided to put that song on the album. And a lot of Sabbath fans hated it. Because it was Ozzy's territory; it always had been. The fans thought that commerciality had invaded the band, and to be honest, they were right. But I thought it was a good song. Bill heard it when he was cruising down the freeway, on FM radio, and he was thrilled to bits. He had his five minutes of . . . that."

Bill denies that there were any rows over "It's Alright" going on the album. "Oh, not at all. To be honest with you, I was really reluctant for it to go on the album. I felt really uncomfortable. I wasn't aware that I was pushing it. I felt the opposite, like, 'This is a bit weird.'"

Side 1 of *Technical Ecstasy* closed with "Gypsy," one of the album's stronger tracks, one that played on Sabbath's key strengths, namely heaviness and unpredictability. Bill's opening rhythm is tribal and busy, but then Geezer and Tony place the simplest of chord patterns over it. Eventually the song collapses into a bold but simple and groovy hard rock, then comes a third transition, and then a (Queen-like) fourth, and then a fifth to close

out: five completely different passages laid one after another, no chorus, no verse, the last being a dark jam that recalls the alchemy of old. "I like 'Gypsy,'" remembers Tony. "We used more of a piano. I think with that album we used keyboards probably more than most. Gerald playing keyboards made it easier for me because I could concentrate on the guitar stuff instead of playing piano here and there." Bill has said that he thought 'Gypsy' was first conceived at Strawberry Studios in London around Easter, and that Ozzy may have had a fair bit to do with the lyrics.

"'Gypsy' was just a throwaway lyric about meeting a gypsy. Stupid, really." The tone in Geezer's voice says so much more than the words themselves — it betrays the fact that the band could indeed write a throwaway lyric at this tired time, and not care. It also contains a reminder that one shouldn't read too much into many of Geezer's seemingly deeper and more poetic lines. In many cases, it was the drugs talking, and a deadpan, thoroughly honest Geezer will say as much.

"'All Moving Parts (Stand Still)' was one of my titles," recalls Bill with a laugh, zoning in on the opening track of the original vinyl's side 2. "And it manages that; I think it was that literal. I just loved it, really odd. The working title for that was 'Claret On The Blanket.' And that referred to a very dysfunctional sexual thing. I'll just leave it at that right now [laughs]." Bill has said at other times that it simply refers to the menstrual cycle.

He's right about the motion of the song though, the track moving laboriously with shallow breaths — elephantine and clumsy and murky — signaled by Geezer's lobotomized disco funk of a bass riff, and the progressive herky-jerk of the break section. Still, this was a rocker and at least a bit of an avant-garde one, not so obvious as, well, everything presented on the album thus far, save for "Gypsy."

Sez Geezer, "'All Moving Parts (Stand Still),' I think it was about Margaret Thatcher at the time, something like that. At that time . . . well, there still hasn't been a woman president in America. It's about a woman who has to dress up as a man to become president, because that's how misogynistic American society is. Britain canceled it out when Margaret Thatcher became Prime Minister — that was another coincidence. By the time the album came out, we had a woman prime minister." Not quite, since Margaret Thatcher was elected May 4, 1979; but indeed The Iron Lady (!) had been the leader of the Conservative party since 1975.

"Aha! Now then, 'All Moving Parts,'" laughs Mr. Woodruffe. "That was really funny, because we were set up in an amazing manor house somewhere in Surrey, and Ozzy disappeared for a couple of hours. And he came back with an armful of marijuana plants that were about eight feet high [laughs]. 'Where did you get those from?!' He'd found a greenhouse just up the road, that was about 100 meters long that was full of these plants. I mean, how he found it, I don't know. So what he did then was, we had a log burner in the room where we were all sitting and he put the whole lot on the fire [laughs]. And then the words to this song 'All Moving Parts (Stand Still)' started arriving."

And the inscrutable lyrics of "All Moving Parts (Stand Still)"? "Well, it means that Ozzy put lots of dope on the fire."

Next up we had "Rock 'n' Roll Doctor," perhaps the album's second least characteristic Sabbath track, Tony remarking that "we made it more into something with a honky-tonk feel, a piano thing, although it didn't start out that way." It is in fact both a boogie woogie song and a party rocker, although the idea of "party" was painted in typical Sabbath grays and deep blues. Essentially, Ozzy's anguished cries sound less like a celebration and more like a dance with the devil, the central character of the lament seeking a temporary respite from bone-wracked ills, a simple salve on the shakes. Bill offers the following comment. "'Rock 'n' Roll Doctor' we did really fast. We started jamming it live, before we even knew it was going to be a song. Because Tony would always do those long solos. And you know, we had half of our material right there [laughs], for the next album. Because he would just be putting riff after riff together. And I think that's where 'Rock 'n' Doctor,' might have stemmed from. The song was pretty good but it needed some-

thing on there, just to give it a bit of a honky-tonk feel, which is why there's the piano."

"I think 'Rock 'n' Roll Doctor' was to do with Ozzy," says Geezer. "I think he came up with that, either the lyrics or the title. It doesn't sound like anything I'd write."

If that's the case, Jezz certainly didn't see any of it. "No, Geezer wrote all the lyrics; he always did. Nobody else ever had a part in that. Right from the very start. For the three years I was with them, I never saw anybody else put pen to paper. But musically, it was all a group effort. Do the riff and see what comes out. We were desperately short of songs anyway. We had to drag everything out of the bag."

"The piano in 'Rock 'n' Roll Doctor'; I like that. Me and Tony worked the riff out, and it was new to them; they didn't do stuff like that.

I've seen reviews saying that that album was one of the worst Sabbath albums they've ever done; I've seen a lot of feedback like that. And I actually think it was quite refreshingly different [laughs]. In the end, it went platinum in the UK. It struggled to start with, but it got there."

Hard feelings begin to surface on this subject of Woodruffe's stamp on the album. "Well, that's a very difficult area, really, because my input into those songs is a tremendous amount. But you'll notice on the rereleases, I don't even think my name is on the covers. The truth of it is that I can't really tell you what the truth is because it's heavy business stuff, and I'm owed massively, but I ain't going into that."

It sounds similar to what went on a few years later between the Osbourne camp and Bob Daisley and Lee Kerslake.

I REMEMBER KISS. A BIT OF A NIGHTMARE WITH THEM, ACTUALLY — VERY, VERY OBNOXIOUS.

"Well, at least they knew they were selling their stuff," says Jezz. "They were paid. A bit. And it was straightforward. Sharon [Ozzy's wife and manager, in the solo years] would say, 'You want to be on the album? We buy it off you and that's it.' That's the hard rock 'n' roll business. With me, back in the '70s, there was nothing, no agreement, anything. No paperwork, nothing. Because actually, to be honest, I never did it for the money anyway. I never have. I never did any of the stuff with Robert Plant for any other reason other than the fact that I desperately needed to do this for myself. But I was involved in virtually everything all the way through. I was heavily involved in the arrangements of all of them. I think it just says 'Additional Arrangements' by me somewhere."

Jezz denies that Ozzy was resentful of keyboards. "It wasn't that as much. It was a massive clash of personalities between me and Ozzy, because of where we'd come from, our backgrounds. I was very fortunate. My dad was a band leader in the '40s, and after the Second World War he built up a retail music instrument business which was, you know, big-time. So I had a privileged lifestyle. Whereas Ozzy was struggling from the day he was born, really. And there was that real clash there of totally different backgrounds. Which didn't bother me, but it sure bothered him."

But things were much warmer with Tony because of their mutual jazz backgrounds, with both being fans of Django Reinhardt, Erroll Garner and Joe Pass. "When we started writing the album, it's not fair for anybody to say that it was his responsibility. In the public's eye, it was, because I didn't really exist. Because if I existed, I was going to cost them lots of money [laughs]. That's the truth of that. So they kept me in the . . . well, behind the curtain, for the first American tour. Eventually I came onto the side of the stage, but was never really given a prominent part in the band. But it was the start of my career, and I caught a lot of experience from that. So that's how I got paid, really."

Can any of the Sabbath guys play keyboards?

"That's subjective to me, because people who I think can play keyboards are people like Oscar Peterson [laughs]. But yeah, they can get a few chords. Tony can." Adds Graham, "I think Tony was a bit more technical than Bill because he used to play accordion, when he was a little kid, so he was much better using both hands."

Nearing the close of *Technical Ecstasy*, an album that is with the world but without it as well, is a melancholy wisp of a ballad called "She's Gone" ("a big production thing," says Bill). Worlds away from "It's Alright," on this one, the state of the band is not alright, except maybe for those flawless orchestrations courtesy of Mike Lewis. Says Jezz of his input on this one: "The intro to the strings, I think that's it. I worked closely with the guy who arranged the strings — I really like that. It was done at Criteria, and they brought in an orchestra to do it."

Closing the album, "Dirty Women" was a particularly rousing piece, meandering depressively then blazing out with a free-burn of a riff from Tony, triumphant, the euphoric heavy metal high point of the record. But as Tony agrees, it is a strange topic for a Sabbath song. "Yes, well, Geezer was writing about more obvious things on this album, but 'Dirty Women,' that's the one we had a laugh about." Bill says that, live, he "loved doing the end of that, with Tony. We do that big buildup with the double bass drums, a lot of nice stuff on that one."

Jezz chips in. "'Dirty Women' was completely mine; I wrote all of that, and you'll see no credit at all. I wrote it in the barn at Glaspant Mansion in Wales, which is where we did the first rehearsal for that album." Geezer volunteers that "'Every day we used to go past this red light district on the way to the studio. We were recording in Florida, and we would see all these prostitutes waiting for the clients, all these dirty old men. It was about that, basically."

"Dirty Women" will forever be paired with "Gypsy" on this record, given that they are both side-closers, both epic, complex, heavy, and both about evil women, a topic that is a heavy metal crutch, but one this band did pretty good to steer clear of o'er the years, (at least the Ozzy years). Throw these into the mix, and what you had was an album that seemed all too deliberately to check off boxes, Sabbath filling out a form to apply for a place in a changing rock 'n' roll landscape; searching valiantly, bravely, but falling short through a compartmentalization of their ideas into digestible nuggets. Gone was the imploding, dark star, black hole, progressive rock possibility of where a song might go, never to return. Lyrically, Geezer behaved and played along. These songs were more "about something," and often that something was unremarkable.

Sabbath remained a main player on the concert circuit, their legendary status intensifying.

BLACK SABBATH WORLD TOUR '76~77

OFFICIAL PROGRAMME

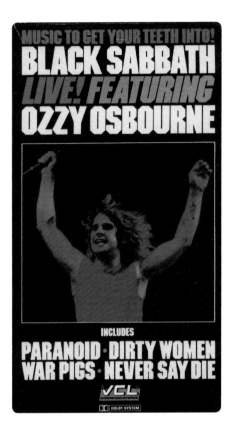

A typical show on this tour would open with the carnality of "Symptom of the Universe," the new songs introduced into the set being "All Moving Parts (Stand Still)," "Gypsy, "Dirty Women" and "Rock 'n' Roll Doctor." "Electric Funeral" was brought back from the old days, with "Hole in the Sky" and "Megalomania" from one record back now dropped, possibly in part to the vocal energy they required to pull off, indeed on the latter, Ozzy was known to give in and drop down an octave on the highest bits.

"Boston, Kiss, everyone," reminisces David of tour mates for the *Technical Ecstasy* tour. "Everybody backed up Sabbath. But they used to do that purposely. We used to get Bob Seger, Ted Nugent, bands that were breaking in America then. It was to sell the shows out, basically. You'd get people who come to see Black Sabbath, but they had also come to see Ted Nugent. There wasn't a great deal of interaction between Sabbath and support bands, but nine times out of ten you would stay in the same hotel as them anyway, so you're going to bump into them. I remember Kiss. A bit of a nightmare with them, actually — very, very obnoxious. There was a lot of money behind Kiss and I think they were just sort of going for it. And they were under the impression that it was their gig, although they were the support act. They were more like, 'Really, it should be Black Sabbath supporting us.' And if you think about Boston, they had an album high in the charts. So it was probably a contractually obliged gig; they did the deal to do the tour before the album was released type thing [laughs]. All sorts of politics."

Bill pipes up on Boston. "Sib Hashian is still, to this very day, a good friend of mine. Sib stays in contact with me all the time. Christmas cards. I watched his family grow. Sib was in the

But slippage in the charts was the order of the day, with *Technical Ecstasy* rising only to Number 13 in the UK, for a six-week stay, and a paltry Number 51 in the U.S. "It's Alright" was launched as a single, backed with "Rock 'n' Roll Doctor" (the two happiest songs on this glum record), but this was not to be a replay of the smash success Kiss had with their shameless ballad "Beth," also sung by the drummer, a mere two months after that track put Kiss on the fast track.

Nam, and Sib used to ride on our bus. Oz came onto our bus, and then eventually Sib came onto our bus, and of course we were drinking heavy back then, but Sib used to tell us all the nightmare stories in the Nam. He went through a lot. Great drummer, great man, and he's doing really well right now; he's an actor."

Other bands performing one-offs or only a handful of shows on the American leg of the tour, included Target, Montrose, Dr. Hook, Black Oak Arkansas, Mother's Finest, Climax Blues Band, Heart, Moxy and Journey.

"Ozzy never drank before he went on stage," says David, when asked about the potential for booze-addled wipeouts. "He'd have a pint maybe, but he was always straight when he was on stage. There were odd gigs where the equipment gave us trouble. I remember a gig in Fort Bragg or one of the American bases. The stage was metal or something and I think the taxicab radio was coming through the PA [laughs]; used it like an aerial. It was never a clear run [laughs]. There was the one in Germany, Ludwig's Arms or something; that was nuts — GIS all jacked up. You used to get the GIS and the locals in Germany, a mixture of GIS, Hell's Angels, and disgruntled heavy metal fans, a recipe for disaster [laughs]. I remember Tony would take forever and a day with his tuning up. Because he used such light strings due to the prosthesis, he had trouble keeping his guitar in tune. It was a bit of a chore for anyone listening. But if Tony wanted it right, he would have it right [laughs]."

After UK dates with hard-hitting A&M blues rock artists Nutz (soon to change their name to Rage), in April of 1977, a young, brash and bounding-like-kangaroos AC/DC hitched a ride on the Sabs' European jaunt.

David Tangye counters rumors that AC/DC stole the show from the tiring veterans. "I don't

WE DIDN'T THINK THERE WAS ANY FUTURE IN THE BAND, AND OZZY HAD LOST ALL HIS CONFIDENCE. HE BELIEVED IN THE PRESS WHO, PARTICULARLY IN ENGLAND, SLAGGED US TO DEATH, PARTICULARLY HIM.

think so, no. AC/DC was a great band, but two different bands altogether. They complemented each other. Some gigs . . . you can have a good gig one night and then maybe a so-so one. It also depended on the equipment and how it runs. But I don't think there were any words spoken about blowing anybody off the stage. The early tour with Yes; that was two totally different spectrums. Yes was very, very technical, and I just think that was a total mismatch."

On December 6, 1976, Frank Zappa introduced the band live on stage, and even that has now become part of bootleg lore. David says, "Frank was absolutely brilliant. I think it was the second time they played Madison Square Garden, and Frank came along to introduce the band. We went for an after-show meal at the Time Life Building. Ozzy said to me, 'You like Frank Zappa? Would you like to work for him?' I said yeah [laughs]. Frank was a big fan of Black Sabbath; he loved Sabbath. He told me that, actually, because I was sitting beside him.

Neil Medhurst

Elvis Presley was a big fan of Black Sabbath. We almost met him. He didn't show, but I think he was in his last days because he died about six months later. Mike, the Warner rep, said he was going to come to the gig, but he didn't, and we were very disappointed."

Occasionally, playing live, it looked like Ozzy might lose his voice. "He used to complain that some of the tunes were too high for him, that he couldn't hit the notes," says Tangye. "Tony would always say, 'Give him some honey! Give him some honey!' [laughs]. 'Sabbath Bloody Sabbath' he always found difficult, and 'Rock 'n' Roll Doctor' was the other. They got through it, like every band. Singers are singers, aren't they, with their idiosyncrasies? And it was difficult singing the things they did; there was a lot of light and shade. It's hard to go from one to the other. It puts a strain on your vocal cords. It's different when you play guitar or drums, but a voice is so personal."

"The *Technical Ecstasy* tour was quite interesting," adds Graham, "with the big chandelier above Bill, and the big 14-foot-wide drum riser on a stained glass pedestal. And they had burning torches and some nice backdrops. We used to lower the big cross. We had cobwebs, and a snow machine for 'Snowblind.' There was supposed to be a live album. We recorded something at the Hammersmith Odeon, because I remember the mobile studio coming and parking outside. But they weren't happy with the final result of it."

"We did do a live album," confirms Jezz. "I don't know what ever happened to that. Just after that tour, we went to Holland, to a studio called Real Light Studios and we had all the masters for a live album. We spent weeks and weeks trying to sort it out. We were doing overdubs in the studio. I remember Bill was trying to sort out some of the drums where he'd

messed up. So it was a serious project. It would've been the first Sabbath live album, wouldn't it?"

I later brought this up with both Geezer and Tony and neither professed any recollection of these sessions.

And that was it for Jezz Woodruffe's tenure with the Sabs. "Ozzy left, and the band didn't know what to do, so they just said, 'Well, that's it; it's all over,' and then they didn't come back to me. And I was off anyway, to Europe, doing some stuff out there. It just fell apart when Ozzy went." Jezz is referring to Ozzy's on-again, off-again status in the band which would persist right up until preliminary work on *Heaven and Hell*. The next significant move for Jezz was a fusiony, funky, quirky keyboard-mad solo album in 1980 called *Opposite Directions*, which helped him get his esteemed Robert Plant gig. "After I left Sabbath, or the whole thing finished, my friend David Anderson, who was the bass player in Hawkwind, he had a studio on another Welsh mountain just up the road from me. So I decided to record my first solo album there in his studio. That was put out by a small independent label called Graduate Records, who, at the same time they were signing me, signed UB40. And the guy who worked for Graduate records, Lord Williams, was a friend of Robert's. He knew Robert was looking for a keyboard player so he gave him a copy of *Opposite Directions*, and then Robert came to find me."

At that point, David Tangye also relieved himself of his service to the band. "For *Never Say Die*, they went over to Sounds Interchange. I didn't go out for that; I finished after the European tour they did with AC/DC. I came back and there was nothing to do. And Mark Forster was there. I was actually working for Black Sabbath then, on the payroll. Because previously I'd been working for Ozzy and Ozzy used to pay me. It was all up in the air a bit. It's a hard life."

In any event, Black Sabbath's seventh album, *Technical Ecstasy*, was to be no more than a bullet-pocked signpost on the road to misery, the band soon to follow up with a record that would be received with even less enthusiasm. As Geezer relates, however, at the time, "the press were saying that we were a bunch of morons and couldn't play our instruments. That's how we were perceived and that's why the original band folded, because we just lost confidence in ourselves. We didn't think there was any future in the band, and Ozzy had lost all his confidence. He believed in the press who, particularly in England, slagged us to death, particularly him. They didn't give him any credibility whatsoever as a singer or a front man. The British press were calling us dinosaurs in 1976. It was unbelievable. We started believing it, though, and we were looking in different directions ourselves and not realizing we had the direction. The record company was that way as well. We'd go to a reception with them and they'd be playing the latest punk album or Bob Marley. They didn't give us any confidence whatsoever. We didn't believe we had any relevance."

9

"IT WENT INTO ME EARS"

– Never Say Die

Black Sabbath limped through the latter half of 1977 a band in tatters. Eventually, they would get it together enough to cobble and bobble a record, but before that, Ozzy would be out of the band temporarily, replaced for about three months by Savoy Brown's Dave Walker. A bootleg exists documenting the band's one live performance, on the BBC Midlands *Look Hear!* show, where Sabbath performed an early version of "Junior's Eyes." The vocals alternate between highly stylized bluesiness (hoary almost) and somewhat Dio-esque choruses. The lyrics are sporadic, slurred and mostly unintelligible: "Louie Louie" has nothing on this guy. Bill drummed with his arm in a cast after slamming it in a door, the accident due to frustration — it still flares up into arthritis to this day. Walker, who the band had known since the early '60s, and his Birmingham band Savoy Brown and The Redcaps, had moved from San Francisco to London to consort with the band, even writing lyrics for the sketchy new songs. By January of '78, all would agree that the match was bad.

In the interim, Tony would produce, quite capably, the debut album by Quartz, who would relinquish to Sabbath one Geoff Nicholls, soon to be their hidden keyboardist, major writer, full-fledged member, then hidden keyboardist again. "I remember some of it," says Tony, of producing 1977's *Quartz*, reissued in '79 in unique paper bag packaging as *Deleted*. "It was something they asked me to do, so I had a go at it. They had some good songs. Interesting, quite straightforward — I had used the same format and techniques as we do with the Sabbath stuff, because that's all I knew. Since then, of course, I've learned more and do things differently."

As it would turn out, the image seared into the minds of all involved in the making of *Never Say Die* was the biting cold of trying to stitch the damned thing together in — of all places — Toronto.

"That was quite strange," begins Graham Wright, "because they had actually been to the studio in Toronto in the summer. And Toronto is a great place in the summer. Lots of leaves outside, and it's warm [laughs]. And the only time they could get the studio was in the winter. And at that time it was flavor of the month, Sounds Interchange. It was like, 'Hey, great studio. Toronto. The Stones had recorded there.' Entering their rehearsals, that was when Ozzy left and Dave Walker had come in. And when Ozzy had left, this was when Blizzard of Ozz began. Even then, Ozzy was thinking about his own thing. When he got the sack, it was like, 'I can go on and do my own thing.' But in Toronto, they were still rehearsing basically.

We took over this old cinema, and they could have it during the day, because they showed movies at night. So they would rehearse during the day, on stage, and then went into the studio on the night and put stuff down. And it was freezing cold — the blizzards were hitting. You know what Toronto is like in the winter [laughs]. Especially a bad winter, and there was one. We all stayed in this apartment block, just around the corner from the Gasworks on Yonge Street. It wasn't the best place to be, because they were used to going to Criteria in Miami, and L.A. [laughs]."

"Being at home in England was strange because we'd never been at home," explains Tony, referring to the despondent break before gearing up to make this record happen. "We were always out touring. Nothing was happening with the writing; it had dried up. And drugs were probably a part of it. When it first started happening, was with *Never Say Die*. Before we recorded that album, Ozzy left. We brought another singer in for a short while, wrote some more songs, and then Ozzy wanted to come back, two days before we went into the studio. We used to play moodies with each other, like a spoiled kid, you know? So you'd have to pamper everybody and it got silly. We all went to Toronto for six, seven weeks. And Ozzy wouldn't sing any of the stuff we wrote with this other guy, because I think he felt like, "Well, I'm not involved in it." He was a bit jealous, I suppose. So what are we going to do now? Here we are, we're due to start recording in two days, and we've got nothing, no material. So we go into a cinema at nine in the morning, freezing cold it was, and started trying to write material to record in the evening. Which was a bloody joke! Some of the stuff, when I listen to it now, sounds really disjointed. Because it was done too quick. We

I DON'T LIVE IN A CASTLE WITH COUNT DRACULA AS A DOORMAN. MY HOUSE IS A SMALL LITTLE COTTAGE.

never had time to analyze it. It was a nightmare! It was done in the morning, and that night we were recording. We did an eight month tour on *Never Say Die*, which was great. But problems were setting in with the band."

"My God, that was when Ozzy left the band," recalls a wincing Butler. "And just as we'd gotten the studio all booked and everything, he decided to come back. So we had to scrap everything we'd done and start all over again. So we got to Toronto, and because the studio was booked from like two in the afternoon, we had to start rehearsals from eight o'clock in the morning so we could write the songs before we could record them [laughs]. We had to be out of there by like twelve so they could start showing the movies. And the cold got to me. It went into me ears, and I was like deaf for about

three months after that. So everything sounded like it was recorded underwater."

"It wasn't very good," says Geezer, of the Dave Walker material. "It wasn't us, anyway. I mean, the *Never Say Die* album wasn't very good, anyway. It was sort of thrown together at the last minute, and that's why it's so bad. I just don't like that album."

"Oh, it was terrible!" continues Graham, remembering the infamous theater. "We were trying to rehearse, and there was this old lady with this Hoover, Hoovering the aisles of this thing [laughs]. It didn't last long ... only ten days or something. And writing too, because there was a shortage of material. I remember Geezer going to see Elvis Costello and The Attractions at the El Mocambo. I was really pissed off I didn't go, because I knew Bruce Thomas. We went to the Gasworks, saw local bands. It was quite funny; we would go on the odd night off and just sit there and have beers and nobody used to bother Ozzy or Tony [laughs]. I mean, they used to walk up and down Yonge Street and nobody used to bother them."

"I remember it being really cold in Toronto," adds Bill. "Some things were conceived in other

places, but I think probably the strongest memory I have is that we were really struggling for material. And I was dismembered a little bit. I guess we were all cold and dismayed. We were in the studio and I think Rush were too, and we would go over to their studio and say hello, screw around a bit. And I think they came to our studio. But that was about it. We would literally just pick up our crates of Molson [laughs], put them in the back of the station wagon, go back to our rooms. It was just like a bunch of apartments. And we would go there and get drunk and try to work on the homework of the day, the stuff that we had put down in the theater."

Ozzy explained, "There's a little bit of each year involved in our new album. It's a subtle combination of the changes we've gone through musically and in our personal lives."

"It was getting too serious," lamented Oz of the perennial tour grind, "so after *Technical Ecstasy*, we decided to wind it down a bit, just to give our heads a rest. The heaviness of it all got so intense for me that I just had to take a break. I was drinking and generally abusing myself, just being an animal, and it was destroying me, killing my ability to do anything. I didn't want to destroy myself or my family. Now I've really got it together on a good level and I really love what I'm doing. We take our time about what we're doing; before, you'd get people screaming at you on the phone about commitments. 'You've got to get this out; you've got to do that.' What's the point of doing anything if you're not satisfied with it?"

"The fans would be very surprised to see the way we live," Ozzy continued. "I don't live in a castle with Count Dracula as a doorman. My house is a small little cottage. I have three children, two boys and a girl, and a wife that's raving mad. All wives are raving mad. Living with me leaves something to be desired. I'm absolutely mad. I change with the wind, always have. Dr. Jekyll and Mr. Hyde a thousand times a day. But I don't change for the bad — basically, I'm a gentle person. I do crazy things to make people laugh, because if people are laughing, then they're not going to be aggressive. Keep them happy and they won't pull a gun, or pull the trigger. Where I grew up, if you weren't good at fighting you were stabbed into the ground and victimized, but I hated that, and felt that the best way to get out of it was to be funny and make them laugh.

"I suppose it was a progression from that to the band. Keep a lot of people happy, let them get rid of their aggression at a gig, and they're not going to be outside mugging some old lady for her purse. When I make the peace signs at concerts, it's like waving at someone, knowing they're with you. I'm like a front man for positive things. If I see any fights, I stop the show instantly; I walk off. I don't want anyone to get harmed. We all realize that we have a big responsibility. I've never said this before, but I'm afraid of people really, because people can hurt in very subtle, evil ways. The challenge of my life is to try and win them over. When we began, we had nothing. I was walking around in rags. My mother never had a nickel, my father was working constantly, we were like the street's tramps. But I had all these dreams. If you're sitting on a gutter and you've got nothing, your ass is hanging out and your mother cries because she doesn't have any food to feed you, you write hard words because that's the way you've been reared. You're a hard person from the word go. We got success from that. We got out of that and now I'm living in a very nice house in the countryside, breathing fresh air. I live a relatively happy life, but it's such a cost to have happiness in this world. I don't believe there's anyone in this world that's 100 percent happy. I'm 29 years old now. I saw what happened to the flower power generation, how a bunch of people got an innocent, beautiful thing going, and the big machine made money out of it. Made it filthy dirty and horrible and destroyed it. Then, when we came in, at the end of the disaster, we got 'em going again. We were telling them the truth, what was happening, and if you've been stoned on acid for five years, you need something to hold onto."

Never Say Die was pulled from the freezer on September 28, 1978, and eventually limped up the charts, to a spirited six-week Number 12 placement in the UK, but a lowly Number 69 in the States, even if eventual gold status was its happy lot. The album was wrapped in weirdly uneasy and uncommunicative Hipgnosis cover art (much like *Technical Ecstasy*), featuring two fighter pilots completely obscured by their uniforms. Faint images were painted into the

clouds, sort of like Blue Öyster Cult's *Mirrors*. Two of these might represent the ghosts of the shot down, and two more "mechanical" ones are difficult to make out. Sabbath had been asked to choose between this particular cover art and the famous doctors shot that wound up being used three years later for Rainbow's *Difficult to Cure*. Some copies list the songs on the back in shuffled order, an oft-used convention of the day, while others list them in the correct order.

Never Say Die kicks off on a hopeful note with the record's title track, a happy, melodic, bashing hard rocker, Tony turning in a spirited and spiraling solo as the song smashes to a close. Instantly, one's attention is drawn to the garagey, distorted, midrange-heavy, ambient sound of the record, production that is vaguely Zeppelin-esque, circa perhaps IV, *Houses of the Holy* and *Presence*. Geezer's lyric is chock-full of enigma, although one senses a cohesion with past themes, this idea of looking to the future, hoping things can be saved before it's too late.

People usually remember the innocuous and comparatively somber chorus, but miss some of the great lines in here — no help from Ozzy, however, who makes them almost unintelligible.

"I liked that one," volunteers Bill. "It was made well. And it did reach the British charts. I remember when we came up with the title for that, Ozzy and I were in the conservatory in Monmouth. He was saying 'die' and I was going 'never' [laughs]." The idea was to find something that summed up the band's ten years

together, in light of the upcoming anniversary.

Indeed "Never Say Die" did make the charts, hitting Number 21 in the UK as a pre-LP single four months before the launch of the album. The track, backed by "She's Gone" from *Technical Ecstasy*, was the first single Sabbath had put in the charts since "Iron Man" and "Paranoid" a lifetime earlier. The band would repeat with "A Hard Road" (backed by "Symptom of the Universe"), issued in conjunction with the album's release in September. Of note, the "Never Say Die" single would feature a graphic of "Henry" the dancing devil, designed by Geezer, which would crop up on Sabbath artwork repeatedly over the years.

"It was about . . . I don't think it was about anything," says Geezer quite amusingly, with respect to "Never Say Die." "I think it was just like trying to be up for once instead of always being miserable and down." Geezer denies "Never Say Die" was a case of a band gunning for a single. "We were gunning for anything we could come out with at that time. Like, desperate."

"Johnny Blade" is announced by a "Mr. Crowley"-esque synthesizer pattern from Don Airey, none other than the synthesizer player on "Mr. Crowley," an early *Blizzard of Ozz* hit extraordinaire. Bill trundles in with one of his trusty single roll snare patterns and it's off to the races, the band creating a caterwaul of a rocker, briefly fired by melodic respites, one of which is the twangy chorus. Later, the song takes a Sabbatherian left turn, Tony breaking out one of his tuneful yet doomy he-man riffs. Airey throws in a few percolating and novel licks, his performance on the album reminiscent of Tony Carey's on Rainbow's *Rising* album. Eventually, the song collapses into a groovy jam, with Tony driving it with one of his freight train solos. But it is Bill Ward's drumming that dominates, captured loudly like Bonham all over Zep IV.

"'Johnny Blade' was partly about Bill's brother," notes Geezer. "He used to be a bit of a tear-away, a bit of a hooligan, when he was a teenager, in gangs and things like that." Adds Bill, "Tony came up with this incredible lick, and I immediately copped to it and I put down a four stroke roll. It was freezing cold in that theater, absolutely freezing — I've never felt such cold. But yes, as soon as Tony started playing that, it just felt like wow, we're back in 1964 or 1965 [laughs]. It was that kind of playing or rock, midnight music. And I knew exactly where to go with the drums; it just matched so well. Because Tony and I had played together and had been in a lot of bands when we were 15, 16 years old. So we had the experience of doing cover tunes from the early '60s and even the '50s. So when I heard 'Johnny Blade,' I recognized that '50s influence. Conceptually, Ozzy and I started messing around with the idea of Johnny Blade, this weird character. I got hooked with the song and took it back up to the apartment, got some things worked up and called up Oz and said 'Come on up; let's have some brews,' and he liked the idea. I knew that was a song already — really nice. I had done some nice fills, Don Airey had played

the keyboards, and then Geez brought everything together with the final lyrics."

"My brother, for a while, was a bit of a Teddy Boy," says Bill, answering to Geezer's assessment of the lyric. "So he would wear a zoot suit and the chain, with the little razor blades with the open edge — they called them flick blades. My brother had a lot of that image about him, and it was a very popular time. People had slicked-back hair and everybody dug Elvis. My brother turned me on to a lot of rock 'n' roll, and was very influential in my life. And yeah, Geezer knew my brother real well. Oh, God yeah, they got on great."

"'Junior's Eyes,' I wrote about Ozzy's father," says Geezer with respect to the record's third, melancholy, boldly good third track. "His father had just died and Ozzy was devastated at the time."

"'Junior's Eyes' was really, really sad," adds Bill. "Ozzy's father Jack had died during these sessions. Jack gave us all the original crosses. We all loved Jack. We all knew each other's par-

TONY ALWAYS HAS BEEN THE
WORKHORSE. I HOPE OSBOURNE
OR GEEZER DON'T GET PISSED
OFF, BUT YEAH, TONY PUT IN AN
INCREDIBLE AMOUNT OF WORK.

ents, and we all interacted. But Ozzy was off the wall, totally. We came up with 'Junior's Eyes' and Oz loved it. We actually did the pre-production work on that at Field Farm. My second wife and I actually lived in the house and we built a little studio in there. When we left, other bands started using the studio. It was kind of a party house. We had some of the guys from AC/DC living in the house. Judas Priest used to go down there and rehearse. So the house actually gave birth to some new songs. Ozzy did both of his songs there, two of my favorites, 'Am I Going Insane' and 'Who Are You,' the preproduction. But yes, Jack was great. Everybody was there for the funeral. And we were definitely in London doing the finishing touches to *Never Say Die*. So in-between, there was a death."

"Junior's Eyes" creeps into existence on a psychedelic and funky bass line, a Bill Ward lope, and an even more psychedelic squall of noise from Tony, who takes a backseat as colorist. Once the chorus hits, the clouds open for a comforting but sorrowful smudge of melody. It is Bill Ward and his big stout-of-heart fills that really imbue the song with passion, not to mention Ozzy's anguished vocal.

"'A Hard Road' was just about being on the road," explains Geezer about the next one, this wide-angled, trundling but somehow stately and melodic track being both a success and somewhat aggravating, especially come chorus time. Interestingly, both Geezer and Tony tackle backup vocals. Bill considers Tony's solo a highlight, and he impressed with the band's handling of the song live. 'A Hard Road' ends with voices darting in from all angles and at all frequencies, the whole band ganging up for the close of this hopeful song, Geezer delivering an inspirational lyric of the world going around, people falling down and getting back up. It's vintage Butler, with one eye to the future, Geezer massaging in, with a sense of motion, gentle reminders that we all should clean up our act.

Side 2 opens with what is, essentially, *Never Say Die*'s most conventional heavy rocker. "Shock Waves" possesses no soft breaks save for a few acoustic guitar strums. Again, Bill bashes the song into fit-as-a-fiddle shape, his drums both played and recorded brutishly. Geezer's lyric about the point of death describes a battle between good and evil typical of the man's more religion-based lyrics. Still, it's a little straightforward, lacking the unearthly patina of his many freaky poems.

"Air Dance" is a poignant dark paean to old age, similar in theme to one half of Rush's "Losing It," Geezer imagining an old woman time traveling to her dance-filled youth. Musically, "Air Dance" is a daring track, a sort of jazzy, progressive rock ballad stabbed by ugly guitar licks from Tony, chopped by jerking rhythms, late in the sequence, hit with a baffling bit of Goblin-esque/Krautrock-like fusion rock. In the end it really drove home the point that Sabbath had lost their marbles. Raised some eyebrows with this one, they did. "Yeah, definitely," agrees Bill. "It was almost like a modern jazz quartet on that one. We were definitely bordering on some jazz feels."

As a kid listening to this album, I subconsciously grouped "Over to You" with "A Hard Road," both being these languished, smeared and smudged walls of sound, heavy in a way (we gave the Sabs this one grudgingly), but melodic and a little underwritten. Says Geezer, "'Over to You,' I stole that from a Roald Dahl book I was reading at the time, called *Over to You*. The song wasn't about what the book was about, but I liked the title." Adds Bill, "We had a problem there, trying to get a melody. I did a

ghost melody on that, to see if I could help it along. Keep in mind, we were going through a major loss." Here Bill is referring to helping vocally, given Ozzy's grief and subsequent diminished will to work. "I'd put my drum tracks down, but I was also trying to be as helpful as I could in the vocal area, trying to come up with ideas. And some of them worked and some of them didn't. But my ghost vocal . . . Oz came in and he liked it, so he just went over my track."

Despite the backing track's lazy churn, the lyric Geezer puts to it is a poisonous indictment of society, a crystallization of the communiqués the Sabs had laid out for their pessimistic, outcast fans since the days of "War Pigs" and "Paranoid." One of those is about strife from the outside and one is about strife from within, and the almost resigned, morally void torment of "Over to You" addresses both.

Kraut-rock returns with a vengeance for the

worst jazz song ever written, "Breakout." Mercifully short, this one is loaded up with nonSabbath-specific instruments, including horn arrangements by Will Malone and some prominent sax soloing. Geezer has said that the sax was added upon Tony's suggestion because Ozzy wasn't around to lay on a vocal. When Ozzy finally showed up and heard the sax on it, he apparently turned tail and walked back out. Ozzy's attitude was getting to Geezer. "I was getting more and more uncomfortable having to write lyrics anyway. *Never Say Die* had me writing lyric after lyric after lyric and Ozzy wouldn't even read them in the end. I was getting really pissed off."

A question to Bill about Tony's resentment over having to write all the music over the course of *Technical Ecstasy* and *Never Say Die* led to a comment on "Breakout."

"Tony always has been the workhorse. I hope Osbourne or Geezer don't get pissed off, but yeah, Tony put in an incredible amount of work. Everybody had their own ideas, but it was like, what's acceptable and what isn't? So there was a lot of sitting around, waiting to see what Tony might bring out. The big band thing, 'Breakout.' Now, that particular riff, Tony had been playing around with it for a couple years. And every time he played it, I would rush into the room and say, 'Let's do something with that!' And it would kind of go by the wayside, until eventually, he found another part to go with it. And I thought, oh my God, this is incredible. What you end up with is an interesting sound collage that is the wackiest thing Sabbath had done or would ever do." Sure, "Breakout" is reviled, but always with a bit of a chuckle and a shake of one's mullet. I mean, this sure as hell wasn't a case of the guys trying to write a radio single.

Never Say Die closes with what just might be the best track from either this record or the one previous. "Swinging the Chain" packs a wallop that sort of embodies all the doom and anguish of Sabbath's situation at this tiring turning point. Tony's riff is sinister, but it definitely swings. His guitar tone is buried, covered with cinder blocks and rebar. Bill is brought in to sing that track, and his world-worn voice seems dragged and ragged beyond recognition when compared to the sweet McCartney-esque pipes behind "It's Alright."

Explains Graham Wright, when asked why Bill's doing another vocal: "Again, it was Bill, the mother hen of the band, trying to help Ozzy out, trying to keep it all together. In singing a song, he thought, 'I'm helping out, we're getting stuff down, I've got some ideas.' With songs like 'Johnny Blade,' he was almost trying to go back to the old days. 'Never say die, come on, we don't want to split this up, we want to carry on.' It was hard for them. The studio was awkward, because when we got there, it was so dead. They wanted to liven it up, so I had to get loads of sheets of plywood and put plywood on the floors and up against the walls to try to brighten the sound up. And because they were having financial problems, they couldn't, like, just cancel it. They'd booked it! They weren't happy with the studio or the weather, and it was a kind of forced album. Everything seemed to be going wrong, which was a real shame, because they were really trying hard amongst themselves, to get back together and produce an album. They made a mistake by going to Toronto. They should have gone somewhere warmer. But there were distractions in Miami and in L.A., distractions they were trying to avoid. A band like Sabbath, you go to Miami or L.A., you've got every coke dealer in the world trying to give them coke. L.A., you've got the whole Sunset Strip scenario. And we'd rehearse in Wales because they were away from all that. At the end of the day,

they were so down to earth; they were great guys, that if they could get away from the distractions, they'd be fine."

"That was Bill Ward at the time," laughs Bill o'er his chain-smoker of a vocal on "Swinging the Chain." "I wish I could still sing like that now, actually. The range on it was just unbelievable. There are a lot of high notes there. I liked what Tony and Geezer had put together. I thought, Oh man, I could get behind this. And I like the big jazz thing we put on the front, 'Breakout.' I know that that came under some comments, but I thought it was fucking great. I was trying to finish the last verses on 'Swinging the Chain,' and I knew that the very next morning . . . we'd finished about 3 a.m. and we had to get up at 6 a.m. to catch a flight to the East Coast of the United States, because we had a gig that night. So we were balls to the wall on that album."

Additional in the surprises department, "Swinging the Chain" includes a harmonica solo, torrid waves of new Iommi riffs late in the tale, and a bunch of seemingly impromptu gang vocals. All told, this is a brilliant, crushing, nonobvious rocker that proved Sabbath still could write well away from the norm. Tony's solo sounds like a cross between Jimmy Page and Brian May in gleeful noisenik mode. There are voices in this song that sound like no Sabbath member I know, but apparently Ozzy is added somewhere in the fade.

"Well, Bill wrote 'Swinging the Chain'; I

think it was about Hitler or something. He knows what that's about," is Geezer's curt assessment of the lyric. Bill answers to the charge — sort of. "There was definitely a reference to Adolph Hitler, in the sense that, you know, at the time, vandalism was pretty rampant. So I did make a reference about vandalism, and Adolph Hitler being the biggest vandal of all. Because he really went to town on that. I just liked the title, 'Swinging the Chain.' When we were doing that at Monmouth Valley in Wales, my all-time favorite place to be, my brother came in. And we had been to the pub, kind of drunk, and Tony was playing that first riff, and my brother came into the room, and he was, like, swinging a chain; but there was no chain; it was invisible, and he was kind of getting down and rocking to it, like dancing to it as if he had a chain in his hand. That's where the title came from."

All told, it was a momentous way to end

what was to be Sabbath's last album with Oz, the God-given original Black Sabbath rocking hard but almost laboriously, and definitely elliptically. Indeed, folks were cast into unlikely roles, with Bill, the secret artist in the band, stepping up and presaging the beauty that would present itself all over his two precious solo albums eons later.

Sabbath's *Never Say Die* tour is one of those that has been continually battered by headbanging historians as a bit of a disaster, in large part due to the contrast between the bitter, infighting and boozing Sabs on one hand, mounting their "ten year anniversary" tour, and the band's backup (at least for a huge stretch of it), four firecrackers from California collectively called Van Halen. Heating up the crowd o'er every crease and corner of a detailed UK jaunt, and then kicking ass back in the States for interminable months on end, Van Halen were on fire, out to prove what became obvious every night, that these guys were shooting stars about to light up the sky.

"They were really very good," says Tony. "But the problem was, you see, they were going on before us, and it was all new again to them. And they were picking up stuff from our show. So we would do a drum solo, guitar solo and all that, and the way that Ozzy would say things, it was gradually getting put into their show. Which made it very awkward. It did cause problems, because they were on the road with us for eight months. It was like our show being played twice [laughs]. The same sort of chat in the middle, the same sort of antics, and then they started getting bigger drum risers and more of this and that. Which was great, I mean, they were learning and they were good players, great band. And I got very close to Eddie. We used to sit in my room and talk a lot. And I just got annoyed one night and said, 'Eddie, are you

going to play a couple numbers off our new album tomorrow?' And he says, 'Hey, man, you know . . .' and of course, 'Come on, let's go in my room' and we had a chat. And he said 'Look, you know, we grew up with you guys and we look to you as our influence,' and what can you say? I said, 'That's great, but you can't

do the same things as we're doing on the same show. When you get your own show, fine.' But they were fine, great. I'm glad they did what they did."

Geezer strongly concurs. "I liked them as a band, but it was their first major tour and they ripped off everything from us [laughs]. I mean, it was unbelievable. The difference from the first night, in Sheffield, England, where they just went on and did, like, the Van Halen show, and by the time they got to America with us, they were doing all Ozzy's peace signs. Everything Ozzy was doing, Dave Lee Roth was doing. Eddie Van Halen was doing his long guitar solo because Tony was. In those days, Tony used to do like a 20-, 30-minute guitar solo. So Eddie Van Halen started doing that. I used to use a wah-wah pedal on my bass, so their bass player went out and got one. And they were doing all that before we went on. So they were doing the Sabbath show before Sabbath went on. And Tony had a go at Eddie one night and he's going to beat the hell out of him [laughs], but he just told him to stop copying him, basically. And Eddie sort of agreed and didn't do it. But David Lee Roth still carried on ripping Ozzy off." Amusingly, Ozzy didn't mind telling the press at the time

that Van Halen were so good, they ought to be headlining the tour.

"Oh, they were just having a ball!" was Graham's assessment of Diamond Dave & Co. "They used to be the house band at Gazzarri's on the strip. They just started to break the club circuit in America, and then they released that Kinks song. They were this young band full of energy, just loving every minute of it."

Bill gets the final word on Ed and the guys, and he's pretty kind about it. "I knew they were influenced in the early days, but they were still in the old format — drum solo, guitar solo, bass solo. In other words, all the other bands that had come before, Zeppelin, you name it, we were all doing that same type of show. But I think on a slightly different issue, yeah, Van

Halen tended to watch the show and pick up a few things [laughs]. But they quickly moved on and formed their own pathway."

Bill figures the *Never Say Die* tour was the first one where he started using oxygen onstage. "During the real hot gigs. I was starting to get tired out. Oddly enough, I don't use oxygen anymore [laughs]. My health is a lot better. But back then, I was still drinking. We were playing for up to two hours, and still a lot of the fast stuff — it was a hardcore show. So the energy I was using up . . . sometimes, I would just burn out onstage, like, 'Man, I can't even breathe, it's so hot.' So I would get a couple hits of oxygen, which would really help me breathe through."

I asked Bill about his philosophy with respect to his drum solo. "Well, it was popular to do drum solos in the late '60s, because, obviously, Ginger Baker had forged the way. Stage shows were different because they would feature the artist, Jimi Hendrix and Mitch Mitchell. All these drummers performed drum solos. So naturally, we would feature Tony; obviously, then I would have a solo for 15, maybe 20 minutes. I knew different parts that I was going to go do, but a lot was left open for change, improvisation. Playing night after night could become monotonous. So one of the great things Sabbath did was to leave out an area of about 30 to 40 minutes sometimes of improvisation, which really does give us a great sense of freedom. Surprises would happen. When we play Black Sabbath now, it's bam-bam-bam-bam and that's it. It's a set order, everybody knows what's going to happen, la-di-da. And unfortunately, I think the kids know what's going to happen as well [laughs]. I think they've been very patient. I don't want to continually come to the stage and play the same things over and over again. It's like a rip-

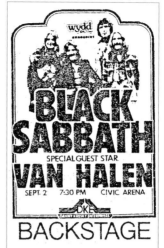

off, almost."

Did you ever choreograph your solo with lights or effects? "No, we never put those things together. That's intelligent stuff. This is primeval. Sabbath, you know . . . we don't think in those terms."

Given his vantage point, I asked Graham to tell me a bit about the engine room of the band — Bill Ward — and how he did what he did live. "When I first started working for Bill, he was unorthodox. He had this totally hodge-podge kit, all different makes. Even his toms — there were different sizes, but they didn't range from highest to lowest; it was a hodgepodge. And it was all different colors, bits of Gretsch kits, bits of Ludwig, Slingerland. His mates ran a drum shop in Birmingham called Drumland, so we arranged to get this white Slingerland kit sent over from the States with the hardware not attached to it. So I spent a couple of weeks on the top floor of Field Farm, where I used to live, and I built this white Slingerland kit around Bill. I'd fit the hardware to the tom toms and

Promotional brochure

drum solos. He used to have Remo Emperor skins because they were the heaviest, hardest skins, so he hardly broke skins. And he didn't like cleaning his cymbals, because he reckoned they would lose tone. He had tympanis, but that was mainly for studio work. He even had tubular bells, but didn't use them that much. On *Sabotage* there were backwards cymbals used, *sssst* sounds, where they just reverse the sounds. But Bill was unorthodox; he wasn't a time man. For the *Never Say Die* tour, he used the old drum riser from *Technical Ecstasy*, but I painted it white. We just had a backdrop with those pilots' heads. There wasn't much going on, maybe some dry ice."

"Sabbath were a goodnatured bunch to work with, I can honestly say that," muses Graham in closing. "They are good people. There wasn't the scandal. Yeah, there was the drug-taking, there were binges. But it wasn't all the time. Never heroin, just coke, pot and booze, and to be honest, there wasn't much pot [laughs]. It was more drink than anything. But even then, it wasn't like a lot of bands. There's a lot of myth that goes on about things."

Graham admits that Bill wasn't capable of taking over the business end of things. "Oh, he tried, he did. He was concerned. When you're talking with top lawyers from London and record company executives, you're going to be out of your depth. But he was trying to keep his finger on the pulse; he just wanted the best for everybody. And you know what? I think the top people at Warner Brothers, Joe Smith and that, when they met the guys, they actually liked them, you know?"

built it around him so it fit like a glove, basically. Bill got a good feel from that. It was nice to just sort of bring these shells out of the box and do all the fittings — we were getting involved in the kit. He used that for a couple of years and then he changed to a silver/gray Tama kit he used up till *Heaven and Hell*.

"He had gongs, one of those big Chinese things, which he used in his drum solo. I used to sit behind him and was always feeding him with these oxygen bottles and his water. He was a hard player. The whole kit used to be bolted down to the riser so it couldn't move. If he did lose his temper, he couldn't trash it anyway, because nothing would move. He could play double bass drums, but that was mainly for

10

"TOGETHER IN BARRY GIBB'S HOUSE"

– Heaven and Hell

By 1978, Ozzy was descending into his own hell of alcoholism, and threatening to take the band along with him. However, amidst the turmoil within the band, the New Wave of British Heavy Metal [NWOBHM] had found its footing by this point, and metal was on the upswing. Black Sabbath, along with other previously lonely hard rockers like Judas Priest, Blue Öyster Cult, Uriah Heep and even the likes of Budgie, Blackfoot and a newly heavy Kiss, found they could do fetching business in this new louder reality.

SABBATH WAS A FUCKING PHENOMENON. THERE'LL NEVER BE ANOTHER BAND LIKE THAT AGAIN. I DON'T CARE IF YOU COULD RESURRECT ELVIS PRESLEY.

"It was the greatest thing in my life," Ozzy mused years later. "Sabbath was a fucking phenomenon. There'll never be another band like that again. I don't care if you could resurrect Elvis Presley. I remember the thrill it was to come from the back streets of Birmingham in England to Madison Square Garden in New York with all those thousands of kids. It's like playing on Mars. You can't buy that. You can't shove that in your arm. But then we'd get off-stage and have all of these fucking jerks pissing away dollars and sucking it up their noses or blowing your dough on cocaine, and you're sweating your butt off on stage every night. I mean, at the end of the day, after spending 11 years of your life, I don't want to be tossed into the trash can like everyone else, and that's what the band I worked with tried to do to me. I can't believe it."

"Sabbath was a walking disaster," said Ozzy, shortly after his rough tumble from the ranks. "Everything it touched, in one hand was gold and in the other was a big piece of shit. The last few tours were just to get enough to fight these various law cases we were involved in, because we got ripped off ruthlessly by our management. Our last tour together was a disaster because Van Halen was opening for us and it

was terrible, because they were great and we were just falling apart on stage every night. I couldn't get into the later music we were doing. The last three albums we did fucking sucked. I hated being part of it. It got to the point where I wasn't putting my heart and soul into it. I was killing the band and the band was killing me. I finally needed to make a move for my own life. I have three kids, and I thought, 'Nothing is worth being dead at the age of 33.' I was not prepared to give my life as the rest of them have for the glorious name of Black Sabbath. I was getting up and literally drinking all day. I was also taking a lot of dope. I was just using junk to get me through the day. I wasn't jacking up or anything. Lotsa booze . . . more booze than dope."

Fortunately, the commercial and creative torture was soon to subside on both sides of the divide. Ozzy would thrive through his first solo album *Blizzard of Ozz*, reenergized by a guitar prodigy known as Randy Rhoads, while a fit and trim Black Sabbath would come up with a ripper of an album called *Heaven and Hell*.

Bill Ward's assistant Graham Wright recalls the events that surrounded Ozzy's departure. "In 1979, we had done the tour with Van Halen, who were tearing America apart — especially when they were supporting Sabbath. There were quite a few shows where they stole the show. I think Tony was getting a bit frustrated. And he was also good friends — and he still is today — with Brian May of Queen. And he was watching Queen grow. And it was like, 'Oh, I wish Ozzy would pull his act together.' And Ozzy was going through a bad time with his marriage. It was typical Ozzy: when he's up, he's up, and when he's down, he's down; he's like the clown. And there were certain people who were around Tony at the time who were down on Ozzy as well. So instead of helping . . . 'Tony, oh, Ozzy will be all right; let's keep Ozzy up and help him,' there was a split in the camp. Me and Bill were being friends with Ozzy, and Tony was getting fed up with Ozzy not pulling his weight. Ozzy wasn't really sacked. He got up and left, more than anything, after a conversation with Bill. It was more like Bill trying to talk to Ozzy, saying 'Look, things have got to change.' It had been brewing for a while."

"As soon as I left, I knew the whole thing was planned behind my back," Ozzy stated soon after his departure. "I had to leave because I couldn't handle hiring these big fucking houses and trying to keep up with the Led Zeppelins and Stones and David Bowies of the world when we couldn't afford it. I said, 'Get it sensible and let's do what we can afford and put something away for ourselves for a rainy day.' Finally I said goodbye and good luck; but it's turned sour like everything else. It's like a divorce where you sit down with your wife and say, 'Darling, you can have this and you have that.' It got sordid and very nasty in the end. I mean, they weren't exactly gentlemanly about it. I physically had to go and steal some equipment from a warehouse to carry on and do my own thing. It was just silly. I just feel sorry for them if that is the situation they want to get into. I am sick that it's carried on. I didn't even get to do a farewell tour. They at least owed me that. But if they want it bad enough to do what they've done, they must deserve it more than I do. God, I'm not prepared to put myself through that torture again."

"I don't think we could have helped him at all, at that time," adds Tony. "It had come to an end; he was totally out of control. We weren't that much better, but at least we were still in control. We were all coked out and doing this and that. It got longer and longer between writing sessions; nothing was happening. We went to Los Angeles, all living in a house

OZZY WASN'T REALLY SACKED. HE GOT UP AND LEFT, MORE THAN ANYTHING, AFTER A CONVERSATION WITH BILL.

together. I was the only one who used to go to the record company. They were saying, 'We haven't heard any tracks yet. When can we hear them?' I told them, 'They are not quite ready yet.' The truth was that we didn't have anything. I was giving them a load of crap. It was difficult as I was the only one who would even face the record company. I finally told them, 'We've been here for months and nothing is happening. We're spending money and we're not doing anything.' It would've gotten to a stage where we would have broken up and we would have all gone our separate ways if we had not told Ozzy at that time."

Recalls Graham, "It was never the same again, was it? Tony carried on the name and spent all them years trying to put bands together . . . and great for Tony — he flew the flag. He tried every formula he could, until they got back together again. But deep down, Ozzy wanted to be himself. He wanted to go do *Blizzard of Ozz* and be Ozzy, and just have like session men playing behind him. And he'd actually had some local guys in England playing with him up at his house, up at Ranton, Jersey Cottage. So he'd been playing with the idea all along. And obviously Sharon got involved, and the rest is history, isn't it?"

"We had to prove a lot on *Heaven and Hell*," recalls Geezer Butler. "We were written off by everyone. 'Well, Black Sabbath is Ozzy, and you can't carry on without Ozzy.' And when [Ronnie] Dio came in, he brought a lot of inspiration and just uplifted us. He was really up for it, had loads of ideas, which is what we desperately needed. We were on our last legs. I actually left at the time, because I was going through a lot of personal things. And I came back to the band and a lot of that *Heaven and Hell* album had already been written. And I just loved it, because I could hear it from an out-

sider's point of view. I thought it was a great direction to go in and it was a pleasure to play on. None of us were against Ronnie. Tony was going to carry on with Ronnie whether it was Sabbath or not. And I didn't know whether I was going to be in the band or not. I think Bill had stayed there just to see how things would turn out. And it turned out well."

"It was really strange because we had all grown up together," continues Butler. "It sounds corny but it was like losing a brother. You go through so much together and then suddenly they are gone. Tony was just desperate to get on with someone who was into the music. It did the band a world of good and it did Ozzy a world of good as well. He was in a really bad state at the time and he just couldn't get himself together. He wasn't turning up at the band rehearsals or the recording sessions. On the last tour he kept disappearing on tour and was always drunk. I think it turned out for the best for all of us."

It fell upon Bill Ward to finally fire Ozzy from the band. "I volunteered, as Ozzy and I were very close. I knew what Tony, Geezer and myself were saying about him. Ozzy was in really bad shape at that time. We were not accomplishing a whole lot. I knew it was coming to an end. I reluctantly pitched in and agreed that we would need another singer. It was the proper decision, but also incredibly sad. It was the right thing to approach him directly and talk to him. After I got sober I realized that I had lied to Tony, Geezer, Ozzy and myself — I didn't want to be in a band without Ozzy. I found that out by making some more personal mistakes, one of which was that I participated in making *Heaven and Hell* with Ronnie Dio."

With Ozzy gone, everybody from David Coverdale to Robert Plant to Glenn Hughes was being considered as a replacement. The Hughes idea was nixed because, at that point, Geezer was astray, and a conflict would have taken place, Hughes being a bassist, with Geezer soon to reenter the fold. But with Geezer still out of the picture, Geoff Nichols played some bass, with even Ronnie helping out in that department. Later, the band considered Rainbow's Craig Gruber and Boston's Fran Sheehan, before coaxing Geezer back.

Says Tony, "Geoff really wasn't a keyboard player as such; he was basically a guitar player when I knew him. When Geezer left for a period, and Ronnie first came, we brought Geoff so that he could just play bass, really, while we were writing the songs. When Geezer came back in, Geoff ended up playing keyboards [laughs]. And he just got stuck with that, really. I think he's helped a lot through the years. He's not a fantastic keyboard player, but he plays the right things, you know? He doesn't overdo it. We just wanted somebody who could thicken it up, play the parts if I was playing a solo and whatnot. But he's had a good role throughout the years."

Adds Bill, "Geoff was there at the live concerts and he just put strings in in a couple of places, where things would need to go. When Tony is doing his stuff, Geoff will sometimes back him up, add to the sound. So they have their own musical relationship. He's kind of the unsung member, an incredibly nice man, a very good musician. We started using keyboard players live from *Vol 4* onward, so we've always had a keyboard player. Gerald Woodruffe did some stuff with us on all of our albums from thereon in. Don Airey was there. On tour, we've always had another keyboard player in the wings. Things like 'Dirty Women' live, we

needed keyboards, just as filler. At the NEC shows in the UK, Geoff played on two or three songs. 'Spiral Architect' is a good example, where he would keep the song full, especially when Tony is off soloing."

Ronnie's joining of Black Sabbath was, in fact, a typically haphazard rock 'n' roll affair. Phone calls took place but went nowhere, plans evaporated. Ronnie worked on forming a solo band, first in Connecticut, then in L.A. Then one day at the Rainbow Bar & Grill, Ronnie runs into Tony (and Sharon Arden, later Sharon Osbourne) and a jam at the house ensues. Early rehearsals would feature Geoff Nicholls variously on bass, keyboards and rhythm guitar.

Geezer has said that, in some ways, this mysterious Ronnie tryout was pretty innocent, that the band barely "existed" as such at the time, and that once Tony had become taken with Ronnie, he might have proposed a Sabbath album, or perhaps merely a solo album, or maybe a whole new band. In other words, it seems that a decision by Tony to work personally with Ronnie preceded the idea of hiring Ronnie to join Black Sabbath.

"Sabbath was a joy to be in, because it was a band's band," says Ronnie, with respect to what was to be a fortuitous, efficient working relationship (even if it wouldn't last). "We wrote together, played together, had good times

Hell-bent. Heaven-sent...

Black Sabbath   Heaven and Hell

together, supported each other. Totally different to what Rainbow did. It wasn't Sabbath featuring Tony Iommi or Ronnie James Dio. It was Black Sabbath. We cared a lot about each other, and there were no restraints or conditions put upon what we could do — complete and total freedom. And that's why we made a magnificent album called *Heaven and Hell*."

"I loved that album," says Tony. "It was a real challenge for us. We were riding high with Sabbath. We were doing big shows, but then we cut it off and brought somebody else in. It was a risk, something we wanted to do. We wanted to make it work with Ronnie James Dio. He was a different voice and made me write differently. I think it really worked. And I loved making that album. Ronnie came in really as a professional. We were able to sit down and write the album without any problems. Ronnie came into the band and was doing whatever we told him, basically because he wanted the gig. But Ozzy had been with us many years. We had a big challenge going out on tour with a new singer. We didn't know if he was going to be accepted by the Sabbath audience."

"I really didn't want to be in a band without Oz," laments Bill. "That's what I had known all my life. And when Ronnie joined, I tried to meet Ronnie with enthusiasm and respect. I knew that we had to move on, but I didn't necessarily like that period. I know Oz was having a really, really difficult time."

Bill wasn't in the greatest shape either. "Rehearsing and putting it together at the house in Bel Air, California, I can still remember some of that pretty good. But when we were starting to bring it to Europe, to finish it up, I have very little memory after that. That's when my mother died and I went on a drunk, probably for about, you know . . . well, until I got sober [laughs]. But I went on a drunk, and the only thing I can recall is Tony being incredibly patient with me. He would give me the nod, cues and stuff like that, because I honestly didn't know what I was doing, I was so ill."

Bill compared working with Ozzy to working with Ronnie. "Ronnie is incredibly talented in the sense that he is more self-serving. He really knows what he likes musically, he's a good writer, he can write his own lyrics. Basically, all-around, he's more self-sustaining, whereas Oz is incredibly open-minded with his music; Oz is far more fluid. Ronnie is very talented, whereas Oz was always very vulnerable, which was great. Being with Oz, you can write something and he'll take it, digest it and spit it out and perform it like no one else can. And I've never seen any other artist be able to do that. So Oz was more fluid and sponge-like. I could throw things at Ozzy and he would pick it up. Ozzy would also pick up a lot of his own things; he's talented unto himself. He writes a lot of his own lyrics; he puts things together."

Continues Ward, on the *Heaven and Hell* dynamic, "Immediately there wasn't a lot of room for Geezer, and I know that Geezer withdrew. Geezer had been our most prominent lyricist. With Ronnie, a lot of the themes I'd been used to had changed. There were many lyrics I simply couldn't get along with. I'd never had a problem with any previous Sabbath lyrics. And I'd always had input, on melody, lyrics, ideas for songs, titles, and there wasn't any place for me. Because Ronnie was self-sufficient, something happened to both Geezer and me. And there was a tremendous loss, not being able to continue with Oz, which I felt on the *Heaven and Hell* tour, when we did songs that Ozzy had sung for over ten, twelve years. And I just couldn't speak the truth at that time.

It took me [till] several years later, when I was sober, to be able to understand what those uncomfortable feelings had been inside me. And what they were was the fact that I missed Ozzy so terribly. I always regarded Sabbath as a phenomenon, and when Ozzy wasn't there, part of the phenomenon wasn't there. Ronnie's a beautiful man — I've got no problem with him personally — but it just wasn't the same. I wasn't adjusting to the change."

"The difference [between working in Sabbath and Rainbow]" says Ronnie, "is that Tony is an all-around player. Ritchie [Blackmore] is a brilliant player, and always will be. He has very good musical ideas. But to my way of thinking, he is not a member of a band. I've always been a band-oriented musician. Tony is a team player. Tony cares about me, he cares about Vinny, he cares about Billy [Ward] and we all feel the same way. Ritchie really only cares about himself. I'm trying not to make this a derogatory statement. The man hasn't said any bad things about me and it's not in my constitution to use the press to say anything bad about Ritchie. I wish him all the success in the world. The difference is an attitude: Ritchie is really a loner. He's a kind of man who uses people for their talents, a sort of musical vampire. I've heard him say this stuff himself, so I'm not really throwing stones at him. He uses the people until he feels that he can't really get any more out of them and he carries on to the next person. You convince Tony that you're a good person, and that has to be the first and most important credential, in Black Sabbath. If you're not a good person and human being, you're not allowed to be in this band. Vinny, when he came in, was a great person. Maybe there are better players, though I tend to doubt it, but if he didn't have his personality, he wouldn't be in the band. Tony is an all-around player who is always an important part of the band, where Ritchie would use the keyboard player to fill the holes and allow himself to only play solos. That's fine for him, because that's what Richie does best."

For his part, Ronnie mused, "Being so much different and being more of a writer than Ozzy is, I helped shape that band into a bit more of

From the collection of Doug Roemer

me. But it was still Black Sabbath. I think that Martin Birch, who produced that album, made an incredible difference. The sounds that he got were really wonderful. It was a real joint effort. It was everybody doing a great job on the album. I thought Bill Ward was great on it; he's always been underappreciated. We did shape the music a little differently. Ozzy used to call it Black Rainbow! I never tried to do that. I mean, the subject matter was very different and the riffs that Tony writes are very different from Ritchie's. We just made it Sabbath Mach II."

"We were all living in a house in L.A. at the time and Ronnie lived there anyway and would come over every day," recalls Geezer. "He wrote all the lyrics, but I actually was listening to some old tapes the other day and we have Ozzy singing 'Die Young.'" Whether on tape or not, Ozzy was also known to be around for skeletal incarnations of "Children of the Sea," "Lady Evil" and as we shall see later, "Heaven and Hell."

"They had a couple of riffs and things they had done because they had been rehearsing with Ozzy," affirms Dio, describing the opening days of the project. "It was going to be their tenth anniversary. They had a studio in the home that they were living in and had knocked some things out. When I first actually met them physically, Geezer, Bill and Tony, they said, 'We are in the rehearsal place. Do you want to have a listen at this thing we've been doing?' So they played something for me, and Tony said, 'Do you think you can do something with that?' I said, 'Give me a few minutes and I'll see what I can do.' In 15 or 20 minutes I wrote 'Children of the Sea' with them. Then Geezer left and it became just Tony and myself and Bill. Tony and I started writing everything else after that. Geezer came back just to play on the album. It was all written at that point with the exception of 'Neon Knights.' Geezer had come back. We needed one more song and were in France when we wrote that one."

Graham recalls the meeting of minds this way: "Well, again, they knew Ronnie because Glenn Hughes, an old friend of the band, being English, was around, and he knew Ronnie, and it's a small world out in L.A. Ronnie wasn't doing anything with Rainbow anymore and was available. It was like, 'Oh, come over Ron, and have a jam.' And he appeared one day and started jamming. He was singing, just sort of making words up, joining in. And they were playing him what they had gotten down. Then off to Criteria and again it was rehearsals and then recording."

Hughes pipes in with his part of the story. "In 1977 when I moved back to L.A. from London, Ronnie and I were talking to each other quite a bit. He was living in upstate New York, married to Wendy Dio, and then he moved out to California, to where I was living in Encino. Wendy Dio and my first wife Karen, and Ronnie were inseparable; very, very close. We used to do everything together. And I've known Tony since '69, so, when Sabbath were looking for a singer, I was hanging out with Tony, and Ronnie was there. I don't want to take all the credit for it, but definitely I could've been part of that process."

"Ronnie is great," adds Graham, summing up the man. "He's lovely. Ronnie is an anglophile, loves England and loves the English. He likes nothing better than to go out for a curry after the gig. He's a wonderful talent, great voice. I know all the crap that went down when he was with Sabbath, but I felt a bit sorry for him in the sense that he walked into Ozzy Osbourne's shoes."

Ronnie, as he's said, was working quickly, creatively, successfully, in marked contrast to what would happen when he was involved in future Sabbath tooth-pullers. "That happens a lot when you work with people that you haven't worked with before. The first projects are usually the most stunning because you have a collection of ideas that are drastically different from each other. So you write and it seems to flow more than it actually did. It was an easy album to write because everybody was given their chance to do what they needed to do. As we carried on, we got more finite about it because we had so much success with *Heaven and Hell*. We started looking more at the next album, saying things like, 'I don't really like what you did there. Maybe you could do it more like this.' Your freedom stops flowing at that point. You're concerned about what somebody else wants. That album actually became successful for a reason other than the fact that it was good! All of the sound technicians for other bands started playing it during the intermissions at gigs. People were going, 'What's that?' 'It's the new Black Sabbath!!' Everybody just rushed out and got it and drove it up to the top."

Fact is, however, that no one was sure at first if the project would even go under the name Black Sabbath. Without Geezer and Ozzy, and with two guitarists, and a proposed keyboardist and bassist of Ronnie's choice, this could have become a six-piece band with two original Sabbath members. Instead it ended up a four-piece with three. In the end, it was decided to call the band Black Sabbath, partly because the boys figured the strength of the album warranted it, partly because it was just good business. As Graham has mentioned, recording relocated from California to Miami's Criteria

Studios (and partly to France), mostly to get away from the ensuing feud between notorious band manager Don Arden and his daughter Sharon over plum management assignments.

But before one encounters the lively, optimistic music enclosed, one is hit with the album's striking cover art an illustration of three angels smoking and playing cards. "I'd like to get the original painting; that's the one I love," muses Ronnie. "In fact, I did try to buy it but it wasn't for sale. I thought that was absolutely magnificent, one of the best pieces of art I've ever seen. To me, it referred so much to the title, *Heaven and Hell*, and to the song I wrote for that."

Where does it currently reside? "I have no idea. I would assume it would be at Warner Brothers, because that's where it was bought, and I'm sure that's where it stayed. They weren't about to give it up. I think we all tried to get it. I know Geezer tried to get it, but likely they said no to him as well."

"We all lived together in Barry Gibb's house in Miami," says Graham, recalling the communal situation for the album's sessions. "We took over his house, this big Spanish villa. It was a typical Sabbath get-together. We would always cook our own food. We'd be cooking spaghetti, chicken cacciatore. Ronnie would have all these Italian recipes, we'd be making our own curries, we'd all pitch in and Ronnie and I would be cooking dinner together. You see, Sabbath were very down-to-earth people. They didn't want fancy catering — I used to make big shepherd's pies [laughs]. 'Oh, yeah, great!' Because it was like good old home com-

fort food. Criteria Studios found this house. The band wanted like a six or seven bedroom house. So we all had a room each. In the early days, it was just me there; I was doing everything, looking after them, doing all the equipment, and later we got this other guy from Florida to come help with that."

To the resplendent end result, *Heaven and Hell*, issued on April 25, 1980, opens with "Neon Knights," a barnstormer of a calling card, the band chugging along briskly, but not without starry stadium rock melodies. "A very nice song, but that was quite a bad time for me," recalls Bill warily. "I don't remember recording 'Neon Knights' to be honest with you. I was still feeling ill. That was me playing drums on the whole album, but I was blacked out. I was so ill that I don't recall playing the songs. 'Neon Knights' felt a little bit light for me in comparison to some of the lyrics we had in the past. I thought it was nice and that it had some good melodies, but I thought hmmm, this is a bit different. It edged towards the mainstream more than what I'd been used to."

As it edged toward the mainstream, it also edged toward a new sonic clarity for the band, something that was evident in its impressive, steely opening salvo. As mentioned, the legendary Martin Birch was at the production helm for *Heaven and Hell*, and his presence was a shot in the arm for the band. "He was a bit of a joker, very laid-back," notes Graham Wright. "Martin was an engineer-cum-producer. He was willing to work with the band and listen to Tony's and Ronnie's ideas on the production side of it. He integrated well with the band. He was in charge of the board and engineered the album. And they were pleased. It was a fresh start for them. They were all excited, partly because we had escaped L.A. and the whole Ozzy sacking."

Graham, Bill's minder for years, takes some exception to Bill's comments about his self-professed state of oblivion for the *Heaven and Hell* sessions. "Yes, where he's said that he doesn't remember playing drums and doing the recording for *Heaven and Hell*, I find that a bit strange. He wasn't out of it or anything. He was cleaning himself up during that album. I think he's just trying to block it out because he was upset about Ozzy leaving the band. It was a bad time for him, them years, because he had lost first his father and then his mother in the course of about a year. And Ozzy left the band. You see, Bill was never drinking really hard. He'd only drink beer if he drunk anything. He'd never drink spirits and he wouldn't touch cocaine [if so, this must be after Bill's horrendous self-professed binges]. Bill was like the cleanest one, really, of the lot of them! The thing with Bill [laughs], he was a bit of a hypochondriac. He carried *bags* full of medicine [laughs]. He's looking back. He's saying these things about not remembering doing the album, but it was a long time ago. He worked hard on that album."

"Neon Knights" was the last track written for *Heaven and Hell*, given that the boys needed a quick-paced rocker to balance the heft of the rest of the album. Consequently, the returning Geezer is more involved with this one than on anything else. The song was issued as the record's first single, vaulting to Number 22 in the UK, backed with "Children of the Sea." Musically, the track challenges the new speed metal and proto-thrash of the NWOBHM, but at a sophisticated distance. Ronnie's lyric is poetic, heroic, but ultimately enigmatic one line to the next. It can be read as a metal call to arms but its rapid-fire images are above and beyond.

"Children of the Sea" followed with a light acoustic intro and some nice bass coloring

from Geezer. Ronnie is utilizing his clean singing voice, no growl at all, until the first classic scream 'n' hum over Geezer's plundering riff. "'Children of the Sea' was one I could appreciate lyrically," offers Bill. "Musically, it's a blues-based song; Tony and I just played blues behind it because that's basically what it is."

Explains Ronnie, "'Children of the Sea' was my first ecological attempt, and that was just saying that we run before we can walk, we do everything the opposite way because we want everything so quickly. Everything has to be instant gratification, which includes what we're doing to the planet. So that was my first attempt at a bit of a social conscience. It did about as much good as getting killed on a Greenpeace boat, which doesn't help much either. It made me realize that you're just not going to change the world, writing a song. At least I'm not going to. Especially when you're in Sabbath for God's sake, and here you are writing a song, 'Children of the Sea,' and no one out there is thinking, 'You know, he's really concerned about the environment.' They're thinking, "'Children of the

Sea,' he's talking about some devil that came out of the water.' So you're stuck sometimes within your own parameters you've created, and nobody ever believes that there's actually a gate in the fence that you can actually come out of once in a while."

"Lady Evil" kicks off with Geezer on bass, his bass line prominent throughout. Ronnie's lyric is a little too B-grade spooky on this one, offering a standard tale of a "magical, mystical woman," one of too many evil woman songs that would crowd the NWOBHM songbook of the day and the wider, expanded dinosaur-inclusive heavy metal encyclopedia of all time. Yet a few of the lines are truly chilling, imagistic and convincing. The song was released as the album's second of three singles, but didn't chart on either side of the Atlantic.

Side 1 of the original vinyl closes with that classic of all classics "Heaven and Hell," the most famous Dio-era Sabbath track of all time, a perennial live favorite for the Dio band, an epic that speaks volumes in an arguably modest seven minutes (the track was excruciatingly pared back from an eight-and-a-half minute goliath, originally engineered by Iommi and an uncredited Geoff Nicholls). Tony's riff on this one is brilliantly malevolent, his circular logic speaking up then laying back and letting

Ronnie disseminate his wicked world warnings. The bass line had been concocted by Nicholls, who took his own Quartz classic "Mainline Riders" as inspiration. Geezer adopted the pattern and went with it, grumbling however that if it had been up to him, he would have done something a little more complicated.

A good reason why "Heaven and Hell" is a classic lies within Ronnie's lyric. In a swirl of lesson-eering, Ronnie throws out brief yet insightful lines on the nature of life and, possibly, life beyond. As the speed picks up, so does the urgency of the lesson, a urgent call to live fast but watch your back. The close is an exasperated climax that leaves more questions than it answers. Circular, succinct, philosophical in a number of areas, "Heaven and Hell" is a true symphony of metal.

Explains Ronnie, on this variously pulsating, lacerating rock classic, "I knew where I wanted to take it lyrically and melodically. Tony came up with the riff and the other parts in between. That one really flowed. We were knocked out

by that one. When we started rehearsing it, we couldn't stop playing it. We played it every day for hours. Finally, after enjoying it so much, we realized that we had to finish it."

"'Heaven and Hell' is a story of contradictions, because that's exactly how I viewed the world," explains Ronnie. "'The world is full of kings and queens who blind your eyes and steal your dreams, it's heaven and hell.' That's really the crux. The song is about everybody trying to take advantage of your talents, whether it be musical talent or a talent in life, which is what happens to those less endowed, who usually want to glom onto and grab all the juice from those more well-endowed. And that was not a sexual reference by the way [laughs]."

But wait, it seems that "Heaven and Hell," or something like it, reaches back to the waning days with Oz, Graham recalling fondly watching Ozzy grappling with lyric ideas for the fledgling track. "Yes he was. We were in the house on the hill in Bel Air. We had already decided. It was actually my idea to call it *Heaven and Hell*. This was a conversation with Bill and Geezer. It was all based on a book by Aldous Huxley from years ago that I read when I was in my late teens. I remember saying, 'I think *Heaven and Hell* would be great name for this album.' And it just took, you know? It wasn't like, 'Oh, you've decided.' But I did mention it and it was taken on. And yeah, Ozzy was there when we first started rehearsing. In Bel Air, we built this rehearsal room out in the carport at the back of the house, and that's when we started rehearsing. It was towards the end of that when Ozzy left. But they sort of got a few songs and riffs down. They were working on the song 'Heaven and Hell.' Because Ozzy was trying to write the lyrics down. He's dyslexic, and he actually said to me, 'Hey, I've got some lines; would you write them down for me?

Help me.' Because me and him just sat in the studio and I was writing these words down. I wish I would have kept them [laughs]."

"Graham had nothing to do with that title," says Ronnie, ire rising in his voice. "That was my title. That was a song that I wanted to write for a long time. I'd written some of that already. We were writing at the time and I said, 'I've always wanted to write this; I've got a great idea.' I mean, I called the song 'Heaven and Hell.' I'll tell you how full of shit he is. Because in truth, I toured a long, long time ago with a band called The Easybeats who did 'Friday on My Mind,' one of my favorite bands of all time. Two of the greatest songwriters I ever heard, Harry Vanda and George Young, who was Angus' brother. And they did a song called 'Heaven and Hell,' and I just absolutely loved the idea of what they were trying to do, with the song, musically. And I said to myself, 'Someday I'm going to write a song called 'Heaven and Hell' and make it different from theirs.' I just loved the concept of what it was all about, and what it sparked in me. In fact, I saw George. I was playing with Sabbath in Sydney, and George came to the show because he was at the time producing Rose Tattoo. George came to the show, and I hadn't seen him in years. And I said, 'I just want to tell you, this song we're going to do tonight, I stole the title from you!' 'Aah, great, great' [said with a Scottish brogue]. So Graham Wright is full of crap."

"You think about these accusations or braggings that aren't true," says Ronnie, clearly on a roll. "Well, so where are the other great ideas you came up with, Graham? Of course, Graham went on to his great writing career after feeding me the words 'Heaven and Hell.' Had Graham done that, and I used that, I would've told you unequivocally. I would've said 'Yes, Graham came up with that title.' And it's just a shame that everybody else can't do that. But you're missing one other person. As I remember, didn't Craig Gruber write most of that song as well? He was the bass player that played with me in Elf; came into Sabbath, and that didn't work out, and Geezer came back. Well, all these years later, I'm hearing that he claims to have written most of the song, or a great portion of the song. And my reply was always the same: 'Well, he must have written that song, so he could carry on with all the other great songs he's written over the years.'"

Dio is forgetting that Geoff Nicholls, in to help out on keyboards, also claims a big hand in writing the song. Graham indicates that Nicholls' presence was quite key. "I was there in the studio for the whole recording. I looked after them in Criteria. Geoff was there all the time with Tony. He took over keyboards during the early days of the album. Geoff was Tony's right-hand man, on the music side."

Graham goes on to articulate Ronnie's role in the proceedings. "Ronnie supplied a lot of the lyrics, and he was directing; he knew what he wanted out of the songs. It was a bit strange. Ronnie was putting a lot more input in than they were used to, because Ozzy didn't put much input in [laughs]. Geezer would give him the lyrics: 'Here's the music; sing along.'"

Side 2 of this boldly engineered Sabbath proposal begins with the hummable and buoyant "Wishing Well," a track that is not so beloved in the canon, perhaps too "happy" given the weightiness of the rest of the album. Still, Ronnie's lyric is strong, subtly expanding on the themes in "Heaven and Hell," those addressing chance, fate and the dangers of believing in luck. "Walk Away," also from this album side is similar musically to "Wishing Well," too sweetly melodic, and arguably the worst track on the album, a song relatively straightforward compared to the rest of the record. In it, Ronnie addresses the wiles and temptations of beauty, exhorting the listener to walk away in the face of it, because with beauty usually comes the corruption and victimization that follows beauty everywhere.

"Die Young" — both musically and lyrically — is nearly as looming and timeless as "Heaven and Hell." Fast, passionate, urgent and entirely exhilarating, "Die Young" is fantastic, from the opening Geoff Nicholls keyboard wash, iced by lofty Iommi textures, through the triumphant intro, to Ronnie's classic "Oomph!", the startling, mellow respite, and a race to the finish. Lyrically, Ronnie drives home the philosophical concept of living for the day — the positive images of endless energy are ironic. One arrives at a sense that pretending and presuming immortality and omnipotence is a doomed, mournful rose with many thorns. "Die Young" was the album's third and last single (hitting Number 41 in the UK charts), backed with a live version of "Heaven and Hell." Of note, the album proper hit Number 9 in the UK charts, staying for fully 22 weeks, with the record notching a Number 28 placement in the U.S. as well as an eventual platinum certification, the band's first million seller since *Sabbath Bloody Sabbath* (excluding the *We Sold Our Soul* compilation, which of course went double platinum).

"Lyrically, it's like the Mick Jagger line," muses Ronnie. "'What a drag it is getting old.'

You know, maybe it's better to die young than to go through all this crap you're going to have to go through as you get old. If I die young, I'm going to die as my exhilarating experiences are happening. So it was obviously just my thoughts at the time."

"Lonely Is the Word" closes the album on a pulsating, uneasy, slow metal note, although its chorus is a fitting coda that talks in words and music about ennui and endings. Contrasting images of impossible astral travel with devastating solitude, millions with ones, immense light and heat with unfathomable darkness, Ronnie demonstrates the gulf between the highs and the lows that can pummel even the most confident. "Lonely Is the Word" is also often cited as the song containing Tony's favorite guitar solo of the entire Sabbath canon.

Hitting the road, Black Sabbath decided Geoff Nicholls shouldn't be playing guitar, but rather should play keyboards. Then it was

decided, perhaps partly so they wouldn't look too much like Rainbow, that Nicholls shouldn't even be seen. The notable stage prop at that time was a flaming cross, which Ronnie would salute with a scary introduction. The lasting tour pairing for the album was the infamous *Black and Blue* tour, which saw the band duking it out with Blue Öyster Cult, Sandy Pearlman having managed both bands. Relations were not always cordial as egos played a role in continuous one-upmanship. Touring began in Europe, April 17, 1980 was Sabbath's first public date with Ronnie as frontman. As indicated, the album saw release a week later. Other bands Sabbath shared stages with included Sammy Hagar, The Babys, Midnight Flyer, Vandenberg, Riot, Molly Hatchet, Journey, Gamma, Girlschool, Shakin' Street (another Sandy Pearlman act) and Cheap Trick. The tour involved a large European leg, followed by all of America (but not Canada), Japan, Australia and then a fairly extensive run through the UK to finish up. The Nassau Coliseum show from October 17, 1980 was filmed for the low-budget *Black and Blue* video.

"The *Black and Blue* tour; that was a strange one," recalls Graham Wright. "It was a business venture . . . you know, we've got Black Sabbath and we've got Blue Öyster Cult, and if we put them together we can sell arenas out. If Black Sabbath did a tour at that time, they wouldn't

> I RESOLVED MYSELF TO THE FACT
> THAT I CAN'T PLAY IN BLACK
> SABBATH UNLESS OZZY IS THERE.

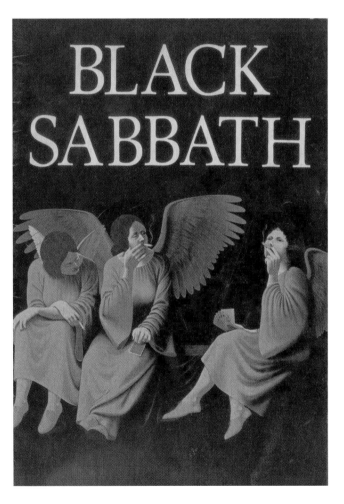

Heaven and Hell tour program

be able to sell, and same with Blue Öyster Cult. But the two together — Sandy Pearlman came along and saw a business opportunity. All I remember is that the Black Sabbath crew were crammed onto one bus, and Blue Öyster Cult's crew had two buses."

And the bands didn't get along. "Sabbath headlined some cities and the Cult headlined in other cities," says Graham. "And yeah, it was geared towards the Cult, that tour. But Sabbath was a bigger band, so there was a bit of friction there. By that time, Bill had left, and I was the only member left out of the original crew. Les Martin, Spock, Luke . . . all those guys had gone by then and I was getting surrounded by Italian Americans from New York [laughs]."

"Vinny was all right," adds Graham, on the Italian-American drummer who would replace Bill. "He came in, and I carried on for a few weeks, because I needed to get my paycheck. He had this little drum kit. All of a sudden, from Bill's huge 22 inch shell Tama kit, double bass drums, gongs and cymbals for days, Vinny had this tiny five-shell kit. But he was a good drummer and a nice guy. But Bill and I were mates. I basically lived with Bill in Worcester. We'd gone through thick and thin. And he said to me, 'Don't leave — carry on.' But in the end I just felt I couldn't take it. Everybody was emotionally involved in those days. It wasn't just like a job. 'Oh, I'm going on tour' with a tech like it is today. I left in New York and flew to Los Angeles, spent a couple of years living in L.A. and I got a little studio together and started painting."

In conversation with Sabbath expert and collector Doug Roemer, Ronnie explains that Bill was along for almost all of the *Heaven and Hell* tour. "We did Day on the Green, the L.A. Coliseum, 100,000 people, both places. Did Madison Square Garden and the Forum a couple times. Did 'em all. And then right at the end of that tour, we were supposed to go to Hawaii. Bill didn't travel well, and, as he has suggested, he was in a very bad state. And he hated to fly; couldn't deal with it. So Bill said, 'I'm going home.' He used to have a Winnebago that he drove around all the time on the road. And Bill went home and left us standing in Denver with a promoter with a gun to our heads, saying, 'You're not gonna play?! You'll never play again!' So we snuck out of town, found Vinny, went to Hawaii, did all the rest of the gigs, and then went back to Denver to make that show up for the guy. But I loved Billy then, I love him now. He's been one of the sweetest people I've ever known in my life."

"I think Ronnie Dio is fucking great and I have no ill feelings towards him," says Bill. "When we did *Born Again* with Ian Gillan it was the same. I love Ian. He is a wonderful man and has an incredible voice, but at the same time it was very difficult. It didn't feel OK on the inside. I tried again in 1984 with Tony, Geezer and another singer but I just couldn't do it. I bottomed out. What I did to amend what I had done was a decision to never get back together with Black Sabbath in any way, shape or form unless Ozzy was in the band. I made one more mistake when the band was thinking about reforming. Ozzy pulled out at the last minute and we already had some gigs lined up in South America. I was itching to play and I was missing Geezer and Tony as well. I went to South America and I didn't know the songs that well and it was not my best performance. We were playing with Tony Martin — great singer and great guy, but I knew it wasn't the same. I resolved myself to the fact that I can't play in Black Sabbath unless Ozzy is there. I didn't tell Ozzy that I was doing that. I didn't find it necessary to tell him. I

From the collection of Doug Roemer

needed to know that I knew the truth. For a long time neither Ozzy nor anybody else for that matter knew that I was privately amending the wrong I did to everybody when I lied to them. The only way I could right that wrong was to not be a part of anything."

"I doubt very much if I would be the first one who ever did that," says Ronnie, modestly, on his now-famous "devil horns" hand symbol, something that he had started doing around this time. "That's like saying I invented the wheel. I think you'd have to say that I made it fashionable. I used it so much and it had become my trademark until the Britney Spears audience decided to do it as well. So it kind of lost its meaning. But it was a symbol that I thought was reflective of what that band was supposed to be all about. It's not the Devil's

TOGETHER IN BARRY GIBB'S HOUSE

sign like, 'We're here with the Devil.' It's an Italian thing I got from my grandmother. It's to ward off the evil eye, or to give the evil eye, depending on which way you do it. It's just a symbol, but it had magical incantations and attitudes to it and I felt it worked very well with Sabbath. And then everybody else started to pick up on it. But yes, I did it so much that it became a symbol of rock 'n' roll of some kind."

The symbol actually dates back at least to Egyptian times, where it was used, in sculptures, much the same way, to ward off evil, most pointedly the attempts of grave robbers to plunder the riches of pharaohs' burial tombs.

I asked Graham for an impression of the legendary John "Dawk" Stillwell, the budding tour sound guru for the band then, now and for years to come, the earsplitter for Manowar. "All I remember is that he upset Tony. He filed down the frets on one of his guitars and hollowed them out, so he could bend the strings or something. I just remember that he ruined the guitar and Tony wasn't happy about it [laughs]. I mean, yeah, how can I put this? The guy is a technician. When I met him, I'd been on the road sort of ten years. I mean, I was a doer. I'd been through all the tours, been up all night, did all the gear. I didn't want to hear

about how he could sort of rebuild a Marshall amp. The guy was on a bit of a weird ego trip."

On tour, "Wishing Well" and "Walk Away" would not be played, but everything else from the album made the set list. "Lonely Is the Word" was played with Bill in the band, but it was dropped once Vinny came aboard. "Lady Evil" was played with Vinny, but not with Bill.

"He was good at making tea," says Geezer, when asked about the usefulness of Geoff Nicholls in a live setting. "I think he's more useful for the later stuff, from *Heaven and Hell* onwards, and occasionally for like when we did 'Spiral Architect.' He was great for that because it's got strings. Keyboards, I'd be perfectly happy to hear them. But sometimes I could hear keyboard notes backing guitar solos, and it really put me off. But anything legitimate, fine."

"And of course we had some disasters," says Tony, pulling out a couple of tour tales. "Some things that didn't quite work properly. With the Dio setup we had this big cross. We had it made that it goes on fire, flashes of light and whatnot. We used to use that in 'Heaven and Hell.' One time, Ronnie's going, 'Look, really concentrate on the cross; concentrate on the cross.' And at a certain point in 'Heaven and Hell,' it used to burst out in flames. And this one time, I think it was Madison Square Garden, it didn't burst out in flames. It was just like *pffft*, a little spark, which was very embarrassing. So that was a dismal failure. Another night, we went on stage when we started using these concussion bomb things, during 'War Pigs.' And again, it's Madison Square Garden — I can't believe it. The guy who had done all the pyro for us, he put too much powder in it. He had built these iron tubes that contained the powder, and he put them under the stage. We went on stage, started 'War Pigs,' the first note where the bangs went off, it lifted the stage and blew all the tubes out of the amplifiers, blew the speakers. The concussion was just unbelievable. So it was the first and last number; really, that was it. We said goodnight. Everything blew up."

Geezer recalls that somehow the band did finish the show. "Yeah, that was the Dio years, *Heaven and Hell* or *Mob Rules*. We eventually carried on the set. But he was just like this overenthusiastic road manager we had. He said, 'Well, it's Madison Square Garden. Let's have a really big bang.' And he put enough to blow the pissing building up. And it just like blew all the equipment out and blew all the seats out the back of the theater. It was our Spinal Tap moment."

Dio still looks back on the whole *Heaven and Hell* experience with fondness, fully 25 years down the line. "*Heaven and Hell* is an album just chock-full of great songs. It will always be my favorite. I can tell you just a little aside. We wrote some of the things here in L.A. — actually 'Heaven and Hell' was one of them. We wrote

From the collection of Doug Roemer

'Die Young' in Florida, at the house, before we went into the studio. But when we finally got into the studio, we would record the song, and not finish it all off — just drums, bass, guitar, a little bit of vocal — and we would take it to the local strip club, right across from the recording studio, and we would go, 'Play this!' And if the dancers liked it, we knew we were onto a good one. And they seemed to like everything we did; they loved 'Heaven and Hell.' And they just generally gave us our rule of thumb for what that album was going to be [laughs].

"We worked really hard on that album. It certainly wasn't a matter of just going out and partying. That band was pretty well dead in the

David Lee Wilson

water before we did *Heaven and Hell*. I certainly took it seriously — so did Tony, so did Geezer when he came back, and Bill was Bill. He always took everything seriously. We had a great engineer in Martin Birch, which made all the difference in the world, because then you didn't have people stumbling around in the studio. You had Martin Birch, one of the greatest engineers who ever lived, in all capacities, giving you sounds you'd never had before. That album sounded like no Black Sabbath album anyone had ever heard before. And there was a desire to tell everybody, 'Screw you, pal! Here we are, we're back again and we're good.' That gave us a lot of satisfaction. It's just a shame it all blew out, because I thought that satisfaction would be something we would be able to live with as a raised banner for the rest of our lives together."

A couple months after the launch of *Heaven and Hell*, a live album appeared on the racks. "*Live At Last* was a bootleg by our manager that we had left at the time," says Geezer, referring to

Patrick Meehan. Tracks on it hail from shows in Manchester, March 11, 1973 and the Rainbow in London five days later. The sound quality is acceptable (Tony dominates, resulting in black sheets of doom), the performances impressive, with Oz singing well. "Killing Yourself to Live" includes some alternative lyrics — the crowd hearing this eight months before the song would be released on record. But most intriguingly, "Wicked World" ends with a segue into an unnamed, fully formed original. The verse sounds like that of a funky blues song, but then Tony rips into a gorgeous set of chords that sound very much the work of the master. The *Live At Last* tapes would later be cleaned up and expanded (with 1970 and 1975 performances) into the *Past Lives* double CD set, issued by Divine/Sanctuary in 2002.

In closing — and in closing off the first year of what looked like a bright new decade for Black Sabbath — *Heaven and Hell*, 25 years down the line, is still Ronnie James Dio's favorite album of his entire illustrious career . . . Dio, Rainbow, Sabbath, all of it. "Yes! And it's not just the music; it's all the things that went together with it . . . the reason it was made, how difficult it was to make, the time it took, the people involved, the changes while we were doing it — that's what made the difference. It was an album that started a cycle for hard rock music, and I'm very proud of that."

11

"THE REST OF SABBATH HATES EVERYBODY"

– Mob Rules

The combination of metal's dramatic rise in 1980 and the presence of a sharp, efficient, disciplined album in *Heaven and Hell* made the newly reconstituted Black Sabbath a success. Now it was time to follow up the record. Bill Ward had been mercifully put on waivers and seasoned drum titan Vinny Appice joined the band in Honolulu in late summer after two days' rehearsal in L.A., with Cozy Powell passing on the gig. "Damn, I did a lot of the States, Japan, Australia, Europe. I probably did half of it," notes Vinny, on replacing a "not well" Bill Ward (who was also clashing with Ronnie for a good chunk of the *Heaven and Hell* tour), making him a known quantity when it would come time to make the new

Previous to Sabbath, Vinny was best known for his work with Rick Derringer, most notably the classic *Sweet Evil* album. "The blue album was my first album," notes Appice, referring to the *Derringer* debut from 1976 (Rick had previous records as Rick Derringer). "Before that, the only big thing I did was that I played with John Lennon for a while. I've got three videos for England and we did a live gig for him at the New York Hilton and we did handclaps on that song 'Whatever Gets You through the Night.' The handclaps on there are me and my band; that's how I met him. We used to rehearse in the Record Plant Studios in New York and that's where he used to work."

After a couple of failed one-offs (Axis and Bruzer), Vinny was now to be part of his biggest band yet. But, as Ronnie indicates, this twist in the tale was to be short-lived. Things were going well commercially . . . you would

Alexander Rack

think the smiles would go 'round the table and back again. "That's probably just the whole point of it, isn't it?" says Dio. "Any time anything went well for Sabbath, they had to decide that it was going to be somehow sabotaged, Sabbath-taged. It just happened to be the way of the band. There's just so much negativity going on and it never came from me. I was always very over the moon about continuing to do another project with the band, but like I said, there was a lot of negativity from some sources and that just made for hard times. Different drummer in, people not hearing what they thought they needed to hear. Because Vinny took chances. Vinny was a player and Billy was more of a percussionist than a drummer. Vinny did a lot more things that were perhaps foreign to the guys. So I think he was restrained a bit, which made it hard for me. But if there was not a problem in Sabbath, one would be created. That's been pretty evident throughout their career — lots of problems. That made for unhappy times and unhappy times make for not great music."

"There are no radical differences at all," said Ronnie back in late '81, comparing the impending *Mob Rules* with *Heaven and Hell*. "Since we have a new drummer, some things will have a different feeling. We're still a very powerful band and there may be a few softer bits, but then they turn into the smashing Black Sabbath sound we had on the last album. We were fortunate to find Vinny, a drummer who has the power and also a technical expertise to do that little extra we might ask of him. Nothing against Bill, because his sound was so firmly entrenched in the Black Sabbath sound, just as Tony's guitars have been, as Ozzy's voice was, and as my voice is, now that I'm in the band. Martin Birch is a perfectionist and technically very good in the studio — it's a more polished sound than what the band had before. You must remember that the first Black Sabbath album was completed in four or five days. From then on the band became more of a people's band and they would need to bash it out. Fortunately, with the success, we've been given the time and money to do a little more of a polished production."

"Ronnie is fast at writing songs," added Geezer in the same interview. "He can almost write them as he sings the melody line. I haven't had to write anything for him. I'm more pleased than I was about *Heaven and Hell*. I'm happy with 100 percent rather than 90 percent. On the last one, there were a couple numbers I got fed up with after a while. Vinny is great, fits in really well. He was a fan of the band before he came in and he knew all the numbers. He's fitting real well as a person, too."

"Ronnie was very good," recalls Tony, 20 years after the fact. "We sat down, much the same as I do with Glenn Hughes, really, and we came up with a lot of good stuff. I mean, certainly on *Mob Rules* anyway. When Ronnie came in, *Heaven and Hell* was partly written. With *Mob Rules*, most of that album was written with Ronnie and myself sitting down in either my house or his house and putting things together."

"Sure, people will read into things what they want to read, just like Dio logo upside down reads devil," says Ronnie of the curious cover art for the album, which some say contains, very cryptically, the message "Kill Ozzy" in the sticks and mud at the bottom (look for "Kill" to the left of artist Greg Hildebrandt's signature, and look for "Ozzy" directly beneath Greg's name). In fact, Greg has answered the accusation saying that the 24" x 20" watercolor was done in the '70s, and was licensed for use by Sabbath. Could it have been altered? One

label rep at the time said Sabbath requested that the message be added but this account is highly dubious. And, is that not future Dio mascot "Murray" on the blank canvas in the middle? The painting was actually originally entitled *Mob Dream*, and that center bit was intended not to be canvas, but the stretched skin of a person, with the face, naturally, as a real face.

As luck would have it, *Heaven and Hell* was set to become the last record for the band's deal with the venerable Warner Brothers. In fact, most staffers had given up on the Sabs and

THE REST OF SABBATH HATES EVERYBODY

Tour program

indeed the record was not properly worked until it became obvious the thing had legs. And due to its success, Sabbath were summarily re-signed; and, on the quiet, Ronnie was signed to a solo deal as well, which, as it turned out, was a blessing for him.

"Once again," continues Ronnie, looking back 20 years after the fact, "we were going

through our 'Sabbath hates everybody' period, or well, I guess, 'The rest of Sabbath hates everybody' period. And we had a new drummer. Vinny came into the picture, and those guys were so notoriously used to the only drummer they'd ever had, Bill Ward. Plus, *Heaven and Hell* was so easy to write, just Tony and I. And suddenly you had Geezer back in the mix again and he was about as positive as, I don't know, what's the most unpositive thing you can think of? A minus sign I guess. And that upsets the applecart that worked so well before; it became difficult."

"Geezer was never pushy that way," clarifies Ronnie, on the subject of Geezer getting back into writing. "I just think that Geezer had this really negative attitude, in his life. I don't know why, but there were times when he was very happy. Most of the time when it came to these things, perhaps he examined them too closely. But we wrote together; Geezer was an excellent writer. It's just that sometimes you have to let go and say 'That's good, that's great, I like that,' instead of moaning. And I had written so much, and as far as I was concerned, a lot more musical things than Geezer. I wasn't about to be told what to do. Not that he tried to do that, but I knew what the process was. And that pervasive attitude of negativity was there all the time. He probably had some problems in his home life at that time. I know he hated being in America, always wanted to be back home in England. But that shouldn't surface when you're in the creative process and I felt that's exactly what happened. It wasn't so much that he was insisting on doing this or that, just that there wasn't that positiveness that Tony and I had all the time when we did *Heaven and Hell*."

I asked Geezer Butler when the first cracks started to appear on the mighty Sabbath armor. "Ronnie thought that *Heaven and Hell* was so successful because it was all down to him. He didn't give anybody else any credit for what was done. I mean, Tony had written the album for God's sakes, musically anyway. And Ronnie thought, well, I've come in and resurrected Sabbath and without me Sabbath would be nothing. And he had that kind of attitude, and he was really hard to work with," Geezer said, adding that, with respect to the material for *Mob Rules*, "it came eventually, but it was nowhere near as easy as *Heaven and Hell*. Things got too strained, and by the time of *Live Evil*, it was all over. Me and Tony would go in one day, and Ronnie and Tony would go in the next day. Couldn't even be in the same studio together."

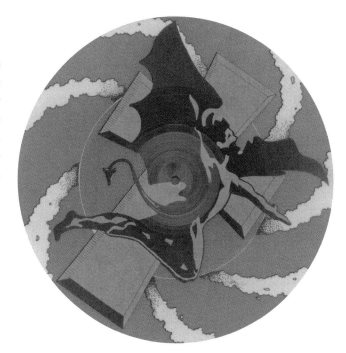

If there was friction between Geezer and Ronnie in the lyric department, Vinny didn't see it. "No, not at all. In fact, Geezer was happy to have him just do it. He wrote a lot of lyrics for everything else; but when Ronnie came in, that was his thing, that was his job. So Geezer didn't mind."

"Well, Bill is the king, as far as I'm concerned," adds Butler, comparing drummers. "Vinny is great as well, but he's got a totally different style; he's funkier. He's great to play with. Of all the drummers I've played with, Bill would be my number 1, and Vinny would be my number 2."

Indeed, back to the subject of writing, for *Heaven and Hell*, the entire band was credited on every track with respect to music (which irks Ronnie to this day, who insists that it was he and Tony who wrote the album), whereas for *Mob Rules*, all tracks were credited "Geezer Butler, Ronnie James Dio & Tony Iommi," Ronnie receiving, full and lone credit for lyrics again. I asked Vinny if he thought he should have been included on the music front, along with that cabal. "At that time, no, I was just too happy to be in the band. But a lot of the songs

weren't written beforehand and we kinda jammed around. Nothing was written beforehand. And, the same thing with *Dehumanizer*, I kept all the riffs on tape. And when we weren't rehearsing, I kind of edited them and put all the good parts together and said 'Here's a bunch of riffs we have; let's listen to them' and they would go, 'Yeah, that's good, let's try that!' But as usual, the powers from above, you know . . . 'No songwriting on this; we'll take care of you on the next one, no problem.'"

And it's Vinny who opens the *Mob Rules* record (released November 4, 1981), four splashy, loose high hat notes giving way to the melodic and trundling "Turn Up the Night," a song that contains a handful of Tony's most prosaic solos, and the second largest dose of melody on the record after "Slipping Away." Never a fan of the song, Ronnie offers, with a laugh, an uncharacteristically terse "It's all right." "Turn Up the Night" was indeed one of two *Mob Rules* singles, backed with "Lonely Is the Word," rising to Number 37 in the British

charts. Oddly, the track seems to get the band in trouble. Many fans at the time and indeed since, have called *Mob Rules* a bit of a rehash of *Heaven and Hell*, a weaker sibling as it were. And "Turn Up the Night" was good evidence of that, with similarity of speed, melody, placement, even title to "Neon Knights." After that, it became an easy exercise to match up, however loosely, tracks from that record with this one. Even lyrically, the song can be seen as a call to arms to the metal nation. "Neon Knights" seems deeper but perhaps that is due to its numerous disjointed mysterious phrases. "Turn Up the Night" holds together better and moves forward with more confidence, and can be read as addressing many heavy metal touchstones, that of rock 'n' roll, that of evil, that of women, pretty much summing up what most metalheads thought about all day.

"Voodoo" is next, led by a mammoth riff from Tony at an insistent mid-paced tempo that allows for maximum drama from Ronnie. It's a classic steeped in Sabbatherian mannerisms, pounded simply by Vinny and Geezer, another great dark horse of an Iommi solo buried back there somewhere in the stomped sludge. "'Voodoo' turned out well," notes Ronnie. "I always liked the title and we plowed through the music as best we could and it turned out pretty good. But it wasn't a happy time. *Heaven and Hell* was, *Mob Rules* started to be unhappy and then *Live Evil* was one of the darkest times in my life. So 'Voodoo' just luckily turned out to be a pretty good piece of music. But it could have been ten times better had we all been on the same page."

Ronnie's 'Voodoo' lyric demonstrates one of the man's many talents. His words can be read as a high quality look at the emotions and (possible?) magic behind voodoo, or something much more universal moving into the realm of other religious disciplines, or universal beyond that into the ugliness at the heart of man.

"Different studio, different equipment," opines Ronnie on this album's fatter, warmer sound, versus the piquant tones of *Heaven and Hell*. "The gear was the same; we didn't change any of that. Different drummer of course. No, I guess maybe just a natural progression for Martin Birch. He just tried a few different things. It's probably down to the reverb or the Eventide processes that we were using."

"*Mob Rules*? Yeah, it's got a sound to it," adds Vinny on the same subject. "I thought it was a little muffly here and there, a little dry. But it's got a lot of low end and a lot of bottom end on the bass drum and the bass. And for that time I thought it was pretty damn good. Martin was a really nice guy, and he liked a lot of drums, which was cool. And he was the kind of producer that didn't get involved so much with the

From the collection of Doug Roemer

songwriting. He was more involved in getting the sounds right."

Next up was the album's epic, "The Sign of the Southern Cross" beginning acoustically before a meltatious wad of Iommi riffs roll like tanks through the African desert. Says Ronnie, "I love that song. That's one everybody mentions when you talk about that album. I've always loved that title. When I was a trumpet player as a little kid, there was a song called 'The Southern Cross.' And I did a little research into it. 'The Southern Cross' is Australian-related as well. But I just loved the idea. So when it came time to write a track, we needed something that was going to be a little more *Heaven and Hell*-ish, and that was the title we put to it. And it was a lot of fun to write." Lyrically, Ronnie weaves one of his more elaborate, mystical, quasi-scientific stories. Again, the power of the song is in the seduction and timeless universality of the words. Each line sounds like the sweet nothings of infinite, awe-inspiring proportions.

"E5150" offered a respite from Iommi's ear-yanking, the track comprising three minutes of spooky electronic music that would be an apt opener for the concerts of the tour. It is essentially paired with the album's title track (sort of title track: the song is called "The Mob Rules," the album, *Mob Rules*), "E5150" being an intro

WE ENDED UP KEEPING 'COUNTRY GIRL,' BUT IT'S ALWAYS HAD A LITTLE BIT OF A CRINGE, ESPECIALLY AT THE TIME.

before the burst of communicative chords announcing the real start of the mayhem. It is said that Geezer wanted the word "evil" represented on the album, and 5, 1 and 50, represented as Roman numerals render V, I and L. Stick an "E" in front of it, and you have "EVIL." Of note, Van Halen have an album called *5150*, and explanations of that have always centered on that number being police enforcement code for criminally insane.

"The Mob Rules" exists in two versions, the song have been written for (and used in) the animated *Heavy Metal* movie, the cinematic realization of the post-psychedelic graphic magazine of the same name.

Ronnie's lyric is a hard one to crack, with general scenes of violence dovetailing with veiled, imagistic exhortations against the stupidity of mob thinking and mob justice. There seem to be more warnings embedded in the short lyric than just the one against not thinking for oneself, but then again, Ronnie always had a knack for stacking up warnings and heedings and bewarings until one just had to take at least a few of them to heart, else the pile would collapse.

Vinny fondly recalls the recording of "The Mob Rules" this way. "Warner Brothers wanted us to write a song for that movie, so we had a couple days off, or we made a couple of days off, and we went into the house where John Lennon filmed 'Imagine,' which was his house, but Ringo owned it now and he had a studio there. So we went there and we all hung out there for like three days. And it was cool because the drums were in the friggin' hallway. It's a huge mansion, and we're in the living rooms, hanging out, writing a song, together, playing, and finally we recorded it and put the whole thing together there. And then they assigned us rooms and I got John Lennon's room and that was right after he got killed, so I didn't want to stay in there. I was scared." The band was, in fact, informed of Lennon's death in mid-flight, as they were on their way to England to set up shop at the legendary studio.

All in all, "The Mob Rules" is the album's anthem, its call to arms, party central for what is a ponderous, slightly uneasy record. Like "Turn Up the Night" and "Slipping Away," it possesses melody, but its hooks manage a heavy metalness that make it a sort of drinking song, what with its pushing and shoving rhythm, its careening from one side to the next.

And speaking of next, we come to side 2 of the original vinyl, "Country Girl," which again is steeped in a sort of triumphant heavy metal sense of melody that presages nicely the tone and feel of Dio's *Holy Diver* album.

"The only person who didn't like that was

Bill, upon hearing it," says Ronnie. "He didn't think that it had anything to do with Sabbath. But then again, I didn't tell him about all the songs that they did early on that I didn't think had anything to do with Sabbath either. But everybody else loved the song, me in particular. I wrote that song for Wendy. Rather, I didn't write it for her, so to speak, but the inspiration was there."

Some complain about the lyric, considering it a little too boy/girl for the band, but outside of the key, memorable, plainspoken line, the rest is classic evil-woman Dio stuff, Ronnie coming up with enough images of hellfire and brimstone to strengthen even the weakest resolve with respect to the temptation of . . . frankly, another witch.

The "Country Girl" lyric is in fact the first that comes to mind for Tony, when thinking about any lyrics he personally wasn't quite sure

about. "It was a heavy riff and we thought, 'Ooh, God, "Country Girl" . . . it don't really go with what we're playing.' And we sort of mentioned it to Ronnie, and it didn't really go down well at all. We ended up keeping 'Country Girl,' but it's always had a little bit of a cringe, especially at the time."

"Slipping Away" follows, and is truly the *Mob Rules* track that has no truck with the other songs on the album. Funky, slippery, almost awkward, it is too darn happy, something that might have fit on the first Rainbow album, or as light relief on the second or third from that band. It includes a very thick and distorted bass solo. "Yeah, we wrote that one in England," notes Ronnie. "We were at a place called Goldrock Road, where we mixed *Mob Rules*. Tony had the riff, as usual, and he said, let's make this a little bit funkier, and that's actually one that Geezer liked. It came together very quickly. I wrote lyrics and melodies to it in the studio, and we liked it a lot. It was a departure for Sabbath and became just one of those natural progressions that should happen as much as possible." On the words front, it's a pretty cool song, Ronnie speaking directly and plainly, with a minimum of mythology. Nonetheless, the message is complex, even the concept of slipping away taking on two definitions: that of willful escape, and that of fading or dying.

Then comes "Falling Off the Edge of the World," a secondary epic for the album, one housing arguably Tony's most malevolent riff

of the first Dio era. "The writing process for that was weird, not just for that song but the whole album," says Ronnie. "We did it at this little studio we had used before, Vinny and I, when we were doing some production for somebody else. We went there and did the rehearsals and it was weird — strange room, strange place. That was one of the latter songs we wrote for that album and it was not as smooth as 'Sign of the Southern Cross'; but again, the locale was different."

Ronnie's lyric seems to be a paean to desperate depression, with the key image being the extreme one, falling off the edge of the world. Answers Ronnie, "Once again, as with the title 'Heaven and Hell,' I have to credit George Young and Harry Vanda, who also wrote a song called 'Falling Off the Edge of the World,' and I always just loved that title. So once again, I borrowed their title."

I had asked Ronnie about stories regarding Tony's fabled boxes and boxes of tapes. If indeed, boxes of them existed, says Dio, "Tony never pulled a tape out, that I ever saw in my life. Tony did not go back and play a riff. Tony just did things the way all of us did, very naturally. Tony would play something and we would always say, 'That's great Tony!' And he would go, 'It is? Do you like that? Oh, OK.' And he'd play something to us another day and we

would go, 'Tony, that's great!' Because he is just a riff master; it just flows from him. But I never saw him pull a cassette out of anywhere. He just pulled those things out of his mind; he's just the best at that."

Closing the album is a track without much of a riff at all. "Over and Over" could be called the album's ballad. Yet it's more like a heavy, sloggy, doomy blues, a musically simple and relaxed song that allows Ronnie's vocals to shine, as well as housing one of Tony's signature mournful blues solos, or rather, a quintessentially goddamn godfather of heavy metal solo applied forcefully over a blues vibe. Says Ronnie, "I like what I wrote in it; it's a very kind of Dio song. I think it was a reflection of how I felt at that time as well, perhaps that idea of railing against negativity. There was one line in it about life being made of paper, and there being a flame. And that flame to me was some of them at that time."

It's hard to agree that the song rails against negativity, rather, it wallows in it, though the depressive images are less stark and extreme than those of the song's predecessor. But there's a hopelessness, a draining of the sands of time, that echoes in the literary echo itself of the words "over and over," as well as in the listing, rudderless quality of the music.

All told, *Mob Rules* did quite well, rising to a Number 12 placement in the UK charts, where it stayed for 14 weeks, the record hitting Number 29 in the States, only one notch less than the U.S. placement for *Heaven and Hell*, although that one went platinum, with *Mob Rules* only reaching gold. "The Mob Rules" as a single failed to chart in the U.S., but the UK mob pushed it to Number 46.

Touring for the album, the band played almost everything off the record, save for "Over and Over," and by the close of the jaunt back home at the Hammersmith, they had

trimmed "Falling Off the Edge of the World," "Turn Up the Night" and "Voodoo" as well. "Slipping Away" housed a Vinny Appice drum solo. "Neon Knights," "Children of the Sea" and "Heaven and Hell" were carried over from the previous record.

Support for the first leg took the form of the ill-fitting Alvin Lee, a bit of a hero to the band. The burning cross was replaced by one studded with a ton of lights, which drained many an electrical system as the tour ground on. The band first hit Canada for five dates, then the eastern U.S. and the Midwest, before returning to the UK for 14 dates. For a second U.S. leg, hard-hitting southern rockers Doc Holliday had the unenviable task of opening (a couple dates at the front and a few more later), with slightly quieter southerners The Outlaws taking the lion's share, with yet another southerner Johnny Van Zant and Canada's AOR-ish Wrabit filling in as well. All did not flow smoothly. Shows were canceled and rescheduled for various reasons: riots, blizzards, food poisoning for Tony, Vinny being injured by dry ice, and of all things, a roof collapse due to heavy snow.

12

"LIKE A HOUSE THAT FELL DOWN"

– Live Evil

Assembled amidst bad vibes, *Live Evil* is actually a corker of a live album. Released tit for spat with Ozzy's *Speak of the Devil* album, both records shared some of the same Sabbath hits played by pounding, instinctual bands, most notably rhythm sections that bulldozed and balleted simultaneously, at will, at leisure. The Dio-era Sabbath material on *Live Evil* was the icing on the doom cake, with Ozzy immaturely making his whole damn record full of Sabbath songs. Both camps, predictably, com-

"Those assholes," spouted Ozzy, to the press done at the time. "They wait 15 fucking years to do a live album, and then they do one at the exact time I do mine. On top of that they're still using some of my songs. I can't believe that they had the balls to put 'Paranoid' and 'Iron Man' on their album. Black Sabbath performing those songs without me singing them is like four guys getting together today and calling themselves The Beatles. That's just rubbish. I'm bigger than Sabbath ever was. All you've got to do is look who is selling more records or more concert tickets and decide for yourself. Actually, it's rather sad that they still have to live off of songs that are ten years old. It's a fucking joke that they don't have more confidence in their new material. Yeah, I do 'Iron Man,' too, but that's my song — people demand that I do it. I imagine Sabbath does it because they don't feel their new songs hold up very well. The strangest part of this whole matter is that I had lost all of my bad feelings towards them. I realized that our parting ways was the best thing for both Sabbath and for

me. But I'm upset about both these albums coming out at the same time. I guess we'll just have to see who does better when it comes to selling copies. That'll be the final word on this matter, and, may I add, I have no doubt who's gonna end up on top. Those fools. I'll admit that Dio is a stronger singer than I am, but no one can deny that I'm a better front man. What I have is a special gift for being able to relate to audiences and what they want."

"He has his fans and we have ours," countered Tony, "and while I'm not naive enough to think that a lot of our fans don't like Ozzy too, I don't think we're in direct competition. They'll just have to buy two great live albums. I'm sure both records will do very well. *Live Evil* is designed to reward all those people who laid down their money in this recessionary period to make our last tour successful. We all believe that it's one hell of an album. When Ozzy was in the band, he had difficulty remembering lyrics on stage. He was so concerned with prancing around and turning the crowd on that sometimes he forgot when and what he was supposed to sing. That's not really a knock, because that was part of Ozzy's

I THINK YOU'D HAVE TO BE RATHER DEAF NOT TO HEAR THE DIFFERENCE RONNIE MAKES WITH THIS BAND ON STAGE.

charm. But I think you'd have to be rather deaf not to hear the difference Ronnie makes with this band on stage."

"It seems strange that he recorded a live album full of Sabbath songs, as he didn't need to do that," said Tony to *Kerrang!* "I mean, he's always going on about us and how we shouldn't go out as Black Sabbath then he turns around and records a whole album that's Black Sabbath!"

"I thought he just made himself look stupid," added Geezer.

On the subject of constructing a live album, Dio said, "It was a very ardous process but we enjoyed it. The shows that were the strongest seemed to be the ones we did at Hammersmith Odeon in London, as well as ones in San Francisco, Seattle, Fresno and Dallas. Most of the time we could eliminate a song pretty quickly, especially if the guitar wasn't mic'ed properly or the vocals didn't sound right. It's so

hard to get a studio-quality sound on stage because there are so many variables that can go wrong. We didn't mind having a few blemishes on the album. But we did want to keep them to a minimum. We didn't want to go back into the studio after we finished listening to the tracks and have to rerecord parts of them. That would have been ridiculous. That would defeat the whole purpose. We only wanted to document what Sabbath sounded like on this particular tour, not create another studio album with crowd sounds mixed in." Further to Dio's comment on specific cities, it is known that the April 23rd and 24th shows in Seattle (with The Outlaws supporting) were recorded for use on the album, as were Dallas (May 12th) and San Antonio (May 13th).

But dealing with *Live Evil* as we must, there was plenty of complaining behind the scenes within Sabbath, let alone the grousing between Sabbath and Ozzy.

Shortly after the departure of Ronnie and Vinny to form Dio, Tony gave his side of the story with respect to the problems during construction of *Live Evil*. "It's difficult to say how pleased we are with the album, we were so wrapped up and involved in it. It was hard to view with any clarity. Personally I had to leave off for ages before I could listen to it. You just can't get a proper perspective of it if you're around it all the time. It was an awkward situation because of what happened with the band. It made the whole thing difficult to produce. Ronnie wanted it a different way to how we heard it. So we'd be in the studio mixing during the day and Ronnie would come down at night and change it. It began to sound like a vocalist with a backing band. He tried to have full control of the album. I mean, we've been waiting for years to do a good live album. We wrote the fucking music so we know how it should sound! But he kept going into the studio and changing everything. In the States he was getting like a little Hitler. He's got a great voice, but personality conflicts took over, really."

"It was a strain doing it," added Geezer. "We'd done a couple of live albums before but scrapped them. In fact, *Live At Last* was one of the ones we'd scrapped. It was terrible! I think we'll definitely produce the next album unless we get a really good straight producer who isn't smashed out of his brains all the time. Maybe all we need is a good engineer. At first we didn't know what was happening, and the engineer was in a funny spot because he couldn't say anything."

"That all got out of hand, honestly," remarks Tony, fleshing out the story. "We were going in and mixing the album. Over a period of weeks, I was seeing the engineer beginning to look worse and worse. He was getting more drunk all the time. I wondered what was going on. I asked him one day if he was all right. He said 'I can't stand it anymore. I've got to tell you what is going on.' I told him, 'Go on.' He said, 'You guys are going home after doing a mix and then Ronnie is wanting to come in and do his own mix. I don't know what to do.' Basically, that is what happened — that's the crunch of it. We tried to ban him from the studio. It got pretty bad."

"Well, *Live Evil*," recalls Ronnie with a sigh, setting the record . . . straighter? "That was a big fixer. That was like a house that fell down and

needed to be fixed again. The only people that didn't get the chance to fix it were Vinny and I. We were accused of going into the studio and turning up the vocals and the drums. And that was the story told to Tony and Geezer by an engineer that was drinking a bottle of Jack Daniels a day, so we know why he said that. As was their wont, they believed it, and that led to the breakup of that one. It was all completely untrue and absolutely stupid! When we did reform in '92, the apologies went all the way around. But that record was made by Tony and Geezer and the engineer with the drinking problem, and I think it took them six months to do it, here and there, fixed and then not fixed."

This event seemed to be the straw that broke the camel's back, in terms of breaking up this now very well-regarded version of Black Sabbath.

"Well, that's what we were told," says Ronnie, specifically on the subject of what cracked Sabbath in two, "but I'm sure there were other reasons. That was a time when we had a lot of success, via the *Heaven and Hell* album and the

Mob Rules album. Life had changed for the guys, going from not being successful to being very successful again. And once you get to that point, all the temptations come about, and there were a lot of conditions. And I think that clouded a lot of intelligence on their parts too."

"There were accusations of people going in and remixing things," says Vinny, getting to the heart of the matter in the manner of a good-natured, impartial judge. "We would go in and turn things up and they would go in and turn things up. But not really any of that was true. The whole problem was, if everybody would show up at the same time, that would have solved the problem [laughs]. So you figure that if some people show up and the other people weren't there for hours, at 200 or 300 dollars an hour, why not get some work done? Or try to get it close? So that played a part in it, too. And the same thing happened with *Dehumanizer*."

And to make matters worse, the back cover of the album awards Vinny with non-band-member status. Geezer, Tony and someone

named Ronnie Dio ("Oh yeah, anything to wind people up," says Vinny remarking on the fact that "James" was deliberately left out of Ronnie's name) get their names in large print. Keyboardist Geoff Nicholls, not a part of the band yet, is listed next in smaller print, then Vin in text of the same point size.

"I don't know how that happened, because we were good friends and I had nothing to do with the breakup. They got pissed that I went with Ronnie. I don't know if I was supposed to play with them or not. But that's what happens in this business; it's a pretty crazy business. But yeah, I got a bad credit on there and a little tiny picture."

To reiterate, though, despite the hijinx, the album is an impressive classic metal feast, and there is nothing wrong with the sound — everybody can be heard just fine. The front cover is actually from an original idea by noted cover artist Ioannis (Blue Öyster Cult, Deep Purple, The Allman Brothers Band, Lynyrd Skynyrd, Fates Warning), who had approached the band wanting to do cover art for them, but the general concept was usurped by and credited to Paul Clark instead. It is indeed similar to what Rush portrayed with *Exit . . . Stage Left*, this idea of a class reunion consisting of characters from all the previous albums.

Opening with the eerie, spacey sounds of "E5150," the band break into "Neon Knights" with Ronnie singing on all cylinders. "N.I.B." follows, with Ronnie taking particular relish in the "Lucifer" line and Vinny storm trooping the groove with big single-stroke snare rolls. "Children of the Sea" follows with Ronnie showcasing his blues chops elegantly, and "Voodoo" closes with a bit of a jam, but Vinny driving the track hard.

Side 2 begins with "Black Sabbath," Tony replacing the rain sound effect with a steely and rainy acoustic-styled guitar segment. Ronnie enunciates the song *real* thespian-like, while Vinny quietly proves that Bill Ward isn't the only one who can play slow and "outside of time." "War Pigs" is downright funky, and includes a drum solo that gives way to the heaving strains of "Iron Man."

Side 3 begins with a rousing, carousing run through "The Mob Rules," which leads to a

kitchen sink version of "Heaven and Hell." And, although the sing-along can be a bit of a chore, the signature riff is lacerating. But more importantly, the gates of Hell open up rather unexpectedly for the highlight of the album: Tony's guitar solo. He begins quintessentially screechy, high-note Tony — a bit hard on the ears like Kirk Hammett. But then Tony introduces a huge stack of sinister, tortured chords, the riffmaster creating for a solo what he does so well for song structures. Tony summarily (but only temporarily) rips to shreds his solo, and the results are frightening.

The last side of the original vinyl features an expansive and very heavy bulldozing of "The Sign of the Southern Cross" with more "Heaven and Hell" inserted. "Paranoid" gets a crushing guitar sound and "Heaven and Hell" returns yet again. Closing the album is the perennial "Children of the Grave," followed by a bit o' "Fluff," a fitting whimper, not a bang,

signaling that it was time for Ronnie to finally form his own damn band.

Most Sabbath fans quite like the album, and so do I. But at the time it was basically panned — or at least, a few years later, the press was pushing that version of events, the post-op denigration of the album practiced by the band themselves. Geezer even went so far as to say that the band never promoted the album because they didn't think it deserved it. The fact is, there was no band left, so what was the point? Meanwhile across town, Ozzy's double album of Sabbath tracks featured a surprisingly fierce Brad Gillis of Night Ranger fame, leading a crack band through the biggest hits of Sabbath's career. The production of the album was savage and powerful, Ozzy sang with the spirit of a man scorned, and one couldn't fault the rhythm section, consisting of Quiet Riot's Rudy Sarzo and Tommy Aldridge, double bass pioneer of the Pat Travers Band. "Speak of the Devil" ("Talk of the Devil" in the UK), zoomed to Number 14 in the U.S. charts, charting at Number 21 back in Britain.

Years later, Geezer Butler talked about the Dio experience, incarnation and the concurrent success of Ozzy as a solo artist.

"I suppose it's crossed my mind, 'Why is Ozzy getting everything when we wrote all the stuff?' There was a little bit of resentment there when he got all the credit for everything and he was probably the least constructive one in the band. We weren't like that; we were really soul mates. We went through so much crap together, so much opposition from the press, and it was at least great to see one of us get to the status that he'd gotten. I think the difference being Ozzy as a solo artist . . . he's got the ultimate control over everything. The *Heaven and Hell* thing was incredible; it was one of the biggest-selling Sabbath albums. He really put us back on top again. But then the band internally started falling apart. It was us on one side and Ronnie on the other. When that started to crumble, we didn't have what Ozzy had and that was ultimate control, because it was his band. If he didn't like somebody, they'd be out. Plus he didn't have to write the stuff; he picked writers to produce material for him. With us, we had to write our own stuff in a bad atmosphere; I think we lost a hell of a lot of ground doing that."

13

"AS ONE MIGHT DISTURB A BIRD SANCTUARY"

– Born Again

A third era in the life of Black Sabbath was about to begin, but how that era could be categorized is a messy issue. It could be considered the Ian Gillan era, but given that it only lasts for one album, maybe it's really the comical musical chairs era, with two albums emerging each with a vastly different lineup. Everything's fragmented and shattered at this point, but that doesn't mean great music didn't get made. To recap, Ronnie and Vinny are both now gone, following the *Live Evil* debacle. Geezer and Tony form the core of the experience still, with Bill being lured back from the wilderness in an emotionally fragile, delicately sober state.

Hans Arne N

The music these three Sabs would create with Gillan . . . well, if any album in the history of Black Sabbath is getting a new set of horns up from metalheads here deep into the new century, it's *Born Again*. Perhaps this is because most subgenres of the form right now are so crushingly heavy and dark, just like this mad, opaque record of demonic vibrations.

The story told time and again of the unholy alliance between Sabbath and Ian Gillan is of a chance meeting in the pub between Tony and Ian. Both drank long and hard and got smashed, and Ian was reminded the next day that over the course of the evening, he had agreed to join Black Sabbath. In actuality a meeting had been set up with this subject in mind, in order for the guys to suss each other out, as it were, over a few pints. Gillan had initially turned the Sabbath office's overtures down, but then his own manager suggested meeting Geezer and Tony. They picked a good pub and apparently set up camp there for 12 hours.

"Ronnie didn't leave, we got rid of him actually, but after that we didn't know quite what to do," explains Tony. "Whether we should go do solo projects or what, because there was only Geezer and myself at that stage. All we really wanted was to have some time off because we were in Los Angeles for so long and got bogged down. We thought of different vocalists, and then Ian came about, though we had not thought of him for a minute. I don't know how it came together but it was arranged for us to meet in Woodstock. We hadn't seen Ian for a time, but we met in the pub there, The Bear. We just sat down and talked over different things, how we felt about the band and each other; it was really exciting. He joined officially at the end of February. He's totally committed to Sabbath. He loves being part of the band because he hasn't been involved in this sort of setup since Purple. He's in as a partner, and he's the happiest he's ever been."

Gillan's ex-bandmates, most vocally bassist John McCoy, were none too pleased with the duplicity and haste with which Ian closed up shop on the Gillan band. On Gillan's part, he blamed a three-month break precipitated by vocal nodes, indicating that the band impatiently drifted apart and away into other projects while he was sidelined.

Hans Arne Nakrem

"Those stories are a little out of line," says Ian of the press reports (Gillan calls the British press his biggest enemies). "They're saying that I faked having vocal problems just so I could break my band up and join Sabbath. That's not true. I was having serious vocal problems, and doctors told me that I should take a number of months away from singing. I didn't expect my band to sit around waiting for me, so I gave them permission to look for other gigs. When the Sabbath opportunity came, I didn't feel any particular concern for the band — most of them were already involved with other groups. I was looking out for myself. How could I turn down the chance to play with Sabbath? I've known Tony and Geezer for years, and I felt I could make an important contribution to their music. We all seem to be on the same wavelength. Sabbath is an all-British band again.

HOW COULD I TURN DOWN THE CHANCE TO PLAY WITH SABBATH? I'VE KNOWN TONY AND GEEZER FOR YEARS, AND I FELT I COULD MAKE AN IMPORTANT CONTRIBUTION TO THEIR MUSIC.

That's surely not a put-down of America or Ronnie and Vinny, but there is a certain sensibility that we share, having the same roots, that is irreplaceable. We've all been through the same experiences. We've tasted success and we know we want to taste it again."

In any event, once the new alliance was formed, "Deep Sabbath" set out for The Manor, the legendary Richard Branson studio ensconced in a country setting.

In press interviews, pre-release conducted at the time at The Manor, Tony was characteristically upbeat about the band's prospects. "We didn't really rehearse that much, which keeps the songs fresh. It wasn't worked out at all, and it feels a lot better, much more raw. It's got the rawness of the early Sabbath. And we've produced ourselves, because we're all experienced enough to go in and say what we want. We fancied getting back to the basics again, doing it in England and not going for the extreme in studios, which we always have done; that costs an absolute fortune. We wanted to record either here or at Rockfield, a place where we could all be around, live in. We've been able to use some stuff that we've had for a few years, really. We could've used it before, but it just wasn't suitable vocals-wise. Now Ian comes along, though, and can sing on it, so it's great. There's a hell of a lot more energy now, it's more exciting, and I'm sure that will reflect on stage. Ian has given all of us a tremendous boost; we're like little kids again. It makes a huge difference when you can work that way as opposed to, 'Oh, I'm fed up with it.'"

Tony also indicated that he thought for a minute about hanging up the Sabbath name for the project, but then changed his mind.

Like Ian, he was also chuffed that the band was all-English again everyone in close proximity to each other (rehearsals took place in Birmingham). Even though Geezer maintained a residence in St. Louis, he had a home in England as well. "I think it makes a tremendous difference," says Tony. "No disrespect to American people because they're fine musicians, but I don't think it's the right combination for us. American musicians don't seem to have the roots we do in Britain. Ian, on the other hand, has been around the same as we have. Purple and ourselves were going at it around the same time. We did it the hard way; a lot of bands that come up now — without sounding like an old man — have it easy. But I still believe that to work hard is the main thing, to lay the foundation. It's like building a house — if you start off at the top, it won't work. This time we've done everything like in the early days. We've gone back to a cheap rehearsal room, the lot, because when you've got a good lifestyle, you can lose the anger that you had in the first place. We noticed it and said 'Straight back, that's it!'

"It's lovely that there are no arguments about what things to do. It's something that none of us really expected. All of us have been in this business a long time, and we all tend to think in terms of our own egos, but not so with Ian. He's a very nice man. But as far as the writing aspect and direction, it wasn't quite right at first, because he's been at it on his own for 11 albums, as a superb player, with his own Gillan band. He was a lot more commercial than us. Doing this album, which was done fairly quickly, we didn't quite know what direction we were in, fully. But, it's worked. Live, he does enjoy doing the older songs. He doesn't particularly like doing the Dio tunes, because with his range, he can sing

more like Ozzy than he can like Ronnie."

"Ronnie was actually quite young and hadn't experienced too many things," Tony continues, in one particularly amusing jab at Dio (Ronnie is older than Tony by at least five years). "Vinny too, was quite new to this. That's when you get the problems. We found out that Ronnie was doing his own solo album, and we felt he was paying more attention to that. Ronnie and Vinny left in the middle of the live album, so we completed and mixed the album on our own." Include the first statement, and there are no less than four inaccuracies there.

Years later, Tony summed up the very early Gillan days. "Coming from Deep Purple, you think, well, I wonder what he's going to sound like on this stuff? Because at first, when we started writing the songs, we never heard what Ian was going to do. He didn't sing, because he had a problem with his throat. He had to keep quiet, because he had this node on his throat. So [laughs], the first rehearsals, he didn't sing anything. He was there, but he didn't sing. So we thought, God, I wonder what he's going to sound like when he does sing? So really, the first times we heard him sing was when we were actually recording the album."

Tony was typically effusive about Ian in his press duties at the time. "We went through a whole list of candidates for the vocal position, including people like Robert Plant and David Coverdale, before finding out that Ian was available and interested. It's been a perfect match. His voice fits our music and Terry and I feel much more relaxed having a singer with Ian's range. He has such an incredibly powerful voice — his shriek is legendary. He makes us play even louder than before. That's one of the reasons that the new album is so good. It may be the loudest album we've ever done. It is a back-to-basics album for us. It took us only four weeks to record, which is about a quarter of the time we've been using on our recent albums. Working that quickly took us back to the same sound and the same musical atmosphere that we had on our first album. In fact, this record is very close in style to that LP."

"He's all right; a bit off the wall," notes Geezer, on Gillan. "He was fine as a person to get on with, but his lifestyle is a bit strange. He insisted on living in a tent [laughs], when we were doing the album. And he had his own boat there so he could go sailing every day. And he definitely likes his booze."

Actually, there were apparently two tents, one for Ian and one for his golf clubs — guarding his golf clubs at night has been cited

Hans Arne Nakrem

as one of the reasons he stayed in the tent. One night, Ian decided not to stay in the tent, so the guys told him that a fox was tearing it apart. Ian went out, tripped some wires and the tent exploded. As well, the guys had rigged up an exploding soccer ball for Ian, and had also arranged some wires to trip off explosives as he drove up the drive to The Manor.

"He was just being Ian," laughs Geezer, when asked why Ian was living in a tent. "And we blew his tent up and we sunk his boat. I think that was about enough [laughs]. He crashed Bill's car so we got revenge by sinking his boat."

With respect to work on the album, Ian, who busied himself with crossword puzzles (he also penned ream after ream of Deep Purple lyrics, often in collaboration with Roger Glover), "wrote all the lyrics and all the tunes, all the melodies" for *Born Again*. Except one.

Says Geezer, "I just came up with the idea for 'Disturbing the Priest.' I think I wrote that one, but [Ian] would like to work on his own. He didn't really want any help and you didn't really see what lyrics he had done until they were ready to be sung. So you couldn't really change them [laughs], once he had done them."

"You practically have to live out of each other's pockets in a band like this," reflects Geezer. "So you have to have an unwritten code among you in respect to others' feelings. It was a shame with the old lineup, really; it was a clash of personalities. Basically, Ronnie couldn't take criticism. I think Tony and I are very egotistical. We don't take anything from anybody. Then again, the demands we make are not that bad. We like to level with everybody. Ian realizes that and in fact, he's told us a few things. He doesn't have to prove anything, and neither does Bev. Bev is not exactly wanting for money. We just get on well together."

The Bev of which Butler speaks is Bev Bevan

of Move and Electric Light Orchestra fame, who was tapped to be Sabbath's touring drummer after Bill fell off the wagon hard. Tony enthused at the time that Bevan was in fact more of a hard rocker than one might conjecture from his work with ELO, and that in his Move days they used to call him The Birmingham Basher for his hard-hitting style.

"Working with this band has been incredibly easy," offered Ian, back in the thick of the situation. "I've never been able to write so easily. We went into the studio and in the first week we were able to complete six songs. My lyrics just naturally fit into their music. One day I was working on a song called 'Death Warmed Up,' and the pieces just fell together. I'm not exactly new or naive about this business, and I've gone through my dry spells with groups before, but I can honestly say that I've never experienced as creative a period as I have working with Sabbath. That's because we are each one quarter of the band. Before, either I was leading a group or I was playing second fiddle to someone. I rarely was equal with the other band members. We all have the same sense of humor and the same way of looking at the world. I don't really know that much about their problems with Ozzy Osbourne or Ronnie Dio, but I know our relationship has been very warm and exciting. I'm willing to become part of the band. I have no desire to dominate the scene. We're not going to do any of my old songs. I just couldn't see Sabbath playing 'Smoke on the Water' or 'Child in Time' on stage. On the other hand, I'll be very pleased to do the Sabbath anthems."

Bill was around for the making of the album, but his drinking got him in trouble again. "He started off being [sober]," says Geezer, "but ended up boozing again."

Says Bill, "It's the first album that I did sober,

no drugs, no alcohol. In 1983, I was pretty shaky, learning how to be in the world without a drink. I felt pretty good about my drumming on the album. There's a lot of hidden work I did as a drummer which doesn't necessarily come through on the tracks. And that kind of means something to me, even if other people can't hear it [laughs]. I know it's on there. To me, it's a victory album, in the sense that I managed to do that. Because my primary objective was being sober. So doing it sober, even though I was flipping out from time to time because I didn't know what was going on with me and I had to be rushed to the hospital a couple of times . . . because I didn't know that living in the new world was difficult. I didn't understand the road maps yet.

"I think I was in there about 60 days without

Paul Sheehan

Paul She

a drink. I'd relapsed a couple of times before that and I think this was my ninth attempt at trying to be sober. So there I am, 60 days, maybe 90 days, without a drink and absolutely just totally insane. But at the same time playing drums. I felt that Tony and Geezer were again incredible. I'm born again as well, and there were really good power licks, power drives. The biggest change was the fact that Ian Gillan was on that album and doing vocals. I guess my biggest fear was, could Ian do Sabbath-like lyrics? I didn't feel really invested, that it was Sabbath. I felt like three members of Black Sabbath and Ian. But he has a greater voice and is just a nice guy, a good rock 'n' roller, one of the guys. But I thought it was a bit of a mismatch. So when Ian started working on the lyrics and the melodies, some of them were phenomenally good. I'm an enthusiast for melodies myself. So a lot of Ian's melodies, I just went 'Man, you know, wow, I wouldn't have gone there.' I had a lot of respect for that. But I went through the same thing as with

Ronnie. I had always been used to Ozzy's, Geezer's, or my own lyrics. Ronnie has great melodies, and then he started to do lyrics for Sabbath songs, and I felt that they were putting themselves out of context. It felt like it was out of Ian's realm to sing specifically about some of the things he was doing. And I had the sense that he might be throwing his true self away in order to make the album work. And I had a feeling Ronnie was doing some compromising when he had done *Heaven and Hell,* because some of the songs he had been doing with Rainbow, the lyrics were different. And suddenly we have two incredibly talented people singing these great melodies, and I had lost that lyrical connection I was used to with Geezer's lyrics, since I was a teenager. I almost felt that we were jumping on our own bandwagon. Because by '83, a lot of bands had established themselves playing metal, especially from the American west coast. So we were having to jump on our own bandwagon to attain success. Other than that, I thought it

was a pretty darn rocking album."

Indeed Ozzy proclaimed, "*Born Again* is the best thing I've heard from Sabbath since the original group broke up." And Geezer was sounding at least a little sympathetic to his old mate. "When I saw Ozzy, we both had those live albums to deal with; we were both going through our own miseries. We couldn't afford not to release *Live Evil*, and Ozzy was forced into making *Speak of the Devil*. I think it was seeing Ozzy like that that brought back the old Sabbath spark!"

"It's all very simple," explains Tony, recounting the situation with Bill coming back into the band and then out again for the tour, very much like what happened post-*Heaven and Hell*. "He came back to play on *Born Again*, after having left the band in Denver two years before. The main reason he left was because he was an alcoholic, basically, and he wanted to try and be cured. He went to get himself into a hospital, and be under supervision, which he needed to be. But we wanted Bill back, and he said he would love to do it. We got a hold of him and he looked absolutely great. And, we were pleased to see him looking so good. We went in to record the album, and he had a few things like a divorce come up, so of course he started drinking again. Anyway, he was again shackled to it and went back to square one. And, he couldn't find the proper help in England, because of where we were recording; the AA and things like that are not as strong there as they are over here. So, he just had to get back into a hospital. It's very sad. And he clearly wouldn't have been able to handle the road; he's a great friend and we couldn't see him go through all that again."

"I felt quite detached from everybody because I was really trying hard to be sober, and I hadn't yet learned," reflects Bill. "The booze, man, it looked so good to me. So there were daily temptations. And that's no put down on Ian [presumably Bill is referring to Ian's drinking]. That's just where Ian was at. I felt really good about what I did with the album, in between my panic disorder and having to be rushed to the hospital [laughs]. The guys were going, 'What's going on with him?' Now, I found that years later, and I don't have those conditions anymore. It's called agoraphobia. And I didn't know that the panic attacks were stemming from that. And of

course, I've been treated for agoraphobia years and years and years ago. It's actually the fear of feeling fear. That's its exact definition. Isn't that weird? [laughs]. But when I finished my drum tracks, I got drunk. What I couldn't come to terms with was touring sober. It had been tough enough to make the record sober. Touring sober scared me to death. So I had some more misery in front of me until I learned how to be able to tour sober. And since then, I've done many tours sober now.

"When Oz was asked to leave — and I'm going back a little bit here — the way that we had the spider web if you like, or this very fragile system that we had, was disturbed. As one might disturb a bird sanctuary. And so, the result of that was I withdrew a lot, from bringing ideas to the foreground. And I also recognized that Geezer withdrew. I saw the same kind of thing going on with *Born Again*. I don't want to be disrespectful to Ronnie or to Ian, but it's just not the same without Ozzy there. That situation allows everyone to bring

far more to the table. And I think there's a lot more energy, period. But Ian was fine, as far as I could tell. I mean, he liked to get a little bit crazy, but I just took that as normality. He was there every morning working on stuff, and way early in the morning. Ian is up and ready to go."

"Oh, I hate the album cover!" says Bill. He grimaces recalling the garish red devil-baby on purple background, chosen to represent *Born Again*, and apparently given the ok by Tony. "After I finished doing my part in *Born Again*, I drank again. So I got drunk and didn't actually see the album cover again until maybe six to nine months later. I thought, Oh man, give me a break!" Ian kept telling the press that he puked when he saw it for the first time. But Tony quipped gamely, "When you see the cover, you know we're not talking about born-again Christians! It refers to the new lineup, which makes us feel rejuvenated — that's all. At one point, we were considering having a cross on the cover, but we felt that might give the wrong impression."

And once the record started turning, things were still . . . ugly. *Born Again*'s sound is harsh, the production powerful but turgid, drums like cannons, the guitars drowning but taking a few would-be survivors with the first swamping of the ship. The band themselves are pretty much in agreement that the sound sucks.

In response to accusations from Ian that Geezer went in and ruined the mix, Geezer exclaims, "That's a load of crap. I'm the one who was saying that it sounded awful. Gillan went on holiday so he wasn't even there. Gillan did his vocals and left on holiday for about six months, so he doesn't know what he's talking about. I was saying the bottom end was too heavy and that it was too bassy. I got sick of telling everyone that it didn't sound right. When I was proved right, Gillan came back and said, 'What the hell is wrong with this?' A lot of people blamed me because I was the one who wasn't there at the time."

Robin Black was the engineer on the album, brought back for the first time since *Technical Ecstasy*. Explains Geezer, "He's the ultimate person in charge, engineering-wise. But I think he was easily swayed. He listened to too many of us. It should've just been him in charge and

that's it. I've got the original tapes. I heard what it should've been like and then when it came out it was horrible. I think we all went on holiday at the end. We were glad to get out of the way. The songs on it are great, it's just a really bad mix; I'd love to be able to go back and totally remix that album. I really do love the songs, especially 'Disturbing the Priest,' 'Zero the Hero,' and 'Born Again,' the song."

"In the end, I hated that they gave it an '80s sound," was Bill's curious comment (it's more akin to something from the Dark Ages, say 1050–1100 AD). "It's like, my God, don't do that. Especially, don't do it to my drums [laughs]. But my drums have an '80s sound and it really dates the album. The drums need to be far, far drier than what they are. They're way too wet. And because of that, they get lost inside. When you have depth, like bass, or layers and layers and layers of Tony Iommi, then the drums need to have a tougher sound."

While it sounds likely that Tony used more tracks for his guitars than ever before on this album, Bill disagrees. "Tony usually utilizes a

number of tracks. It was kind of a delicate mix. I would have loved to have heard Geezer and my bass drums a hell of a lot more. I heard my drums when I laid the drum tracks. Because I was sober, I spent a lot more time working on my sound. And the drum sounds, before anything was laid, they were really, really solid. I was extremely pleased with the way they were sounding. But I'm not blaming anybody. It just turned out to be a bit washy."

Tony summed up the situation this way. "We never heard the pressed version because we were in Europe touring at the time, and it was out, and by the time we heard it, it was Number 3 or something. It was all distorted and sounded awful, and then we find out later that nobody had oĸ'd the pressing — no one had oĸ'd it! I found out later that someone had had the lacquers, and if you leave them too long,

they go off and the sound goes funny before they press them. Apparently they had sat around for too long, so when they pressed it up, the sound was all distorted. We couldn't figure it out. These tapes we've got sound good, but you put the album on and it sounds horrible!"

But no one was complaining about the songs. *Born Again*, issued August 7, 1983, opens on a rock 'n' rolling note, "Trashed" valiantly trying to keep up with "Neon Knights" and "Turn Up the Night" but just falling short. Like those two anthems, the song is melodic but heavy, and within this mix, mercilessly so. Tony turns in a piercing arch-Iommi solo at the end that caps off an amusing introduction to this unlikely marriage of metal minds. "Trashed" contained by far the silliest lyric yet on a Black Sabbath song, and it is Gillan's favorite song on the album.

"The stuff we've done on the album is the most commercial material Sabbath's ever done," said Gillan, while working on the album. "That's not to say that the band has sold out its roots; rather, it means that the material is excellent! The writing I'm doing with the band is less complicated than the things they did with Ronnie. The gothic images and the Greek mythology things have been worked to death. I'd rather get a touch more sex in there and a little less mythology. I'm not going to copy Ozzy or Ronnie. They had their style and I have mine. It just so happens that Tony and Terry had quite a bit of material they had written that they hadn't used because it didn't work with Ronnie's operatic singing style. They've dug up some of those tunes and we're working on them."

"'Trashed' was about Ian crashing Bill's car," explains Tony. "At the studio we were at, which was Richard Branson's home, there was a go-cart track, and we all had our own individual cars that we had bought for the band, just to use for the tour. And Ian decides to get pissed one night and take Bill's car around the go-cart track. Of course, it wasn't a very good idea. He completely wrote it off, smashed it up, it caught on fire, and that was it. And Ian decides to write a track called 'Trashed' [laughs]. This was a proper car. We had bought four cars for the band to use while we were recording, and for the tour. And instead of Ian taking the car that he had, he decides to take Bill's. Not a very good idea." The cars were reported to be Ford Granadas, and, contrary to the above, rented, not bought.

"Trashed" was issued as a single (it didn't chart) and was also one of the compositions chosen

SO WE WENT FOR A BEER, ME AND THE VICAR; WE BECAME VERY GOOD FRIENDS.

from Ian's past to rerecord for Ian's *Gillan's Inn* album, a sort of Gillan-commandeered tribute record to his 40 years in the business put together mostly in Buffalo, New York.

Next up was the progressive and mad "Disturbing the Priest" (originally considered as the title for the album), preambled by a spot of noise called "Stonehenge." There's something forced about the track. It's sprung and

AS ONE MIGHT DISTURB A BIRD SANCTUARY

209

then shot, a little over the top in its doomy, evil tonality, especially given the fact that there's Ian singing a spooky satanic lyric.

Says Ian, "'Disturbing the Priest' has a lovely story about it. Because I remember getting a phone call from Tony Iommi, and from Al Dutton, who was their tour manager at the time, also my tour manager during the Gillan days, and they were in some town in Mexico. And Al says, 'I've got to go. We're being run out of town.' It was a Catholic town, and they had taken offense. They'd taken the title of this track, 'Disturbing the Priest,' as absolute clearcut evidence that these guys were the Antichrist, anti-God, anti-church and everything else. Of course, it's not true at all. I mean, I never saw anything nasty about them in the year I spent with them. But the story behind 'Disturbing the Priest' is very simple. I was doing the vocals one day and the studio door was open, at Richard Branson's recording studio in Oxfordshire. And I became aware of the vicar from the church next door, who was standing in the control room. I went in and said, 'Hi, good afternoon. What can I do for you?' And he said, 'My, isn't this amazing.' He said 'Look, I've only come to ask if we can organize our times. Because I'm having choir practice at the moment and your music is quite loud, and we can't concentrate on our pitching.' And I said, 'Well, I'm so sorry; of course, we'll stop right now. How long is your choir practice?' And he said, 'Tuesdays and Thursdays from, I don't know, four until six or something.' And I said, 'We'll stop, straight away.' And he said 'No, no, just close the door. We can change if you want.' And I said, 'No, no,

we'll keep the doors closed. And we won't make any loud music between four and six on Tuesdays and Thursdays. No problem at all.' And he said, 'Really, that's very kind of you. Fancy a beer?' And I said, 'I'll see you in the pub at six o'clock' [laughs]. So we went for a beer, me and the vicar; we became very good friends. So I told the guys the story, and when I saw Geezer in the studio, and Geezer Butler said, 'Well, that's a great story.' It's a play on words, of course, disturbing the peace/disturbing the priest. And it was out of nothing but respect for the fact that they were having choir practice."

The whole gong (or cymbal or plate or something or other) in water technique from "After Forever" is revived for the "Stonehenge" segment. "We wanted a sound like a bell that lost its pitch," says Bill. "And how you do that, is you take a metal plate, hit it, and then as you lower it into water, it changes pitch. So that's real simple, fun stuff. For the lyric, I think there was a bit of a barney going on, a barney being a bit of an argument, with the local priest. There might have been more going on, but doing that album, I was basically hanging on to the bedpost, trying not to drink, you know?"

Side 1 of *Born Again* closed with a massive earthmover called "Zero the Hero," preceded by 48 seconds of murk known as "The Dark." Arguably the band's heaviest song ever, its circular riff has been cited as the inspiration for the smash Guns N' Roses hit "Paradise City." Ian's amusing, halting, English-as-a-second-language phrasing, most prevalent on the Gillan albums, is in full force, his poetry being ironic, all its meaning veiled in subtle wisecracks, the lines quite memorable and repeatable.

"'Zero the Hero' is one of my favorites," offers Bill. "I had a bunch of fun on the song because I love that pace, a 'Heaven and Hell' feel, a really solid pace, doomy, laid-back. It's just enough where it can sound really heavy, like 'Into the Void' or 'The Writ.' Geezer was experimenting with those very loud bass chords at the beginning, and it was like, 'Hell, what's that?!' From my point of view, it was a Geezer lick that kicked it all off and we just threw it all down."

Side 2 opens with a jarring title, "Digital Bitch" combining two words that seem out of step with Sabbath themes. Ian's lyric about some spoiled broad (she's real, but Ian ain't talking), doesn't do much to help Sabbathize the song. Tony's riff is richly dark but powerful — and with those production values, well, Tori Amos would sound doom metal. Tony gleefully drenches the songs in very electric soloing while Ian howls and screams and improvises. The chorus is practically punk rock circa London in '76. A good, solid track, helping to make this record the well-regarded dark horse that it is.

Next up is "Born Again," the album's only ballad, and even this sounds locked in the dungeons at Clearwell, not to mention growling and heavy and nasty.

Recalls Bill, "I went into the studio to watch Ian do his thing. I watched him go in with pencil and paper. And I love lyricists, so I thought, OK, I wanted to experience this. And I watched him put the vocals and the melodies and the lyrics together for 'Born Again.' And he went to places I would never have dreamed of going. I just went, 'Maaaannn! You went there?!' So it was fun for me to watch. Ian was outstanding on the slower songs. His blues influence was really obvious, shines through really good."

"Hot Line" is quite similar to "Digital Bitch," but Bill's rumbling drum intro and gangland rhythm pushes it into more malevolent terrain.

Ian is manic on it as well, while Tony and Geezer lay down a steady riff of doom — Tony resolutely slashing, Geezer plying that one-track AC/DC pulse, namely the "teenaged eighth notes" made famous by Roger Glover.

Born Again closes with "Keep It Warm," an excellent dirge that breaks into a squishy melody come chorus time. With this mix, the song positively thrashes slow-motion in enveloping quicksand. The tone on Tony's guitar is agonizing, and Ian responds by howling in blues-battered pain.

"That was just a wonderful form of self-expression — pure Sabbath," opines Bill, "Ozzy is the singer for Sabbath — what we were all doing was just having an interlude. That song

Paul Sheehan

sentable extra track called 'The Fallen.' Nothing B-level about this one, with the band swirling up a metal cauldron, spiced with a curious double-speed chorus that is as charming as it is unexpected. What's more, against an album chock-full of bold soloing, the succinct but carnal solo here might have been the record's best. Upwards of five additional tracks are rumored to have been written, one being the aforementioned "Death Warmed Up." Curiously, Canadian act Kick Axe had been asked to submit songs to Sabbath at this time. Four tracks were quickly written, two ending up with King Kobra, one to "an artist who shall remain unnamed," and one . . . well, guitarist Larry Gilstrom is not sure. He's never heard *Born Again*, or, unsurprisingly, the outtake tracks.

Born Again somehow found its way to Number 4 in the UK (that country's high regard for Gillan might account for the deep placement), but only Number 39 in the States. "I thought it would've done better than that," laments Tony, "but there again, I was disappointed, and I had the album in front of me, so the kids were bound to be disappointed. When we left the studio, the album sounded fine to us. It came out while we were in Europe on tour, and I had helped with the album pressings, up to that point. But I hadn't heard it. In fact, Bev found the LP, and said, 'Have you heard the album?' and I said, 'No, I haven't played it yet.' He said, 'Put it on, and have a listen, then,' so I put it on, and it sounded bloody awful! The quality of the production is dreadful! I just couldn't believe it. I just don't know what happened. Nobody seems to have an answer."

Incredibly, at this juncture, says Tony, "Ozzy wanted to get the band back together, yes. He came over, and asked if we wanted to reform

was pure grunge [laughs], and Tony Iommi was the godfather of grunge. That was just one of those amazing, dirge-y riffs Tony used to come out with. I like the way Ian sings 'Born Again.' But my particular favorite is 'Keep It Warm'. . . . *rat*! [laughs, referring to the inexplicable syllable Ian adds to the chorus lyric]. It reminds me of a blues standard, and I like playing the old blues things. We did a similar thing on *Heaven and Hell* — 'Lonely Is the Word,' also a blues feel. Not unusual for Sabbath, considering its mid-sixties roots."

And that was it for *Born Again*, although bootlegs of the album's demos circulate, including what is basically a finished and prethe band. Because, basically, all the disagreements that we'd had had gone by the wayside. And, he realized that we were true friends to him, and not just saying things or getting on his back because we hated him. We really all got along great, you know, because we really love him. But it wasn't really the right time."

Unfortunately, the lasting memory of this strange era for the band — apart from getting one lethal head-smack of an album out of it — is of Ian Gillan rummaging around in the dry ice for his lyric sheets. Ian was obviously casual about doing his homework. Tony however defended Ian by saying that he was new and using cue sheets, and that Ozzy had done it all the time. As well, fans complained that Ian's wardrobe made no adjustment for his new posting, that his accursed bongos were inappropriate, and that encoring a Sabbath show with "Smoke on the Water" was beneath this mighty institution ("Apache" by Iommi's fave The Shadows, was also occasionally pulled out of the bag). Speaking years later, Ian said with a laugh that he was the worst singer Sabbath ever had, and that the fans spent the year of his reign in utter confusion.

There were also reports of lousy vocal performances. Said Ian in his own defense, "Even our first night in the U.S., we had a bad time at the Meadowlands, but next night, we change the monitor mix. I've never used monitors in my life — hate 'em. But Tony and Geezer wanted to hear the voice. I say, about 99 percent of the time, it's a ghastly sound. Having gone through three mixers, we now have one who knows his ass from his elbow. And we have a decent sound. I never do sound checks — I refuse. After doing one or two, I realize I get into it, very strong, start singing and all your energy explodes, and then suddenly you're down again. I really like the idea of

Hans Arne Nakrem

WE THOUGHT THE DWARF WAS IN IMPECCABLY BAD TASTE BUT WE WERE OUTVOTED. DON REFUSED TO GET RID OF HIM. I WAS LAUGHING MY FUCKING SOCKS OFF.

coming to the show just ready to explode, not with my energy dissipated like that."

"Ian's such a loon that he makes every day in the studio or on the road a wonderful experience," reflected Tony in press duties during the tour. "It's not like Ozzy, who was a rather scary loon — Ian is just a little crazy. He's a barrel of laughs. He still has one of the most incredible voices I've ever heard. I remember listening to Deep Purple on stage when Ian was with them and being floored by the power of his singing. He has the perfect heavy metal voice. You can never play too loud when Ian's singing. I can feel the difference out there every night. The crowds are responding to us with more enthusiasm since Ozzy left. With our type of music, you have to have patience. If you keep playing long enough, the taste-makers will rediscover you. Metal was out of style for a long while, but now it seems that there are more, good hard rock bands around than ever before. I have to believe that Sabbath was a major influence for most of them."

The *Born Again* tour skipped the UK but blanketed Europe and North America. In Europe, Sabbath picked up Pretty Maids as openers in Scandinavia and then Diamond Head for the rest of the jaunt, a few dates augmented by Girlschool. In North America, Nazareth, Quiet Riot, Night Ranger and Helix did the honors, the tour ending in March of '84. Most of the new album was played at one point or another, with "Trashed" being a notable omission from documented set lists.

Out on the road, Sabbath was the sorry subject of the much ridiculed Stonehenge debacle. "It had nothing to do with me," says Geezer with a laugh. "In fact, I was the one who thought it was really corny. We had Sharon Osbourne's dad, Don Arden, managing us. He came up with the idea of having the stage set be

Stonehenge. He wrote the dimensions down and gave it to our tour manager. He wrote it down in meters but he meant to write it down in feet. The people who made it saw 15 meters instead of 15 feet. It was 45 feet high and it wouldn't fit on any stage anywhere so we just had to leave it in the storage area. It cost a fortune to make, but there was not a building on earth you could fit it into. I last saw it on the docks in New York on the same tour. They were probably thrown into the Atlantic Ocean. They'll think it's Atlantis."

"It was the biggest bloody thing I've ever seen," adds Tony, curiously blaming Geezer! "It was an idea that Geezer had had. 'Oh, what about doing Stonehenge for a stage set?' And they went away and built this Stonehenge. Of course, we never heard anything or seen anything of it until it turned up at the rehearsal. Which, we hired the NEC, here in Birmingham, which is a big place, a very big building, where they held all the concerts. And this thing arrived and we couldn't believe the size of it. I said, 'Bloody 'ell, where are we going to fit this?!' We ended up only doing two shows with it, and they had to be open air, because we couldn't fit it anywhere, with the full set. We ended up taking just a half set around on tour with us. We did Reading Festival and we did a festival in Ireland, where we could use the whole thing. We took it all to the States, but we just couldn't set it up. We couldn't set the huge columns up in the back; it was too much. We told them to quickly get rid of it. We tried to give it to someone to stick in the desert. But where it went, I don't know."

Ian remembers the events a little differently. "Well, normally when I tell the story it lasts about a week," chuckles Ian. "I don't know where to pick it up. Basically it starts with the idea that we had. As we completed the album,

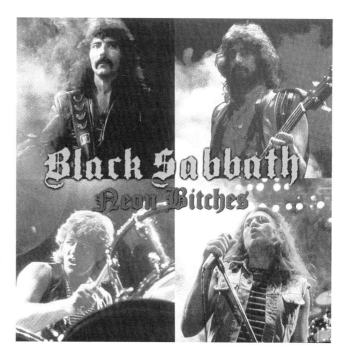

we went to a company in Birmingham called LSD, Light and Sound Design. They said, 'Does anybody have any ideas for a stage set?' We all stared at each other, trying to think of something and Geezer goes, 'Stonehenge.' The bloke said, 'What a great idea. How do you visualize it?' Geezer says, 'Life-size, of course.' They built an exact replica of Stonehenge, which is huge, out of fiberglass and carbon fiber, in sections. No one gave it any thought that we could only get it into two of the halls and even then it was only three [sections of it]. The rest of them are in containers in a dock somewhere and they have been for the last 20 years. I remember it being set up at the first gig at Toronto, Maple Leaf Gardens. We had hired the place out for a week to rehearse for the first gig."

"You can see most of this on *Spinal Tap*, because I told the guy who was the associate scriptwriter this entire story. *Spinal Tap*'s budget wasn't as big as Black Sabbath's, so they produced a miniature Stonehenge and we produced a life-size one, which filled God knows how many containers which came over by ship. We could only get three of them up in Maple Leaf Gardens and the rest stayed in the truck."

"I remember that there was a dwarf hanging around. The manager looked around like, 'Why is this guy hanging around here?' And then Don Arden, the manager, decided there was going to be a dwarf dressed up as the baby on the cover, with little yellow horns and yellow fingernails. The dwarf would appear at the top of the stones screaming, get to the middle, and then the Druids would come out, which were basically the roadies in robes — very convincing apart from the Reeboks under the robes. And the bells would toll and chime and the dwarf would fall off the back of the Stonehenge onto a pile of mattresses and then the show would start. We thought the dwarf was in impeccably bad taste but we were outvoted. Don refused to get rid of him. I was laughing my fucking socks off. I don't think a Black Sabbath show on tour the first night should start with the singer and the drummer rolling on the ground laughing about what was going on onstage. We knew what was going to happen, and perhaps nobody else did. Because the dwarf came out dressed in the leotard, got to the middle of the stage and fell off backwards 20 feet as the baby scream flanged on the tape, and he disappeared into the smoke, and the Druids came out for the toll. But the screaming didn't disappear as it normally did because somebody had removed the mattresses. We didn't see the dwarf anymore. I think he bounced right out the door."

14

"THIS IS GETTING A BIT RIDICULOUS"

– Seventh Star

Did Ian Gillan quit Black Sabbath or was he fired? It's neither here nor there, because the real reason Ian left was that a lucrative deal was struck to put the original Mark II Deep Purple together again, which resulted in the highly suc-

> BLACK SABBATH HAS AN INCREDIBLE REPUTATION TO LIVE UP TO, AND I'D QUICKER DISSOLVE THE GROUP THAN DO SOMETHING THAT WOULD HURT SABBATH'S LEGACY.

Ian has further stated that he signed on for one Black Sabbath album and one tour; probably quite true, and all parties probably thought that wise and sensible. But to the press he would often add that everybody knew he was going back to Deep Purple after that, which is not true. In no way was that deal sealed. In the months before *Born Again* was birthed the band's discussions were at various times, preliminary, partial, rumor-filled and supposition-based; although it is true that real attempts at progress were made. Talk to any of the Rainbow guys and they'll tell you it was all quite last minute, although the speed with which *Perfect Strangers* emerged leaves cause for wonder — the album was issued not 14 months after both *Born Again* and Rainbow's swansong (until reunion) *Bent Out of Shape*. Rainbow was part of the brew because both Ritchie Blackmore and Roger Glover were needed to make Mark II complete. In the mix, there was also talk that Geezer did not want to tour for more than six weeks, against the wishes of the others, and that a certain onstage tension could be seen in Ian's performances, leading people to believe Ian wasn't happy with his lot.

In any event, Ian was out and the tour ended rather abruptly. More dates were being planned since *Born Again* was doing well and a video for "Zero the Hero" had just been issued. The promotion machine ground to a halt and Tony and Geezer found themselves with less of a band than ever, given that Bill wasn't even part of the mix at this point. However, once

Bev Bevan had also departed for ELO II, Bill's name was brought up for whatever was to happen next, be it a Sabbath album, a solo album from Tony, or a completely new band situation. Then, finally, Geezer would leave the fold as well, effectively putting Sabbath as a valid construct on ice.

The plan thereafter was to get an unknown to fill the vocalist role, the band beginning its serious search with Ron Keel of Keel. Next, one David Donato was seriously given a shot, the situation resulting in a premature photo session and a full-blown feature in *Kerrang!* on David as the Sabs' new frontman. Fading from view after a few months, David went on and formed White Tiger, who issued one album before he would disappear from the music scene to build motorcycles. Bill, living in L.A., was jogging regularly and using a rowing machine, having emerged from what he calls a four-month depression. Having apparently quit drinking, he said yes immediately when asked to re-join, having missed the friendship of his mates. But just as quickly as he "joined," Bill now found himself bolting. "When I got sobered up a few months later, which is the last time I've had a drink, I tried to involve myself once again with the fellas. David was a nice guy, really nice person. But again, I wasn't getting it, and had to face the truth and say goodbye. I just said, 'No. This is twice now I've tried to leave.'"

So with Bill out of the picture again, next up for serious consideration was the mysterious Jeff Fenholt, who was wrapped up in both the post-Keith Relf Armageddon and a possible band with the remnants of Rainbow and Elf. The drummer of choice was Eric Singer from Lita Ford's band (Tony was briefly engaged to Lita), soon of Kiss and Alice Cooper fame. Demos exist of Fenholt working on songs that

David Lee Wilson

Eric Singer

would make their way, quite altered for legal reasons, to *Seventh Star*, with Geoff Nicholls being extremely involved in the new material. At this point, you had Tony and the unjustly invisible Nicholls, and that's it for Sabs, with Tony starting to see the light that this collection of players about L.A. was not Black Sabbath.

BLACK SABBATH

Their Satanic Majesties... 15 years on.
The complete story–exclusive interviews!

Next to be part of the brew, and to stick around for the eventual record, was bassist Dave "The Beast" Spitz, important as well, given that he was the link to *Seventh Star*'s producer, Jeff Glixman. Glixman had produced Americade's unreleased second album, *Rock Hard*.

"This is getting a bit ridiculous," said Tony in late 1984, after having dispensed with Donato. "We thought we were ready to begin recording our new album, but then we realized the band really wasn't as good as we wanted it to be. Black Sabbath has an incredible reputation to live up to, and I'd quicker dissolve the group than do something that would hurt Sabbath's legacy. David acted like a star from the day we met him. There's nothing wrong with that, but we've had enough trouble with egomaniacs

over the last few years. We want someone who's confident, yet we're also looking for a bloke we can get on with. The answer may be to find somebody British."

Intriguingly, Tony goes on to say that there were clashes between Donato and the producer — none other than Bob Ezrin. "It was a matter of opinion, pure and simple. We want a singer to fit in to our approach, while some of the people we've had in the band recently want us to basically become their backing band. I've been involved with Sabbath for 15 years, and I'm not about to let anyone new come in and tell me how things should be done. We're a very British band, and we've learned that we need to have British blood in the group. That's what we tried to do with Ian Gillan last year, but Ian's mind was everywhere but in Sabbath. The stories of the Deep Purple reunion had already begun, and we knew that his tenure with us would be short. We were located in California at the time that Ian split, so we decided to see if the local talent would meet our needs. We thought we had found the answer with David, but unfortunately that didn't work out. Now we'll head home to England and find a singer who can be with us for the next ten years. We're looking for someone new who can come in and blow everyone's mind. The days with Ozzy are a thing of the past. Our future lies with finding the best young vocalist in Britain and showing everyone that Black Sabbath is still the best heavy metal band in the world."

Well, he wasn't young, but he was British. The job fell upon none other than Glenn Hughes to put the crowning touch to the collection of souls that would create *Seventh Star*. In fact, in many ways the record is more of a Hughes record than a Sabbath one, or at minimum, an Iommi-Hughes album, of which

there are sort of two to date, *The 1996 DEP Sessions*, issued in '04, and *Fused*, issued in '05. Glenn's been involved with many projects, but his most famous is Deep Purple, for which he recorded three studio albums, *Burn, Stormbringer* and *Come Taste the Band*. However, Hughes first made waves with Trapeze, whose *You Are the Music . . . We're Just the Band* album Glenn calls a turning point in his musical development. "With that one, I was finding my legs as a writer, writing more in the soul, R&B heavy rock style that I've been known for. *Medusa* was my first stab at singing lead vocals for a whole record, and the first black-and-white album. I was only 18 and I was learning my trade."

Glenn charts the origins of Trapeze, leading to his mixing with Birmingham's finest. "I'm from Cannock, which is near Stafford, 70 miles north of Birmingham, and in '69, in the Midlands of England, from that era in the north of England, there was still a heavy contingent of American bands like The Beach Boys, and The Beatles and the whole harmony thing. Between '67 and '69 there really wasn't much intense hard rock. And then Zeppelin and Cream, in '68, started to raise their heads, and when we started putting Trapeze together in early '69, we were also on the Moody Blues' label and the Moody Blues were extremely mellow. We were sort of in the same genre as they were, with the big harmonies influence and Hammonds and the Mellotrons. That black-and-white record and that first band was only around for nine months before we switched into the trio. We realized that America was going to be our calling ground and we needed to go hard rock.

"I'd sort of known Robert Plant from bands before Trapeze. I was in a band called Finders Keepers which was the same sort of harmony thing. And John Bonham, I met. He came to one of my shows with Finders Keepers, and then with the trio as Trapeze, we would play at Mother's in Birmingham. Zeppelin played there, Black Sabbath, every major band. I played there half a dozen times, and every time, John Bonham would come and he would sit in with Trapeze. And also I'd see in the audience all of Black Sabbath, and there was Roy Wood, Jeff Lynne, all the local bands. Because Trapeze were a cult band that was about to make it big — and then of course, I left to join Deep Purple. But yes, Bonzo was a really good friend of mine. Apparently Judas Priest were there too. Actually they opened up for Purple, as The Flying Hat Band, Glenn Tipton's band before Judas Priest. A lot of great bands came from Birmingham."

So the roots go deep, Hughes being hired on for some of the same reasons that Dave Walker was looked at — hometown roots. But Hughes was also known as one of the greatest voices in the business, so high hopes were circulating within Tony's band about the union. The record that was to emerge March 1, 1986, was going to be a Tony Iommi solo album for much of its making, but then changed to the messy Black Sabbath Featuring Tony Iommi at the last minute. Even the acetates for the finished album simply list Tony Iommi as the artist; but then again, the official status of the typed information on these sorts of items is always debatable. The band was to include Tony, Glenn, Dave Spitz, Eric Singer and Geoff Nicholls, Geoff finally getting his due as a member of Black Sabbath. Gordon Copley, there for much of the preliminary stages of the new band concept, was credited as bass player on "No Stranger to Love."

Interesting parallels have been drawn with respect to the cover art of *Seventh Star*. The 1506 copper plate engraving (behind the photo of Tony) by the German Lucas Cranach the Elder is called *The Torment of Saint Antony*. This was the Saint Antony who led an ascetic, monastic life in the deserts of Egypt. Our present Tony, Tony Iommi, had been summarily tormented by the making of this new band and album, and is seen on the cover, standing and looking glum in a desert. As well, there is an instrumental track on the album called "Sphinx (The Guardian)" and the title track, "Seventh Star," can be fit quite handily to the story of Saint Antony.

"Originally, I was talking about doing a project like I did with my solo album," explains Tony, addressing the contents beyond the art, "where I used ten different singers, that kind of idea. But it didn't materialize. Glenn came along, and we ended up using Glenn on all of them. But *Seventh Star* was very, very difficult. I'd written most of the stuff before we got together with Glenn; then Glenn came in and sort of sang. But it was very hard in those days because Glenn was going through a serious drug problem. And quite honestly, I wasn't much better [laughs]. But it made it hard to communicate with each other at that time. The difference, when we got together again in '96 . . . bloody 'ell, he was like another person, cleaned up, and he looked good, sang great, of course, as usual. And he was just a pleasure to be around."

All songs were credited to Anthony Iommi, a big disservice to Geoff Nicholls and Glenn Hughes. "Let's just say for contractual reasons I couldn't participate in the credits," explains Hughes, "as with other albums I have done. When you don't see my name, there are reasons for that, which I'm not allowed to discuss because of contracts. I'm being as polite as I can be about it. I've been asked many times, 'Why didn't you get credit on this album?' Simply because I can't really speak about it."

"The album itself was wonderful," continues Glenn. "Tony and I are really good friends. The album was basically recorded in Atlanta and Los Angeles over the period of the summer of '85. It was a good time, and the actual recording of the album was sweet. A lot of people like that record. It was a Tony solo album even when we finished recording it. His management at the time and Warner Brothers just put their heads together and went 'Well, this is a really strong record. We'll tour behind it and call it 'Tony Iommi's Black Sabbath' or whatever. I wasn't singing it, if you can imagine, as a Black Sabbath record! I was singing it as more of a Tony record. I was writing lyrics within that framework as well. It was about the human

condition, which all my songs are. But Tony was really happy with it. But that album was initially his solo album and he was going to have three singers on it, me possibly being one, and Dio and Halford were going to be asked to be the others." Tony, when asked specifically about these plans, draws a blank.

When asked about other major parties to the crime, namely Geoff Nicholls and producer Jeff Glixman, Glenn admits that "the Glixman connection was a little unfocused for me. I wasn't really comfortable working with Glixman for personal reasons. Geoff Nicholls was . . . I can't really say too much about him. He's just a friend of Tony's, really. You know, I'm the kind of guy who will never dish up the dirt, but I think Geoff is Tony's buddy, you know what I'm saying?"

"Well, he was weird," says Glenn, elaborating on Glixman. "He was a troublemaker. And anybody I'd ever known who has worked with Jeff Glixman — I won't name names, but you can look at a discography — have mentioned that he's been a pain in the ass, just a gossipmonger, a troublesome fellow. He was also riddled with the disease of drug addiction that was plaguing the whole music industry in the '70s and '80s. But he was a very strange cat to work with, always pitting Tony and Glenn against each other, and it didn't work because we're very,

Fred

very close. He was up the label's ass, telling lies to the label about this and that, complaining. He's got a lot of problems. *Had.* Once again, he *had* a lot of problems."

With respect to lyrics, Glenn confirms that "In a small way, Nicholls and Glixman helped a little bit. But I came with the bulk of the work, of course." Glenn insists, however, that Nicholls didn't write any of the music — that was Tony's area. Nicholls has provided a lot of detail to the contrary.

On the press trail for the album, Tony defended forming a band with relative un-knowns. "It's all very intentional. Dealing with superstars is a pain in the ass. I didn't want to go through all of that contractual stuff again.

Every time you let somebody in with any kind of a name, it's do this, do that. I just wanted to get out on the road and play. By the time you get through all of the legal stuff, you forgot what you were supposed to be here for. We tried to get the old band back, but it just never seemed to work. I felt if we were going to go out on the road, everything had to be spot on, where we're going to really enjoy ourselves and do it. The last time we went on tour, there were so many problems going on; so much added spice. I wanted to get fresh blood and really get cracking. Have a good go, and really work hard. I like this situation now. I'm seeing fresh vibes come into it. They're really energetic. It makes me feel bloody old! I have to let them play for two hours before I turn on. Wear them down a bit! I much prefer working with somebody when they just want to play. They don't have anything in terms of money or reputation; they just really want something. The so-called 'experienced' people have forgotten how to do it. It's exciting."

"The last time we were all together was for the Live Aid thing," added Tony of the original band's panned gathering for three songs at an ungodly 10 a.m., July 13, 1985. "Which was great. It was disastrous for the band, really, because we didn't have a check or anything, and we didn't know what we were doing. Couldn't hear the monitor, so that was bad. But the event was great. It was quite funny. We started rehearsing and originally we were going to have two nights of rehearsal. That's all. The first night ended up being talk night. We just sat there and talked about old times. It was quite funny; but even then we started having problems. During those two days, it was like going back ten years. We have all become things in our own right. We came together it was like 'Riiippp,' it could work. We could make it work. But we don't. I mean Ozzy's got his own thing; and Bill, the only way he'd get back on stage is in [the original] Black Sabbath; and Geezer is just going to do his solo projects.

"If we ever did get together, it would be quite awkward at first. As we know, just from Live Aid, that there's just so much involved in putting the band together. Just legally. Because we split, now were all individuals, signed to different companies. It's involved, and to make it work, you have to really want it. That's what's so nice about these guys. They're really keen and eager. It's like looking back 15 years. If we put the old band back together, it wouldn't have had it live, because everybody is too . . . mellow. When you actually get together you

realize it was a good idea, but not that good an idea. We had an offer, if we did a tour, of 20 million [laughs]. Which, is quite a bit. But we'd all be suing each other. The money would go there. It's like on some tours, one's got his attorney, one's got his accountant, and you end up having 50 people on the road, and they're all attorneys and accountants. It's bloody ridiculous. I much prefer it this way."

Back to the matter of the platter, *Seventh Star* opens with an adrenaline rush, "In for the Kill" being modern speed metal of a sort, but very un-Sabbath-like. The drum track on this one is highly technical, actually in 7/4 time. The lyric is of a marauding, bloodthirsty king and his forces, and not much more than that, even if it is said to include Vlad the Impaler and Armageddon touchstones. Adds Glenn, "There was the demon and drug stuff in 'In for the Kill'; that wasn't one of my favorites." Glenn obviously seems to imbue that lyric with a sort of battle with drugs metaphor, but it's frankly hard to see. Glenn's vocal is jarring, his twanging Hughes-isms pronounced, not in the least muted, love it or hate it. It was all a bit much to take after two Dio records, one with Ian, and now this. Sabbath as a brand had become a fuzzy thing indeed.

Fred Tollin

Fred

"No Stranger to Love" was next, "Sabbath" turning in a shockingly commercial, very American power ballad, but one that works for two reasons. First, Glenn pours his soul and his consummate and bluesy vocal skills into it; and second, as the song progresses, Tony shades the piece with huge malevolent chords that, if nothing else, cause a chuckle from the shocked metalhead. Nicholls puts a synth wash on top of Glixman's corporate '80s production job, and the two together, along with Singer's dramatic drum track, turn the song into the synthetic beast it is. It is of no surprise that the song was issued as a single, although Spitz laments that the first offering should have been the heaviest song on the album. The video coughed up the shot of Tony for the cover. It also included Bing Crosby's niece Denise (soon to be a major and prolific actress) in the story line and had Geoff Nicholls dressed as a policeman. The austere, film noir video had Tony wandering around an empty, run-down city after the story's broken love affair while a vicious black dog ran around and Denise appeared and disappeared like a ghost tormenting Tony's mind. Not very Sabbatherian, to say the least.

Seventh Star's pace picks up with "Turn to Stone," an acceptable speed rocker with one of Tony's patented melodic but heavy and simple riffs. Eric puts up another storming drum track, while Glenn sings a standard, unremarkable evil woman lyric. Tony's solo isn't much to write home about either.

"Sphinx (The Guardian)" is a little smudge of keyboards before the record's title track shuffles center stage. Arch-Sabbath but also similar to Zeppelin's "Kashmir," this one strikes me as a bit of a second guesser — as in, "We gotta write a typical Sabbath song for this thing." This attitude mars much of the material from the ensuing Tony Martin years, and here, it doesn't help matters that Glenn Hughes isn't a spooky Dio-esque singer. The lyrics came from Geoff Nicholls, who is referring to Armageddon arriving when the seven stars align, although the seventh star has also been equated to the morning star, basically the blazing fall of Lucifer from the heavens. Both make sense here, as does the (unintended) aforementioned interpretation that falls in line with the cover graphic.

"Danger Zone" is perhaps the most successful song on *Seventh Star*, Tony's riff being dark, passionate, potentially accessible, like the very best of what might come on, say, *The Eternal Idol*. This one sounds heartfelt coming from Glenn, in that it is indeed, a drug and damnation lyric similar to Thin Lizzy's "Got to Give it Up" and select sentiments from that band's *Thunder and Lightning*.

A big, boring blues number is next, "Heart Like a Wheel" nonetheless containing a few doomy Iommi stylizations to the predictable idiom, as well as lots of room for Tony to demonstrate his bluesy soloing chops. Geoff Nicholls' lyric draws ever so slightly from a movie he had seen regarding a female race-car driver. Call this one an Iommi showcase though, because it's really so underwritten as to barely exist at all. As well, with this sort of cannon-like drum production, don't look for it to groove.

"Angry Heart" follows, and like "Danger Zone," this is a melancholy rocker that works. Tony and the blues collide best when transformed into something modern and sped up. With Nicholls' Hammond on here, and with Glenn singing, this one's more Deep Sabbath than anything on the caustic and drastic *Born Again* record. Geoff Nicholls tells the story of turning in a lyric about the death of his mother, but says that Jeff Glixman plumped for his own lyric about the death of his dog. Tony weighed in on Nicholls' side and what

Fred Tollin

you hear on the record is his idea, although Nicholls had made it both vague and universal, in the spirit of true art.

Curiously, Glenn offers the following. "All the lyrics were pretty much written about the way I was feeling at that time. 'Angry Heart' was written about some love interest that had gone wrong. 'No Stranger to Love' was about stuff that had happened to me. I wrote the lyrics in the studio. Pretty much in a hotel room. But that period for me wasn't my best as far as me being in the greatest of health — very foggy. I just remember showing up at the studio and singing. But I think the album's great. Tony loves the record and it sold pretty well." Sift through the details, and you'll find lots of examples of conflicting stories as to who should be getting credit for what. Much of it revolves around the controversial Nicholls, but some around his predecessor as well. Jezz Woodruffe, sounded perfectly reasonable telling me about logging on with the Sabs for

THIS IS GETTING A BIT RIDICULOUS

David Lee Wilson

Sabbath expert David Lee Wilson and Ray Gillen

the *Sabotage* tour, but he also allegedly wrote, in a fan club newsletter missive dated February 17, 2002, that he was all over the *Sabotage* record as well as its predecessor, *Sabbath Bloody Sabbath*!

"Well, you know, it still haunts me that one of the last things, the acoustic thing at the end, is written about Tony's father," continues Hughes, on *Seventh Star* closer "In Memory," one of his favorite lyrics on the record. "Tony's father had just passed away and it was really crushing for him." This short but fully realized song serves, in conjunction with "Angry Heart," as essentially one of those soft codas one would get with a Sabbath rocker on the mid-to late '70s Ozzy albums. Of course the mystique and manic depressive creativity isn't so passionately at play here, but nonetheless, it's an interesting way to close the record. The album continues to rise in the estimation of many a Sabbath fan, particularly if they subconsciously group it with the DEP *Sessions* record and *Fused* — 1986, '96, '05 . . . 20 years of Glenn and Tony dabbling and doing.

But it all fell apart on tour. Glenn admits to stinking up the joint and then getting tossed after five mostly bad shows. "The performance on tour was abysmal for myself. I had an ailment due to the fact that I had a disagreement with somebody. I got into a fight that I didn't really provoke and then subsequently ended up in hospital and damaged my throat." In fact, Glenn was hit by a Sabbath employee, production manager John Downing, who was only trying to restrain a loaded Hughes and corral him into his hotel room. But it was quite a blow, resulting in a chunk of Glenn's eye socket lodging in his sinuses and all manner of facial bruising requiring Glenn to cake on makeup for photo shoot's then and well after he was gone from the band. Downing would eventually disappear for good: he boarded a ferry, got into a fight, and was not among the disembarking passengers at the end of the journey.

"Somebody asked me, 'Is there anything in your life you would like to erase?'" opined Glenn years later, clean and sober, born-again Christian, and father of a spate of ripping solo albums that have all critics calling him once again, The Voice of Rock. "It's those five concerts. I lost my voice even before we did the first one. There was a bunch of blood that was caught in my throat from a punch in the nose, in the socket, so I had to have a throat scrape, so I couldn't sing. Can you imagine going on in front of 15,000 people knowing that you can't sing and you can't cancel? We should have canceled, but lucky for myself, Ray Gillen stepped in and finished the tour. And I was so glad for that. I was really grateful because it was really embarrassing for me."

Drugs and drink were a big part of it as well, but add to that the last-minute change from *Seventh Star* being a solo album to a Sabbath album, and you've got psychological psych-out

Fred Tollin

David Lee Wilson

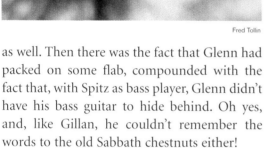

Ray Gillen

as well. Then there was the fact that Glenn had packed on some flab, compounded with the fact that, with Spitz as bass player, Glenn didn't have his bass guitar to hide behind. Oh yes, and, like Gillan, he couldn't remember the words to the old Sabbath chestnuts either!

"I didn't feel comfortable in the Sabbath format. Simply because I don't believe in the Devil; I don't believe in singing about the Devil. You know, I'm going to tell you the truth. It's a well-known fact that Glenn Hughes is one of the greatest rock singers on the planet, which is really great, for people to say that, when they say it. But I really believe that Black Sabbath belongs to Ozzy Osbourne. Those songs are really his songs and only he can sing them. I didn't feel comfortable singing those songs."

As the tour began in March of 1986, songs from the record in the set included "Turn to Stone," "Heart Like a Wheel," "Danger Zone," "Angry Heart" and "No Stranger to Love," with the title track played in medley form with

"Sweet Leaf" and "Symptom of the Universe." Backups were W.A.S.P. and Anthrax. After Glenn's infamous five gigs (at the last one, Geoff Nicholls sang much of it while Glenn lip-synched!), Ray Gillen took over, and "Angry Heart" and "No Stranger to Love" were dropped from the set. Interestingly, "Neon Knights," "Heaven and Hell," "Children of the Sea" and "Die Young" proved that the first record with Dio was still fondly looked upon by Tony and, presumably, the Sabbath fan base.

Ray Gillen's first show with the band was on March 29, in New Haven, Connecticut, after Ray had been, somewhat comically, traveling with the band for a few days, to the growing suspicion of Hughes, who eventually exploded in fury when he found out who this guy was, almost breaking down Dave Spitz's hotel room door in the process. Ray, 24 years old at the time, was a New Jersey native who had done

Fred Tollin

work with bar band Harlett as well as Bobby Rondinelli's band Rondinelli.

Ray had two days rehearsal in Boston and was thrown into the fire, touring North America through April and then to the UK from May into early June, dismal ticket sales all around, shrill German hair metalists Zeno in tow. Ray looked great, sang great and proved to be a motivating, talkative front man; although like Ian Gillan before him, he needed cue sheets all over the stage, and even had the same accursed problem with the demon dry ice obscuring his view. Interestingly, Ray professed little knowledge of the Ozzy material, but claimed to have known all the Ronnie-era songs word for word, being a big fan of Ronnie during his tenure in both Rainbow and Sabbath.

While all this was going on, other Sabbath alumni were busy getting on with their lives. In February of '86, Ozzy had launched what would be yet another hit album in *The Ultimate Sin*. Dio would be a bit of a shambles after the departure of guitarist Vivian Campbell; the *Sacred Heart* album and tour had done well, but band dissention was at a peak. In October of '86 Bill was telling the press about his "Bill Ward Band" wielding, as evidence of its existence, a confusing high-tech

song with Jack Bruce and Vinny Vincent called "Tall Stories."

But most obscurely, Geezer and Jezz Woodruffe were involved in a debacle all too typical of the music business in the mid-'80s. "Iron Maiden management decided that they needed to form a supergroup," explains Jezz. "And it started out with Geezer. Geezer had signed to Iron Maiden's management, Sanctuary Music, run by Smallwood and Taylor at that point. And then they started putting out the word to find people for the band. So the first they came for was me. I wasn't doing anything, and the retainer was a good one [laughs]. I signed up. And then they got Gary Ferguson, the drummer from Gary Moore's band, who's really good. So that was the nucleus of the band. And then it was flying people in from all over the place, including Ozzy's old guitarist, someone who Sharon sent over anyway, long black hair, from New York, Jimi Bell. If he wasn't one of Ozzy's guitarists, he was one who would've been. Sharon would've sent over the top rejects. The band was actually called Strikeforce. We had 30 tracks done, vocals and everything, and I think five of the tracks were broadcast on American radio once.

"It was middle-of-the-road rock with a soft edge to it, melodic, REO Speedwagon-y sort of stuff. They spent something like a quarter of a million pounds and never put it out. I don't think any of the songs would've shown up anywhere because they spent so much money so the publishing was held up back there somewhere. And what was funny is that they sent me a bill for 67,000 pounds, said I owed it to them. I still have the letter, but I didn't pay it back — I thought that was really funny at the time."

15

"A PARTICULARLY HARD BREED OF FANS"

– The Eternal Idol

After Black Sabbath's inglorious UK tour (Tony, The Beast, Eric, Geoff and Ray: great band, but who were these guys?), Sabbath set up in Birmingham for rehearsals. Significantly, the band that had shifted management from Jim Simpson to Patrick Meehan to Don Arden, had now hooked up with Patrick Meehan Jr., although the father was still involved. Money problems were to rear up, but the immediate crisis was that the band was having a hard time writing. Most pertinently, Eric and Dave realized that their new lead singer was a bit of a Graham Bonnet — great voice, but alas, he doesn't write songs.

ting done, word came down that the band was, quite surprisingly, going to fly off to the plush and pricey Air Studios in Montserrat to record their next album. Before the smoke cleared from the tropical debacle, Black Sabbath would have a new bass player and new singer. With respect to the former, the man who got the call was none other than Bob Daisley of Widowmaker, Rainbow, Ozzy Osbourne, and most recently, Gary Moore fame.

"I wasn't actually in the band," clarifies Daisley. "I came in to do the album. I had been working with Gary Moore at the time; this was October of '86. I got a phone call from Jeff Glixman, who was producing the album. He had done some of the Gary Moore albums, and Sabbath's bass player Dave Spitz had to go back to America. They were in Montserrat, in the West Indies, and he had to take care of some business or personal things, and they wanted to get on with the album. So we worked out the financials and within a couple of days I was in the West Indies. And Tony Iommi was great to work with; I like Tony. They did ask me to join the band, actually several times. Both Tony and

Patrick Meehan, the manager, asked me to join. But I heard things about their management and I wasn't sure. And I was happy with Gary Moore, so I said no, I'll just stay where I am. So I did the album and that was it."

Spitz's departure had to do with a host of things. He had found out, through the press of all places, that his girlfriend had hooked up with Eric Carr from Kiss. There were money problems within the band, and his relationships were bad with both Jeff Glixman and Patrick Meehan. Case in point, Spitz mentions the aggravating phone system, while Glixman says Spitz was always on the phone to his girlfriend, and not around to work when he was needed. In any event, he had had enough and decided to leave — or was slightly pushed.

In prerelease press, Ray explained, "Dave

Spitz is a good friend of mine. In fact, he got me into the group. But when we were recording the album in Montserrat, he was having a number of personal problems, and people told him he should think about going home until he could straighten them out. So Daisley came in — I think he was an old friend of Tony's — and he's been a major help. He's a very gifted songwriter — he wrote virtually all of Ozzy's solo material — and he really helped me with my song-writing. I'd come up with the concept of a song, write it and give it to him. Then he'd add some things and really polish it up."

Geoff Nicholls was also involved in the lyrics, as we shall shortly see. But first, there's the shocking departure of Ray Gillen, which, again, was complicated. First off, Ray couldn't write, and then it was found that he knew nothing about recording or working in a studio. Compounding this, he didn't seem to want to compensate by concentrating on the job, instead partying until all hours of the night with women ready at his feet. Money was an issue as well, as it was with Dave and an increasingly cantankerous Glixman, and then Ray had left to join Blue Murder, which fell through when he and John Kalodner didn't see eye to eye. (Ray would end up making his mark on two torrid and classic Badlands albums, shortly thereafter dying of AIDS-related complications on December 3, 1993.)

And, as Iommi explains, that's how we get to Black Sabbath's Tony Martin years.

"My best friend from school managed Tony Martin in his band," says Iommi. "And when we were looking for a singer, Albert said to me, 'Why don't you try Tony?' And I said, 'Well, he's with one of your bands.' And he said, 'He is, but he could do with a break. Why don't you try him?' So I did and I liked what he was doing; I really liked his voice, and we've done quite a

PROMOTIONAL USE ONLY – NOT FOR RESALE

4 songs from 'the eternal idol'

few albums together. But it's hard, to bring a new singer in again. It's always been very difficult under the Sabbath name. You can understand that people won't accept something just like that, Sabbathers being a particularly hard breed of fans. And if you bring somebody in, and they don't like it . . . my answer to that was, I brought people in just to keep it going. People say, why do you have so many people in? Well, the recent years, if you can't make somebody stay in the band, you've got to replace them."

Says Martin, when asked why Ray Gillen was out and he was in, "As far as I understand, Ray wasn't cutting it, because he wasn't turning up or something like that. He was kind of lazy . . . actually, that's a horrible word to use. I don't mean to be disrespectful. But he wasn't there, doing it, when they needed to do it. I've got the

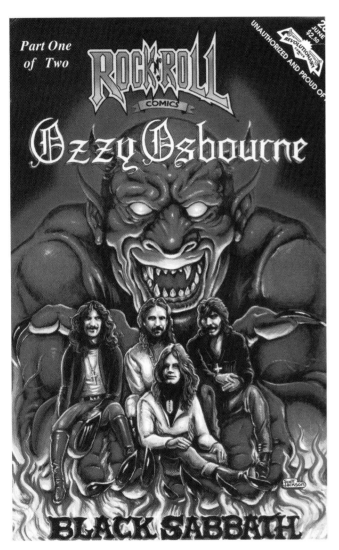

Daisley have also pointed out that Ray was a "vowel" or vibrato singer like Ronnie, and that they found themselves reworking the words so you could understand what he was saying. In any event, his six-month stay with the band was over.

Tony Martin explains the circumstances around his hiring. "Birmingham ain't that big, and everybody tends to know everyone else. So the manager I had at the time knew Black Sabbath, because they all went to school together and they even worked in some of the same places when they were growing up, and they'd been lifelong friends. In fact, he worked with the band as tour manager when Ozzy was in the band. So it's down to my manager, really, which was kind of weird. Because he kind of did himself out of a job, almost, because they had their own management, and they didn't allow anyone else to make management decisions. So he kind of sat twiddling his thumbs for quite a while."

Turns out Martin is quite talented among the vocal ranks. "I play everything. Bass, drums, guitar, keyboards, violin, harmonica, just do everything [laughs]. But I've been in it 37 years. I just pick up things along the way." Martin says, however, that his musical prowess didn't help him land the gig. "If I'm getting an idea, if I can just pick up a guitar and show them, 'You know an A?' 'Oh, right, ok.' So it does help in that respect. But it didn't help me to get the job. It's just something I do. If I'm trying to get an idea across, I'll just play it."

Martin says that while he enjoyed being in Sabbath, the band was starting to get black-listed by others. "It was one of those situations where nobody was interested in working with Sabbath. Because, either they wouldn't turn up or they canceled gigs. They were a risk. My manager told me he would have to drag Ozzy

recordings of Ray singing *The Eternal Idol*, the demos, and it was ok. The thing I had about Ray was that his voice sounded great, but you couldn't understand what he was saying — the words, his diction." Geoff Nicholls and Bob out of hotels and out of bed and God knows what else, just to do the gig. They'd have him locked up, just so they knew where he was. It's just that you had to be insured. Like, if the band doesn't play, somebody has to pay for all that, like the posters that get done, the T-shirts that get printed. It costs money.

"And record companies were a bit leery. There were problems with the *Seventh Star* shows, and even with the Ronnie version of the band. But the general pattern was that Sabbath was difficult to work with. So when I joined, they had gotten about as low as they could get. They'd gotten an unknown singer, this young kid [laughs] from Birmingham, not really been in the industry. They went that low to find somebody to sing for the band. So I kind of take credit for building the band back up a little. Because I never missed a show. My association is from 1987 until 1997, and in those ten years, I never missed a show, unless it was canceled by them, for some reason. Even if my voice was really hopeless, I still went on and did it. So it helped to build the band's credibility back up. But it was a real shock when it came to an end. I put so much work and effort into it, and I didn't get a gold watch or anything [laughs]."

"He more or less did note for note what Ray Gillen had already done," says Bob Daisley, on Martin's performance once he had been ushered in to top off what was to become *The Eternal Idol* (one alternate title was *Blood God*). It must be said that Tony's instructions were to match Ray's parts as closely as possible, and that he was hired on his ability to do that. Still, hearing the Gillen demos, there are divergences, especially with respect to "Hard Life to Love," where the creative choices from Martin are considerably all-new and quite plentiful.

"It was difficult for me to evaluate him,"

continues Daisley. "I haven't heard anything else that Tony's done, just that album. I felt a bit sorry for Ray Gillen not having his performance left on there. He did a great performance on that album, singing, and that was all his phrasing. I wrote some of the lyrics for it, but that was all his phrasing and vocal ideas, and then they replaced him with Tony Martin. I can't remember if Ray just left or if he was

> TONY'S AMAZING BECAUSE
> HE STILL LIVES FOR THE MUSIC.
> HE WALKS INTO A ROOM, AND
> THE WHOLE SABBATH
> VIBE IS THERE WITH HIM.

fired. And Jeff Glixman was a nice bloke to work with; he's got a good ear and he's pleasant. That album's got some good tracks on there."

Mr. Iommi contrasts Martin with Glenn Hughes. "Glenn comes with a lot of experience and is totally original in his soul; he's got great feel and can make things happen just purely by opening his mouth, and it comes out really soulful. With Tony . . . it's already been done by Glenn [laughs], if you know what I mean. Glenn was Tony's idol. But Tony's a great singer; don't get me wrong. He's very, very good. But I just found with Glenn, we bounce off a lot easier. He comes up with so many ideas."

To further confuse the making of this record, Air Studios' Montserrat location was used (Jeff Glixman producing) as well as Air's London location (Vic Coopersmith producing). Finally the band utilized Battery Studios in London, where noted metal man Chris Tsangarides took on the all-important role of getting Martin's performance down, while mixing the album, and recording a couple of bonus tracks in "Some Kind of Woman" and "Black Moon," to surface on the 12-inch maxi-single of "The Shining." "Some Kind of Woman" was wholly

inappropriate for Sabbath, sounding very much like a David Lee Roth solo track, from its speed metal boogie riff to the girlie lyric to Tony's vocal melodies — in actuality, this one was recorded with Dave Spitz in Montserrat but was finished in London. "Black Moon" is actually a really cool evil woman song with a thumping Sabbatherian rhythm and dark, stormy melodies — bass courtesy of Geoff Nichols. It would be revisited and rerecorded for the band's second album with Tony Martin, 1989's *Headless Cross*. Deciding to clean house and bring on Tsangarides, Tony Iommi had complained about Glixman wanting to take over the project and hire even more people to help finish it. Tony also complained about Glixman's lack of knowledge with respect to digital technologies.

"I was told there were a couple of guitar solos I had to record on it," muses Tsangarides, who had also worked with Y&T, Thin Lizzy, Anvil and Tygers Of Pan Tang by this point. "When I got there, I had found out that all the guitar solos still needed to be done, and many of the arrangements, and then the singer left in the middle of it, so we had to find a new singer to re-sing the whole album, and three weeks became six months [laughs]. And there were a lot of politics going on, with previous management and record companies, a whole can of worms that was opening up right before my eyes, and I didn't even realize what state the whole thing was in. Basically they had a manager, prior to the one that they had, and apparently the old guy had run off with the advance for this record. Monies were running out, and they were being held ransom by various studios, with the tape, because bills hadn't been paid. But it got itself sorted out somehow and it all fell together. But yes, the singer left to join Gary Moore, and the bass player, Bob Daisley, left too, so I didn't know who was going to be in the room from one day to the next [laughs]."

Martin says a few words about Geoff Nicholls, the man now, for two records straight, listed on the album sleeves as an official Sabbath member. "Geoff has contributed a lot. Geoff was never taken seriously for a long, long time. He's the funny man of the band, makes everybody laugh. He's a clown, great to be around. But he's like that all the time. Sometimes you want him to shut up because he's just so funny all the time. 'Will you just stop?!' I don't know what it was that put people off, but they never really took him seriously. But his input was huge. A lot of the *Eternal Idol* album was put together by Geoff, riffs and lyrics. He's not been given his due. He's like the Black Sabbath bible."

"We used to call it *The Eternal Idiot*," jokes Martin, getting back to the record — the joke comes from a comment uttered by Tony Iommi's Irish gardener. "But seriously, they gave me about eight days to record the whole album, which is great, because they had been in Montserrat for a year and a half in the sunshine, and then they come back to rainy old London, and I have eight days to finish the whole album. It was thrust upon me with great speed, so I didn't really have time to think about it."

Those eight days it took to do the vocals likely went by much quicker than the eight hours it took to shoot the album cover. What happened was that Iommi had wanted to use the 1889 Auguste Rodin sculpture *Idole Eternelle* for the front cover shot, but his request was turned down. Not to be deterred, management hired a couple of models to reproduce the sculpture, and had them spray-painted gold. After the eight-hour shoot, the two models were sent to hospital with paint poisoning.

Ray Gillen commented on the cover art. It was while he was making the press rounds prior to the issue of the record, and more pertinently, prior to him knowing he was not even on that record. "The title doesn't really apply to any members of the band," laughed Gillen. "We got the title from a Rodin statue of a naked woman and man where the guy is kneeling with his hands tied behind his back while he's kissing her breast. It's very erotic and very beautiful. It elicits very strong responses in people, and that's exactly what we're trying to do with our music."

Gillen goes on to plump for the album. "We're real excited about the way things are going. Tony, in particular, has been revitalized by playing with a bunch of new, young guys, and he says he's having the best time he's had in a long while. We're out to show the people who said some nasty things about Black Sabbath the last time out that we're really strong now. We'll take a lot of pleasure from seeing lot of critics eat their words. People have been really nice to me. They're a little skeptical until they hear the album, but after that they realize I belong. Tony really lets me do what I want on the album as far as writing and singing goes, and that's all I can ask. He expects a lot from people, but no more than he expects from himself. Tony's amazing because he still lives for the music. He walks into a room, and the whole Sabbath vibe is there with him. He has an incredible aura, and working with somebody like that is very exciting. He invented the sound that really is heavy metal."

Many gravitate to *Headless Cross* as the best record of the Tony Martin years, but this writer much prefers *The Eternal Idol*. The album opens elegantly with a triumphant, epic track called "The Shining," a song that went back in Sabbath lore at least three years. A swirling cauldron of an intro gives way to one of Tony's "Geronimo" riffs, one blessed with a sweet darkness found within Soundgarden's most Sabbath-like

moments. As the verse cracks, the song becomes Deep Purple-ish with Nicholls' pulsating keys. Martin delivers a Dio-esque vocal and then the song explodes for the chorus. Tony Martin's audition for the band was a run-through of "The Shining," and only "The Shining," and that was it, he was in. Unfortunately the song's lyrical sentiment is clouded by an association with the popular Stephen King/Jack Nicholson film of the same name.

Amusingly, for the video, because Sabbath was bass player-challenged during its shoot (Daisley having opted out of touring), the band plucked a rocker-enough-looking guy off the street and put him in that role. Given that he could play guitar, he was deemed suitable for their purposes, but the fact that he said he was the reincarnation of a "red Indian chief" caught the boys off guard. The video actually shows this mystery man quite a few times, not to mention, inexplicably, a hawk flyin' around. "Tony hated that video," laughs Martin. "They've got him rotating on a turntable, going round and round. And there was somebody at his feet gently turning this turntable with him on it, playing guitar. And he said, 'I feel like a right fucking twat, doing this.' He said, 'Do we have to do this?' And they're saying, 'Oh, gonna look great, gonna look great.'"

The well-constructed, accessible but heavy song was launched as a single, but failed. Oddly, the first two verses of the lyric are missing from the printed lyric sheet. Said Ray, obviously early in the process, "I really like 'The Shining.' I read Stephen King's book of that name a while ago, and it made a big impression on me. When I started working on material for the album, that was one of the topics that stayed in my mind. And quite honestly, I think I sing the hell out of it."

Next up was "Ancient Warrior" (original title

"The Axeman"), a thumping, spooky, circular rocker, Daisley obscuring an antiwar message in mythological language. Tony's riff is inspired, and the break takes the song even higher, the next transition housing some screechy, shredly but also Middle Eastern/Blackmore-esque flavorings from Iommi. "Hard Life to Love" follows, and is this writer's favorite on the album, Sabbath coming up with a party rocker with soul and a certain aristocratic feel, like Whitesnake at their best. The lyric is nicely couched in a reality Sabbath themselves could have paid more attention to, Daisley and Ray writing a blues song to a life spent with booze and drugs. The verse section is richly melodic, allowing for a wandering bass line and soaring work from Martin.

"Glory Ride" closes side 1 with a bang, trundling boldly on a one-note bass line, Iommi in epic mode somewhat akin to his riff from "The Shining" four tracks earlier. Martin's vocal is as sky-high as the lyric sentiment, the idea revolving around World War II pilots and their dogfights, with overtones to the suicide mission of Kamikaze pilots as well.

"Born to Lose" finds Iommi incredibly topping most of his riffs from side 1, coming up with a driving freight train of a pattern, Martin echoing with a vocal scat to go along with the riff before diving back into his lyrics. Curiously, the whole thing revolves around a character that emphatically won't be losing this battle. But then again, getting into battles in the first place, means you've already lost and slipped a rung on civilization's ladder. Next is "Nightmare," on which Tony uses his slow-then-fast formula again, the riffs solid and bankable, although strangely simple and accessible. As a nice touch, an evil laugh by the disappeared Ray Gillen was left in the mix, this being the only bit of Ray's performance not meticulously replaced by

THEY'VE GOT HIM ROTATING ON A TURNTABLE, GOING ROUND AND ROUND. AND THERE WAS SOMEBODY AT HIS FEET GENTLY TURNING THIS TURNTABLE WITH HIM ON IT, PLAYING GUITAR. AND HE SAID, 'I FEEL LIKE A RIGHT FUCKING TWAT, DOING THIS.'

Martin. Lyrically, the band slips a bit into formula — perhaps a good time for a break, which happens next with "Scarlet Pimpernel," an acoustic instrumental awash in eerie keyboard atmospherics from Nicholls.

"Lost Forever" is a kick-ass rocker verging on speed metal but well-behaved in its squared-off chug, somewhat akin to "Symptom of the Universe." Iommi's solo is spirited, musical, logical, as Tony delivers the goods, admonishing a man on the verge of execution for continuing to plead innocence when guilt is so plainly in his stare. The "burning with fire" break is horrible, possibly the first truly bad musical segment on this inspired record.

The Eternal Idol closes with the record's title track (sans the "The"), Sabbath delivering a lumbering epic reminiscent of "Black Sabbath" or select movements of the megalithic "Megalomania." Lyrically, the front two thirds seem to mimic a religious Geezer lyric while

Mike Eriksson

the back bit inexplicably seems to attack the world's power structures. Once again, this sounds like the new Sabbath trying to be the old Sabbath. And one must surely draw the conclusion that that is a fool's game, and that this band was doing just fine with earthy, traditional romps like "Hard Life to Love," "Born to Lose" and "The Shining." And yes, take those songs and the slight divergences together, and what you've got here is a record much more cohesive than *Seventh Star*, even if the bandness of it isn't much of an improvement. Martin adds an unmistakable gesture to the Dio years, and Tony seems much more inspired writing in this vein, as compared to the wayward stylings of the last record.

Touring for *The Eternal Idol* was both brief and disastrous. On bass for some of the tour was Virginia Wolf's Jo Burt (Dave Spitz stepped back in as well) and on drums, a combination of Terry Chimes — once Tory Crimes of The Clash, most recently of Cherry Bombz — and *Born Again* touring drummer Bev Bevan. In fact, Eric Singer had been long gone from the band, having left in January of '87; his drum tracks were done long before work was finished on the album. Eric would unsuccessfully audition for Gary Moore's band and then next surface with Ray Gillen in Badlands, their stunning debut to be issued in June on '89.

Says Martin of Sabbath's highly publicized Hammersmith debacle, "We were supposed to do a show in England — we had the big private jet and the whole thing — flew into this place, and it got canceled. And then we went to Greece to do a show in Athens. In 1987 we had a cancelation in Rome when the Pope was playing an arena and they took us from a 10,000-seat arena and put us in a 3,000-seat theater instead. There were kids outside and the army was in and somebody got shot. We

did three quarters of the show and then we had to pull it because they were rocking the buses and whatnot. But we had a good run. Mostly in the Tony Martin years, we were doing between 10,000 and 20,000 capacities. The odd 40,000 in there, and the odd 5,000 in there. But average that, there were 10,000 seats or something. We were doing OK."

"When I first joined the band," Martin explains, "I had absolutely no input into what was going on. I was basically swept away into a void of Black Sabbathdom, the Black Sabbath kingdom, this place where I'd never been, and I had no idea how any of this worked. You're just sort of whipped around to all these places. And when they said, 'We're going to South Africa,' I think almost everybody went, 'What?! What's this about?! You can't go there!' And then they came back to us and said, 'OK, this is the score: we'd agreed to do the gigs, as long as they allow a mixed audience.' And we said, 'Does that make any difference?' Because the apartheid shit was still going on, so, how does that, like, help us get in there and not get shot or something? And they said, 'No, it's all cleared, we've done this, everybody's agreed with it, all the varying parties and interested parties. They've said it's a great idea, it's cool, as long as it's a mixed audience.' So everybody in the band said, 'Oh, all right then.' We went along with it. And when we got there, it *was* a mixed audience. There were white and black people in the same venues, but then, I guess, ultimately, that was just a staged event. I mean, it had to be. I couldn't see how else it could have been arranged. It was a completely bizarre situation to me. But I have to say, the crowd was great. They really appreciated what we were doing. I suppose with a name like Sabbath, it's going to draw people anyway. We were doing 10,000 capacity and were there for about a fortnight."

"Bev Bevan wouldn't go, and it didn't matter what management said to him," continues Martin. "He just would not go. So he did Athens — the first show that I did with them — and then from Athens, he flew home and we had Terry Chimes from The Clash on drums, in South Africa. When I was with the band, we had seven different lineups — it's a constant changing story, Black Sabbath. Terry was put in touch with us via the management, and I guess they were just scratching around to find anybody that would go to South Africa. I got on OK with Terry. He's actually an acupuncturist now, in London, in High Street somewhere. But he'd got a good strong style, and was able to get around his kit. He had a huge cage. It was like a square frame and all these drums hung off this frame. He had like 20 skins on there. He played real hard and he got it all pretty much right. Fair play to him; he did a really good job. But the South African thing stayed with us for a while and then it just went away."

Contrary to the above depiction of events, Iommi explained to the press at the time that Patrick Meehan's lawyers had convinced them that Sun City wasn't actually in South Africa, and that the geographically challenged Sabs were dumb enough to believe him. Status Quo and Queen were to receive similar denouncement for playing the white enclave. Six nights were logged, with Tony said to have received a Rolls Royce as part of the compensation

package. Tony called this claim rubbish, adding that he'd had one for 12 years. But there was no denying the payday was substantial. Tony had indeed talked to Queen about the situation beforehand, and said he was encouraged to do it, adding that it was all in the service of delivering music to those starved for it.

Back home, with respect to the Hammersmith cancelation, the band was in the embarrassing position of having their gear confiscated due to debts that had been piling up. As well, Iommi cited tennis elbow and the Singapore flu. In conjunction with one other UK cancelation, not a single UK or U.S. date was played in support of *The Eternal Idol*, Sabbath closing 1987 with what was to be their 13th lineup since 1980.

"OVER-THE-TOP DEVIL DEATH EVIL KIND OF THING"
– Headless Cross

Much of 1988 was spent with Sabbath slumbering fitfully in a ghoulish grave. Nothing much happened until Tony emerged with a new record deal, chuckling that "After 20 years with the same record company, I began to feel like part of the furniture. I felt really happy when Miles Copeland called me and said, 'I want you to make a Black Sabbath album.' No disrespect to our old label, Warner Brothers, but it's certainly nice to be on a fresh label that is really behind the band, and makes us a top priority. It got to the point before that people didn't even know we had a new record. One of the problems is that we weren't getting the exposure that we should have been getting. This again boils down to our old record label."

Well that's how Tony framed it anyway, but there was no denying that Copeland's I.R.S. was a step down for this venerable, previously Warner-only institution. It didn't seem to hurt the situation though, with *Headless Cross* being a generally well-regarded and well-distributed record, rising to Number 31 on the UK charts, doubling up on *The Eternal Idol*'s Number 66 placement. Neither charted in the U.S. however, with Tony, after the fact, putting it down to things going sour with I.R.S. after the initial spot of hope.

"They weren't getting the albums in the stores," said Iommi. "It wasn't what I expected it would be. Miles Copeland personally wanted to take it on. He's why I signed with them in the first place. Because all the other record companies that were interested wanted artistic involvement. I didn't want that. I wanted to do my own thing and Miles saw that. He said, 'Look, you know how Black Sabbath stuff's got to be. You write it; I'll put it out.' And I liked the way he approached that. Once I signed with them, Miles, as much as he wanted to be involved, wasn't. It went to somebody else — and it was somebody else who didn't like us. But *Headless Cross* was the biggest album I ever had in Europe."

As a trivia note, before all this happened, Sabbath technically notched their 17th lineup when the two Tonys, Terry Chimes and Geoff Nicholls on bass played a brief charity set on May 29th of 1988, marking the first time Tony Martin would perform with the band on home soil. Sabbath played three songs, "Neon Knights," "Paranoid" and "Heart Like a Wheel," the only time a *Seventh Star* selection had been played outside of the tour for that album. In August, drummer Cozy Powell joined the Sabs, and Geezer's wife and manager, Gloria Butler, indicated that Geezer wanted to rejoin the band. However jazz rocker Laurence Cottle was the bass player on deck to record the album, so Geezer joined Ozzy's band instead. Four-string veteran Neil Murray joined Black Sabbath once the tour commenced — Cottle emphatically didn't want to tour the record, and Murray was a safe bet, as he had experienced success with Cozy in Whitesnake. Laurence Cottle came recommended by Cozy, since he'd played many sessions, including work with Eric Clapton and Forcefield.

Oddly, Tony Martin still felt rushed about the whole thing. "*Headless Cross* was really weird, because I had not been in the band that long. Off the back of *Eternal Idol*, we went straight into *Headless Cross*. So I was still not sure about my footing, trying to find what I was doing. We went straight into it after coming back from that little tour. I hadn't really had a chance to socialize with the guys. And it wasn't really until we did Moscow, Leningrad, those kinds of places on the *Headless Cross* tour, that it dawned on me where I was. I was in Black Sabbath, but it didn't really catch me until two and a half years after I joined. I was too busy. Which is kind of a weird thing to happen to you [laughs]."

Now actually writing with the band, Martin comments on Tony's famous penchant for coming up with riff after riff, which then go on tapes and into boxes. "It always started with those, but never finished with those," says Martin. "There were that many boxes. We start going through the tapes . . . and we did it every

time. We had the boxes and boxes of tapes and we started pulling them out and listening to them, and then it was just quicker to write some new ones. We just ended up putting the tapes back in the box, writing whole new ones and recording them, which made the pile bigger and bigger."

Despite these tapes being the holy grail for metalheads, Martin doubts there will ever be a box set called The Tony Iommi Riffs. "I can't imagine how. There's just that much stuff. And

OVER-THE-TOP DEVIL DEATH EVIL
KIND OF THING

Mike Eriksson

nitely go for the over-the-top devil death evil kind of thing. Let's be really crass and obvious with what Sabbath is supposed to be about. But musically it was a lot more '80s AOR than some people liked."

Said Tony, dubiously, while on the press trail for the record, "This is the most important Black Sabbath album ever and the first to feel like a Sabbath album in years. From the start, Cozy and I sat down and put this material together at my house and built the whole album up from nothing — all the riffs are newly written. Headless Cross is a sixteenth century village about two miles from where I live. Back then they had this plague that threatened the village and they thought that if they were to erect a cross that it would remove the plague, and of course it didn't and the people died. The cross is still there to this day."

The title had been suggested by Tony Martin, with Cozy gunning for *No Compromise* instead. Iommi's history lesson is a bit of a dog's breakfast, since this particular town did not have the rich plague-riddled history others in the area had. To make matters murkier, little mention is made of the plague in the title track's lyric, Martin turning it into rote "devil rides out" blather. Martin tells the story of local concern over a new highway being planned, which would necessitate the upheaval of mass graves of the plague-ravaged dead. There was concern that the plague bacteria itself was not dead, and that a new epidemic might arise from the digging up of these graves. Martin also remarked that he still lives in Headless Cross and that his neighbors were peeved that he would name a new Sabbath album after their town.

"I'm in a constant battle for words," says Tony, bringing the story into focus. "They mean a lot to me. The way I work, is from the

it's not as if they're really complete songs. They're just riffs that go round and round. And the other thing is, what do you call them? If you're trying to label these hundreds and hundreds of cassettes with little ideas on them, what do you call them, Idea Number 1? Then what is Idea Number 1? [laughs]. After 20 years, you're not going to remember what Idea Number 1 was. So they get lost in this black hole."

Neil Murray concurs. "Tony's got millions of riffs, either in his mind ready to come out, or already on tape from years and years of sitting at home and putting them down. So it's more a question of constructing a song out of them. I think they decided with *Headless Cross* to defi-

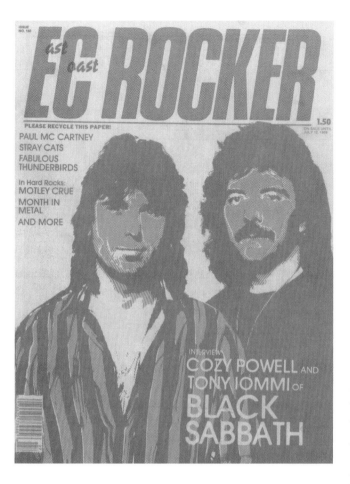

Mike Eriksson

initial inspiration, whatever that might be, the music or a story or a title. Then I have to make a story that has a beginning and middle and an ending. I can't just do the fantasy lyric thing like Dio did, wizards and rainbows. So I'm in a constant battle, always, to find words that fit. And once I start off on a story, if one or two words are wrong, I just can't let it go. It drives me nuts. Sometimes it takes me months to get one or two words in place that let me continue with it. So with *Headless Cross*, that one was basically about people's faith in symbols, like the crucifix or the Star of David or whatever symbol for that particular religion it is. They put so much faith in symbols, and in England

for example, when the plague set in — 1600 and frozen to death, whatever it was — they nailed crucifixes to the door, to the front door actually, not the back door, the front door, to stop the plague from getting in the house. And to us that's ridiculous. But it just demonstrates to me over the years, the faith people had, and still have, in symbolic nonsense. So I researched words that would fit the time, the period, the story. I do research what I'm singing. It's not intimately dateable; I don't like to nail it too specifically to a historic period, but I want that lyrical effect.

"*Tyr, Headless Cross*, they were both very much themed that way, lyrically. And only I know when they're correct. I know that's a weird thing to say; you think you can hook up with somebody and get together and write some words. I've tried that, and it works to a point, but when you've got something in your head that you can't convey . . . all that stuff to me, devils, I don't believe in any of it, basically. I don't think anybody really does in the band. I'm certainly not a believer in God, so it's not an easy thing for me to put across. But if you

OVER-THE-TOP DEVIL DEATH EVIL
KIND OF THING

believe in the story that you're trying to sell, that makes it more important to get across."

Tony Iommi and Cozy had considered getting either David Coverdale or Ronnie James Dio to be the singer on the next Sabbath album. Tony Martin's standing in the band had been up in the air, given his halfhearted attempt at joining Blue Murder, the fragmented project band of John Sykes, who ended up complaining about Martin's thinning hairline. Cozy, perhaps remembering all too well those battles of will with Ronnie through *Rising* and *Long Live Rock 'n' Roll*, was plumping for Coverdale. Eventually, Tony and Cozy agreed that Ronnie should be seriously considered. However, it is said that once Cozy heard the original version of "Black Moon," he was taken with Tony Martin's treatment. And in the end, it became more a case of relief that Martin would be rejoining the fold. It's all a bit incongruous with the aforementioned recollections from Martin, whose words indicate an erasing of a whole series of events.

Leading up to his joining the ranks, Cozy also lets on that he had been asked to join Sabbath both at the turn of the end of the '70s and again in '82 and '83. He regrets not joining the first time, as a year later he would split with Ritchie Blackmore, post-*Down To Earth*. At this juncture however, he had done a couple years with Emerson, Lake & Powell, which he judged "a disaster," and thus, he was finally ready to become Black Sabbath's drummer.

"Every song on the record," says Cozy, "has a story attached to it. Our singer Tony Martin is more into the darker side of life one could say,

but mostly the songs are about interesting phenomena. It has lyrics that one could perceive as satanic, but it just blends into the story. When we do the tour we'll be playing a complete selection of older and newer material, and we know that there'll be a lot of kids in the audience that have heard of the name Black Sabbath but don't know the tunes, so we hope to educate them. With this record we're going to put Black Sabbath back to where it should be in the scheme of things — at the top! We've now added Neil Murray from Whitesnake on bass, so now we're a totally complete unified outfit that'll rank along any of the previous Sabbath lineups."

"Sure it would have been nice to have the same people stay together for all these 20 years," added Tony Iommi, "but life changes and everyone is different. I still hear from Geezer when we're at home, but Ozzy I hear from very rarely, only by letter. And I haven't seen or heard from Bill since we did Live Aid a few years ago. The period with Ronnie was a very good period, but from there to now I try

to forget that period 'cause it really didn't feel like I actually had a band. All bands after many years together go through the stages of 'When will it end?' But if it was to happen it would have been during the *Seventh Star* period. But I believe in Sabbath and all I needed was the right band, which I now have. All the doubts are gone and things are full steam ahead! Cozy and I just talked the other day about how involved we are with the band, literally eating and breathing Black Sabbath every moment of the day."

"Yes, he would like to nail it and get it done," confirms Iommi on the oft-repeated character-ization of Cozy Powell as a one-or-two take kind of guy — love it or leave it. "But again, Cozy was really helpful when we did *Headless Cross*. He came to my house, and we just sat there, the two of us, with a little amp and guitar and him with his sticks and a tape recorder, and we just put the ideas down and it worked great. I'd play a riff and he'd say, 'Oh, I like that one,' and then we'd make it into a song. We worked well as a team. So all the things that were said about Cozy by various other people, I worked well with him and he was a real good person, a lovely guy. When he's on your side, he's on your side. He's a very loyal person and a really nice character. We'd have a laugh with Cozy. He's a prankster, much like myself. And as a drummer, yeah, he speaks for himself."

"I've been on most of his takes when he was in the studio," adds Tony Martin, on Cozy's quick working methods, "and he would do them pretty much first time, if he knew what the song was. If he wasn't quite sure what the song was, he would sit in the studio and say, 'For God's sake, somebody play the song or sing something so I can put this stuff down,' and he would actually drop in on the drums. He would play along with it and just drop in —

I STILL HEAR FROM GEEZER WHEN WE'RE AT HOME, BUT OZZY I HEAR FROM VERY RARELY, ONLY BY LETTER.

Mike Eriksson

and that's amazing, because if you hit a cymbal softer than you did originally, there's a notice-able drop in level. But this guy, he would be able to drop in on drums, and you could never tell where he dropped in. Fantastic! But the amount of takes? One or two, maybe three, but usually by the first or second take he would have it nailed."

OVER-THE-TOP DEVIL DEATH EVIL
KIND OF THING

Headless Cross, as mentioned, seems to have a bit of a preferred placement among those who debate the ins and outs of the Martin years — it was particularly well received in Germany. And it was about bloody time. For three records straight now, the press, especially in Britain, had the knives out for Sabbath, drubbing each record as it emerged, conversely praising Ronnie for what he had done with the fine Dio albums, especially the first two, *Holy Diver* and *The Last in Line*. Deep Purple and Ozzy weren't doing too badly either. In the press, Iommi was diplomatic and almost grandfatherly about it all; but the opinionated and hotheaded Cozy was fighting mad, even though this version of Sabbath wasn't exactly the one he was referencing when making all sorts of claims about the band's hallowed accomplishments.

In any event, Sabbath was most definitely going for a full-on occult vibe, garish and crass perhaps, but it's almost as if the fan base was tricked into eating it up. Whether this was really what the affable Tony Martin was all about

never seemed to come up for debate. *Headless Cross* was seen only in a positive light, as Sabbath doing what they do best, even getting back to their roots, which, as we've seen, are much more complex and cerebral than this lot.

The album opens with 1:06 of horror movie nonsense called "The Gates of Hell," lest anybody be confused about the tenor of the album. However, it's mildly inspiring that what follows is a side of three long songs. In 1989, basically the heady peak year of the hair metal explosion, five chewy anthems a side was *de rigueur*, yet here was Sabbath stretching out (although not too far, at 6:28, 4:29 and 6:56 respectively). So yes, the title track essentially opens the album, "Headless Cross" framed on a rhythm bed much like that of "Heaven and Hell," Martin calling us over for a sit-down as he tells us a scary story. The video was similarly unimaginative, Sabbath miming the song live amidst hooded monks with torches; lots of that classic Cozy shot, namely the full-on frontal, Cozy's wingspan in service of bashing a couple cymbals. Tony Martin's looking a little less boyish,

attempting both a moustache and a beard at the same time, falling a bit short on both.

Immediately one notices the powerful production, the bold, blunt and brutish drumming of Powell, and those piercing, melodramatic, Dio-esque melodies from the singer. "That's always amazed me, actually," says Martin, on his memorable crosshatched melodies. "It just seems to happen. I'm not a writer, as such, like a poet. I don't sit down with a pen and scribe; I always work from the music first. And it depends on what sort of feeling I get from the track. But even then it changes, once we've got a basic idea going. If I want to put in verses or take it in different direction, it can still change. So it's a really complicated mix of music and vocals together."

"Devil & Daughter" gallops a bit too pertly, not helped by the braying keyboards obscuring the lackadaisical riffing from Tony. This one is quite Rainbow-esque, and is one of those

Devil and Daughter

THE CROSS IS ON FIRE. AND WE WERE SORT OF SHOUTING, 'STONE DOESN'T BURN!' AND THEY'D COME BACK AND SAY, 'IT'S BLACK SABBATH. ANYTHING FUCKING BURNS.'

tracks studiers of the Sabbath point to when accusing this record of being a bit too sweet and melodic, despite the Halloweeny lyrics from Martin.

A video was filmed for the track, which saw the band further load on the trappings of All Hallow's Eve, burning crosses accompanying the all-night, freezing-cold shoot, reminiscent of Rainbow's frostbitten experience with "Death Alley Driver." Comments Martin, "The funny thing was the sky; look at the sky on the video. It goes from black to blue to navy blue to white, to like, black again, because as the video was shot through the night and went into the morning, they just took off the bits they wanted and didn't think about the continuity. The sky changes color instantly. And the cross is on fire. And we were sort of shouting, 'Stone doesn't burn!' And they'd come back and say, 'It's Black Sabbath. Anything fucking burns' [laughs]."

Tony cites this as one of the hardest Sabbath tracks to sing live. "Weird notes on things like 'Devil & Daughter,' which was top; A5 or A-sharp or something. I remember thinking, 'This is a stupid note; why am I singing such a note?' Because I thought it was just an album track I wouldn't have to do live. We had to drop the

OVER-THE-TOP DEVIL DEATH EVIL
KIND OF THING

Which is side 1's closing selection, a bombastic epic that works, due to a strong chorus and a set of speeds that Sabbath does well. The loud and bleeding production (credited to Iommi and Powell) works a spell as Martin growls over a surging sequence of Iommi riffs. There's a Crue-ish party rock element to the fast riff on this one, but with what is a noisy barrage from the guys, it takes the listener away with a hefty headbang. Over the fast, groovy bit, Iommi's pal Brian May cameos on guitar, turning in an uncharacteristically brash and murky sound collage. The intro to the song includes a chiming pattern that is in fact a bit of a bass guitar trick. Once on tour, Neil Murray took great pains to reproduce this, actually having a second bass set up and ready to go, specific to the task.

"I had one of those really weird nightmares," notes Martin, "an out-of-body experience, where you're supposed to float and look down upon yourself. I had a dream that that was happening to me, where I was just getting further and further away, and I was getting smaller and smaller. And it was like, when death calls, you're on your way. And then it got twisted into a devil and God battle-type lyric [laughs]."

Side 2 opens with another almost AOR-ish track, "Kill in the Spirit World" sounding like NWOBHM accidentalists Demon, right down to Martin's gruff Dave Hill-like vocal. Midway, a faux-spooky stab at a chorus turns into a ballad-esque break, over which Tony turns in a pleasingly psychedelic solo. "'Kill in the Spirit World' was fantastic," remarks Martin. "Cozy thought it was really good as well. That was like, there is something to the hereafter, and people who are bad take that deceit and badness with them; and, if they murder somebody in the spirit world, what happens then? It's all supposed to be glory and wonderful and fantastic

Mike Eriksson

keys to make it work. And when we do that, it works, because then you can get the note. Also, when you drop the keys, it makes it a bit heavier; there's a bit more grunt to it. But on the other hand, you're sort of ducking and diving. Each of the albums had something in there that was technically difficult for me to do. I guess the *Headless Cross* album was the worst one, though, with this one and 'When Death Calls.'"

on the other side, and I guess if you're bad, you go to hell. OK, if you're in hell, then what happens if somebody does something wrong?"

"Call of the Wild" continues in this melodic hard rock vein, recalling Demon or perhaps Witchfynde, two bands that incongruously sang of Satan while humming a happy tune. A ludicrous sitar lick accompanies the silly chorus, before a pumping bass line from Cottle takes us back into the verse. "Call of the Wild" was originally entitled "Hero," but was changed because Ozzy ended up using that title on '88's *No Rest for the Wicked*.

"Black Moon" is buffed up and Sabbath takes a run at it again — if you recall, the band recorded it last record 'round, the "Evil Woman"-like song showing up as a bonus track. This one possesses an overt sense of melody, especially come chorus time. Interestingly, the song was nearly renamed "Angel from Hell" — the band was still on Warner when it was originally penned, and now having moved to a new label, legal issues would have arisen had the original title remained.

Headless Cross closes with another epic in "Nightwing" (ostensibly about an owl), the requisite mellow intro morphing into an elephantine riff or two; the track is a power ballad, and it offers Iommi's best solo of the album.

Recalls Martin, "'Nightwing,' I remember only because Cozy Powell wouldn't let me sing it [laughs]. I did a rehearsal first take of it, and they shut me off and said, 'That's it, we've got it.' And I went 'What?! No, no, no. That's not it.' And Cozy just sat in the chair and said, 'That's it; that's the one.' And I said, 'No, that was just messing about.' 'No, I don't know what you've done to it, but that's like, you just sung it the way it should be.' 'Oh, no, no.' And I argued with him and we almost got into a fight over it, because I was determined to sing it again. And

Mike Eriksson

he said, in the end: "I'll let you sing it again, but we're going to use this one' [laughs]. And I said 'No, you can't. You've got to let me do it again.' And I did, and tried and tried but you know what? I just could not get it again. And whether that's because we had an argument and I'd lost it, or I just couldn't do it, but we ended up keeping the very first take we did."

A song called "Cloak & Dagger" was also recorded during the *Headless Cross* sessions but

OVER-THE-TOP DEVIL DEATH EVIL KIND OF THING

only shows up as the B-side to "Headless Cross" and at the end of side 1 on an obscure picture disc version of the album. A big thumping blues, this one is also Rainbowesque, even a little southern rock — quite nice, with rich, arcane melodies in both the verse and break, and an excellent, thespian vocal from Tony, who turns in a lyric that could apply to the arche-typical heavy metal evil woman, or perhaps the Devil himself.

To the band's credit, much of the new album got played on tour, Sabbath typically opening with "Headless Cross," later including "Call of the Wild," "When Death Calls" and "Devil & Daughter." Much of the rest of the set was nec-essarily a greatest hits pack, with "Children of the Sea" being the only curious old school entry, while "The Shining" represents the first Tony Martin album. Martin has said that "When Death Calls" also gave him trouble

because of the complex, multi-tracked harmonies. Indeed, Martin has always had some degree of trouble pulling it off live, a fact he freely admits, a fact that hasn't escaped the notice of the fans. He has his ways around it, some more obvious than others, and Geoff Nicholls and his array of technology has been an aid as well. Still, the ride for Martin has not been easy, with respect to his sabbath albums and his performance on stage.

Though the record was issued on April 1, 1989, the tour belatedly got going May 31 in New York, with Kingdom Come and Silent Rage in tow throughout the June dates in the eastern U.S. Attendance was so low that all of the latter June and July dates had to be canceled. The band limped back to the UK, where the solid, major-label German act Axxis opened, continuing on into a well-received spate of European dates. On two occasions, Ian Gillan showed up to help with encores; Brian May appeared on another occasion, the second of two Hammersmith dates.

Sabbath next hit Japan and then Russia for their first dates there in the history of the band. Girlschool opened for this protracted visit, which saw the band setting up in a few select halls, playing multiple dates in huge venues to huge crowds who were incredulous they were seeing any version of Sabbath at all. St. Petersburg was a semi-conventional concert setting, but in Moscow, the band played directly to a glum set of officials and their extended families sitting up front, behind which was empty floor, with the true diehards crammed into the stands about the place. With the temperature being 40 below outside and stifling hot in the venue, the band quickly became irritable, and Martin's voice suffered in the process.

OVER-THE-TOP DEVIL DEATH EVIL
KIND OF THING

Says Martin, recalling the tour with amusement, "Because we were one of the first bands into Russia, they were quite strict, pretty heavy on crowd control. They didn't like crowds gathering. And so they had 40,000 of them in the Olympic indoor arena thing, in Moscow. We were doing matinee shows. We would do one in the afternoon and one on the evening. And they got 40,000 people in, see the show, 40,000 people out, and then instantly, 40,000 people in to see the show, and then 40,000 people out. And they just did it like clockwork: 'Of course we can get 40,000 people in, no problem. Watch!' And they did [laughs]. They just like streamed in politely and just sat down and they wouldn't move. Mind you, they had the army with guns. It was an amazing thing to watch — military almost.

"Russia was mad. It was completely different each place that we went. In Moscow, the first row of people were like 50 feet from the front of the stage. And in between us and them was the army, facing the crowd. And on the front row, you could just make out that it was full of dignitaries. They had the mayor and his wife, his mom, her mom, brother, sister, kids, grandma, and it just sort of went down through all these people. And then we were doing 'Iron Man,' actually, and I had to call Tony Iommi to the front of the stage: 'Just look at this!' He was playing some solo part, and I said, 'Look at this!' And grandma is knitting to 'Iron Man.' Fantastic! She was knitting, she had the whole thing out — stitch one, pearl one, stitch three — and she's doing it! Knitting to 'Iron Man.'"

Still, as Tony Martin has mentioned, this was the first time he really took stock of the situation and realized what he and the band had accomplished. Excepting the American letdown, Sabbath was in pretty good standing. Sure the mania in Moscow had to be put in perspective, but on the balance, *Headless Cross* — some say despite itself — did its job in establishing both continuity and even a bit of uplift for Iommi and his troops.

17

"ABOUT NORDIC GODS AND WHATEVER ELSE"

– Tyr

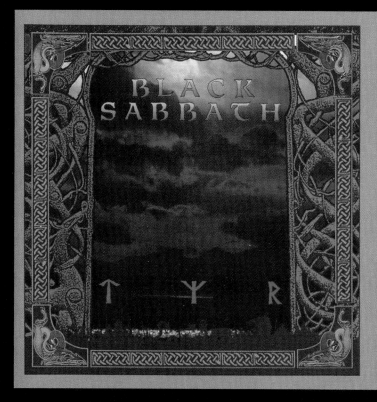

Sabbath's next record, *Tyr*, would feature exactly the same lineup that toured *Headless Cross*, the only significant difference from the last record was a new bass player, Neil Murray. *Headless Cross* had been well received, but there was some snickering at the lyrical direction of the album, coupled with complaints over the cartoony cover art.

THERE ARE A LOT OF KIDS IN
OUR SHOWS THAT ARE SO YOUNG,
THAT WEREN'T EVEN BORN
WHEN SABBATH RULED.

Jerry Fielden

Sabbath would take these criticisms to heart, and arguably overcompensate with Tyr's improbable Norse mythology themes. Much to the band's chagrin, the snickering continued.

"My favorite is *Tyr*," opens Tony Martin, looking back on the career a decade down the line, nonplussed over the album's lyrics. "*Tyr* was just a great album to work with. It was produced by Cozy and Tony, who had it right for those first few albums. Those albums were brilliant. *Tyr* was one of those albums that came together in the studio; it didn't develop either on stage or in a rehearsal room. We came up with some very basic ideas. Cozy had been working on one track for a couple of hours, which wasn't like him, because he always had it nailed within an hour, less than. He said, 'Chap, you're going to have to tell me how the vocals go on this, because I'm playing in the dark here. I've got no idea what you're doing.' So I picked up a microphone and I just started singing, and it just worked! And he went, 'Ah, perfect!' So he played and I sang, Tony came in and did the rest of the guitars, and that was it — brilliant. That's what I love about music — sometimes it really happens, and other times it's a real pain."

How much does he consider *Tyr* to be a concept album? "They all are, kind of. None of it's real. I don't think anyone could really believe all that, without trying to dispel the myth. There is a mystery about it, and that's really cool to have, but I tried as much as possible to have the lyrics follow the truth; but it's not all true, you know what I'm saying? It's a story, it's theater, it's what we do on stage. But it has truths in it."

Years later, Tony Iommi cast an eye askance at some of the lyrics from this era. "I've come across it with Tony Martin; we'd have discussions about certain lyrics. Because Tony would sort of end up getting into his theme thing, you know? *Tyr* was all about Nordic gods and whatever else, so he got a bit heavy on that. He sort of wrapped himself up in it."

In *Tyr* the songs along this Norse mythology theme are scattered amongst others that are

Tony Martin

Jerry Fielden

the album *Tyr*, because of the Viking theme. That was just a spurious title."

"My general idea is to put a direction to words," explained Martin, on this idea of being conceptual. "I also had an idea to do something with the red Indians of America or the samurai warriors of Japan. It's a little difficult to keep coming up with new ideas for songs, but people still do. Amazing that there's only eight notes in a scale, and people keep coming up with new songs out of those eight notes. Music's fascinating. You can keep drawing inspiration from things that just pop out of the air. Fucking 'ell. And then when somebody else does it, you think, 'Why didn't I think of that?! That's brilliant!' Anyway, I picked out names, *Tyr* being the son of the Odin, and there's Hell. And then I put the story together. It ended up being quite close to the legends. I had a mail from one of the Nordic school tutors and he'd been using the album to teach his pupils about their legends [laughs]. I thought that was amazing. He'd bring it into the classroom and get the pupils to read the lyrics and learn by it."

"*Tyr* was kind of an extension of *Headless Cross*," says Neil Murray. "The band that was on *Tyr* was the touring band for *Headless Cross*, so we had this lineup sorted out. *Tyr* was musically not that different, but in a couple of cases there was an attempt to be heavier. But lyrically, we very much decided to get away from the devil worship type of thing. But then, that lineup didn't last much longer." Murray was never happy with the bass sound on the album, or at least its volume — indeed, it is kind of buried, although the end effect is a record with

not, which is curious, because most "half" concept albums, like Rush's *2112* or *Hemisphere*, group the songs together. The title, of course, plus the cover art, inner graphics and an instructive quote as to the meaning of Tyr reinforce the theme, one that, frankly, is so separate from anything Sabbath-like as to be fully laughable. But as Martin indicates, all of this might not have happened. "We were messing with titles for the *Tyr* album, and one of the ideas was *The Satanic Verses*. Salman Rushdie had written a book called that, and he had this fatwa issued against him by the Muslim community, for his death. And so we thought, maybe that wasn't a good idea [laughs]. It's a great title, if anybody has the bottle to use it. *Tyr* was interesting because we didn't have a song called 'Tyr' on the album; they just called

WHO'D WANT TO SOUND LIKE OZZY? SERIOUSLY, OZZY'S A GREAT SHOWMAN, AND HAS HIS OWN SOUND, BUT IF I HAD TO, I'D CHOOSE THE DIO SIDE.

Alexander Rack

Neil Murray

enough of the frequency of bass, if not plainly heard bass guitar.

"It was a learning process for me, because the music I was playing before was more Journey-like," said Tony Martin on the press trail for the album back in 1990. "*The Eternal Idol* took the raw edge off my learning, then the finesse came with *Headless Cross*, and now my influence can be heard on *Tyr*. The general feeling of the band is that I've come in and given them some new blood and ideas, having come from a totally different background. I've

introduced harmonies and choruses that have given that extra twist to the Black Sabbath feel, making Sabbath more powerful than ever before. *Tyr* is a much more accessible album from the start than *Headless Cross*. There are a lot of kids in our shows that are so young, that weren't even born when Sabbath ruled. So it looks as if we're beginning to be more accessible, which is great. It's a challenge to us, as we obviously have to not only put ourselves across, but tell them the history of the band by playing the early hits. We want to put Black Sabbath back on the map."

"Not unlike *Headless Cross*, this album is based on people's beliefs," continued Martin. "I like to take real stories and turn them into lyrics. Being that I'm really into history, and Vikings especially, I thought they'd be great to write about as they were particularly nasty people. So we did three to four tracks around the Viking idea. But the rest of the album has nothing to do with it. There used to be a lot of references to Satanism in Sabbath lyrics. I even did them on *Headless Cross* — the underlying story was about the black death — but that's not what I, or the band, are into. I think it's had its due. Kids come to see this satanic band, but we're not like that at all. Our lyrics have these connotations, and we have those kind of interests, because historically it's been a part of our culture, with witchcraft and all, but it's not as prominent as it was."

Tyr was issued in late August of 1990, eventually beating both of its Martin-era predecessors to a Number 24 chart placement in the UK. The album — arguably the first of the CD era for Black Sabbath — opened with a brooding, ponderous thud rocker called "Anno Mundi" (the working title for the album as well), the intro amusingly recalling that of "Children of the Sea." Martin is full-on into those Ronnie

Jerry Fielden

Jerry Fielden

James Dio melodies while Cozy bashes away in the background, grand fills everywhere.

"I hope I sound more like Dio than Ozzy," said Martin at the time, about those relentless Dio comparisons. "Who'd want to sound like Ozzy? Seriously, Ozzy's a great showman, and has his own sound, but if I had to, I'd choose the Dio side. Me, I'm fortunate — or unfortunate, depending on how you look at it — to have that Dio-ish kind of voice, which I can't change, because I was born with it. I'm fortunate though to have a very large range, more than Ronnie. So I'm at home singing both Ronnie's and Ozzy's material, as well as my own. If you take the different eras of Sabbath, the band has gone right back to the old riffs — just now we have melodies and choruses."

Adds Martin on the "Anno Mundi" lyric, "At

that time, everybody was starting to do this 'save the planet' thing. Everybody seemed to be going mad, I thought, going insane, 'We've got to do this and that,' and *anno mundi* translated, means 'year of the world,' and it came from the fact that everybody was going mad trying to save the planet. So it was the year I thought everybody was trying to save the world."

Next up was "The Law Maker," a pleasing enough fast rocker imbued with much melody. The song drives home the drum-heavy but full-spectrum production values of the Iommi/Powell team. In fact, the sound is bass-heavy but not excessively so. Cozy's snare sound is a little synthetic, but that's a small complaint. A highlight of the track is the old school Rainbow melody of the chorus.

"Jerusalem" was a solid heavy rocker with a

hooky chorus and a buoyant enough forward thrust to it. Again, Powell turns in a finessed performance, finesse not being something one normally associates with Cozy's hard-angled bash. Tony Martin had indeed taken away the rough idea to the song and finished it off, actually heavying up what was first intended to be one of the album's most commercial tracks. Martin would go on to rerecord "Jerusalem" for his '92 solo album, *Back Where I Belong*. Says Tony, "'Jerusalem' was because I saw, on TV in England, a thing about an American evangelist who had been taking everybody's money, and using it to get himself a big house and car. And I thought how ridiculous and how ironic that this guy, 'Praise the Lord, Praise the Lord,' and he's taking everyone's money and then spending it. The chorus goes, 'Where will you go when it all goes wrong, Jerusalem?'"

"The Sabbath Stones" (named as such to represent the Ten Commandments) is not so successful a track; pounding a bit melodramatically, the riff does not improve markedly once Cozy and Murray break in with their spooky

plod. Incidentally, this one began life as "Lunchbox," then "Fire and Water" and then "Fortune the Flame."

"Odin's Court" is prefaced by a minute of ambitious, dark symphonic music called "The Battle of Tyr." "Odin's Court" itself is an intro at two and a half minutes — acoustic with two verses — to another ludicrous lesson in Norse mythology, this one called "Valhalla" (originally, "The Cold Winds of Valhalla"). Again, it's hard to get around the clearly enunciated lyrics, hard to get around memories of the Stonehenge set and the contrived nature of these concepts. Still, "Valhalla" is distinguishable as a showcase for Neil Murray's bass skills.

Major change of pace for the record's second-to-last track, "Feels Good to Me," Sabbath turning in a power ballad that predictably saw issue as a single, backed with a live version of "Paranoid" in 7-inch form, the 12-inch adding a live "Heaven and Hell." The CD single unsurprisingly contains both tracks. This item partially rights a wrong: Cozy had felt strongly that an opportunity was missed,

Jerry Fielden

that the band should have recorded a live album during the bizarre and protracted visit to Russia. At the time, he had commented that the crowds were huge, the band was as tight as it ever was going to be, and that the multiple dates in the same venue would have made for easy and logical assemblage of something like that. In any event, these two tracks are lifted from that experience.

Unremarkable but competent in this high-traffic power ballad field, "Feels Good to Me" nonetheless contains a soulful enough pre-chorus before a looming, brooding chorus takes hold and shakes the listener. There's a bit of the blues and southern rock to this one, Martin reinforcing the image in the video, in which he looks like a hirsute "new country" rocker. The video also features the band in an elegantly staged lip-synched live setting, with a vague storyline concerning a rocker guy and his motorcycle-riding rocker gal. Then he cheats on her. The end.

"I never settled into the video thing in those early days," recalls Martin. "The live ones were better for me. The directors they put with us

had some weird ideas. With 'Feels Good to Me,' if you look at the video, it starts out in like an old English theater, and then it suddenly flashes to Los Angeles with a girl on a motor-bike — I don't understand the connection. They did strange things to us that had nothing to do with the song. And it cuts in all away along the track, Gothic English theater, sunny Los Angeles, Gothic English theater, sunny Los Angeles . . . what's that about?!"

"'Feels Good to Me' is actually a love song," said the singer in 1990. "On *Headless Cross* I did one and they said, 'Um chap, this is a bit too soft!' But I managed to sneak this one in. It's kind of strange in context with the other material, but it shows that we still have room to grow. What we hope to get is some radio play

Alexander Rack

Alexander

this time out. The reaction to the new songs by radio, people we've met, has been good. They seem to want to hear from us again."

Tyr closes with Tony's best riff of the bunch, "Heaven in Black" (that title winning out over "Into the Black") trundling to a simmer; Cozy is in Rainbow "Long Live Rock 'n' Roll" mode, the band finding a groovy pocket not found in many other spots on this stiff, artery-clogged record.

"'Heaven in Black,' I wrote about the Kremlin in Russia, which was built by the great czar," says Martin looking back. "If you explain either too much about it or not enough about it, it kind of spoils it — leave some mystery. You've seen the pretty cathedral in Red Square, with all the pretty towers on the top? St. Basil's. The czar had some guy build this thing, but so he couldn't build another one for any realm in the world, he had his eyes burned out. And then he sent him away for five years, and he still wasn't satisfied. So he had this guy back and said, 'Do you think possibly you could actually still remember what this thing looks

AFTER TYR AND THE TOUR THAT FOLLOWED, THEY DECIDED, 'OK, WHAT CAN WE TRY TO DO TO REGAIN A BIT OF GROUND IN AMERICA? WE'LL HAVE TO GO BACK TO A PREVIOUS LINEUP.'

Jerry Fielden

Tyr tour program

like?' And he said yes. So he killed him [laughs]. It's just like one of those stories that inspired me to write something for Sabbath, because it's dark and mysterious. So there are truths in it, but it's not all the truth."

"We were always headliners, but not in very big places, when I was with the band," says Neil Murray, recalling Sabbath as a touring commodity. "I was with them in '89 and '90, so after *Headless Cross* and after *Tyr*, quite a bit of European touring, a bit in Japan, a bit in the States, but only after *Headless Cross*. It was really down to the record company situation. The band was quite well known in Germany, and not nearly as well known as it used to be in Britain and almost unknown in America as far as having any profile. It was theaters and that's it. And that's probably why after *Tyr* and the tour that followed, they decided, 'OK, what can we try to do to regain a bit of ground in America? We'll have to go back to a previous lineup.' And you get Ronnie Dio back in."

The *Tyr* songs trotted out on tour included "Anno Mundi," "The Law Maker" and "The Sabbath Stones," with three numbers also representing the previous two records, in total. Two additional *Tyr* tracks, "Feels Good to Me" and "Odin's Court," were played the first night of the tour then dropped. U.S. raunch rockers Circus of Power were the main backup act (Thunder also played), Sabbath making a detailed jaunt around Europe (with their faithful German fans holding up the side), again admitting defeat by skipping North

Alexander Rack

Jerry Fielden

America. A memorable night was had at the Hammersmith on September 8th when Geezer and Brian May put in cameos — Geezer's two-night appearance might be seen as the first seed of the Dio lineup reunion to come.

Several other UK dates were canceled due to poor ticket sales. To be fair, the number of UK dates was a mite ambitious, since Cozy felt the band had to hit some more remote markets in the kingdom. The European tour would have to be truncated as well. One highlight was an Amsterdam gig, where, upon being told not to use pyro, Cozy had the idea to use huge blasts of compressed air during his momentous "1812 Overture" drum solo, a carryover from his Rainbow years. At the show, the system malfunctioned and blew bits of the ceiling away, with a choking dust descending on the perplexed crowd.

18

"MORE SPAT OUT THAN MELODICALLY CARESSED"

– Dehumanizer

If generalizations can be ventured, *The Eternal Idol* was a tank, with *Headless Cross* and *Tyr* also fitting that characterization, even if both of those had Sabbath doing acceptable business in mainland Europe, especially Germany.

SEEING RONNIE AGAIN AFTER ALL THOSE YEARS, IT JUST . . . CLICKED! ALL THE ANIMOSITY WAS GONE.

Heavy metal's Black Sabbath is reborn

Band member says he's mystified by their evil reputation and influence

But there was Tony Iommi reestablishing relations with Geezer at those two Hammersmith shows, and then Ronnie did much the same in Minneapolis, hauling Geezer up to play "Neon Knights" with him at a Dio gig, August 28, 1990. Geezer was told, "Don't show up without your bass," but he did just that, losing it on the flight, so he had to borrow one for his cameo. A drunken reminiscing session ensued after the show, and the seed of reunion was sown.

"Probably not speaking to each other for nine years," deadpans Geezer, when asked at the time about what had thawed relations. "Me and Tony have always maintained contact, and then I got on stage with Ronnie in the States to jam, and we just got a really good feeling together. Seeing Ronnie again after all those years, it just . . . clicked! All the animosity was gone. I think Tony Martin had gone just about as far as he could in the old Sabbath lineup. As for Cozy, Warner Brothers wanted some demos from us, and at a pretty crucial stage, Cozy was injured in that accident he had. The label was pressing us to hear what we were up too, so they suggested that we get Vinny Appice in and the rest just went from there."

And that was it. Black Sabbath had pulled off an exact reunion of the *Mob Rules/Live Evil* lineup, Warner in the driver's seat, much to the relief of the band, who had by this point decided I.R.S. had had a big part in blowing the band's recovery in the crucial American market (I.R.S. remained the band's label internationally). Appice's return was not as predetermined as were the reinstatements of Geezer and Ronnie.

Cozy was supposed to be the drummer of choice, but had somewhat resented the ploy, citing loyalty to Tony Martin and Neil Murray. But then Cozy suffered a broken pelvis in a horse-riding accident when his horse landed on him. It was thought he wouldn't walk again, let alone drum. Then Cozy complicated matters by getting in a car accident. Cozy indeed did make a full recovery, but the band had long since moved on.

But was the horse in fact a red herring? Perhaps, so given these comments from Ronnie. "When all this came to be, I say yes to it, but with some reservations, the first one being that Cozy Powell was the drummer in Sabbath at the time. That was a problem for me. I played with Cozy in Rainbow and I knew what kind of player he was. He's a great player, and a great drummer for Rainbow. But I didn't think he was the right player for this band. But he was Tony's mate, and Tony, being a very loyal person, said 'No, I want Cozy in the band.' I very well could have said, 'Well, if you want Cozy, you won't have me.' But I wanted this to work, and I wanted to try. Tony assured me that Cozy was a different person than the guy I knew from Rainbow, and that he doesn't play the same way. Which shows you that Tony doesn't know what he's talking about when it comes to drummers, because he played exactly the same way. I made Tony realize that we were wasting our time, and it came about that we made the change. And this is not to downgrade Cozy, it's just a matter of him not being the right player for Sabbath. It would be like me not being the right singer for Yes. Once I made my decision to be in Sabbath, it was like, let's get down to business, and never to look back."

With respect to what would be revealed as an uneasy alliance at best, Ronnie added, "I think it was always going to be tense. It had been ten years since we'd done anything, and we hadn't talked to each other. A lot of success and a lot of failure had gone down the road in that time. They hadn't exactly been knocking the socks off anybody, and we had had great success with the first three Dio albums. We both kind of reached a medium ground, and we were presented with each other as equals as opposed to the first time when they were Black Sabbath and I had just come out of Rainbow,

YOU KNOW, I LOVE THOSE GUYS — I ALWAYS HAVE, I ALWAYS WILL … I STILL CARE FOR THEM VERY MUCH, AND WE DO SPEAK, BUT THROUGH OTHER PEOPLE.

and Vinny was an unknown. So, the footing was very different. There was tension, but we made the best of it. We had intended for it to not be anything but a lot of albums to come, a lot of touring, and perhaps end our careers that way. But once again, circumstances and personalities dictated other things. But it was a great album, and the reason it's a great album is because there was tension. If we had fallen into each others' arms with love and adulation it probably would have been the biggest, sappiest piece of crap on Earth! You know, I love those guys — I always have, I always will. It was never a personal thing with me, never! It just turns out that way more in the press than anything else. I still care for them very much, and we do speak, but through other people."

Tony also admits things were a little tense at first. "It was something that happens with most bands, when you've been apart for a while, particularly if you've been doing your own thing. Ronnie's had his own band, I've had Sabbath, Geezer's been working with Ozzy. It just takes a while to settle into working together again. We did go through a sticky patch though, I must admit." Added Geezer, "We've been working together for the best part of a year so far and

David Lee Wilson

life through the computer and he was turning people into organic computers. We didn't have time to put all those lyrics into 'Computer God,' so I still had this title, *Dehumanizer*. For the title, we all agreed that we shouldn't pick one song title off the album. It should be something that sums up the whole album."

Years later, Iommi would say, "*Dehumanizer* was tough. It was more working as a band, but it was more difficult. We were trying to change Ronnie's way of singing, instead of singing about rainbows and things. There's nothing wrong with that, it was Ronnie's thing, he'd always done that, he would mention that in albums. We just wanted to try and get away from that."

"Tony was a great singer; there's no knocking him at all," adds Iommi. "The only thing he does lack, which he'll admit to himself, is experience. It's very difficult to come into a band like this to play to thousands of people when you're used to playing in smaller places. It was really difficult for him, and I thought he handled it really well, but he'd admit himself that sometimes he was lost for things to do, things to say. He was following people like Ozzy, Ronnie, Ian Gillan, names and people that he's always looked up to. In the studio he was pretty much faultless, but I think Tony had gone as far as he could touring-wise."

In what is actually slightly more communication than the norm, Tony Martin got the news through a phone call from his manager Albert Chapman who told him not to show up to rehearsal that day. In fact, if he did, he would be refused entry. To this day, Martin has never been officially fired. And what I mean by that being more than the norm . . . well, often with these matters and the Sabbath guys, the phone just wouldn't ring to come in to work. One supposes this one got made because an action

though it started off really well, we did have a little cool period for a bit, and we really didn't know if we had it in us or not. Obviously the music's got to live up to the lineup and this last three months, it's been going really great, it's really clicked."

Dehumanizer was to be issued on June 30, 1992, the curious title coming from a list of about 20 names Geezer had concocted. Explains Butler, "Originally, that was part of 'Computer God,' but not in the lyrics. It was a story about this guy who tries to get a program on the meaning of life and God. The computer takes over God's role and tries to become God. The Dehumanizer was like the grim reaper come to had to be reversed. As things turned out, with Sabbath struggling with Ronnie, Tony's services would be requested a couple of months later (nothing happened) and then again a few months after that, at which point he actually visited Rockfield and re-sang the *Dehumanizer* vocals. Martin was in fact back in and then kicked out again — sales of his solo record suffered when Polydor dropped him for his apparent duplicity, and the album ended up being issued only in Germany and Japan.

"I was doing *Back Where I Belong*," confirms Martin. "Tony called, but I didn't accept. I was actually determined to do my own thing. And then they deleted my record, because they found out I had been talking to Black Sabbath again; they dropped it completely. Oh, well, thanks guys! That's pretty shortsighted of you. But there you go, that's the industry. But yes, they offered me the gig, within four or five months of getting together with Dio, because they were having such a hard time."

"I got in there after Cozy," says Vinny, of the unfolding events. "I love Cozy, great drummer, but they were just not getting along with certain people in the band and it was taking forever, going over budget and all this shit was hitting the fan. I came in and everybody got along. Ronnie and I moved into a big house in the middle of nowhere, I was arranger of the riff tapes again, and songs were popping out and they were pretty good songs."

Vinny actually finished his tracks and left a full six weeks before the rest of the band had completed their parts. And with respect to the writing, there had been a subtle shift in the chemistry there as well, with Geezer writing more music in the preceding two to three years than he ever had. Geezer would compose on guitar, record that, add a drum track and some bass, and then present it to Tony in that form.

In rehearsals, the band would run a couple of DAT machines and record all of that day's jamming. Homework would be for all to go through the tapes and come back the next day with suggestions of which riffs worked best. Of note, Vinny was excluded from the credits, the band opting for a simple "Butler/Dio/Iommi" for all the songs. Geoff Nicholls was on board but, according to Geezer, not coming into the process until three-quarters the way through.

"From my perspective, it was really something that never got finished," said Ronnie upon the release of *Dehumanizer*, about the original Dio era's link to the present situation. "We were doing so well at the time, then suddenly, within a relatively short period of time, it all flew apart — a chapter unfinished. So, having done my own thing with Dio for this length of time, I thought it was a good time to start finishing that chapter. So when Geezer came along with the opportunity and kind of felt me out, I told him that I had also been thinking about it. From that, he called Tony, and things just fell into place from there.

"I really don't think that anything was lost. I feel that within the ten-year period that everything had gotten better. Geezer, who's always been a great player, has gotten incredibly better and more involved, which was an unexpected gain from my perspective. Tony has become a better player with age; he's like a fine wine. I think I approached it differently too. I didn't want to be Ronnie Dio on this record. I think

Vinny Appice

that this album was more spat out than it was melodically caressed. Vinny has gotten better in the ten years too. If there was anything lost, it was ten years of our youth, not being able to go from the *Mob Rules* album and grow together. But maybe in retrospect it was the right way to do it, to just come back cold, and bang, here we are again. That may turn out to be more important than to have grown together, as we may have wanted to make the same album five or six more times.

"What we didn't want to do was a Who situation, which is not even doing an album, and just try to cop the money by touring. We didn't get a fortune to do this particular project; I would have made more money just staying where I was with the solo project instead of having to share virtually the same amount of money I was making alone. So it wasn't for the money. It may have been done by them for the money, but my situation was a hell of a lot better than what theirs was. We set out to stay modern, to live in this world. I removed the vestiges of wizards and dragons that I've always done in Dio, just removed Dio from Sabbath."

Indeed that was the case, with Ronnie writing cutting-edge lyrics, most definitely of this world but still enigmatic and intelligent. Musically, somehow Ronnie's will seems to have seeped into the Sabbath sound. Sure, sludgy doom and darkness is the domain of Tony Iommi, but there is a curious likeness between *Dehumanizer* and the sum total of *Lock Up the Wolves*, *Strange Highways* and *Angry Machines*. This strange sluggishness was a big part of Ronnie's music during the first half of the '90s, even when it said Black Sabbath on the album's wrapper.

Dehumanizer opener "Computer God" was all of this and more, most definitely sluggish and sparse and crude musically — and it was more than modern lyrically, Geezer, in a rare lyric on a Ronnie record, talking about computers and their thorough control over our lives, opining that some day they'll turn on us and start fixing the mistakes of our makeup. "I came up with that," says Butler simply, "that whole concept that God was the ultimate computer."

Adds Ronnie, "The idea is that we as human beings have created so much technology that it seems to be overtaking mankind itself. If we get to the point where computers are more important than human beings, you're gonna find that the next God is going to be a computer. Computers will dehumanize mankind. Human values and humans in general seem to be a bit redundant at the moment — and should we let this happen and not care about ourselves? We're all going to be dehumanized and the next God we'll pray to is going to be called Apple or IBM, unfortunately."

Ronnie, who really pens everything on the album except "Master of Insanity," charts the philosophical path to *Dehumanizer*'s lyrics. "In the early days with Elf, we wrote things that were perhaps more juvenile, being younger men then. And the music itself was a little more honky-tonk rock 'n' roll, which didn't really lend itself to a lot of deep things. And then when I was in Rainbow, the music and the lyrics kind of tailored themselves together. So I wrote more escapist, fantasy-based things. Which I carried on into Sabbath, which was a perfect vehicle to be even darker and more doomy, which is what I really wanted to be more involved in anyway. Then the world changed; it had become a place where, even if

GEEZER NEVER REALLY WANTED TO BE THE LYRICIST IN THE BAND. HE HAD TO BE BECAUSE OZZY COULDN'T.

you tried to escape, you could never escape the reality of it, because when you came back, it had become a pretty rotten world, especially for a lot of young people, with the lack of employment and disease and wars all around the world, just all the horrible things out there. And I found it really hard to talk about having your dreams come true and really applying yourself, and things will work out fine at the end of the day. It's just not like that anymore. So from *Dehumanizer*, I started to write in a much more realistic, observational kind of way. I've been a lot more factual and observant about the realities of life today."

Of the three Dio-era albums, says Ronnie, "The only lyrics that Geezer ever contributed to at all were on *Dehumanizer*. Most of the song 'Master of Insanity' was a song written by Geezer and a guitarist named Jimi Bell, and I loved the song. I changed it around a little bit, and Geezer said, 'Well, we'll all take writing credit for that one.' 'OK, fine, if that's what you want, but it's your song. Why don't you take credit for it?' 'No, no, I don't want to.' 'OK, fine.' But no, the only lyrical credits would be for that song and 'Computer God.' I mean, he never would come to me and try to say, 'Here, I've got some lyrics; want to use these?' Never; he would never do that. I would say to him,

'Got any lyrics or anything you're really interested in? Something you'd like me to try to deal with?' 'Well, no . . .' 'Of course you do! C'mon!' 'Well, I've got these.' 'Oh, great!' Geezer writes very strange, really good stuff, but those are the only contributions."

Ronnie adds, "Geezer never really wanted to be the lyricist in the band. He had to be because Ozzy couldn't. That's the whole purpose of Geezer having to do it. He always said 'Thank you very much for being the lyricist. I don't want to do it. I don't want to go through the trauma of doing it. I'm a bass player and I'd rather be a bass player than a writer in that manner.' But it's a shame because Geezer's a good lyricist."

"What we all felt in our hearts was, let's not be dinosaurs," says Ronnie. "Let's make a great modern album, an angry album. It's angry because we are all so disenchanted by what we see around us. We all thought the world would be free once the Berlin Wall came down, but it's now in worse turmoil; we're angry because of the way our governments are treating us. We're just angry about the worldwide social problems, which are getting worse and worse. That's why the album has the textures that it does, as people are angry, and so are we — we're pissed off!"

Reiterates Tony, "We had to make sure that we didn't sing about rainbows and wishing wells. Not to knock Ronnie, but Ronnie agreed to get away from all that, the magical side and the knights and armor."

"After All (The Dead)" is *Dehumanizer*'s second selection, not one of the album's stronger tracks. Ronnie turns in a fragmented lyric about the afterlife, paying the piper etc., divinity or damnation as one's destiny. This one's slower and more carnal than the last. Musically, the song is half Tony's, half Geezer's. Said the band collectively in the record's official bio, "It's about communicating with the afterlife. 'What do you say to the dead? Will you forgive me for living?' I guess the dead would be pretty pissed off. These are questions that anyone would ask of the dead: Is there a hell? What happens to your soul? Of course, these questions won't be answered until 'after all,' that is, when we're dead."

"We didn't want to follow the trends of the last ten years," said Ronnie, on the subject of the album's many "slow" songs. "We figure there's enough thrash bands out there to take care of that. What Black Sabbath have always done best is to be very dirge-y and very slow. Fast songs, by the way, are the hardest things on the earth to write. Two were difficult enough to do."

By this point in the record, one also can't help notice the merciless whack of Mack, the producer. Mack is a controversial figure that some say wrecked Queen when he was in there, applying his crackly, broken-speaker tone to Billy Squier, working with ELO and Extreme as well, although neither of those are quite so Mack-like. The band recorded in the homey comfort of Rockfield in Wales, but they mixed on Mack's turf, Musicland in Munich. For Sabbath, Mack also tones down his Mack-isms, but still, in conjunction with an Appice that leans the same way, he creates a drum sound that is fat and Bonham-esque though hard on the ears from too much midrange. It's a strange, earthy, interesting effect.

"It's exactly what we wanted," defended Ronnie. "It sounds as if we were right there playing it. Except for a few keyboard spots in some other bits, it's just exactly as we'll be playing it live. It's somewhat like a Dio album in that respect — you can hear each part being played; the mind can erase the other instruments and just focus in on one. And if you want to listen to it as a band, it's also there. Doing it this way has always meant that you deliver a great product. That's why we chose Mack. Not only was he a great engineer, but we knew that Mack was sympathetic to this attitude that we wanted, a real raw product. We also wanted someone who had enough musical integrity that if they made a suggestion, that we'd certainly listen. We're long in the tooth and set in our ways, but we went in open-minded. Some of them were great, some weren't, but we listened."

Adds Geezer, "We were looking around and given a list of producers to choose from. Our first choices were already booked up for a year or two years. Mack wasn't even on the original list. Somebody suggested Mack, which nobody ever really thought about. So we got him over from Germany, and he came and listened to the stuff and he really liked the direction of it. The best thing about it was that he didn't want to interfere with any of the songs, and that's what we were looking for, more of a great engineer rather than a producer that interferes and tries to rewrite the songs. It takes so long for us to agree on one song, so by the time we agree on it, we know it's the right stuff. So he really filled the bill."

Next up is arguably *Dehumanizer*'s finest track, "TV Crimes" being a frantic rocker bent over a venomous Iommi riff. Lyrically, Ronnie spits out admonishment of religious opportunists, his phrasing brilliant, his insights legion. "It's about televangelists," wrote the band. "A 'give-me-eight-million-dollars-or-I'm-gonna-die' track. These guys prey on the

David Lee Wilson

lonely. One day they see a miracle on the TV screen — somebody to love them, somebody they can love. Televangelists lull these people into a false sense of spiritual security, and eagerly steal as much of their money as they can. That's certainly a TV crime."

"TV Crimes," one of the few up-tempo numbers on the record, was issued as a single, backed by "Letters from Earth." It hit Number 33 in the UK charts, with the album finding its way to Number 28 (a worse showing than *Tyr*!), with America chiming in with a Number 44 placement — *Tyr* didn't chart there at all.

"This is inspired by people who have written to us; people whose lives are in crisis," is the band bio's quote on "Letters from Earth." "The letters we receive are from the real world; some are from prison. Because we've always written for the individual, they sense that we genuinely care. They say 'I know I've made a mistake. I will get out of here and rehabilitate myself. Your music has allowed me to carry on.'"

Again, Sabbath turns in a sinister, slow simmer of a track, Dio aggressive in his vocal, high-quality Iommi riffs ebbing and flowing.

"Master of Insanity" finds the band picking up the pace again, Tony producing a melodic but note-dense riff along with a lot of pregnant pauses, and the end effect is evocative of Zeppelin's "The Wanton Song" or closer to home, Rainbow's "Lady of the Lake." Said the official press release, "We're talking about what we as human beings are doing to the rest of humanity and what we are doing to our planet. All the problems that no one seems to want to address — AIDS, overpopulation, acid rain, people living on the streets. The way to defeat it is by reaching out to other people and doing something for the world around you."

"I had written the riff to 'Master of Insanity,'" offers Geezer. "I had done that with my own band I had in '86. I was trying to get a record deal at the time and finding it hard. And that was one of the songs that was on the album I had written, and I played it to Ronnie and Tony, and we just incorporated it into that album." This was the supergroup we discussed at the end of the *Seventh Star* chapter, although Geezer says, "but it wasn't a supergroup. It was just me."

Another excellent *Dehumanizer* composition and a bit of a hit for the band was "Time Machine," another groovy, fairly brisk number, with one of the album's most upbeat choruses. A strange history to this one, as Vinny explains: "We were trying to find a producer and all these names came up. We tried Max Norman; he came out and they said they wanted us to write a song for *Wayne's World*, the first movie, so we wrote 'Time Machine.' And that one, we actually worked with Max Norman on; he came over for a couple days to record. But he didn't fit well with the band. Max is a great

Alexander Rack

producer and everything, but Sabbath cannot be told what chords to play [laughs], and in what order. It doesn't work that way. You don't tell Iommi to play this way. He plays the way he plays. I mean, they will take direction and suggestions and stuff, but you can't smother the riffs that are coming out of these guys. They don't understand being told what chords to play — it's not them. So we came to a compromise on how to put the song together and then recorded it at some studio, a farm in England by an airport, because I remember the planes going over. And that version is on the *Wayne's World* soundtrack, same situation once again [laughs]. It's funny how history repeats itself exactly. Because we did the same thing with *Mob Rules*, a song in a movie, recorded twice,

the band was happy, then broke up, after one record."

What Vinny is referring to is the two versions of "The Mob Rules," the early version used for the *Heavy Metal* movie and soundtrack, the second recorded with the album's other songs and put on the album. On *Dehumanizer*, however, you get the early version, recorded seven months earlier, tacked on as a CD bonus track (in North America). Geezer tells the "Time Machine" story slightly differently, saying that the band already had a couple of songs roughed out, and that song was one of them. The band's comment on the lyric is, "You don't have to live under the confines of what people tell you you have to do. You can change your own attitudes and values;

MORE SPAT OUT THAN MELODICALLY CARESSED

Mike Kibby

just dream a little bit." Ronnie had always liked the *Wayne's World* segment on *Saturday Night Live*, so he was into it. "Time Machine" was demoed and sent off, and Warner Brothers simply used the demo. Saying something about the Mack sessions, this demo is actually more produced and polished sounding than the album version (and some of the lyrics are different as well).

Vinny finishes the tale. "And when we actually started recording *Dehumanizer* a few weeks later, we rerecorded it. And then we settled on a producer, Mack. The drums were mic'ed by these two special overhead mics that just cranked, and that's what gave the drums that biting kind of sound to it. But he did a good job and it's a good sounding album and I liked mostly all the songs on the album. 'Time Machine' was really cool. Everybody was really happy with it, so that's why it became a happy time again."

"Sins of the Father" is an underrated, overlooked "deep album track" on *Dehumanizer*. At the start, alternately psychedelic, atmospheric and warmly melodic, the song then explodes into circular, celebrated Sabbatherian doom, and then, incredibly into another riff, this time a stomping, fairly quick one. The earlier, songworthy themes are never revisited as the band jam out in a manner befitting certain *Sabotage* things. Comments the band, "It's a first-person account of a kid whose father was the whole world to him. Unfortunately, his dad made a lot of mistakes. The line that ties it all up is, 'How much longer are you going to pay for yesterday?' He must learn to fly with his own wings. People shouldn't live in the shadows of others, no matter what has been done to them, good or bad; be your own person."

"They let us be. They said, make the heaviest record you want to make; we don't care," says Ronnie, on the premise of an album that can include such deconstructed songwriting. "They weren't looking for songs that were singles. In fact, there were a couple of things we did and the record company suggested that we do them heavier. And we went, 'Oh well, no problem!' Sometimes you get yourself locked into that mind-set of being radio-oriented, so that an album can be successful. But in this case, this hasn't happened to us. With this album, the stations have played seven or eight of the tracks, instead of focusing on one track, which really isn't good when it shows up in the trade magazines, as many don't get breakout on any one song. We were told by the record company not to worry about it. Just go and be Black Sabbath. It's made life real easy. But I do find it constricting as well, with the Sabbath name, when you're writing, because people expect one sound."

The madness continues on "Too Late," which begins acoustically and then collapses into a series of doom riffs, murky and carnal, underscoring the slow-motion thrashing of the album as a whole. Wrote the band, "The acoustic beginning lends the album some nice light and shade. This is about a guy who made a pact with the Devil. He was able to get anything he wanted, but at the end, he's got to pay the piper. He says 'Sorry, I was only joking,' but it's too late: 'The race is on/And you've run out of road.'"

"It's an individual declaration of independence: I am invincible, I don't need other people to help me do things," was the band line on track 9, "I" (as in me, not the Roman numeral for one). This one's a logical enough number with an accessible, forward-amassing verse riff and a chorus that is relatively hooky.

The album closes with "Buried Alive," another sludgy trudge prescient of Dio circa *Angry Machines*, or indeed many of the riffs that would come out of Tracy G, the noise-tormented guitarist for that controversial era of Ronnie's band. Vinny lays down one of the record's many basic, crashy rhythms, offering none of the grooving sweet science of the classic Dio albums, simply pounding into these songs like a brute. As the band said, "It's about a person who's been told you better do things this way or else. So this guy is crying out for help; he's being buried alive. The world is closing in on him like the lid on a coffin about to be nailed shut."

"Some of it's lighter, but a lot of it's very experimental," said Geezer, on the many songs and song ideas that didn't make *Dehumanizer*. "I can't categorize it. It reminds me of when we did *Vol 4* or *Sabbath Bloody Sabbath*, the difference that those albums were to the first three albums, when we were experimenting. We wanted to come back with a real heavy album, and we did that, but then towards the end of it, we were getting into some different stuff because we'd heavy'ed ourselves to death and were getting a bit fed up coming up with the

Mike Kibby

same heavy riffs. But unfortunately we had to stop. Warner Brothers was saying, 'Where the hell's the album?' because we were already six months late, and we just had to concentrate on the album that we did."

Not unsurprisingly, Ronnie said one shouldn't hold one's breath looking for any Tony Martin–era songs to be played live on the *Dehumanizer* tour. "Why the hell would I want to do those for?! I mean, here's a guy who, in the beginning of his career with Sabbath, was

MORE SPAT OUT THAN MELODICALLY CARESSED

AND THEN THE BAND GOT INVITED TO PLAY ON OZZY'S LAST RETIREMENT TOUR IN CALIFORNIA, A TWO-DAY EVENT. AND RONNIE DIDN'T WANT TO DO IT AND TONY AND GEEZER DID. SO THERE'S THE END OF THE BAND.

Purple as opposed to Black Sabbath. But it wasn't Tony's fault, as he had some pretty big shoes to fill. He had to step in and make the band's career work once again, and that's a damn hard thing to do. You have to know how to do that; to know why it has to be done. That's the basic difference between Tony and myself." The *Dehumanizer* set list drew heavily from the album, Sabbath including "Computer God," "After All (The Dead)," "Time Machine," "I" and "Master of Insanity" in the proceedings. Absolutely nothing surprising filled out the rest of the set. Hitting the road, the band spent a week before the album was launched by playing South America. Sabbath followed that with a brief North American leg, main backups being Danzig and Prong, before returning to the UK and a toe into Europe, Testament being the most regular backup at this point. Then it was back into North America for more than 20 shows, Exodus and Skew Siskin in tow. In the press, Ronnie expressed dissatisfaction with the brevity of the tour and the bare-bones nature of the stage set.

And then Ronnie abruptly quit, basically because the band agreed to play with Ozzy in Costa Mesa, California, to celebrate Osbourne's "retirement" from touring.

"Everything was going along good," sez Vinny, picking up the story, "and we did the album and we got a good reception and the tour was going good. We were playing bigger and bigger places again. And then the band got invited to play on Ozzy's last retirement tour in California, a two-day event. And Ronnie didn't want to do it and Tony and Geezer did. So there's the end of the band [laughs]. Ronnie said 'I'll finish up in San Francisco, and that's it.' And I'm in the middle again, 'OK, what do I do?' I wanted to play with them and I don't want to leave them hanging, so I had to go on

trying to copy what I did. But I don't blame Tony, poor guy. He's a good singer, but he felt he had to do what he was told to do by [Iommi], which was to be like me. Well, I didn't try to be like Ozzy when I joined the band. To be successful, you have to be your own person, and with Tony, the band began to sound like Deep

BLACK SABBATH

280

both sides and sort it out. And they said, 'Yeah, that's cool.' And Ronnie said, 'Yeah, go do the gig.' So I played and we got Rob Halford to sing the two shows, which is pretty cool [laughs]."

"I was very disappointed when Sabbath busted up this last time," said Ronnie, talking to the press for the back-to-Dio album *Strange Highways*. "We went through so much to get from the beginning to doing anything, and suddenly it was over. After giving up the careers we had for ourselves — whether it be Dio for me or WWWIII for Vinny — it was real disappointing. I feel that we needed more than one album to make a statement. I was happy with *Dehumanizer*, but we needed more output. *Dehumanizer* wasn't my proudest moment, due to the way it was made and the lack of care it afforded individually. I was let down when Sabbath fell apart for what seemed to be greed, to me. It was like, 'We can get back together with Ozzy for another reunion and make a lot of money and all retire to Hawaii,' or something. When I rejoined Sabbath, I didn't view it as a short-term venture. For me it was forever! Myself and Vinny possibly wanted to finish our careers with that band; 20 years down the line,

we could have all been sitting in wheelchairs, going, 'Remember the *Dehumanizer* album?' while they wheeled us onstage! I wanted it to last; I really did! There was this big mud-throwing contest when Sabbath broke up after *Live Evil*. No one wants to see people chuck mud at each other, so I was determined for that not to happen again. I knew a month and a half in advance that the reunion was planned, and that we would be playing with Ozzy. I said 'Thanks but no thanks,' but for the remaining six weeks I played and enjoyed myself every night. I never let anyone down and was never angry with anyone in the band. I was happy to be onstage with Tony and Geezer and especially Vinny. Vinny and I talked about it, but the rest of us never communicated. During that time, no one ever asked why I didn't want to do the gig and never focused on the issue of whether it was more important to keep our band together. The subject was never approached, and I'd be damned if I was going to bring it up!"

So Ronnie refused to perform at the show and one can understand why, as it was likely a trial setup for a reunion of the guys with Ozzy. This lineup was on a crash course, and Tony

Martin had been waiting in the wings. On paper, Costa Mesa wasn't supposed to be any sort of display of one-upmanship, or, more accurately, it didn't have to be viewed that way.

Added Ronnie in 1996, "I didn't do it out of a personal thing with Ozzy; I couldn't care less about him. But it was . . . here we were trying to get this band back on the road together, trying to reform this band and make it special again, and now, suddenly, we were going to be the opening act for the ex-lead singer. And I also knew that when that show came that they were going to announce the reunion between the four of them — which did happen. So what was the sense of my doing the show to bolster their careers? They obviously didn't care less about mine. The thing is that everybody continually believes the things they hear about me — that I'm some kind of 'Hitler' figure. People who know me will tell you absolutely different. I don't need to defend myself. Was I misunderstood? Yes, I think so, because of the perception people have that of course it's my fault; that two unassuming gentlemen, Geezer and Tony, couldn't possibly make any kind of wrong decision. In that matter, it had to be Dio who was wrong. I gave up the Dio band and they gave up nothing! They had Black Sabbath and were lucky enough to get Vinny and I to come back and do it. And at the end of the day our preferences weren't given any credibility. When that happens you have no communication, and that spelled the breakup. I think a lot of it was the Ronnie versus Ozzy thing that cropped up. I don't know why, because it's never really bothered me what Ozzy does — I'm happy for his success. But it was that more than anything else, you know . . . 'Oh, I disrespected Ozzy' or something. Like I really care!"

"The Costa Mesa gig was done purely out of greed," echoed Vinny, continuing Ronnie's thought in the same interview. "We had a show booked at the L.A. Sports Arena, which is a big place, paying the same amount of money, so why not do that? We could've done our gig there and then driven down and played with Ozzy on the last night. But they chose to do Ozzy's show instead."

"Ozzy called us up," said Geezer Butler, offering his version of the dance card debacle that would help scotch the Dio era Mark II. "Well, his wife called my wife and said that Ozzy would really love it if we'd do his last gig with him; sort of put the seal on the end of his whole career. He wanted to do an encore with the original lineup. So we said we'd do it. We weren't sure if we'd be in L.A., but if we were, we'd do the encore. Then it came to doing the gig with him, we said fine, we'll do a set before he goes on and then we'll finish off with the encore. We didn't think of it as a supporting gig for Ozzy, we thought of it as a one-off event. It wasn't as if it was going to be a tour. We thought it would be great for the fans to see both versions of Sabbath. Ronnie just saw it as him supporting Ozzy, and Ronnie's exact words were 'I'm just as big, if not bigger than Ozzy, then why should I support him?' And that was the way he looked at it. So we just said, 'Well, that's your opinion. We've got our opinion about it and we're going to do it with or without you.' He said, 'Well, you can do it without me then.' That's when Rob Halford came in. Working with Rob was so great, so relaxed. We rehearsed three hours with Rob, played his favorite stuff. To us it was a fine afternoon. Although the other gigs with Dio had been going well, we weren't having any fun whatsoever. It seemed to be strained. We had forgotten what fun was like. When we got together and rehearsed with Rob Halford, it was great. We did all the old stuff then we did

Tony and Rob Halford

the actual gig. I think it brought back what it was like to have fun in the music. We realized then that the only way we could carry on was to have a good atmosphere."

"I would have liked to see them do a reunion tour," says Ronnie, perhaps a bit incredulously, elaborating on the debacle. "A lot of kids would have liked that. But like a cheap pair of tights, it just fell down again! You can't blame that one on me. You have to go to Mr. Ozzy for that one. If I saw Tony and Geez, I would give them both big hugs and be very happy to see them. We made great music together. Ozzy, though, says he doesn't even know me! I don't want a reconciliation with him as I felt I never had a conciliation! I don't wish him any ill will. My

refusal to do the show had nothing to do with him as a person, but apparently in their eyes it did. What's important is that our band broke up and our disappointment at busting our balls for a year and a half to make *Dehumanizer* and suddenly having it all taken away."

With Halford on vocals (Rob had shockingly just split with Priest, and was close by in Phoenix — plus he was a "Brummie"!), the band included only "Computer God" from the new album, although four other Dio-era songs made the grade. With Ozzy, as well as Bill, Sabbath performed "Black Sabbath," "Fairies Wear Boots," "Iron Man" and "Paranoid." Incredibly, Tony Martin had also been asked to do the non-reunion part of the gig, and had

THE CROWD WENT INSANE, AND IT WAS JUST NICE TO SEE THE INTERACTION GOING ON BETWEEN OZZY AND TONY AND GEEZER.

accepted, only to be told later by Gloria Butler, Geezer's wife, that the agreement was off. The Halford thing went off so well that plans were afoot to get Rob into Black Sabbath, but that fizzled as well.

"It never really left the launch pad," says Halford. "I think that moment was just so special and unique, and created a lot of interest and a lot of focus and possibility for everybody. But that's as far as it went. The world knows I'm a huge Black Sabbath fan, and I always will be. And I was lucky to have a couple of opportunities to actually go on stage and sing with the band. But I think that that's as far as it will ever get."

"I felt something special was happening," says Bill of the experience leading up to his short four-song set as part of the original lineup. "I was a little tired, because I had just traveled 650 miles down from my house in Northern California. I was up there with my kids and basically taking my time out that I do up there, and I knew we had the gig coming up so I traveled down that day. I think I arrived literally a few hours before it was time to do the first show. And we didn't really know if we were going to be doing it or not, because how it was

set up was that Oz was going to call the shots depending on his energy level. He was pretty tired — it was the end of a tour for him — so we didn't know if he was going to be able to do some songs or not. So we were all on standby the first night and I was told, I think it was about six in the evening, that Ozzy definitely wasn't going to perform that night, so I went, 'OK, to hell with it, I could use some sleep,' and I came home. Because Costa Mesa actually is not far from my home at all; in fact it's about a 30-minute drive. So I just came back home to get some rest; I was pretty tired, having been trucking down from Northern California. So I came back to my house. I was starving, so I ordered myself a pizza and I was just in the middle of trying to get it down me and I got a phone call saying, 'You better come back down; Ozzy might want to do it,' and I'm going, 'Oh shit, here we go.' So I got in the car and went back down to the gig and then basically just sat around all night and drank tea. Finally, I got pretty excited when Ozzy said, 'It's a go.' I got some adrenaline then, and playing felt really, really special. The crowd went insane, and it was just nice to see the interaction going on between Ozzy and Tony and Geezer."

Geezer offers the following post-mortem on the *Dehumanizer* era, which shows that even excepting the above test of wills, the rest of the program didn't run so hot.

"Ronnie takes such a long time to get anything done with us. We'd sit in rehearsals coming up with riff after riff after riff and Ronnie would be sitting there reading the paper or something. And Tony and I were thinking, when is he going to get involved in the stuff? It just took him ages to come up with anything. With Tony Martin, we'll come up with a riff and he'll put a vocal on it straight away. *Cross Purposes* took six months from

absolutely nothing to the finished product. With *Dehumanizer*, it took eighteen months, and it was six months until we came up with one song. We knew it wasn't going to work, but by that time, we were too far into it, we couldn't pull out. We didn't have any big arguments or bust-ups, we just felt it wasn't working. We set out with good intentions, but it took like eighteen months to do *Dehumanizer* and it just wasn't working. We really

RONNIE WAS FLOUNDERING AND
HE DIDN'T REALLY KNOW WHAT HE
WANTED TO DO. WE JUST FELT
HE'D LOST WHAT HE HAD.

Alexander Rack

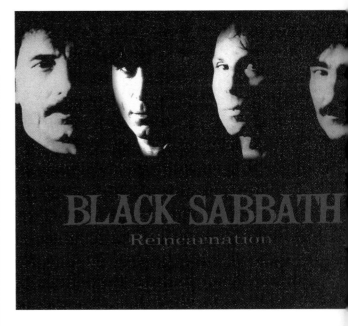

labored. Ronnie totally changed his way of doing things from *Heaven and Hell* and *Mob Rules* to *Dehumanizer*, which was quite painstaking. On *Heaven and Hell* he had a thousand ideas, and was very quick to work with. But like I say, on *Dehumanizer* it took him a long time to get any ideas about anything, although it's good because he doesn't then repeat himself."

Says Geezer in summation, "Ronnie was floundering and he didn't really know what he wanted to do. We just felt he'd lost what he had. It was a good album, but it could've been a great album. I just thought he was the missing factor in it. There were a hell of a lot of good riffs that weren't used on that album. We just went with the ones that pleased everyone, to get finished. We'd never work with Ronnie again, not in Black Sabbath anyways; maybe on something totally different. If he phoned me up and asked me to play bass or something, then I'll work with him. We were good friends; we haven't spoken since the split. I don't hate him or anything and I wouldn't put him down. When Tony, Ronnie and I get together, something just doesn't happen. It sounds pretty good on paper, but when we came together, it was really weird."

"I WAS STUCK THERE WITH THIS KID DARREN"

– Cross Purposes

BLACK SABBATH

CROSS PURPOSES

Incredibly, given the problems with Ronnie, the germination of the *Cross Purposes* album had begun even before the *Dehumanizer* tour took flight. If you will recall, Iommi and Butler had surreptitiously called Martin back in to re-track the *Dehumanizer* vocals (the boys had told Ronnie, who was cooling his heels in Henley-in-Arden in the West Midlands, that they were on break), only to be pressured back to the original and lucrative *Mob Rules* lineup deal. Still, the guys figured they would work on some music with Martin at that time and found it much easier going than the strange, non-communication business they had with Dio. So, in yet another gesture toward some level of continuity, the Tony Martin Era Part II would take shape.

Alexander Rack

Bobby Rondinelli

Martin recaps the years leading up to his reinstatement in the band. "I can't say that I was entirely happy about it," says Martin, about being ousted for the *Dehumanizer* situation. "But hey, I wasn't going to sit in the corner and cry. I actually went from that point to making the solo album. I got a deal with Polydor Records and it was released in Europe. I had 43 musicians play on the record, including Brian May. I was quite busy. It soon became clear that Sabbath had made a mistake trying to get Ronnie back into the lineup. They called me again and said, 'Help! We'd like you to come back and continue.' But I couldn't, because I had already started my solo thing. They had to

continue with Ronnie and they went out on tour, while I kept working on my project. When we were both free, Tony called me up again and we got back together. These things happen in rock 'n' roll. It's a very incestuous business. It's very awkward sometimes, but you have to take your next step forward. Although it wasn't very nice, I got on with my life. I have talked to Dio on a few occasions and I do know him, but I can't exactly say that he's that interested in what I have to say. He kind of avoids me whenever he can. I don't know why, and I've tried to speak with him on a number of occasions."

The Black Sabbath lineup for *Cross Purposes*, issued January 31, 1994, would also include a returning Geezer Butler on bass, Geoff Nicholls as a full Sabbath member (although Nicholls would remain out of the writing credits), and on drums, Bobby Rondinelli of Rainbow fame.

"The tour manager, Robert Gambino, when I played with Doro Pesch, used to be Tony Iommi's personal guy," says Bobby, on getting the Sabbath gig. "So I told him that I loved Sabbath, and if he ever heard that they needed a drummer, let me know. So I get a call from him, and I said, 'All right, give them my number.' He and Tony weren't really talking at the time, so he gave me Tony's number. I called, spoke to Tony's wife and left a message, and Tony called me back ten minutes later. He said that my name was on the list anyway and that they were going to get in touch with me. So I got the gig. There was no audition. He had listened to some stuff I'd been on and he had heard me with Rainbow and just said, 'Do you want the gig?' And I said yeah. Of course, if you go there and you don't play well, you don't get it. And they liked the way I played [laughs]."

"They're both great, you know?" adds Bobby, when asked to compare working with Ritchie

Blackmore versus Tony Iommi. "The main difference is that Tony is left-handed [laughs], and Ritchie is right-handed. No, it was great working with Tony. Tony gave me a lot of freedom, allowed me to play whatever I wanted. This is one of the originators of rock, so it was a great experience. Ritchie is a little more low-key. Tony is pretty easygoing; and Ritchie kind of knows what he wants, and you've got to give Ritchie what he wants, which is understandable. Comparing [Rainbow lead singer] Joe Lynn Turner to Tony Martin . . . Joe is pretty easygoing and Tony Martin is pretty easygoing. They're both world-class singers and writers. They were both pretty quick with their takes."

"The studio kind of made me nuts," said Bobby on the process of making the record, "because on the weekend, everybody would go home, and I was stuck there with this kid Darren. He's a good guy, but it was just me and him, one of the studio assistants. So I would be stuck on the weekends by myself, and I was going a little stir-crazy. I'd go out, do a little shopping, go for walks. There wasn't a hell of a lot to do. But it was a good studio and I enjoyed working there. I'm really happy with that record. I think it's a shame that it went unnoticed."

"I don't know where Tony began and Geezer ended," notes Rondinelli with respect to lyrics. "We wrote the music all in a room together, and some of it was even written before I got there. Geoff always got his two cents in. He had things to say and he was a good, talented, creative guy. But I think Tony Martin did most of the lyrics. It was a really heavy band [laughs]. We rehearsed for about six weeks, writing stuff in England, and did the album in about a month. I'm pretty proud of that."

Echoes Martin on the experience, "Working with Geezer Butler was great. It's actually the only album I've ever done with Geezer Butler

THESE THINGS HAPPEN IN ROCK 'N' ROLL. IT'S A VERY INCESTUOUS BUSINESS.

— lovely man, but he's got a very dry sense of humor. You have to work out what he's saying. He says something, and you look at him, and you can't actually work out whether he's for real. Did he really just say that? So once you get used to that, it's great. He's a fantastic player, of course, and I like him a lot. But that album was probably the most fun."

Tony Martin ended up writing the lyrics, but not for want of trying to get Geezer involved. "Oh, I tried. I tried so hard! 'You know, Geezer, you can help me out here. Do you want to write something?! Just tell me; write it down on a piece of paper and give it to me and I'll work it out.' But he never did. I don't know. I didn't quiz him about it. He was not reluctant; he just didn't want to do it. I can only blow my own trumpet, and just think that he was happy with what I was doing, which made him not want to get involved. But because he's a professional, I'm sure if he thought the music or lyrics were really dire, he would've said something, but he never did. In fact, a couple of times he said, 'I really like what you're singing on this; it's really great stuff.' I can only imagine that what I was doing was OK."

"I thought he was a really good singer," mused Geezer on Martin. "I think he did the Dio stuff better than the Ozzy. He was more

David Lee Wilson

suited for that; he did really well, considering the boots he had to fill. I didn't really mix with him that much. Lyrically, I had a few suggestions for him, when he had run out of ideas. But I really didn't want to do the lyric side of it. I was doing more into the music for that album. I just let him get on with the lyrics. I think 'Virtual Death' was the main one I wrote for it, and I liked that whole virtual thing, which was very trendy at the time [laughs]."

And what of Bobby? "I remember him buying the English newspapers because they had naked women in them, and he couldn't believe that. So he used to buy them all every day [laughs]." Appropriately enough, Geezer and Bobby differ on what the stated purpose of *Cross Purposes* was. Bobby affirms that the whole experience was the making of a Black Sabbath album where Geezer seems to believe the record was intended, at least at first, to be branded as something other than Sabbath; this, perhaps, because talks with Ozzy were

ongoing with respect to a reunion.

Cross Purposes opens with a resounding affirmation of Sabbatherian life, "I Witness" finding the band moving briskly with Martin turning in a vocal along the lines of a David Coverdale, Tony's lyric referring to the Amish and their complete isolation from modern society. "Cross of Thorns" finds the band back in *Tyr* territory, Sabbath combining dark, mellow passages with brooding textbook heft. Iommi has said that the song's lyric originates with a visit Martin made to Northern Ireland, a bit of lyric research ensuing with someone he met in a pub. Affirms Martin, "Up until recent years anyway, we've had an Irish situation, with the IRA and that. And when I was with Cozy Powell's Hammer, we went to Ireland and I was talking to this guy about it, and as these people do, they talk about the Troubles [laughs]. And this Irish guy said something like religion or being religious was like wearing a cross of thorns. And I thought, 'That's brilliant.' And

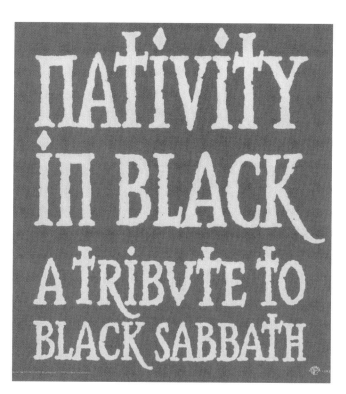

NATIVITY IN BLACK
A TRIBUTE TO BLACK SABBATH

Promotional flat

then I tied the whole thing into the Irish situation and everyone thought it was cool. Much more the considered kind of lyric rather than fantasy and devils and God thing."

"Psychophobia" is an interesting, almost progressive piece with arcane, vaguely psychedelic melodies, the band looking for something different and finding it. Martin says the song is about David Koresh and the Waco, Texas disaster, pointing out that psychophobia translates as fear of the mind. The aforementioned "Virtual Death" is nothing different at all, and neither is "Immaculate Deception," although this one seems to be more successful in this squarely second-guessed Sabbath direction.

One notices as well on these two tracks the plush, professional, but not overwrought production work of Leif Mases, mixer on *Tyr*, engineer on Led Zeppelin's final album, and producer for Lillian Axe, Bang Tango and

Europe. "He was good, I liked Leif," sez Martin. "I didn't have any problems with him, and I don't think he had any problems with me. I thought he was very attentive to what he was doing, and he had some funny stories. And I really like the end product."

Martin says Iommi was able to take instruction from everyone, to a point. "The thing with Tony is, he knows what he doesn't want; let's put it that way. If somebody says something and he really hates the idea, he would dismiss it immediately; he won't even go there. But if somebody comes up with a really good idea, I always found him willing to listen. I mean, I wrote all of the lyrics in the time I was with Black Sabbath. I asked him if ever he wanted to write any lyrics, then he should just give me something. If he wanted to write it down on a piece of paper, I'd have a go at what he'd written. And he'd say, 'No, no! I'll never do that. No, no.' But then when it came to guitar parts and things, he'd sometimes let me suggest little bridges and little chord structures."

"Dying for Love" follows — it's an average and typically morose Martin-era ballad with an above-average chorus. "Back to Eden" is

Alexander Rack

to look after kids, why would you want to kill them? But she obviously had a screw loose somewhere, a very unstable character. She got put in prison pretty much for life."

"Evil Eye" closes the album, and somewhat secretly (he is not credited on the album) Mr. Eddie Van Halen, in Birmingham for a gig, cowrites the track and adds a guitar solo. Or does he? The opening atonal squall is thought to be Eddie, but then again, Geoff Nicholls has said that Tony might have duplicated Eddie's part — indeed Eddie might not have been able to play on it at all, due to scheduling conflicts. Other brief firings within the song could go either way as well; the solos are awful in fact, and they're buried in the mix. One could imagine these as Tony's work, or Eddie playing in that specific zone of his own that happens to overlap with the sparingly used, shred-like facet of Tony's playing. In any event, the song is acceptable brooding blues metal — not superlative, but then again, not forced.

Promoting the album in the press, Iommi said Tony Martin had been easy to work with on these songs. "We had some riffs, Geezer and myself, and we played them for Tony, and he took them home and worked on them and had come up for three or four good ideas. It took about six weeks, and we basically recorded live. I just set up with my stage guitars and Marshall amps, and went for it. Tony's an excellent singer. You're sort of going forward instead of backwards. He comes up with a lot of different ways of approaching material. You can throw anything at him and he'll have a go at it. It's good because it expands the band. You go, 'You can probably do a better melody than that,' and he'd come back with another one. It's great to see because you don't have to accept the first thing that comes into his head."

"This one was really enjoyable for a change,"

perhaps the album's best track. A rocker with a sturdy, halting, elephantine riff, the song gets downright soulful come chorus time. Neither "The Hand that Rocks the Cradle" (for which a video was produced) or "Cardinal Sin" do much to advance Sabbath's game. Martin has said that "Cardinal Sin" was to be called "Sin Cardinal Sin," but was incorrectly printed for the booklet. The lyric refers to the true story of an Irish Catholic bishop, Eamon Casey, who kept hidden his love child for 21 years, and when his secret came out, he was relieved of his duties and left the country.

Adds Martin, "'The Hand that Rocks the Cradle'. . . we had a woman in the UK who was a nurse. She worked in a children's hospital and killed something like ten or twelve children, in the hospital. And I have no idea why she would want to do that. You know, if you're given a job

Cross Purposes tour program

said Geezer, back in early '94, agreeing whole-heartedly with Iommi's assessment of the situation. "It was a really good atmosphere. Sometimes you may go a few days without coming up with anything. But this one, we had so much material coming out it was incredible. We had tapes and tapes of stuff. With Tony Martin, you can play him a riff, and he'll come up with the vocal straight away. He'll know if that riff's going to work or not. It was really back to the way we did the first album with Ozzy. Tony Iommi told me how good he was to work with and it soon proved itself right. He's great; he's a dream. And when we do the live stuff, he fits in well with the Ozzy stuff as well as the Dio. He's got one of those adjustable voices."

"*Cross Purposes* holds up well," continued Geezer. "The only problem I used to have with Tony Martin was the lyrics. They were either Satanic or too mystical or mythical. This time I said to him that I preferred to have the lyrics like I used to write with Ozzy, and he accepted that. We had about six different titles for the album. *Souled-Out* [Tony Martin's idea] was the original title, and then we came up with that artwork. By that time it had become *Cross Purposes*. A lot of people have this perception of what Sabbath artwork should look like, and that was probably the most subtle, not overly satanic."

Frustratingly, the Japanese bonus track "What's the Use" would have been *Cross Purposes*' finest track, bar none, had it been included in the official running order. A fast rocker with an intricate, novel Iommi riff, its chorus is a little underwritten, but Rondinelli is on fire and Iommi's solo strikes an inspired

THE LAST NIGHT OF THE TOUR,
I TURN AROUND AND MY GONG IS
MISSING, AND LEMMY IS STANDING
THERE WITH AN INDIAN HEADDRESS
ON AND A LITTLE EIGHT-INCH
CYMBAL ON A STRING.

CD & VIDEO DOUBLE PACK.
CD ALBUM AVAILABLE EXCLUSIVELY WITH THIS DOUBLE PACK.

BLACK SABBATH
CROSS PURPOSES~LIVE

balance between control and chaos. The song closes with a spirited windup that portends what could have been.

The North American tour for *Cross Purposes* found the band out with a somewhat notorious lineup, Motörhead and egregious black met-allers Morbid Angel as part of the punishing bill through February and March of '94. Five dates in Japan preceded the UK leg, which saw Godspeed and doom-meisters Cathedral in tow. Sabbath then addressed mainland Europe in detail before venturing down to South America, where one Bill Ward guested on drums. Bobby Rondinelli, it seems, had hired himself a new manager, and she asked for a

raise for Bobby. The band was offended, Bobby ousted, and Bill brought in just in time for the South American jaunt, where a shortened set list was used. Unfortunately, the band had all sorts of technical problems, with Tony Martin using a mic with a chord for the first time, com-ically wrapping it around everything in sight as he roamed the stage. The fact that these were big festival dates, with the band opening for Kiss and Slayer, didn't help matters.

The new album contributed "I Witness," "Psychophobia," "Cross of Thorns" and for a time, "Immaculate Deception" to the set list. Interestingly, after the "Supertzar" intro, the band ripped into "Time Machine" from *Dehumanizer*. Few other surprises ensued (some might consider "The Wizard" and "Symptom of the Universe" eyebrow-raisers),

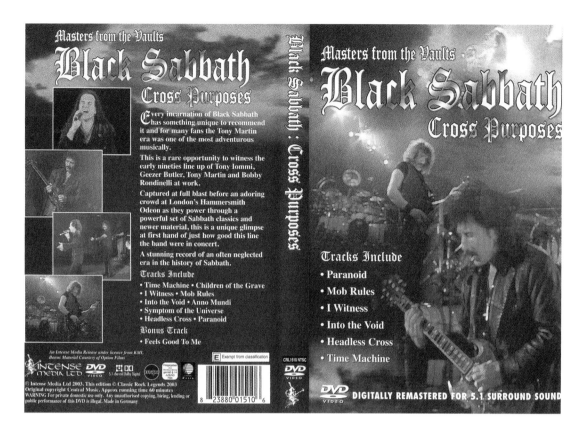

although "Headless Cross" was brought back as the lone full-tour representation of Martin's first run with the band ("Anno Mundi" and "When Death Calls" were late additions). This downplaying of Martin's earlier material had ticked the singer off, and once again, he considered quitting the band.

"In the States, we toured with Motörhead," says Bobby, relating a tour tale. "For my drum solo, I've got a big gong behind me and at the end of the solo, I stand up, get the crowd going, turn around and bang the gong. The last night of the tour, I turn around and my gong is missing, and Lemmy [from Motörhead] is standing there with an Indian headdress on and a little eight-inch cymbal on a string. But I've got this big mallet in my hand, so he stood pretty far away [laughs], thinking that I was

going to hit him. So every time I see Lemmy, he comes up to me and goes, 'I stole your gong!' Tony's a pretty funny guy too. He walked around the studio a lot with this wig that was all dreadlocks looking like a Rastafarian."

An odd and little-marketed live video and CD pack fell out of this tour, 13 months after the issue of the source album. Called *Cross Purposes — Live*, the video included three extra tracks over the CD, but on both, the sound quality is excellent as is the performance of Bobby Rondinelli, who comes off as a much groovier drummer for the Sabs than Cozy ever did. And despite reports that Tony Martin was ill for many of the dates, he sounds excellent as well, most pertinently nailing "Time Machine" (though he opts out of the high notes for "Sabbath Bloody Sabbath"). The fine "I

THE ULTIMATE IN HEAVY METAL

Witness" and "Psychophobia" rock with a little more fire than on the record; again Rondinelli is fluid but dependable. Bobby's performance on "The Wizard" is also quite enjoyable, his drum solo a furious flurry, but his choice of fills of "Symptom of the Universe" don't quite do justice to Bill's more manic, scattershot approach. Also proven: "Black Sabbath" should be dropped from the set if anybody other than Ozzy is up there singing it. Ronnie and Tony both treat it too melodramatically. But yes, all told, this is an underrated (well, ignored) live album, Geezer and Tony both playing well, Butler's bass warm in the mix, Tony's tone rich, powerful, lethal.

When asked how he keeps his voice in such fetching shape after all these years Martin says, "Because I'm good [laughs]. No, I'm not a smoker, I drink a little bit, but I don't do anything to excess. And I've never taken drugs. I've

been fortunate with recording; not quite so fortunate with live work. Just recently, I've had a couple of disastrous shows with the band that I was working with over here. And when the voice goes, that's it, it's gone. Ain't nothing you can do to bring it back. It's not mechanical, like a guitar, changing a string. So you have to work around it. And what I'm able to do live, generally, is to duck or dive the note that I know I ain't gonna get. If there's a high note coming up and I know I ain't gonna get there, I'll take a lower fifth or third or something, anything to get around that note I can't get, which changes the songs slightly. I still sing the same words, obviously but it's taken as your own interpretation of the track. So I struggle live. But recording, generally, I can get right on the button."

20

"WRITE SOMETHING AND WE'LL SEE HOW ICE T FEELS"

– Forbidden

Black Sabbath were back with astonishing quickness a year later, in 1995, towing in their wake a new album, although that didn't stop Tony from altering the lineup once more, making the new record, *Forbidden*, with the exact assortment of fellows that had made *Tyr*.

Courtesy Scott Roderick, swag.com

Although really, what you had was not the *Tyr* lineup, at least as it pertains to band chemistry. Back in that situation, and more pertinently *Headless Cross*, Cozy Powell was very much a partner in the proceedings, but this time, he was a subordinate to Tony. Perhaps one could view the *Forbidden* project as an attempt to relive the bit of a sales and excitement blip the band had experienced during that European *Headless Cross* tour — that right there is the most relevant lineup link to *Forbidden*.

Indeed, Cozy wanted to write and record something that harkened back to *Headless Cross*, but the music industry was a strange and very non-metal place in 1995. No one else was in agreement with Cozy, although the end result isn't noticeably different in cumulative tone than any Tony Martin album, despite the decade span of them all. It's as if all these attitudes became watered down, and no strong direction emerged out the other end, other than that of a sturdy though mediocre Black Sabbath album in the Martin-era style.

"Least favorite is really easy," laughs a beleaguered Tony Martin, when asked to rank his work with the band. "Definitely *Forbidden*. Yet there are still guys that mail me now and say "This is the best album you've ever done,' and I say to them, 'Why?! Why?! For God's sake! Tell me what it is about that album!' Because it was a nightmare to make. I had no idea if I was in the band or not. I mean, they were messing about even then. They weren't telling me, but I could read between the lines because I had been out of the band once before. I knew there was something going on. And they got Ice T to supposedly sing on the album, which he did eventually, but on one track. But they wouldn't tell me if he was singing the whole album or one track, or guesting on one track or what. So for the whole period, it was really uncertain

and it really put me off. Trying to sing in that kind of environment was really difficult. And the songs that we came up with worked great in the rehearsal room and live, but when we put them on record, they had Ice T's producer Ernie C, come over, and it just didn't work!"

"It was the most shit album," laughs Martin. "The thing about *Forbidden* was, by that time, everything was feeling a bit sour. We had this huge meeting in London and they kept promising us that it was going to be great to hook up with some rap guys, and I just couldn't see it and neither could Cozy. He would say, 'This is Black Sabbath.' I know Run DMC tried it and they got off OK with Aerosmith, but this was Black Sabbath, for fuck's sakes. Time put us right in the end, that it really didn't work. And

they kept saying, 'Well, write something, and we'll see how Ice T feels,' and I said, 'That's shit — how am I supposed to write?!' I just couldn't get into it. I just didn't have the impression that I was really there. It was like I was handing it off to somebody to do."

Asked to clarify this Ice T situation, Martin says, "I think what happened was, they waited for us to do the tracks, and then sent them all over to Ice T. Then I think he chose one of the tracks to sing on. And I know Tony Iommi went over to see him; like, they're good friends. But I was in the dark. Singing, I did a couple of harmony things but not much; it was kind of uninspiring to me. It didn't strike me as a production album. It seemed like the sort of album you could do stage-wise. And actually, when we played them in rehearsals, they sounded quite good; I've got various videos of us doing it. But as a studio album, I don't know. They got Cozy playing bass drum beats he normally wouldn't play. We were in rehearsals and the guys were trying to get him into pump bass, like commercial rap-type stuff. And he did try that and they came to a compromise in the end. And he said, 'After all, at the end of the day, I'm still Cozy Powell. I still have to be able to play what's comfortable to me.'"

Doing press at the time of release, Martin unsurprisingly put things in a brighter light. "We decided before we went in that we wanted to make more of a raw-sounding album. Basically what that meant was going back to how records used to be recorded originally — setting up the equipment and simply playing. You kind of get spoiled when you're working in studios a lot. We just left all the squeaks and funny noises in this time around. These are some of the best albums that you remember, the ones where you can hear the guitarist

USING SOMEBODY LIKE ICE T GAVE US A HUGE AREA THAT WE WERE NEVER ABLE TO GET INTO BEFORE.

playing. In recent years, people are trying to eliminate stuff like fret noise. That means you spent a lot more time and money in the studio."

"In terms of the lyrics and melodies, I approached it in a totally different way," continued Martin, speaking in the summer of '95. "I just approached it from the human emotions side. The only way I was going to achieve that was by not writing anything down. Pen did not touch paper the entire time. The first time the lyrics were actually written down was on the album sleeve. I just set up a microphone, took the backing track and sang. What you're hearing is in fact the way the lyrics and the melodies came out. I sang the lyrics; I didn't write them, which is a totally different way of working with vocals."

With respect to the Ice T cameo, Martin said at the time, "It means that we can break out of some of the confines that we've been put into. People like to put you in a box and stick a label on it. We want to break all this stuff down. Using somebody like Ice T gave us a huge area that we were never able to get into before. We could get radio play, we could get fans of his going to the shows, and that stimulates back catalog. You can see how it starts to spread, and it breaks you out of that box and you can move on to other things. Even the artwork lifts us out of that normal, serious element and gives us a new starting point. These were natural movements."

"I really don't know how it happened," remarked Ernie C, on getting the production gig. "I just know that Tony liked our band, and he was wondering who produced the record. He thought that I did it. He came down to one of our shows — we played in Sheffield — and we met him and we talked about possibly doing something with him. He was really nice; I think he liked us, and he wanted me to do the record. Body Count *is* Black Sabbath. I mean, basically it's a little bit of Black Sabbath, a bit of Slayer, a bit of everyone. But Black Sabbath is definitely an influence. Plus Tony, being a left-handed guitarist, I identified with him automatically when I was a kid. At first I was really intimidated and nervous, and I'd say, 'OK, I have a job to do and I have to get over that.' So I had to put behind me that they were Black Sabbath."

"He's a bigger Black Sabbath fan than me!" says Ernie, when asked about Ice T. "He's the Black Sabbath man! He wanted to do something, so he was just on the one song. He didn't really have the time to be around, so I asked him to come down for the one song." On the guys and their ways, Ernie adds, "They're pretty mellow these days, surprisingly. You know, dinner at six, coffee at eight, breakfast at nine, get up, go to the gym. They're really straightened out."

You can add to the saga of Martin and Ice T the fact that the whole reunion with Ozzy was still up in the air. Iommi has said that eight months of negotiation and fairly open dialogue between Sabbath and Sharon and Ozzy ended abruptly with a fax and no further phone conversations. Tony, it seemed, was getting a taste of his own medicine.

Confirms Martin, with respect to the Ozzy-concerned machinations grinding in the background, "They wouldn't admit it. I'd always said, 'This is your band. What am I going to do? I'm not going to steal your band away from you or anything.' If you've got something going on, just tell me. That's all I need to know. That's the least you could expect. But they don't. And they never did. You always had to read between the lines with Sabbath, and it got really tiring in the end, trying to work out what they were up to."

"I think it was absolutely the wrong move," said Iommi, years later, on the Ice T collaboration. Ice T was a hot property at the time, a rap star further lauded for his crossover into fairly extreme metal with his Body Count franchise, notorious for their "Cop Killer" single from the band's self-titled album from 1992. "But again, we were talked into it. That was a low point in our career. We were listening to other people. Why don't you use this guy? He's hip. He might

show you a different direction, brighten it up a bit. And of course it didn't work that way. It was supposed to be Ice T, and somehow this Ernie C got involved. But no, it was a definite, definite wrong move; totally unnecessary and I really regret that."

Wrong move maybe in the sense that the press picked up on it and hammered away. But, the production on *Forbidden* is fine, basically clean and professional just like all the Tony Martin records. Nor are the songs any sort of disastrous departure, the only footprint left by the two rappers being Ice T's cameo on the opener, "The Illusion of Power." Cozy, at the time, lauded Ernie C as both a Sabbath fan and a musician capable of the job. Still, he admitted the album was a bit rough, a bit like an Ernie C album — pretty good on the guitars but not so hot with respect to drum sound. Later, Cozy would get more pronounced in his complaints, citing lack of polish. But one almost has to debate the definition of polish. *Forbidden* can be classified as having too much polish of one sort, and not enough of another. The songs aren't great, although this isn't much of a step down

from the previous three Tony Martin albums.

Says reinstated bassist Neil Murray on Ernie C (Tony had had a disagreement with Geezer's wife/manager Gloria; hence, no Geezer), "Ice T was supposed to be the producer and he said no, and he said, 'Why don't you use Ernie C?' But I might be wrong about that. And to some extent, he had the sound engineer, and they did things the way they wanted. But some of his ideas, which might have been quite good, got ignored. And he didn't have the personality to bend us to his will. As a band we wanted somebody to come along and give us direction, but Ernie really wasn't quite giving us enough and the whole thing ended up being a bit of a compromise. Most of us weren't really happy with the way it turned out. But it was a noble experiment."

"When *Headless Cross* happened," continues Murray, "it was very much Tony Iommi and Cozy leading the band and having the say, whereas for *Forbidden*, it was more back in Tony's control; Cozy had much less say in it. And the idea behind it was to do something more current, and get a producer that would make the band sound more mid-'90s. And

Sean Denomey

there was a fair bit of arguments about it. For some reason the theory was good, but the execution didn't turn out the way I thought it was going to. I really thought it was going to be bone-crunchingly heavy, more powerful than it actually was.

"It isn't as heavy as I anticipated," Iommi concurs. "We did the album in eight days, which was quite unusual for us. We haven't done that since *Paranoid*. I wanted to make the album more of a live feel, to get back to setting up and just playing, as opposed to going in and recording drums for three days, then guitars for three days. I wanted to just walk in and play."

Tony has also put down the writing process for the album, saying that much of it was done in a three-way between himself, Tony Martin and Geoff Nicholls — Cozy and Neil weren't

around all the time, having been contracted to finish other projects.

"I think Tony did a great job," continues Iommi, with respect to Mr. Martin. "We'd done quite a lot together, but it was basically me, my baby, if you like. I had to finance the whole thing. It was very difficult to keep the band running. Tony had actually stuck there a long time and he was very good, and we'd done *Headless Cross*, which I really enjoyed. I thought that album was really good, with Cozy Powell. But the last album, *Forbidden*, I thought just took another road and I don't really like it."

Somewhat undercutting the seriousness of the latest spot of product was the cartoony grim reaper on the cover art, a throwback to *Headless Cross*, essentially. "That's exactly what

Alexander Rack

we wanted," defends Tony. "We got fed up with as soon as you mentioned Sabbath, the gloom and doom. I just wanted a lighter side of it to be looked on. When I saw the rough drawings, I thought, 'That's great. That's just up our street.' The back of the sleeve got the most talk, as people tried to figure out all the folks drawn into the dog pile of the thing. The band was all there, but so was Miles Copeland, Cozy's ex-wife Val, Ice T, Ernie C and the artists of the piece themselves."

Issued in early June 1995, *Forbidden* commences with the aforementioned "The Illusion of Power" (actually the working title for the album), not a good way to open the record. Martin's initial lyric is strangely irritable, the Ice T cameo jarring and pointless, not to mention the fact that the song is an unremarkable and slow composition forced into a Sabbatherian box.

"That was just about politics," says Martin. "I don't usually dabble with political lyrics. It's not really my thing. But Ice T picked up on that, being a rap guy, and he put his voice towards that. But there's nothing really behind that."

"I mostly wrote all the lyrics myself," says Martin, asked if Geoff Nicholls had a hand in this one, or in any of the others. "Have done since I joined, apart from *Eternal Idol*, of course. And I have to say, *Forbidden* had probably more time and more commitment and a bit more assuredness about it. But we could've made it much better. But having that rap thing and having those guys in there trying to steer us into something else . . . it just lost it."

"Get a Grip" picks it up, with Iommi turning in one of his circuitous, note-dense riffs strapped to a catchy chorus — an animated video was produced for this engaging track, although Martin's vocals are a bit weak. Next up is "Can't Get Close Enough," its initial melody recalling the eccentricity of "Psychophobia," its transformation into a heavy metal rocker sounding like a B-grade "Megalomania." "Shaking Off the Chains" is much

Alexander Rack

Alexander R

fresher, with two sets of proggy riffs set in motion, the second being somewhat *Sabbath Bloody Sabbath*-worthy. Says Martin, "'Shaking Off the Chains' was mostly about losing the image that people put on you. Getting rid of the past and starting over."

"I Won't Cry for You" comes next, Martin's impassioned, blues-balladeering vocal somewhat pushed back in the mix. Once again, Sabbath prove modestly successful at the power ballad format through Iommi's knack for infusing elegant and dark riffs of impending doomfoolery. "Guilty as Hell" is successful and heavy and quite groovy in a direction not unlike "The Shining." "They were just current feelings I had at the time," offers Martin. "It just felt like the band was being messed about, ripped apart, doing this rap

thing. Everyone was saying, 'It's gonna be great, gonna be great,' and nobody believed it. And when they turned around and said, 'Well, it wasn't me.' I said, 'You're as guilty as hell. You were the one who thought of it.'"

"Sick and Tired" is a big thumping blues similar to "Heart Like a Wheel," although the verse construct is fresh and melodic tripping down a Whitesnake pathway. Lyrically, this one looks at both relationships and the crap that goes on in the music business, a harkening back to *Sabotage*.

"Rusty Angels" is a strange but quite attractive melodic hard rocker, like hair metal too late. Comments Martin, "There's a graveyard for airplanes in Texas where they store all those military and commercial planes. They all just sit in the desert and they cannibalize them for spares, and there's just miles and miles of these rusting planes. Well, I guess they don't rust, but they sit there. And I saw an image of it; they shot it from above. They might have even gotten it from space — acres and acres of

BLACK SABBATH

306

ander Rack

planes. And it somehow spurred me on to the Enola Gay thing, the B-29 with the nuclear bomb. And it all kind of merged into one story and came out as 'Rusty Angels.'"

The record's title track shows up second to last, Sabbath going for a thudly, oppressive, unremarkable riff before the verse sequence redeems things, while Iommi finds an interesting and buoyant riff to accommodate the prominent keyboard wash from Nicholls.

Forbidden closes with "Kiss Of Death," a languished epic that breaks into a head-smasher of an Iommi riff at very close to two-thirds the way through its width and girth. The chorus is also quite memorable, with Martin singing slowly over a doomy smear. More like this one would have propped this record up considerably.

It's not surprising that the "sunniest" two songs from the album, "Get a Grip" and "Rusty Angels" made Sabbath's set list for the tour, but it is surprising that these two, plus "Can't Get Close Enough," were the only *Forbidden* tracks that did see active duty. "Kiss of Death" how-

ever replaced "Rusty Angels" for the European leg of the tour. A perennial problem, the Martin-era songs were not that well received. June and July saw the band playing the U.S., mostly with Motörhead and Tiamat in tow. September through November saw Sabbath mount one of their most intensive European tours ever, mostly supported by Tiamat.

Comments Martin on the tour, "*Forbidden* wasn't a big seller, but we had a good fanbase in Germany and Italy. We did a lot of the Eastern bloc countries, when the wall was just coming down, and we were still looked on very suspiciously, just being Westerners. But it was good. We had a good following over in Japan, so we went there. We were making our way over to Australia, but we never quite got that far. We went down to Korea, and for some reason we didn't make the leap over the water to Australia; it got pulled."

In April of '96, a compilation called *The Sabbath Stones* was issued as the final obligation record Tony had to deliver to I.R.S. Essentially a highlights pack from Sabbath's I.R.S. catalog, the album nonetheless went that extra quarter mile, including a track each from *Born Again*, *Seventh Star*, *The Eternal Idol* and *Dehumanizer*, also offering up *Forbidden*'s Japanese bonus track "Loser Gets It All." After the compilation's release, Martin bade good riddance to the cold

WRITE SOMETHING AND WE'LL SEE HOW ICE T FEELS

world of twilight-years Sabbath.

"Tony . . . that's a big question," says Tony Martin in closing, when asked for a psychological profile of the riff-master. "Nothing like putting me on the spot. As a player, I rate him very highly. How he plays some of that stuff is just beyond me. He's a great guy; I don't have a problem with him. He's not a bad person; he's a nice guy. And when you're in the frame, he's great to get on with; he's OK. But when you're not in the frame, he's completely isolated from you. The phone just stops ringing. I mean, one minute you're friends and all, and the next minute, you're nothing, nobody; you don't even exist."

21

"A SELF-MADE FUCKING DOOM-TOMB"

– Reunion

And we all know what happens next. Black Sabbath sends a blizzard of faxes, paperwork goes flyin', the wives all talk, and Black Sabbath is back to their original lineup, save for the heartbeat of the band Bill Ward, who is replaced by Faith No More and Ozzy Osbourne drummer Mike Bordin.

Alexander Rack

Speaking to Geezer four days before the first momentous show of Black Sabbath's reunion ascension, I ask him how this could all, incredibly, finally happen. "Sharon Osbourne, Ozzy's wife and manager, called my wife and manager and mentioned it to her. She said Tony and Ozzy had met and sorted all their problems out and were working together on Ozzy's solo thing. So she thought about the Sabbath reunion for the Ozzfest and would I be interested? So I said I'd meet with the guys and take it from there. I wasn't exactly on talking terms with Tony, since the last version of Sabbath. I don't know. I just don't get into many conflicts head-on with people."

"I had butterflies in my stomach for about two weeks before," continued Geezer. "I hadn't seen or spoken to Tony for about three years; a lot of bad things were said to each other, things we'd heard through other people. But when I left Ozzy last, it was on good terms, so no problem with that. But there was trepidation about how things would work out. So going into it I was just

incredibly nervous. I'd grown up with these guys and now I'm nervous to see them — really strange. But as soon as I walked in, it was like we'd never been away from each other.

"Mike was there as well — just us and a couple of the road crew — and we sorta got into it, a bit of small talk, basically went through what songs we were going to do. And we did them like we'd only played them the week before. 'Beyond the Wall of Sleep,' we hadn't played since 1970, and we did it straight off [laughs]. But we just sat down and played the whole set. Ozzy said 'These are the ones I'm comfortable singing.' We left it all down to Ozzy, because he has to do his show first, so he's got songs he feels comfortable singing for 40 minutes after his set's finished."

So Sabbath embarked on Ozzfest '97, playing their first show on May 24th in Washington, DC. The band were billed, somewhat disparagingly, below Ozzy Osbourne, second to headliner, on the main stage, following sets by Powerman 5000, Machine Head,

Fear Factory, Type O Negative, Pantera and, at some stops, Marilyn Manson. The set list was minimal, the band sticking close to the expected, offering "War Pigs," "Into the Void," "Sweet Leaf," "Children of the Grave," "Black Sabbath," "Fairies Wear Boots," "Sabbath Bloody Sabbath" and "Paranoid."

On why Bill Ward was not part of these dates. Geezer says, "I've stayed out of all that. Sharon Osbourne put the whole thing together, so she decided. I don't know if Bill didn't want to do it or what. And Mike loves Bill Ward anyways, and Bill's style — he's a Sabbath fanatic. So he wants to play exactly the way it was recorded. And the same goes for me and Tony, because over the years, I'd changed a lot of the bass lines. So we're going back to playing them exactly the way they were recorded originally."

Inevitably, proceedings got mired down in contracts and lawyers. "It's still even happening now as we're speaking," says Geezer. "It's like one of those simple things that you get together, and you think it's simple until everybody's lawyers get together. I just said, 'Have all the arguments, and when you've all finished arguing, send me the papers and I'll sign them.' You know, I'll do it for free; it doesn't bother me. It's the same old thing, as soon as something's up and there's money to be had, the lawyers all get involved to get as much money out of you as they can."

"Ozzy's a total health nut," said Geezer, about what the band would do on their downtime. "I'm completely off any mind-altering substances whatsoever. One hundred percent nothing whatsoever. Once a month I'll have a non-alcoholic beer. It makes me feel horrible just thinking I used to do what I did [laughs]. I just go around to all the toy shops and comic book shops, buy old books and things."

I'D GROWN UP WITH THESE GUYS AND NOW I'M NERVOUS TO SEE THEM — REALLY STRANGE. BUT AS SOON AS I WALKED IN, IT WAS LIKE WE'D NEVER BEEN AWAY FROM EACH OTHER.

Alexander Rack

A SELF-MADE FUCKING DOOM-TOMB

> FOR YEARS AND YEARS AND YEARS, I LIVED IN MY KIND OF HELL. THEN I LOOK AT SOMEBODY LIKE KURT COBAIN, AND I COULDN'T BE THAT BAD.

"It didn't come easy," sighed Ozzy on the state of his health at this point in his frazzled life. "I still work as hard as ever and I'm working out every day now. I came to a point in my life where I said to myself that if I want to continue what I'm doing, it's going to take its toll. It *was* taking its toll. I was drinking two bottles of cognac a day, beer, coke and God knows how much other shit. It was what I did. I'm not somebody who wants to preach a fine example. If you enjoy it, fair play to you. I'm not one to say don't do it. If you said to me seven or eight years ago, 'Look at me; I used to do it,' I would have told you to go fuck yourself. I'm not one of these fuckin' born again rock 'n' rollers. You can only do it if you really want to do it. If you really want to, you've got to get outside help, 'cause I had to get outside help. I had no choice. I burnt all my bridges. The choice was either sink or swim."

"Every single day I would have the feeling that I was terrified of living, but so afraid of dying," continues Oz. "Every single fuckin' day. For years and years and years, I lived in my kind of hell. Then I look at somebody like Kurt Cobain, and I couldn't be that bad. There's got

to be a lower place than where I was. That's dreadful. When you wake up in the morning with that feeling, it's beyond shame, it's beyond fear, it's beyond anything else. You just don't fit in this world. You can't find a place to go. To carry those feelings away, you have to do exactly the same thing that got you there the night before. It's like a merry-go-round of madness. Then you've got to perform in front of people. In the end you're taking valium, tranquilizers, drugs and booze, and you've got the fear itself. I started to black out. I started to fall to pieces. I'm still not right now. I still have to speak to people. I still have to take medication, but for a different reason now. I have to take anti-depressants and whatnot."

Ozzy says he's now motivated by exercise. "I love to get up and get straight on my bike. I love breaking a sweat. It makes me feel like I'm putting something back. I know I'll never be able to put it all back and I know I'll live a shorter life than most, but I've lived twice a lifetime than most, but in a shorter amount of time. I get panic attacks, I'm on Prozac, I'm on fucking everything. I was so fucked up on drugs and alcohol, that I had to literally clean my system out so that I could go on Prozac. It took me a long time to succumb to the Prozac pills because anything that didn't give me euphoria I didn't want to know about. Eventually, I had no option because I was so fucked up mentally that my doctor and therapist said, 'Ozzy, you have to accept the fact that you have a chemical imbalance in your head.' Then I thought maybe it's the chemical imbalance in my head that's allowed me to be so creative. What if I start taking this Prozac and I lose my creativity? I'm fucked, it's finished, it's over. I'm already living a year ahead of what's happening now — I was thinking that I'd be living on the beach collecting empty fucking Coke cans and whatever. I'm terrible, I wake up in the morning and I'm a disaster area. Then I worry because I have nothing to worry about.

"But the exercise keeps me going — if I don't do it for two days in a row, I go fucking crazy, with or without the Prozac. I take the Prozac all the time. I still get these horrible thoughts, but they just come and go, whereas, before, they would come and grow into these ugly little fucking monsters in my head by the end of the day. I'd run to the bar and to the drug dealer. I'd be thinking stupidity like, 'I'm gonna fail, my voice is gonna break, I'm not gonna win, if I don't get to the elevator quickly, something bad is going to happen.' I'm fucking superstitious. I'd think if a dog looks at me before it crosses my path, my record's going to go down the toilet. And I'd walk around looking for excuses for my fucking head. I'd walk down the street, close my eyes, count to ten — if I opened my eyes and I'd be stepping on a crack in the pavement, I'd think that everything is going to fall to pieces. I'd play these fucking games all the time; I still do. It's a little bit under control; it's definitely not as severe as it used to be because, I go 'OK, I didn't

THEN I THOUGHT MAYBE IT'S THE CHEMICAL IMBALANCE IN MY HEAD THAT'S ALLOWED ME TO BE SO CREATIVE. WHAT IF I START TAKING THIS PROZAC AND I LOSE MY CREATIVITY?

Alexander Rack

make the light before the hotel door closed.' I live my life in a fucking tomb, in a self-made fucking doom-tomb."

"There were some reservations by some, or one, or two, or all the members of Sabbath," said Bill, picking up the story on July 28, 1997, a little under a month after the Ozzfest '97 dates had wound up in Columbus, Ohio. "Ozzy apparently had some reservations about my sanity and my ability to play. At least that's what I've been told. And this would be based on quite a number of years ago. I saw the announcement of the other three members getting together on MTV and it blew me away, and I sent faxes immediately to everybody, not

necessarily to say 'Hey guys, can I be a part of it?' but more asking how they might feel about doing this without me. And I didn't get any responses at all. I got one terse telephone call from Sharon Osbourne who said that my services weren't required, and I thought OK, whatever. I went through a lot of hardship and a lot of pain behind this, and the guys went and did what they had to do. What happened since is that Tony shared with me that everybody missed me, and I said, 'I wished you would have let me know, because I would have loved to have played.'"

And not being up to scratch physically didn't seem to be the issue. Had anybody bothered to check, according to Ward, they would have found a sturdy Bill. "Definitely. I played a drum clinic in Detroit at the Guitar Center, in front of about 150 drummers," said Bill, back in the thick of the debacle. "And the night before I played a sellout concert in Detroit. So my answer would be that I'm more than in shape. I'm playing drums, I'm singing, I'm playing keyboards. It's far more active than what one would do as a drummer in a band. So I don't have any problems with the physical end of it."

Speaking with Ozzy in November of '97, I asked him pretty much the same thing — why no Bill Ward? "I don't really know. I haven't worked with Bill on the road since 1979. And whether I want to do the show or whether I don't want to do the show, I do it anyways because that's my job. Now, nine times out of ten it's great, with the rare occasion that I thought it was absurd to play at fucking four in the morning when I'd already done an afternoon show or whatever. Circumstances where you have to be crazy, or I'm sick or whatever. A commitment is a commitment. But I've worked with Bill. After the *No More Tears* tour, there was an attempt to get a reunion together, to do 25 shows. Somebody was going to buy the shows, blah blah blah. But the problem is, I have a manager, I have an accountant, I have an agent, I have a business manager. So does Tony, so does Geezer, so does Bill. Now it started out, the negotiations, all fine and dandy, fine. Then all this fucking entourage of business managers and accountants got involved and it just got crazy. I just came off a worldwide tour, I don't need the aggravation, it's costing me money I don't really want to spend. I've got better things to do. I'd rather invest some of my time with my kids. So I went my way, and they went theirs, and then Bill sends me a fax saying, 'Look, I always said I wouldn't do Sabbath without you, but I'm going back with Sabbath.' And I said, 'Bill, I don't have a problem with that. I'm tired, I've been on tour for two years, I need a rest.' It's 25 shows we could have done, bang, done them and got on with it. But it just ended up in a big headache, and I wasn't prepared to go through it. And I thought that's it, it's never going to happen.

"And then Sharon came to me and asked me. Because last year with Ozzfest, we only did four shows. And she said to me this year, 'What about doing the Ozzfest again?' And I said well we better do a few more shows, because last year, only doing four shows, it was hardly a big, you know, wow. And I said, well rather than book a year, I'd like to build it slowly, do a bit more every year until it gets established. So she said 'Great, what if we got Black Sabbath together to do the show; what would you think?' and I said, well, yeah. I said to Sharon, I'm going to tell you here and now. You're my manager, but you're my wife, but I'm talking to you as my manager. You're asking me would I do Black Sabbath. As an artist to his manager, I'm saying to you Sharon, yes, and now I don't

John McMurtrie

want to hear any more about it. You've got the problem of getting the other fucking guys together. I don't know, I try to stay away from it. Naturally, because she's my wife and she's on the phone, I have to hear some of it. But I don't know who she's talking to or what's going on. I try to keep my distance, because I'm not a manager, I'm not an agent. To be an agent and a manager you have to be a different person than an artist. You can't do both and do them sincerely. I don't understand managers. They're a special breed of people.

"So I met up with Tony and we got talking and I said, 'How'd you get on with Bill when you last played?' And he said, 'Well, we didn't get on as well as we'd expected.' So I said, 'What if we do these 22 shows this summer; what do you think it would be like for Bill? I would love Bill to be there but could he do the gig?' Because you can't play a gig one day and then

to Tony, 'To be honest with you, I don't feel comfortable about it. Let's establish it first and then see what it's about.' So we got Michael Bordin, who is Faith No More's drummer playing on my set and the Sabbath set. And he wasn't Bill Ward, but then again, neither is Bill Ward Michael Bordin. They're two separate drummers completely. So it went OK. So these two shows we're going to do in England, I said to my wife, I've really got a feeling in my gut, and when I get a gut feeling, nine times out of ten, I'm right. I said to Sharon, 'What happens if halfway through the set, the fucking guy falls over? What happens if he loses his chops? What happens? What the fuck am I going to do?' I can't play drums out of my fucking mouth, you know. And I might fuck up, but as long as you've got solid music and can jam around . . . . I'm not saying for one minute that the sun shines out of my ass and I'm the greatest and everybody else comes second behind me. I'm not saying that for one second. But the drummer is a very integral part of the band. If he starts to sway and fuck up, then the whole band moves. And Sharon went to see Bill in Los Angeles a couple weeks ago and she comes back and goes, 'Fuck, I don't know what to say.'"

Was it a good report or a bad report? "I'd rather not say. But she was very concerned. Let me put it this way. It was a different form of music than what he used to play. It was a different vibe entirely. So I said, you know what, Sharon? I'd like to have a fallback guy. If something happens to Bill and you have to get somebody up there, if Bill can't make it or he gets winded or he breaks his leg or whatever, you've got to keep the show going, you've got to get somebody up there in a second. And she says, 'I think you're right.' So I think she's going to get somebody. I don't care who the fuck it is, as long as it's somebody. But it would be really

be good in some circumstances and not in others. Because I did some shows on that tour and I wasn't feeling good at all, but I got up there and did it because you have to get on with it you know? And I can fucking jump around and fly around the stage, but the drummer's got to keep the beat you know?"

"I was just worried about him generally," sighed Ozzy, asked for specifics on Bill. "Because all these years of people wanting to see us, if we go up there and we fucking look like four idiots, they're going to go what the fuck's this all about? It's a joke anyway. So I said nice to answer the question, to have Bill pull it off. I would really be happy. And I'm keeping my fingers crossed."

Ozzy's not sure how he's maintained himself as an active performer all these years. "I don't run around the block every morning and have to say 15 Hail Marys. I don't know, I'm just a very lucky guy, I suppose. I put a lot of it down to my wife. My wife is very in tune with what's going on in the industry. I mean, I don't know where she finds the fucking time to be my wife, the mother to my children, manage me, she manages Coal Chamber. She's in with what's going down; she works like a fucking slave. I don't know where she gets the time to take a piss.

"I try and work out when I can, but I found working out and doing the shows was killing my legs. I work out on the Lifecycle. But I haven't been doing it, because I've been traveling and I have jet lag. Once I'm back in New York I'm stuck there for about a week, so I have a Lifecycle that I'm used to, and I'll get back on track and do it for an hour or so each day. I've got to get fit for these Sabbath shows. I'm kind of like on a vegetarian diet at the moment, semi-vegetarian. Because I went and had some blood work done a couple months ago and lo and behold I had a really high cholesterol count, and they told me to lay off the animal fats. And with me it's all or nothing. I can't have just a little bit of meat, so I just knocked it on the head, and when I had a blood test a couple weeks ago it was way down. So that's the way it's going to be for a while. But I'm not one of these 'because of animals' people. I'll have chicken soup or a bit of chicken. But I won't have any red meat anymore. None at all."

I asked Ozzy how he's changed psychologically over the years. "I don't know whether I have. It's a difficult question. Every day you get

WHEN I STARTED WRITING SONGS ALL THOSE YEARS AGO, I DIDN'T THINK FOR A SECOND ABOUT THE BUSINESS SIDE OF IT. I JUST WANTED TO BE A ROCK STAR.

up, you're a different person anyway. Sometimes my coping mechanism is worse than the last or better than the last day. Some days, I literally feel that my head's going to explode. I find it hard. Once, I had the release of going to the bar and getting soused out of my head. And I can't do that anymore. Or if I do do it, I get pissed off at myself for doing it. But I'm not as bad as I used to be. But I've got no releases anymore. I've got to find a way of getting my head clear. It's causing problems for me. I can't get in that space again of abuse. I can, but I don't want to do it that way. I don't want to cause too many fucking problems in my life. My kids don't like it, my wife doesn't like it, my peers don't like it. Yet, more than anything else, I feel I've let myself down. Yet it's a continuous fucking battle. It's like, for fuck sakes, will you quit? It's like somebody tapping you on the shoulder.

"I can't have three beers after a show. If I have a drink after the show, I'm going to get fucked up. Once in a while I want to go, 'fuck it,' and smoke a joint or something. Then that leads to other things and everybody gets pissed off around me. I mean I've been in a terrible state with all that shit, dreadful state, near death every fucking time."

Alexander Rack

Alexander R

To add immensely, and almost comically, to Ozzy's stress, it was announced that before the year would end, the original Black Sabbath — Bill Ward now included — would be performing December 4th and 5th, 1997, at the Birmingham N.E.C. Sure, the hits would be there, they would have to be. But as a nod to the more serious fans, and frankly, to keep the guys from getting bored, Sabbath would include such obscure tracks as "Dirty Women," "Spiral Architect," "Electric Funeral," and most shockingly, "Behind the Wall of Sleep," in this milestone celebration of doom. Indeed Vinny Appice was in the wings lest Bill Ward should blow up Spinal Tap-style. Further weirdness saw Ugly Kid Joe's Whitfield Crane on vocals for the sound check, at which he proved his fandom through mastery of the lyrics — "Hole in the Sky," "Hand of Doom" and even "Heaven and Hell" were trotted out mischievously for the check.

Nearly a year later, on October 20th of 1998, a platinum-selling album called *Reunion* would emerge documenting the experience. But first, on April 5, 1998, Sabbath history would be rocked with the death, at the age of 50, of Cozy Powell, a well-known car and motorcycle enthusiast, in a high-speed accident aboard his Saab 9000 on the M4 near Bristol.

The *Daily Mirror* had said that Cozy was talking on his cell phone, was over the legal drinking limit (although later reports said just slightly), and was not wearing a seatbelt. Bad weather may have also been a factor. Additionally he was going 104 miles per hour. We know this because incredibly, he was talking on the phone with his girlfriend Sharon Reeve telling her as much and expressing reservation about the transmission seizing up. His last words, as far as Reeve was in a position to ascertain, were "Oh shit," after which she heard a loud bang. It was thought that a slow leak in his tire had caused him to lose control on a turn and he hit a railing, the car cartwheeling, Powell catapulted, the car landing on top of him. Cozy died at the hospital of his injuries. At the time, there had been talk of a Rainbow reunion, sessions with Glenn Tipton and Brian May, plus touring and recording with Yngwie Malmsteen. It is thought that Cozy's final work was for a record by Colin Blunstone of The Zombies.

"He was really into it," said Cozy's ex-bandmate Tony Martin, on Powell's fateful need for speed, specifically his fancy of motorcycles. "He would race them, go to race meetings. One story, he went to the Yamaha company, and said, 'Can you get me a motorbike?' And they said, 'No, we can't; it's not the same company.' 'Come on, it's the same name.' 'Yes, but it's a different company completely.' So he got a Honda [laughs]. He had this thing that was road legal, but it had the race sophistications on it. My God, this guy used to fly around on it. He was a natural on it; when he was on the machine, it was like he was glued to it — fantastic really. But he died, obviously, driving his car, so something went wrong there. But I spent many miles with him in his car, and he was fast, but I never felt any danger. He always seemed like he was in control."

Reunion (working title: *Songs from the Black Box*) was issued as a two-CD set with a plush, informative booklet. It was also issued as a limited edition digipak. The album included all 16 live tracks, ostensibly from the second night. The album would also include two brand-new studio tracks from the band. "Psycho Man" would see issue as a promotional digipak and as a commercial sale jewel case single featuring the album version, a radio edit and a Danny Saber remix edit. "Selling My Soul" would be distinguished by its use of drum machine, Bill Ward's drum track found to be too inaccurate.

On the subject of writing a studio album, "I've been asked that question and this is what I've come up with," said Ozzy. "If the magic is still there, if we could still do what we could once do, then I wouldn't mind. But I wouldn't do it for the four of us doing a record together, and it didn't turn out. Because I don't really need to do that, you know? It's going backward."

Ozzy then clarifies that nothing had been written with Tony to date, meaning that the two new songs were put together post-Birmingham, in the ten months it took to get the actual record on the racks, and not, as had been rumored, in and around the sessions for Ozzy's solo album *Ozzmosis*.

Sez Oz, "No, see the problem with everybody is that instead of finding out the real truth, no one will phone me up and say, 'Hey, are you writing with Tony?' It's like, I did sit down with Tony and attempt it, but it kind of fizzled out because he wasn't really serious about it. It's like, I've always said that if it was easy to sit down and write songs, nobody would have a

AS FAR AS I'M CONCERNED BLACK SABBATH CONSISTS OF BILL WARD, OZZY OSBOURNE, GEEZER BUTLER, AND TONY IOMMI. AND THAT'S IT.

real job. Everybody would say, 'Oh I'm going to sit at home and write four hit songs today and make a ton of dough and that's me for the next month.' It's not that easy. You have to be inspired, you've got to have the will to write, you have to be in the right frame of mind. Certain things have to be right. I'll try to write with anybody, but sometimes the record company doesn't like the political situation and won't let me. When I started writing songs all those years ago, I didn't think for a second about the business side of it. I just wanted to be a rock star. I thought the money and the wealth would just be there. I didn't think there were greedy bastards that were going to steal it all off of you and tell you to do these fucking stupid things so they'll make an extra five hundred an hour or whatever. It's kind of like you suddenly realize you're in a big business and there's a lot of money to be made from it, and I'm not business-minded. And that's why I'm very lucky that this second time around in my career I have Sharon. But saying Sharon is a good thing, sometimes I have to wonder: is she talking to me as a loving wife or as a bastard manager? It's really easy to get swallowed in, you know? But you just have to bite your lip and get on with it."

The sound quality and the performances on the live album are excellent, Ozzy yelling like a maniac and singing strongly (although, like Tony Martin, he ducks notes on "Sabbath Bloody Sabbath"), Bill deep in the pocket, boomy and powerful, Tony's guitar tone pervasive, absorptive. Highlights include the aforementioned "Behind the Wall of Sleep" slapped in bizarrely as the second track, right after the "War Pigs" opener — let's not overlook the fact that Ozzy's job isn't easy in this one. Geezer then bobs and weaves into "Bassically" before "N.I.B." explodes. "Fairies Wear Boots" gives way to "Electric Funeral" which brings an added sense of downer to the show. Then it's "Sweet Leaf" and finally, what is perhaps the highlight of the record, "Spiral Architect," Tony's intro truly magical, partly thanks to its rarity. The band plays the song with spirit and heaviness. Ozzy's vocal is a little wobbly, but we should be thankful he even consented to give it a go. "Into the Void" and "Snowblind" finish the first CD, these being concert classics but not big hits, two strong album tracks fortunately included.

The second disc opens with a tribal and oppressive "Sabbath Bloody Sabbath," and then Tony's "Orchid" intro into "Lord of This World." "Dirty Women" is another crushing high point, with its climactic jam section near the end. As this part begins, one hears quite prominently (and intrusively) Geoff Nicholls on keyboards, who has kept quiet for much of the rest of the album. Indeed, even in the preamble to it, at which time Tony solos, there is no underlying rhythm track added by Nicholls. If he's not used as a foundation for solos, it made no sense to use keyboards at all. *Reunion* could have been recorded as a power trio, and we would have had the pure, undiluted original lineup experience. "Black Sabbath" and an interminably long "Iron Man" follow, allowing

for a hotdog break, maybe even a smoke, while "Children of the Grave" and "Paranoid" close the show in fast and faster fashion.

The album proper closes with the two new studio tracks. "Psycho Man" is a bit low-rent, with a standard lyric about a psycho murderer serial killer guy. The song's dour *Dehumanizer* galumph picks up at the three-minute mark with a somewhat inspired Iommi riff or two. In fact, the "When he's killed again" passages approach prime, classic Sabbath, in melody to the waning light, in doom fast on the approach. "Selling My Soul" is much better (and you would never guess there was — shock of shocks — a drum machine being used). The lyric is at least a little more abstract than that of "Psycho Man," and the band approach it a bit prog-minded, laying in some keyboard textures as well as dovetailing in more than a few high quality riffs.

"To be honest with you, there was no fucking spark," says Ozzy, on coming up with these two songs. "Bill and Geezer weren't there at the time, and the record company said at the time, 'You know, Ozzy's got an hour to live, could you write us a quick song before you die,' so we went into the studio. So we're in the studio, and people amaze me. We've got a double album, and they're saying 'Do you have any fucking bonus tracks?' And I'm there, 'You have a fucking two-hour show, and you want two more songs?!' But that's the name of the game; you always have to put more on the album than you've got. Tony and I looked at each other and said, 'Fuck this, what are we going to do? We've been jamming around for hours, and somewhere in these hours and hours of tapes somewhere, there has to be something.' But Tony started playing some riffs, and I did some vocals, and then we got the band in, and it came so quick. It kind of frightened me. Because in four days we'd written and recorded them. And I went 'Whoa, this is scary.' I froze after the two songs, because I was scared, you know?"

When Bill says, "I thought Ozzy did a great job with the melodies and the lyrics," Ozzy counters with "I don't know where the fuck they came from! I wrote 'Fairies Wear Boots' and other bits and pieces of things and a few riffs, but I went home and it just came out — it was meant to be. I've still got this experimentation vibe in me. On the verses of 'Psycho Man,' I hate that formulated thing where you

A SELF-MADE FUCKING DOOM-TOMB

go verse-chorus-verse-chorus. In Sabbath that never used to work anyway. So I had 'psycho man' and 'angel of death' as two separate verses, and then by mistake I sung one over top of the other, and that's how most things come by, by mistake. And I thought, that's interesting, so I put that chorus at the end of the song. It's all experimentation, I can't read fucking music — if it feels good, it goes on."

"Like I say, it was scary," continues Oz. "I was asking myself is there some weird shit going on here? I've never written all the lyrics I don't think to any song ever; I always have help along the way. But these just came out. And then when the record company heard it, they said, 'Carry on!' That's the danger; it's like sharks in a fucking feeding frenzy. They want more. My wife was having an office party and I had a tape of 'Psycho Man,' and there were all these record company people there, and I said to the label guy, 'Come to my car, I'm going to play this, and tell me honestly what you think — is this a piece of shit or is it great?' So I put it on my car stereo, and they all have these blank looks, and I'm going 'It's shit, isn't it?' And they said, 'What took you so fucking long?!' It was like I was saying, we were musically constipated for twenty years. I had a great run on my own, and I will continue to have a great run, hopefully. But Black Sabbath is a unique formula no one else can reproduce. And I never wanted to reproduce it."

Does it feel right then, to do something further in terms of a new studio album? "Absolutely! Fuck, you must be crazy! If we didn't think we were going to do something we'd go out of our fucking heads."

"You and I've been out of our heads for years anyway," points out Bill, to which Ozzy adds, "I'm still having my head looked at now. All they see is fucking daylight. I'm sitting here, a cup of coffee, eight thousand cigarettes . . ."

IT WASN'T LIKE A BAND REUNION, IT WAS LIKE A FAMILY REUNION.

Ozzy proclaimed he's "more than happy," with respect to how the *Reunion* album turned out. "I can only answer for myself, but we've had plenty of time to listen to it over the last few weeks and it's a fine album. The goal as far as I'm concerned is that it's been on and off for so long that the only way we could make it work is if we do it for real. We toured last year, but I may as well have been playing with a different fucking band. Because as far as I'm concerned Black Sabbath consists of Bill Ward, Ozzy Osbourne, Geezer Butler, and Tony Iommi. And that's it. I could have Ginger Baker or Phil Collins on drums and it wouldn't be Black Sabbath. So the vibe and the emotion wasn't there. So when we agreed to do the Birmingham shows, it had been so up and down, we just said let's record it and see what happens. And it was better than what everybody thought. Everybody was so constipated about playing the music after letting it sit for so long, it was like taking a giant musical shit."

"My job as a front man is to get the crowd going," adds Ozzy, with a strange note of exasperation. "Ronnie James Dio I think is a fine singer. I've never seen him perform, but he just stands there. The singer has to be a front man. I never professed to be the greatest singer, but I've never had problems with the crowd, you know? There's only one Ozzy . . . thank God.

"When I got back from the hotel, I thought fuck, we did it. Not only that. It was becoming a fucking joke. Every time we would get

together it would fall apart, then two out of four would go out, then one out of four, then another two out of four. It was such a relief, and I thought, is it going to pay off? Are people going to think it's for real? Had we bit off more than we could chew? We said let's record it in case it never happens again. But we'd suddenly found that we'd missed each other. It wasn't like a band reunion, it was like a family reunion. Emotionally, over the years we've had our ups and downs, but we'd still been very close, and not always in a positive way."

Says Bill of the rehearsals, "For the first two or three days, Tony and I really had to work to connect up. For the first two or three days I was getting some memory lapses on bits and pieces and I wrote out some score sheets. But by the fifth day of rehearsal the band was really starting to sound good. I thought we were ready for the stage by about Day Nine. In fact, it reached such a point that we even took some time off, dispersed for the weekend. We knew it was in the bag."

Ozzy, on the reunited lads: "It was like we'd never separated, swear to God. The first week we were talking about, 'You remember when we did this, did that?' We were a bunch of clowns fucking around. The biggest misconception about Black Sabbath is that we're Satan fucking worshippers. We're just like Vincent Price, who spent a lot of his time doing cookery shows, making fucking meals in Hollywood. We're just a different angle of playing music. If all music was the fucking same it would be a pretty boring world, wouldn't it?"

Oz laments there were a lot of songs they might have wanted to perform. "One thing that happens for a vocalist, is that my range has dropped over the years. I can't do 'Hole in the Sky' or a lot of the things I did when I was 21. For 'Sabbath Bloody Sabbath,' I had to change the vocal a bit, because my range has dropped somewhat. It comes with age; you do the best you can. But apart from that on the live album there was no fucking studio trickery. What you get is what was played that night. When we played before, we would play, but there would be a guitar solo and a drum solo and I could take a break, and we'd be off in an hour and ten minutes. I would be singing for 55 minutes and the rest would be a jamming. But this time I was straight out there from fucking start to finish."

Ozzy adds some color commentary on the actual production work done on *Reunion*.

"The album was being mixed and I kept saying to these fucking morons, I don't want it to sound like a studio album with an audience slapped on! I want it to sound like you close your eyes and you're at the fucking gig, even if it sounds like I'm singing out of a sock or whatever. I want that overall feeling that you're at a live Black Sabbath concert. Because I don't speak in a musical language, it's really hard for me to get that across. I couldn't even figure out how to turn the lights on, let alone run the fucking mixing board. So it's really hard for me to say that the guitar is wrong or that the drums sound like they fell down a fucking flight of stairs. And then they go, 'Oh you want this.' And I go 'No, I don't want that!' Now it sounds like we're at Premier Drums doing a fucking drum clinic, you know? Live shows have mistakes; I don't care who the fuck you are. Everybody that plays live makes mistakes, even Pavarotti. Everybody has a good night, everybody has a bad night. If you didn't have a

> SO THE NEXT NIGHT WHEN WE PLAYED WE JUST FUCKING FORGOT WE WERE RECORDING THE SHOW AND WE JUST WENT HELL FOR LEATHER, AND THE NIGHT WAS OURS, THE NIGHT WAS MAGIC.

bad night, you wouldn't know what it was like to have a good night. As it happens, the first show was a good night, the second show was a fucking brilliant night. And we recorded them both. The first night, we went, 'Well, if tomorrow night doesn't work out we've got a save show, right?' So we can always fuck around and polish it up in the studio. So the next night when we played we just fucking forgot we were recording the show and we just went hell for leather, and the night was ours, the night was magic.

"So when we first mixed the album, it was magical, it was like a divine experience. That's how it felt, a fucking spiritual magical feeling. And the guy couldn't capture that on the album, so we got another guy to mix it, on a fucking Pro Tool of all things. So we separated the sounds and got it the way we wanted without making it too clinical. My thing is that as a front man, on stage, it sounds like a soccer crowd singing back to you, and on the record it sounded like three guys in a pisshouse. You gotta get it sounding like you close your eyes and you're at the fucking gig."

we started with that song. 'Symptom of the Universe' was supposed to be on there, but a certain singer wouldn't do it."

"We won't mention any names!" adds Tony.

Notes Geezer, when asked about the work that went into turning the show into an album, "Tony really took charge and oversaw the mixing part of it with Bob Marlette. If everybody had a hand in it, they'd be making their bass louder, or their drums louder or their vocals loud. So it's nice to just have one person go in. But Tony had an overall feeling in mind."

Says Tony of the two new songs, "Suddenly the record company suggested, 'Could we have a couple of tracks to put on as a bonus, something that had already been done?' Bloody hell, just like that. And there wasn't anything done. So I said, I suppose we'll have a go. And there was just Ozzy and myself there. So we came up with some ideas, and before we knew it, we had the basis for some songs. In the '80s, the sound changed so much. Soon as you get the different singer you start writing differently. And that's what I noticed coming back to this album again. Doing 'Psycho Man,' we started writing in the same old vein, because you write for that singer."

"New stuff may happen or it may not," said Geezer, asked about delivering a full studio album. "We're not pushing it. We've just learned to take one step at a time, because in the past we've always said, no, there will never be a Sabbath reunion, and now there is one. It could be incredibly interesting or it could be the biggest disaster of all time. But the one thing we all know now is that it has to be a bloody good album for us to do it. We can't do a halfhearted, money kind of album. Ozzy certainly has a good ear for music, and he knows what he wants and what he doesn't want. I think in terms of doing the lyrics for the blues song, he asked me if I would rewrite some

John McMurtrie

"It proved a nice challenge for us," adds Geezer, interviewed the same day in a separate chat, with respect to "Spiral Architect" being part of the brew. "It was like doing it for the very first time. We had done all these songs 20 years ago and of course have forgotten them. It was almost like totally relearning everything. And that song just sounded great in the rehearsals. We had forgotten all about it really, and never really thought about doing it before because of the orchestra and everything, but we all loved it. We tried 'The Wizard,' but for some reason that didn't make it. And we tried 'Heaven and Hell,' but it didn't sound right [laughs]. From beginning to end really, it was magical. That's the way we planned it, like from 'War Pigs' on, that's why stuff, and I said, 'Why should I change them? They're good the way they are.'"

Tony hoped that working on the live album might rekindle the desire in the guys to do a full-on studio album. "That would be the icing on the cake, for us to do a studio album. Because like I say, between the four of us we have so many ideas, it's fantastic. But once you start saying things, you have to do it. If you say we're going to go in in March, everybody will be saying 'Hey it's March, where's that album?' And we'd like to do it the way we did these songs, boom! No pressure."

Both Geezer and Tony denied ownership of the ghoulish, patchy, somewhat stupid cover art for *Reunion*. "It had nothing to do with us," says Tony. "They just showed us some pictures, and actually, we thought the album cover was going to be something else, the cover of the 'Psycho Man' single with the four faces. That's what I thought we all agreed on, and then boing!, this other thing comes up."

Crap album cover or not, we were staring at tangible evidence that the original Black Sabbath could indeed reunite. Still, Vinny Appice had been waiting in the wings, confirming that Ozzy, Geezer, Tony and Sharon were concerned Bill couldn't make it through a demanding Sabbath set (Ozzy had humorously said it was in case Bill "fell off his drum stool and broke his leg or something"). Substantiating their fears, in mid-1998, between the December dates in Birmingham and the release of the *Reunion* album, Bill had indeed suffered a minor heart attack, and Vinny, in fact, got to play some '98 dates.

"Well, it's no secret. Bill has had his ups and downs for years," points out Tony, to which Geezer adds, "And ever since we did three songs at the Ozzy farewell concert, Bill found it quite difficult even to get through those three

songs. That was in 1992. Which is the reason Bill wasn't on the original Ozzfest thing last year, when the three of us got together. Because none of us were sure, including Bill, that he could tour. The *Reunion* album was a two-day thing and it was the first step to get Bill back into the band. When we did Ozzfest last year with Mike Bordin, the whole tour seemed weird. Mike's a great drummer, but he's not Bill Ward, and you just can't replace any member of this band, really."

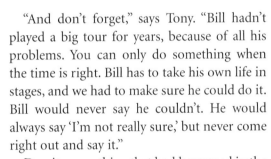

Alexander Rack

Alexander F

"And don't forget," says Tony. "Bill hadn't played a big tour for years, because of all his problems. You can only do something when the time is right. Bill has to take his own life in stages, and we had to make sure he could do it. Bill would never say he couldn't. He would always say 'I'm not really sure,' but never come right out and say it."

Despite everything that had happened in the past, Tony says his relationship with Ozzy was fine at this point. "A lot of things are really blown out of proportion. Things that happened in those days happened for a reason, but that was twenty years ago. Yeah things weren't exactly great; we went through it, though. But we all get along great and we go out there and enjoy what we do."

"I'm afraid it still goes on. We still have some great fun with Bill," says Tony, with respect to the practical jokes that always seemingly fall upon Mr. Bill Ward. Quips Geezer, "What do you mean [laughs]? No, but he was born for it. He's the only one that doesn't really mind. He's like a sponge for it."

"He leaves himself open to it," adds Tony. "And if you don't do anything to him he think something is wrong. 'Why haven't they done anything to me today?' That's the sort of person he is. You constantly have to play him up."

"I KINDA FORGOT HOW WE USED TO DO IT"

– Epilogue

Chris Monshizadegan

To recap, in mid-1998, Black Sabbath was all set to tour Europe — the original Black Sabbath. Then Bill suffered a mild heart attack and Vinny Appice was brought in to drum these 13 shows, running June 3rd to June 30th of '98, each in a different European country.

THE LAST SUPPER

Understandably, Ronnie was not happy with Vinny leaving the Dio band to make tracks 'round Europe with the Sabs. Says Vinny, "When we were on tour with the last Dio tour, '98, the first show, I got a message from Tony Iommi in my hotel room saying call him, and then Sharon called and explained that Bill Ward had a heart attack and the boys want you to come and play and we want you to leave tomorrow [laughs]. So I went ok, fine, *frick*, great, great opportunity, I want to do it, I want to play with them. But I didn't leave the next day because I didn't want to leave Ronnie hanging. So I told Ronnie and Wendy, his manager, and we immediately got on the phone and got Simon Wright in to play. It was a long rehearsal. It was pretty funny hearing all the songs without me playing them. Then the next night I played the last show, on Friday night, and I left on a Saturday to go play with Sabbath. So Ronnie got kinda peeved off with that. That's the kind of person he is. You have to understand, great opportunity to do it, and

it was only for six weeks anyway. So I could come back and finish the tour, plus I went from playing clubs to playing 70,000 seater places, and ten times the money. But he doesn't understand that."

Ronnie was so upset when Vinny left to join Sabbath temporarily that he refused to let Vinny rejoin the band upon his return, as he explains. "Well of course, when Black Sabbath got back together, the first time they had gone out, they had brought Vinny along for . . . yes, that's a good word for it: insurance. So Vinny insured through the whole tour, and didn't play at all. And then when they went out again, they said to Vinny, 'Nah, we don't need you; everything is going to be ok.' So when Vinny left, he left at a very inopportune time. It was like just after the first show of the tour we had just started in America. Luckily Simon had played with us before, and he was free, and after two or three gigs we got it really together. Well, it seems to me that if someone does that to you, I don't think you're going to have your

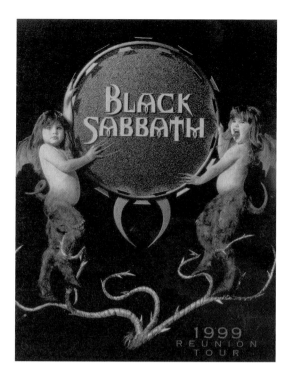

arms open to them. It's not going to be like 'Thanks for filling in, Simon. OK Vinny, you're back in here.' It goes so much deeper than a musician. I mean, Vinny is a great player, he was like my dear friend, and I still consider Vinny to be a dear friend, but that really hurt. So I thought, hey, you made your choice, you'd rather go stand around on the side and do nothing with Sabbath, than to play in a band that you helped create, and a band that you helped perpetuate. I said what's the sense? And truthfully, I'm very happy with Simon. Because, somewhat like Tracy G, Vinny was starting to get full of himself, as a player. I don't mean as an ego — wrong word again. He just started to overplay everything. Whenever Vinny started to get dissatisfied or edgy, he just . . . it didn't really matter, it was just the Vinny show; he was always busy filling all the holes. That's the reason Vinny is not back. I just couldn't take the chance of it happening again. What happens if Sabbath calls again and says, 'Hey we're going to do a tour.' And in reality,

some of the people in that camp would like nothing better than that anyway. I'm sure it was a real point of pride to have wrestled Vinny away."

Black Sabbath wouldn't play live again until the Ozzfest dates of 2001, preambled with a 1,000-seat charity gig in Birmingham on May 22nd, followed by a stop at Milton Keynes four days later. Ozzfest 2001 would be a North American experience exclusively, save for the Milton Keynes date, Sabbath logging 31 shows from June 8th until August 12th. Other key acts on Ozzfest included Marilyn Manson, Slipknot, Papa Roach, Disturbed, Linkin Park, Crazytown and Black Label Society. Bill Ward was back behind the kit for these dates, performing admirably.

I KINDA FORGOT HOW WE USED TO DO IT

THERE WON'T BE ANY OTHER DRUMMERS WAITING IN THE WINGS — THERE'S ONLY ONE BLACK SABBATH.

"Bill is a complete vegan now," said Geezer, also a vegan, two months before the '01 dates. "He used to smoke like 80 cigarettes a day and he stopped cold. There won't be any other drummers waiting in the wings — there's only one Black Sabbath. Bill always had stamina; that was never a problem. I don't know where he gets it, though."

Eight shows that were to follow Ozzfest in August, were canceled when Epic pressed Ozzy, who still carried on a robust solo career, to get back into the studio and finish up work on his long-awaited *Down to Earth* album. In terms of set list, notable inclusions to Sabbath's show were "The Wizard," "Snowblind," but most intriguingly "Under the Sun" and a wholly new track called "Scary Dreams," an improvement on both "Psycho Man" and "Selling My Soul," seven minutes of classic Sabbath re-grooved. In rehearsals, Geezer had said the band worked up "Hand of Doom," "A National Acrobat" and "Back Street Kids," but none of those made the final grade. "They're trying to get us to do Australia and Japan as well, but I think that would have to wait until a new album is finished," added Geezer.

And on the subject of new music, Geezer ventured the following. "We were working on some new stuff and we just wanted to see what we could come up with. We came up with about six or seven songs. No song titles yet, but it's back to the roots back to the old '70s, early '70s sound. It's nothing like the *Reunion* tracks. That was done on Pro Tools. Bill and meself weren't even there until the songs were done. This time we did it the way we did the first three albums, just sit in the studio, North Wales, jam and record everything, listen to it

John Bownas

John Bownas

all back and then work on the stuff we like. And Ozzy would come up with the vocal melodies which is never a problem. So it's very much a group effort. We're writing the way we used to on the first three albums. We all have to like it; if only two of us likes it, then we don't keep it.

"Some of them are sort of finished, but no real lyrics yet. That's always the last thing that we put on. But there are about three of them that we're probably ready to record. And all we need now is about 12 others as good as that and we'll be fine [laughs]. We're not going to rush the album because if it doesn't sound right, we won't put it out. Rick Rubin wants to do it, and that's all we've spoken to so far. Song-wise, there's one really strange oddity, sort of like a ballad, very radio-friendly, and that was the first one to be dumped [laughs] — very commercial. From my material there's a really doomy one that Bill wants to snatch for the Black Sabbath album [laughs]. As well, I'm not the designated lyricist anymore. Ozzy might write something or Bill or Tony."

"Well, we started to mess around writing in a casual way at the beginning of the year and that's all that happened," said Ozzy with respect to Sabbath work speaking in October of '01, two months after the Ozzfest dates. "We gave a few ideas to Rick Rubin and that's the last I heard of it. Anything's possible. We just got together and had a bit of a laugh. At the end of this new Ozzy album, it might materialize. I'm kind of not excited to do this Sabbath album because we all decided if it's not as good as it was in the old days, then we wouldn't do it. I kinda forgot how we used to do it, you know?"

But as we all know, nothing was to come of this enticing Sabbath-as-writers-in-residence story line. The band would hang it up for a couple years, producing nothing much at all. *Past Lives*, basically an expanded version of *Live at Last*, was issued in August of '02. Bill toiled away at the criminally delayed *Beyond Aston*, issuing the more than elegant "Straws" single, fittingly on November 11 of '03. Ozzfest would also happen in '03, with the Ozzy Osbourne band as headliners.

Summer '04, the original Black Sabbath was dishing the doom yet again. The occasion was a couple dozen Ozzfest dates, other loud luminaries along for a turn on the mainstage including, in ascending order, Black Label Society, Superjoint Ritual, Dimmu Borgir, Slayer and Judas Priest.

"It was so off-the-cuff," says Geezer, on the extent of the machinations this time. "Totally unexpected. I was preparing to go into the studio to do my own album, and it came right out of the blue. They asked me who I would play with . . . you know, what drummer. And I said if it's Sabbath, obviously Bill Ward. I think Tony felt the same, that it had to be with Bill or nobody. I'm not sure what the problem is with Ozzy and Bill, but I think they've sorted it out now. I don't know what the politics are and I don't want to know. I was around to Ozzy's house, listening to his new musical that he's doing, and he didn't even mention anything about Ozzfest. It was purely a social visit. It was a week after that when Sharon called."

A highlight of Ozzfest '04 would come to pass when Ozzy, begging off ill, gets replaced by Rob Halford in Camden, New Jersey, August 26. The performance is wincingly bad, displaying graphically two things: that Rob isn't very accurate low in his range; and because of that, preparation is needed (i.e. at Costa Mesa,

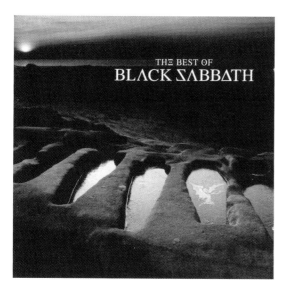

THE BEST OF
BLACK SABBATH

he was quite good). Of course, age had diminished Ozzy more than The Metal God, with Oz's limited range and increasing lack of confidence constricting and diminishing the set list even more, the '04 menu offered nothing adventurous.

"He looks healthier than I do," laughed Geezer, on the fragile subject of Ozzy. "I've put on about 60 pounds. It feels like I have, anyway. It's probably about 20 pounds; I'm going to try lose some of it. Ozzy seems fine to me. He's lost a lot of weight from the last time I've seen him, works out every day. I think after his accident [he'd flipped over on his ATV] he had to get himself into shape as well."

Bill had told me he'd lost 17 pounds and was going for another 15. "He's given it to me, then," says Geezer. "No, Bill, after he had his heart attack, he obviously had to take it easy, immediately give up his 80 cigarettes a day [laughs], stop eating pizzas and ice cream. He just put himself on a better diet. Having said that, the way he drummed on the last Ozzfest in 2001 was unbelievable. He was like more in shape than anybody else was."

Notes Geezer, on Ozzy's curious use of a teleprompter scrolling the band's lyrics, "I don't think he would refer to them, unless you took them away. Then he gets flustered. I think it's almost become a superstition for him now. If it's not there, he doesn't feel right without it. I mean, I've been on stage with him, and he's done totally different lyrics to the song we're on. So he doesn't really pay any attention to it."

Finally, talk about new music was beginning to wane. "I haven't heard anything about it," says Geezer. "We tried it before the last Ozzfest, in 2001. We came out with about five or six songs, but they weren't really up to standard. It just didn't work that particular time. It was too forced, like, you know, we've been offered X amount of dollars to do the new album, and you go 'Oh yeah, if we do a new album we'll get all this money,' and it's just the wrong attitude to go in for. But luckily, we were honest enough to realize we weren't up to scratch. No amount of money would induce us to record something that was substandard."

Talk of a new studio record would be fully extinguished as the band wobbled into '05. Nonetheless, Sabbath continued to valiantly deliver the doom in a live environment, all the originals in place, with cracks beginning to show. Black Sabbath would reemerge on the scene touring Europe in the early summer, mostly with Soulfly as backup, but also hitting the early big festivals, such as Download in California and Roskilde in Denmark. The set has been spiced up, with "Dirty Women," "Symptom of the Universe" (instrumental), "After Forever" and "Electric Funeral" piled on top of the predictables. These 15 dates would bleed into July, and a week later, the notorious Ozzfest 2005 would creak and groan to life.

Ozzfest 2005 would find fan grumblings over the band's predictable set list reaching a

> HE LIKES TO SING THE SAME THINGS
> OVER AND OVER AGAIN. IT'S THE SAME
> WITH HIS OWN STUFF. I DID A TOUR
> WITH OZZY, AND HE WOULDN'T
> EVEN PROMOTE HIS NEW ALBUM
> HE HAD OUT AT THE TIME.

David Lee W

Live in '99

fevered pitch. All Tony could do was throw up his hands.

"Oh God, absolutely! We've got so much material, from even just the Ozzy years. I think we should put other songs in," said Iommi, speaking in preparation for the doomed '05 trek. "And the problem is, it's difficult for us, the band, because if Ozzy doesn't want to sing it, what do you do? We rehearsed some of the songs that we'd never played onstage and they sounded really good. And of course, you get onstage, and Ozzy would go, 'Oh, I don't want to play that one! Let's not do it now!' So you suddenly drop it. So it's very hard. And it's just a thing of himself. He gets this fear, because he's done the others so much, that I think they become second nature and he's frightened to do anything different.

"We had done a show here in England, and had done a two and a half hour set [laughs]. Which I thought, bloody 'ell, we'd done all these songs, and they sounded really good, and he remembered the words and everything, so, I don't really know what the problem is. I must say, the last tour, he was singing better. His attitude is

better, since he's got off some of his medication."

"I'd love to try as much obscure stuff as we can," seconds Geezer, "but it's usually an uphill battle with Ozzy [laughs]. He likes to sing the same things over and over again. It's the same with his own stuff. I did a tour with Ozzy, and he wouldn't even promote his new album he had out at the time. I don't know what it is with him but he doesn't like to veer too far off his usual path. I mean, I think we're all desperate to do new stuff, but Mr. Osbourne won't do it. I'm almost dreading playing the same ten songs again."

"I've made a list already," said a hopeful but charmingly naive Bill Ward, also speaking in preparation of the '05 dates. "We ought to look at new songs. The things I've looked at, is the possibility of doing 'Changes,' with possibly

David Lee Wilson

Tony playing piano [laughs] — how it was originally done. I've even thrown in maybe doing an old blues song, something we would have done when we were 18 years old, like a John Lee Hooker or Muddy Waters song. But what I'd really like to do is write a couple of kick-ass, really hard rocking new songs, or do something that represents Tony a little bit more, something with some nice solos. Or something we haven't

played for a while. The first song I put down was 'Hand of Doom'; 'Dirty Women' as well. Oh yeah, and an acoustic version of, believe it or not, of 'Spiral Architect.'"

Bill affirms that no part of playing Sabbath's set in 2005 is daunting to him — nothing physically anyway. "We do about an hour and ten right now, which is actually a really nice time. I'm good for an hour and 40 minutes if

Chris Monshizadegan

need be. My energy is strong. We just completed a ten and a half mile walk yesterday. We walk about 28 miles, 30 miles a week. And I walk on sand as well, which is totally different from walking on asphalt."

But Bill professes another problem with keeping the heartbeat of Black Sabbath regular. "The only thing that is technically challenging for me on stage is making sure that I know where the 'one' is at all times. Because we play mostly live in open air arenas, and I just need the wind to blow the wrong way, and the sound shifts across the stage. So I have three backup systems that I use to know where my one is. And one of them is a visual where the lyrics are. At any given second, I have a monitor where the lyrics are, just in case I can't hear Ozzy. Then I have a separate direct link to Tony. However, there's a decay. When we've done about 50% of the show, I do start to get the deterioration in my ears. And so, even though it's a direct link to Tony's amp, the sound becomes more of a wash and it's not that distinctive. And I'm working on having it direct with computer feed, no latency whatsoever. And you know, you see these things in the hospital where it shows where the heartbeat is? Well, I'm working on having a computer that shows me where Tony's guitar stroke is at any time. So basically, I can tell, by that, if it's like loud, I can tell where we are. It's another way of keeping knowing where the one is. And finally,

David Lee Wilson

David Lee Wilson

my ultimate backup system, is my personal road manager, Walter Earl, who's an excellent drummer himself. He sits behind me, and when we play live, Walter continually counts the one. So I can look behind me at any spot. If I lose Tony, or Geezer, or Oz, for one second, I just look around, and Walter's got my one, and I can pick it right up."

And what do you see on this monitor?

"What it is, it's just like an image, a sound image. I can tell by looking at the sound image what's going on. If the sound image is all over the place, in other words, if it's real broad, I get an idea of where we are in the song."

Ozzfest 2005 would feature Black Sabbath firmly and expectedly in their usual headline slot, followed by a fiery and surefooted Iron Maiden nipping at the heels of the masters. Below Maiden, one witnessed the likes of In Flames, Black Label Society, Shadows Fall, Mudvayne and Slipknot, in that ascending order.

As it came to pass, Sabbath's live set list was not too, too bad, matching up with that of the aforementioned 2005 European dates. But new issues were afoot — a number of shows had to

be canceled and/or rescheduled due to Ozzy's voice giving out. It all came to a head at the two-thirds point of the tour's couple of dozen stops. There were already "illness" cancelations recorded, and then on August 11th in Auburn, Washington, Ozzy threw his mic down in frustration near the end of "Dirty Women." Things improved two nights later, as Ozzy wisely stayed away from this specific "Dirty Women" vocal altogether. But then two things happened, more cancelations, and the swift uprooting of Iron Maiden from the tour, due to their very public feud with Sharon Osbourne. It was deemed that a few high-tech tricks (piped-in "Ozzy" chants) and low-tech tricks (egg throwing) had to be set in motion in response to Bruce Dickinson slamming Ozzy and the Sabbath organization from his pulpit aboard the stage. Bruce's reputation as a crank had been slowly but surely growing, and this was the icing on the cake. Steve Harris and Ozzy were both gentlemanly and reserved about it, but not so Maiden manager Rod Smallwood, who fired off a rant to the press, and the mudslinging match was on.

"I THINK THE MAIN SURPRISE IS THAT WE'RE ALL STILL ALIVE,"

I spoke to Geezer August 8th, just before all of this was about to blow up, and a solution of sorts had been devised. "Ozzy's never been a fan of doing back-to-back gigs. That's where the problem lies. I don't know if it's psychological with him or what. It's like, from the first back-to-back gig we did, the second night, he blew his voice completely, and he hasn't really recovered since. So now we've had to drop all the back-to-back gigs, and we're rescheduling one of them. Soon as everybody saw that there were going to be back-to-back gigs, we said to the promoter, there's no way he's going to do those gigs. He never has done. It totally depresses him. He's really, really down; I think it's so much to the point now, where it's psychological as well. He goes onstage every night thinking that his voice is going to break, and he's not a very happy person at the moment. We've had to change the Sabbath set around to suit Ozzy's voice even more. So it's just been one problem after another."

When asked about the band's warm-up regimen in '05, Geezer lets on that it takes a lot to get the machine humming, although he says Bill was no longer taking oxygen, and as far as he was aware, hadn't even brought any along. "I start playing bass for about 20 minutes, through some little practice amp, to get me hands flexible, and then I do about half an hour of yoga, stretching exercises, nothing strenuous. Because if I pull something [laughs], that's all. And I think Tony just plays guitar for about an hour. Bill does tons of exercises too, lots of stretching, and he lifts weights. Ozzy does skipping rope, his Lifecycle thing, and then he does half an hour of voice exercises. I think he better change his routine."

Remarks Geezer, prompted by a question about Bill's elaborate comments about finding his "one," "I think if you think too much about something, it puts you off, you don't get into the rhythm of it. I've never wanted to rely on anything else. That's why I don't even use effects on my bass. I just plug me bass in and play. Bill, he's tried lots of different things. I think he's got this permanent monitor problem, which nobody seems to be able to overcome. So he relies on various means of getting his tempo. I think he usually talks to you guys more about it than us."

"I just think Bill has his own way," said Tony, September 1st, 2005, just as Ozzfest — and maybe Black Sabbath itself — was a handful of shows away from being over. "Bill is just such a special drummer, on his own. I've never come across another drummer like Bill. He's a real character and more of a percussionist. He really gets into what he does and he really does analyze it — probably sometimes too much — and he tries to cover every single side of what he plays. As you've said, he's got teleprompters. He doesn't always have Ozzy in his monitors. But if it works for Bill, that's great. Whatever odd things he might have, he gets things done."

"I think the main surprise is that we're all still alive," laughs Geezer with respect to highlights of the '05 tour. "Jimmy Page came along with us when we were flying in Europe, which is nice, but other than that, nothing really. We've had enough problems with Ozzy's voice to fill the next ten Ozzfests. The set list, it started out adventurous enough, but unfortunately it's been filtered down again, to suit Ozzy's voice. We do add a few instrumental bits of songs, like 'Symptom of the Universe' and 'Sabbath Bloody Sabbath' and 'Sweet Leaf,' things that Ozzy just can't sing. So we've incorporated various riffs into some of the songs, so it's like a medley of things. But I always enjoyed doing 'The Wizard'; that's gone. 'Into the Void' is gone; quite a few things are gone. I especially enjoyed 'The Wizard,' with all the harmonica. My favorite part is probably the end of 'Dirty Women' — thank God we've still got that in

the set. It's different every night and it gives Tony a chance to do a solo, and for us to improvise. Sometimes it will be like three minutes, other nights it will be seven minutes long. Sometimes we do an extended version of 'Black Sabbath' with improvisation, but mainly it's 'Dirty Women.'"

On the subject of Ozzy, who may really ponder retirement properly this time, Tony says, "I think he just wants to finish the shows and have a bit of a break, really. I think he probably needs that. He's going to have a little break, which will do him well." Since he is ever game to keep the beast called Black Sabbath alive, Iommi optimistically sees the cancellation of consecutive nights as a solution, a ray of light. "I think so. It's never seemed to have worked for a long time with Ozzy doing two nights in a row. He likes to put everything into the show he can, and I think by doing two

David Lee Wilson

David Lee Wilson

nights in a row, he puffs himself out and wants to have a break in between."

So that was that. Sabbath went out — possibly, sadly, all the way out — fulfilling almost all of their obligations, with the irascible Bruce Dickinson from a band two generations back (Priest would be one, if five years is a rock 'n' roll generation) goading them mercilessly, impudently on to retirement. Yes, younger by two springs of leg-warmered step, Iron Maiden tore it up and tore a strip. It wasn't classy, what Bruce did, but it was telling and graphic. Sabbath had been knocked on its head.

And that's where we stand now. As I write this, Ozzy has just released the covers album from his box set, with bonus covers — hardly a cause to rejoice, as the lowly Billboard placement and opening week sales of scarcely 9000 copies would attest. Geezer, or GZR, has released, since May '05, a third album called *Ohmwork*, and Tony seems to have a fresh spot of life with his old pal Glenn Hughes, their *Fused* album heavy, amusingly slow, but bright and hopeful. And Bill? Well, I've always considered him the most intense and brave artist in the band — surprising, yes, for he is just the damn drummer. But the man's two solo albums are breathtakingly creative, and the long-delayed *Beyond Aston* appears to promise more of the same.

Talking with Tony Martin, we somewhat came to the same conclusions, that the mounting of three Ozzfests plus peripherals has so

Chris Monshizadegan

intertwined the band with the business empire of one Sharon Osbourne, that it would be hard to envision the Sabbath hooking up with a Ronnie James Dio or the man at the other end of the line, Mr. Martin himself. But hey, we all know that all three are options of a sort. As is yet another singer (very unlikely), or solo careers . . . or retirement . . . or . . . a retirement tour. And yet the latest news had Ronnie and Tony possibly working together on a couple of tracks to add to a long-considered Dio-era Sabbath compilation on Warner/Rhino.

But if it all ended now, that wouldn't be so bad. The band that first jammed together almost four decades ago, the band that first brought the doom, pushed out the doom, smothered us with the doom, could be seen as flaring out on top, as headliners, the originals intact, the classics delivered to an insane mania

that could only be conjured for these four working-class lads.

Once the scattered painful memories of summer '05 abate, Sabbath will have firmly reclaimed their thrones as the ultimate heavy metal band, the original soot-stained workers and shapers of the form, the loud bringers of much doom, and, if you look for it, even more hope . . . which is just the way a world-weary and ever-worrying Geezer Butler would have wanted the mad tale of Black Sabbath to end.

And one wonders if some higher force has been at hand, solemnly and even eagerly writing such an ending. On March 13, 2006, after many quiet and contemplative months for the Sabbath camp, Black Sabbath was finally inducted into the Rock and Roll Hall of Fame, at a typically swanky ceremony at the Waldorf Astoria in New York. There were others inducted as well, including Miles Davis, Herb Alpert and Jerry Moss. Lynyrd Skynyrd, as expected, saluted the fallen Ronnie Van Zant by trotting out "Sweet Home Alabama" and "Free Bird." The Sex Pistols, as expected, didn't show up (profanely disparaging the thing from a distance) and Debbie Harry unexpectedly wouldn't let the original Blondie band come up and play a tune — a bit of public unpleasantness, but rock 'n' roll all the same.

Ozzy sidestepped his past perturbed denouncements of the Hall (Sabbath were being inducted 11 years after their first eligibility), and was gracious in accepting, thanking his family, while Tony restated his solid belief in the band's artistic validity in the face of braying detractors, and Bill noted quite correctly, that the induction spoke to a new respect for heavy metal in general. Black Sabbath decided not to coat the proceedings in a sludgy slick of decibel-mad doom, but saw no problem in letting their inductors, Metallica, do so — Lars, James and company proceeded to beat the daylights out of "Iron Man" and, to a deep fan's delight, "Hole in the Sky." It was an event that showed how influential, inspirational, and essential Black Sabbath had become in their almost 40 years in music. Ulrich, himself a member of a band that's almost as legendary as its predecessor, paid homage to the guys who had made him want to become a musician in the first place: "If there was no Black Sabbath, I could still possibly be a morning newspaper delivery boy."

Chris Monshizadegan

DISCOGRAPHY

My predisposition is to always go for a pared-down discography, the idea being that this is the place one double-checks where songs came from, gets the story straight, flips to 'er when listening to ascertain structure etc., and little else. I've always found video discographies dreary, and, especially in the case of Sabbath, offshoot band info would take pages of space that we ain't got. I've not discussed singles either, but much of that is covered in the book.

With the band's break with Meehan, I am respecting the spirit of their feelings by leaving out *Live at Last* and *Greatest Hits*, and one wonders how "official" other Castle-type compilations are — I was told once not to mention the mini album sleeve reproductions in front of Ozzy, because he considers them bootlegs. Heck, even *We Sold Our Souls*, out through Warner in North America, elicits grumbles from the guys. But that one I've always considered quite official, also prompted by the visual cue of it (it "looks" part of the catalogue). So anyway, I've not included Sanctuary compilation *The Best of Black Sabbath* or the expanded release of *Live at Last*, now called called *Past Lives*, also issued by Sanctuary. So yes, I've not included any live albums other than *Live Evil* and *Reunion*. *Cross Purposes — Live* was in with a video pack . . . a bit muddy, and also not widely available.

Also of note, I figured this would be a good place to lay out the (official, significant) recording lineups for each album, so that's there — provided only when different from the previous album's team. Label and date of issue is from the home country, the UK. Side 1 and side 2 designations are noted only for albums issued in the vinyl age, ending in 1989, semi-coincidentally with the last Sabbath album I bought on vinyl, *Headless Cross*. Finally, I've included a Notes section to be used only when I thought essential.

A. OFFICIAL STUDIO ALBUMS

Black Sabbath

(Vertigo, February '70)
Side 1: Black Sabbath, The Wizard, Behind the Wall of Sleep, N.I.B.,
Side 2: Evil Woman, Sleeping Village, Warning
Lineup: Ozzy Osbourne — vocals; Tony Iommi — guitars; Geezer Butler — bass; Bill Ward — drums.
Notes: North American issue substitutes Wicked World for Evil Woman (a Crow cover). '96 Castle remaster includes both tracks. Original and very rare pressing has gatefold in black, text in gray; second pressing is white with black print. Some pressings have the intro to Behind the Wall of Sleep designated as Wasp, the intro to N.I.B. called Bassically, and the intro to Sleeping Village called A Bit of Finger.

Paranoid

(Vertigo, September '70)
Side 1: War Pigs, Paranoid, Planet Caravan, Iron Man
Side 2: Electric Funeral, Hand of Doom, Rat Salad, Fairies Wear Boots
Notes: War Pigs includes Luke's Wall and Fairies Wear Boots includes Jack the Stripper — depending where you look, it's not clear with respect to either's intro or outro status.

Master of Reality

(Vertigo, July '71)

Side 1: Sweet Leaf, After Forever, Embryo, Children of the Grave

Side 2: Orchid, Lord of This World, Solitude, Into the Void

Notes: Some versions list Solitude as 8:08 with Into the Void as 3:08, with no blank band between them. Solitude is in fact 5:02 with Into the Void clocking in at 6:12. Embryo is also erroneously timed on some issues. Original pressing was housed in "flip-top" box with poster. Some issues of *Master of Reality* include the following "extra song" shenanigans: 1) After Forever listed as After Forever (including The Elegy); 2) Children of the Grave being followed by The Haunting (:45); 3) a named segment called Step Up (:30) between Orchid and Lord of This World, and a listing for Death Mask (3:08) before Into the Void.

Vol 4

(Vertigo, September '72)

Side 1: Wheels of Confusion, Tomorrow's Dream, Changes, FX, Supernaut

Side 2: Snowblind, Cornucopia, Laguna Sunrise, St. Vitus Dance, Under the Sun

Notes: On some copies (and as with previous albums, only in some locations) outro to Wheels of Confusion is called The Straightener; outro to Under the Sun is called Every Day Comes and Goes. Original pressing with four page stitched-in insert. Other later pressings with full band live shot only.

Sabbath Bloody Sabbath

(Vertigo, December '73)

Side 1: Sabbath Bloody Sabbath, A National Acrobat, Fluff, Sabbra Cadabra

Side 2: Killing Yourself to Live, Who Are You, Looking for Today, Spiral Architect

Notes: Killing Yourself to Live has had the subtitles You Think That I'm Crazy and I Don't Know If I'm Up or Down, but these are rare. Lyric sleeve in some issues, lyric insert in others. Original pressing was gatefold with psychedelic naked-in-bedroom band shot.

Sabotage

(Vertigo, July '75)

Side 1: Hole in the Sky, Don't Start (Too Late), Symptom of the Universe, Megalomania

Side 2: The Thrill of It All, Supertzar, Am I Going Insane (Radio), The Writ

Notes: Some pressings include a quiet 23-second joke song called Blow on a Jug tacked on at the end of The Writ, but not designated in print as being there. The most basic packaging of all the Ozzy-era Sabbath albums, i.e., no gates, inner sleeves, inserts, goodies.

Technical Ecstasy

(Vertigo, September '76)

Side 1: Back Street Kids, You Won't Change Me, It's Alright, Gypsy

Side 2: All Moving Parts (Stand Still), Rock 'n' Roll Doctor, She's Gone, Dirty Women

Notes: Lyric sleeve in some issues, lyric insert in others.

Never Say Die

(Vertigo, October '78)

Side 1: Never Say Die, Johnny Blade, Junior's Eyes, A Hard Road

Side 2: Shock Wave, Air Dance, Over to You, Breakout, Swinging the Chain

Notes: "Schematics" sleeve included, but not lyrics.

Heaven and Hell

(Vertigo, April '80)

Side 1: Neon Knights, Children of the Sea, Lady

Evil, Heaven and Hell
Side 2: Wishing Well, Die Young, Walk Away, Lonely Is the Word
Lineup: Ronnie James Dio — vocals; Tony Iommi — guitars; Geezer Butler — bass; Bill Ward — drums.

Mob Rules

(Vertigo, November '81)
Side 1: Turn Up the Night, Voodoo, The Sign of the Southern Cross, E5150, The Mob Rules
Side 2: Country Girl, Slipping Away, Falling Off the Edge of the World
Lineup: Ronnie James Dio — vocals; Tony Iommi — guitars; Geezer Butler — bass; Vinny Appice — drums.

Born Again

(Vertigo, August '83)
Side 1: Trashed, Stonehenge, Disturbing the Priest, The Dark, Zero The Hero
Side 2: Digital Bitch, Born Again, Hot Line, Keep It Warm
Lineup: Ian Gillan — vocals; Tony Iommi — guitars; Geezer Butler — bass; Bill Ward — drums.
Notes: Lyric sleeve.

Seventh Star

(Vertigo, March '86)
Side 1: In for the Kill, No Stranger to Love, Turn to Stone, Sphinx (The Guardian), Seventh Star
Side 2: Danger Zone, Heart Like a Wheel, Angry Heart, In Memory . . .
Lineup: Glenn Hughes — vocals; Tony Iommi — guitars; Geoff Nicholls — keyboards; Dave Spitz — bass; Eric Singer — drums.
Notes: Released under band name Black Sabbath Featuring Tony Iommi. Lyric sleeve.

The Eternal Idol

(Vertigo, November '87)
Side 1: The Shining, Ancient Warrior, Hard Life to Love, Glory Ride
Side 2: Born to Lose, Nightmare, Scarlet Pimpernel, Lost Forever, Eternal Idol
Lineup: Tony Martin — vocals; Tony Iommi — guitars; Geoff Nicholls — keyboards; Bob Daisley — bass; Eric Singer — drums.
Notes: Lyric sleeve. Two non-LP tracks Some Kind of Woman and Black Moon showed up on the 12-inch issue of The Shining.

Headless Cross

(I.R.S., April '89)
Side 1: The Gates of Hell, Headless Cross, Devil & Daughter, When Death Calls
Side 2: Kill in the Spirit World, Call of the Wild, Black Moon, Nightwing
Lineup: Tony Martin — vocals; Tony Iommi — guitars; Geoff Nicholls — keyboards; Laurence Cottle — bass; Cozy Powell — drums.
Notes: An extra track, Cloak & Dagger was used as a B-side to Headless Cross as well as on a rare picture disc issue of the album. Lyric sleeve. First LP issue includes poster.

Tyr

(I.R.S., August '90)
Anno Mundi, The Law Maker, Jerusalem, The Sabbath Stones, The Battle of Tyr, Odin's Court, Valhalla, Feels Good to Me, Heaven in Black
Lineup: Tony Martin — vocals; Tony Iommi — guitars; Geoff Nicholls — keyboards; Neil Murray — bass; Cozy Powell — drums.

Cross Purposes

(I.R.S., January '94)
I Witness, Cross of Thorns, Psychophobia, Virtual Death, Immaculate Deception, Dying

for Love, Back to Eden, The Hand That Rocks the Cradle, Cardinal Sin, Evil Eye

Lineup: Tony Martin — vocals; Tony Iommi — guitars; Geoff Nicholls — keyboards; Geezer Butler — bass; Bobby Rondinelli — drums.

Notes: Japanese bonus track is called What's the Use. A sorta live album, as discussed, fell out of the tour for this album, namely a CD and video pack called *Cross Purposes — Live*. The set was later reissued on DVD, without the CD.

Forbidden

(I.R.S., June '95)

The Illusion of Power, Get a Grip, Can't Get Close Enough, Shaking Off the Chains, I Won't Cry for You, Guilty as Hell, Sick and Tired, Rusty Angels, Forbidden, Kiss of Death

Lineup: Tony Martin — vocals; Tony Iommi — guitars; Geoff Nicholls — keyboards; Neil Murray — bass; Cozy Powell — drums.

Notes: Japanese bonus track is called Loser Gets It All.

B. OFFICIAL LIVE ALBUMS

Live Evil

(Vertigo, January '83)

Side 1: E5150, Neon Knights, N.I.B., Children of the Sea, Voodoo

Side 2: Black Sabbath, War Pigs, Iron Man

Side 3: The Mob Rules, Heaven and Hell

Side 4: The Sign of the Southern Cross/Heaven and Hell (continued), Paranoid, Children of the Grave, Fluff

Notes: First officially released Black Sabbath live album. Gatefold. Some CD issues deleted War Pigs, while others deleted parts of Ronnie's inter-song banter and some of Fluff.

Reunion

(Sony, October '98)

Disc 1: War Pigs, Behind the Wall of Sleep, N.I.B., Fairies Wear Boots, Electric Funeral, Sweet Leaf, Spiral Architect, Into the Void, Snowblind

Disc 2: Sabbath Bloody Sabbath, Orchid/Lord of This World, Dirty Women, Black Sabbath, Iron Man, Children of the Grave, Paranoid, Psycho Man, Selling My Soul

Lineup: Ozzy Osbourne — vocals; Tony Iommi — guitars; Geezer Butler — bass; Bill Ward — drums.

Notes: Also issued in digipak version. Psycho Man and Selling My Soul were newly written and recorded studio tracks.

C. OFFICIAL COMPILATIONS

We Sold Our Souls for Rock 'n' Roll

(Warner Brothers, August '76)

Side 1: Black Sabbath, The Wizard, Warning

Side 2: Paranoid, War Pigs, Iron Man

Side 3: Tomorrow's Dream, Fairies Wear Boots, Changes, Sweet Leaf

Side 4: Sabbath Bloody Sabbath, Am I Going Insane (Radio), Laguna Sunrise, Snowblind, N.I.B.

Notes: Two LP compilation; gatefold. Above information is for the U.S. pressing (different from UK). Given that the album was released on Warner in North America, but on NEMS in the UK, this one is somewhat more "official," especially given that the band discredits its issue on the whole (see comments in book). Japanese version includes Wicked World as track 4 on side 2. Warning and Laguna Sunrise deleted from CD reissue, and then later issued with both songs reinstated plus Wicked World on a two-CD set. Canadian issue adds Wicked World and Children of the Grave.

The Sabbath Stones

(I.R.S., April '96)

Headless Cross, When Death Calls, Devil & Daughter, The Sabbath Stones, The Battle of Tyr, Odin's Court, Valhalla, TV Crimes, Virtual Death, Evil Eye, Kiss of Death, Guilty as Hell, Loser Gets It All, Disturbing the Priest, Heart Like a Wheel, The Shining

Notes: Not issued in North America. The only official cross-label compilation to date, with one track each from four Warner Brothers albums.

Symptom of the Universe 1970–1978

(Warner/Rhino, October '02)

Disc 1: Black Sabbath, N.I.B., The Wizard, Warning, Evil Woman, Paranoid, Iron Man, War Pigs, Fairies Wear Boots, Sweet Leaf, Children of the Grave, Into the Void, Lord of This World

Disc 2: After Forever, Snowblind, Laguna Sunrise, Changes, Tomorrow's Dream, Supernaut, Sabbath Bloody Sabbath, Fluff, Sabbra Cadabra, Am I Going Insane (Radio), Symptom of the Universe, Hole in the Sky, Rock 'n' Roll Doctor, Dirty Women, Never Say Die, A Hard Road

Notes: Notable for the fact that all the songs were mastered from the original source tapes. Issued with 52-page booklet.

Black Box

(Warner/Rhino, April '04)

Discs 1–8: all of the songs from *Black Sabbath* through *Never Say Die*

Disc 9 (DVD): video for Black Sabbath, Iron Man, Paranoid, Blue Suede Shoes

Notes: North American issue only. Notable for the fact that all the songs were mastered from the original source tapes. DVD is the infamous Beat Club footage. Issued with a 77-page, hardcover, black velvet-wrapped booklet.

CREDITS

Appice, Vinny. Interview with the author. May 15, 2002.

Arfin, Mike. "Black Sabbath Dehumanizer." *Foundations.* Vol. 5, Issue 12, June 15, 1992.

Bangs, Lester. "Black Sabbath — Black Sabbath record review." *Rolling Stone.*

"Black Sabbath — Laying Off." *Hit Parader.* 1972.

Bogert, Tim. Interview with the author. August 1, 2005.

Bonutto, Dante. "Black Power." *Kerrang!* No. 49. August 25–September 7.

Bronson, Howard. "Black Sabbath: No Downer Group." 1972.

Butler, Geezer. Interview with the author. May 20, 1997.

Butler, Geezer. Interview with the author. November 1998.

Butler, Geezer. Interview with the author. April 10, 2001.

Butler, Geezer. Interview with the author. June 14, 2004.

Butler, Geezer. Interview with the author. April 29, 2005.

Butler, Geezer. Interview with the author. May 16, 2005.

Butler, Geezer. Interview with the author. August 4, 2005.

Cohen, Scott. "Black Sabbath's Ozzy Osbourne: 'I've Got Bats and Eight or Nine Stray Black Cats.'" *Circus.* No. 122, November 1975.

Condon, Sean. "Sabbath LIVES!" *The Standard.* July 15, 1995.

Cummings, Winston. "Black Sabbath — See No Evil." *Hit Parader.* No. 244, January 1985.

Daisley, Bob. Interview with the author. January 2005.

Derocco, Dave. "The Forbidden Journey Continues." *Pulse Niagara.* July 12 – 25, 1995.

Dickinson, Bruce. "Interview with Ernie C. from Bruce Dickinson Rock Show, Radio One." *Southern Cross.* Issue 28, March 1995 and Issue 16, January 1996.

Dio, Ronnie James. Interview with the author. 1996.

Dio, Ronnie James. Interview with the author. June 30, 1999.

Dio, Ronnie James. Interview with the author. April 8, 2002.

Dio, Ronnie James. Interview with the author. December 5, 2002.

Dio, Ronnie James. Interview with the author. September 15, 2004.

Dio, Ronnie James. Interview with the author. February 20, 2005.

Doreian, Robyn. "Dio: The Eternal Flame." *Rip.* May 1984.

Evans, Rick. "Black Sabbath: Born Again, Again." *Hit Parader.* 1987.

Gabriel, Paul. "'Sabbath Bloody Sabbath': The Enduring Riff-Rock of Black Sabbath." *Discoveries.* Issue 97, June 1996.

Galbraith, David. "Black to the Future." *Rock Power.* No. 8, January 1992.

Galbraith, David. "Detox." *Rock Power.*

Gillan, Ian. Interview with the author. June 19, 1998.

Gillan, Ian. Interview with the author. June 17, 2001.

Gillan, Ian. Interview with the author. January 14, 2004.

Gillan, Ian. Interview with the author. February 18, 2005.

Graustark, Barbara. "Black Sabbath." *Circus Raves.* Vol. 1, No. 1, January 1974.

Graustark, Barbara. "Why Black Sabbath Hates America." *Circus.* Vol. 7, No. 5, February 1973.

Green, Robin. "How Black Was My Sabbath." *Rolling Stone.* No. 94, October 28, 1971.

Halford, Rob. Interview with the author. November 11, 2005.

Hanser, Mark. "Two Hours with Tony Iommi of Black Sabbath." *Record Review.* Vol. 8, No. 3, August 1984.

Henderson, Tim. "Back Where I Belong!" *Brave Words & Bloody Knuckles.* No. 9, August/September 1995.

Henderson, Tim. "Black Sabbath — A Cross to Bear with Geezer Butler." *Brave Words & Bloody Knuckles.* Vol. 1, No. 1, March 1994.

Hogan, Richard. "Is Sabbath Turning Purple?" *Circus.* February 29, 1984.

Houghton, Mick. "Sabbath's Sabotage." *Circus.* No. 119. October 1974.

Hughes, Glenn. Interview with the author. August 28, 2000.

Hughes, Glenn. Interview with the author. April 24, 2001.

Hughes, Glenn. Interview with the author. August 2001.

Hughes, Glenn. Interview with the author. September 17, 2003.

Hughes, Glenn. Interview with the author. November 5, 2004.

Hush, Michele. "'Snowbird' — Black Sabbath Tumbles

into Mantovani's Orchestra Pit." *Circus*. October 1972.

Iommi, Tony. Interview with the author. November 1998.

Iommi, Tony. Interview with the author. October 17, 2000.

Iommi, Tony. Interview with the author. November 10, 2004.

Iommi, Tony. Interview with the author. February 21, 2005.

Iommi, Tony. Interview with the author. September 1, 2005.

Joel, Mitch. "Ozzy: Retirement Sucks!" *Brave Words & Bloody Knuckles.* No. 10, November/December 1995.

Kelleher, Ed. "Black Sabbath Don't Scare Nobody." *Creem.* Vol. 3, No. 7, December 1971.

Kirke, Mikael. "Black Sabbath." *Faces Rocks*. Vol. 1, No. 6, April 1984.

"The Land of Oz: A Talk with Mr. Osbourne." *Circus*. 1980.

Liveten, Sharon. "Close-Up: Metal. An Exciting Interview With Black Sabbath." *Creem*. September 1985.

Logan, Nick. "Black Sabbath: Simple and Basic." 1971.

Makowski, Pete. "Come to the Sabbath." *Kerrang!* No. 35. February 10 – 23, 1983.

Martin, Tony. Interview with the author. April 2003.

Martin, Tony. Interview with the author. October 15, 2005.

Martin, Tony. Interview with the author. October 20, 2005.

Masters, Drew. "Black Sabbath." *M.E.A.T.* Issue 2, June/July 1989.

Masters, Drew. "Black Sabbath." *M.E.A.T.* Issue 17, October 1990.

Masters, Drew. "Black Sabbath." *M.E.A.T.* Issue 35, August 1992.

Michalski, Cliff. "Black Sabbath, 1975." *Scene*. Vol. 6, No. 29, July 24 – 31, 1975.

Moses, Peter. "Black Sabbath: Forefathers Reunite." *Metal Maniacs.* February 1993.

Murray, Neil. Interview with the author. July 23, 2001.

Osbourne, Ozzy. Interview with the author. November 5, 1997.

Osbourne, Ozzy. Interview with the author. November 1998.

Osbourne, Ozzy. Interview with the author. October 5, 2001.

Phillips, Kate. "Observe the Sabbath." *Ram*. No. 20, December 5, 1975.

"Raw Rock from Birmingham England." *Circus*. 1971.

Roemer, Doug. "Long Live the King." *Snap Pop*. Vol. 1, No. 11, May 2000.

Roemer, Doug. "Keeping the Sabbath." *Snap Pop.* Vol. 2, No. 4, November 2000.

Rondinelli, Bobby. Interview with the author. January 30, 2004.

Rondinelli, Bobby. Interview with the author. November 17, 2004.

Schroer, Ron. "Bill Ward & The Hand of Doom." *Southern Cross*. Issue 15, May 1995.

Schroer, Ron. "Bill Ward & The Hand of Doom Part IV: Living Naked." *Southern Cross*. Issue 21, May 1998.

Scott, Peter and Alexander Rack. "Tony Iommi Interview." *Southern Cross*. Issue 21, May 1998.

Secher, Andy. "Black Sabbath: A New Beginning." *Hit Parader*. No. 232, January 1984.

Secher, Andy. "Black Sabbath: Exclusive Interview With Ian Gillan." *Hit Parader*. No. 229, October 1983.

Secher, Andy. "Born Again." *Hit Parader*. 1983.

Shapiro, Marc. "Roots: Tony Iommi." *Hit Parader*. August 1984.

Sharken, Lisa. "The Masters of Reality Return." *Vintage Guitar*. Vol. 13, No. 4, January 1999.

Simunek, Chris. "The Wizdom of Oz." *High Times*. No. 283, March 1999.

Smith, Mike. "Eternal Idols: Black Sabbath Return With their New Disc Cross Purposes." *Live Wire*. Vol. 4, No. 5.

Smith, Mike. "The Great and Powerful Oz!" *Live Wire*. Vol. 7, No. 9, September 1997.

Stein, Kathi and Robbie Granit. "Black Sabbath's Bill Ward Reveals the Black Brotherhood." *Circus Raves*. Vol. 1, No. 5, July 1974.

Stein, Kathleen. "'Sabbath Bloody Sabbath' — Black Sabbath Hits a Happy Note." *Circus*. Vol. 8, No. 6, March 1974.

Sutherland, Jon. "Long-Playing Black Sabbath Now Re-formed By Mob Rules." *Record Review*. February 1982.

Tangye, David. Interview with the author. October 25, 2004.

Various fan club members. "Interview — Tony Iommi." *Southern Cross*. Issue 19, March 1997.

Wakeman, Rick. Interview with the author. May 7, 2004.

Ward, Bill. Interview with the author. July 28, 1997.

Ward, Bill. Interview with the author. November 1998.

Ward, Bill. Interview with the author. April 11, 2001.

Ward, Bill. Interview with the author. June 2, 2002.

Ward, Bill. Interview with the author. November 15, 2003.

Ward, Bill. Interview with the author. June 14, 2004.

Ward, Bill. Interview with the author. March 29, 2005.

Webb, Julie. "Black Sabbath: Gradual Change and Live Gigs." 1973.

Woodruffe, Jezz. Interview with the author. October 20, 2004.

Wright, Graham. Interview with the author. October 29, 2004.

Wright, Jeb. "Interviews with Geezer Butler, Ronnie James Dio, Ian Gillan, Tony Iommi and Bill Ward." *Classic Rock Revisited.* www.classicrockrevisited.com

Zimmerman, Deane. "Ozzy Osbourne interview." 1978.